AF412014

Staging Existence

Staging Existence

Chekhov's Tetralogy

Svetlana Evdokimova

THE UNIVERSITY OF WISCONSIN PRESS

The University of Wisconsin Press
728 State Street, Suite 443
Madison, Wisconsin 53706
uwpress.wisc.edu

Gray's Inn House, 127 Clerkenwell Road
London EC1R 5DB, United Kingdom
eurospanbookstore.com

Printed in the United States of America
This book may be available in a digital edition.

Library of Congress Cataloging-in-Publication Data
Names: Evdokimova, Svetlana, author.
Title: Staging existence : Chekhov's tetralogy / Svetlana Evdokimova.
Description: Madison, Wisconsin : The University of Wisconsin Press, 2023. |
Includes bibliographical references and index.
Identifiers: LCCN 2023006219 | ISBN 9780299344801 (hardcover)
Subjects: LCSH: Chekhov, Anton Pavlovich, 1860-1904—Philosophy. |
Chekhov, Anton Pavlovich, 1860-1904—Criticism and interpretation.
Classification: LCC PG3458.Z9 P4836 2023 |
DDC 891.72/3—dc23/eng/20230713
LC record available at https://lccn.loc.gov/2023006219

VeryGood
sandra
G -1-01-054-001-769
Staging Existence: Chekhov's Tet
2/3/2025 11:49:40 AM

769

To Theo

CONTENTS

ACKNOWLEDGMENTS

This book evolved over the years of my teaching at Brown University and my participation in various Chekhov conferences in Russia and the United States, and I would like to thank my students, colleagues, and friends for their invaluable support. I am especially grateful to American Chekhov scholars Carol Apollonio and Radislav Lapushin for their most insightful comments and expert opinions. They provided me with numerous recommendations and corrections that I incorporated throughout the book. I owe an enormous debt of gratitude to my longtime mentor and one of the forefathers of Chekhov studies in the United States, Robert Louis Jackson, who inspired me with his love of Chekhov and who in the course of many years lavished on me his intellectual generosity and support. I am greatly indebted to my colleague and friend Alexandar Mihailovic for his thorough reading of the entire manuscript and his keen suggestions, and to Vladimir Golstein for reading parts of this book and commenting on drafts. I am also deeply grateful to many Russian Chekhov scholars for the collegial atmosphere of the exchange of ideas and intellectual stimulation during the various Chekhov conferences in which I have participated, especially Alla Golovacheva, Vladimir Kataev, Margarita Odesskaia, Anatoly Sobennikov, Andrei Stepanov, and Igor Sukhikh, among many others. My undergraduate research assistants Emma George and Alan Dean were an invaluable aid. I am also deeply grateful to the editorial staff at the University of Wisconsin Press for their patience with my project and help at every stage of the review and production process.

My very special thanks go to the Bogliasco Foundation, whose generous residency fellowship made it possible for me to spend a month and a half at the Bogliasco Foundation Study Center on the Ligurian coast of Italy. This more than a month's stay in an idyllic setting of the Study Center and its stimulating and supportive atmosphere provided me with perfect conditions for the uninterrupted work needed to complete an important part of my research on Chekhov.

Some parts of this book appeared in different versions in other publications. I would like to acknowledge the following publications with thanks for the permission to reproduce sections of these earlier versions with emendations: *Slavic and East European Journal, Chekhov the Immigrant: Translating a Cultural Icon, Sankirtos: Studies in Russian and East European Literature, Society and Culture, Chekhov through the Eyes of Russian Thinkers: V. Rozanov, D. Merezhkovskii, L. Shestov and S. Bulgakov, Anton P. Čechov—Der Dramatiker, Chekhov's Letters: Biography, Context, Poetics.*

Last but not least, my greatest thanks go to my son, Theo, for always being encouraging and patient with me in moments of anxiety over impending deadlines; for his love and invaluable moral support; and, most importantly, for making me appreciate life beyond Chekhov.

NOTE ON TRANSLITERATION AND TRANSLATION

I have used a modified version of the Library of Congress transliteration system with the exception of commonly known names in the interest of readability. Soft signs have been omitted in personal names. Unless otherwise indicated, all the parenthetical citations of Chekhov are taken from A. P. Chekhov, *Polnoe sobranie sochinenii i pisem*, 30 vols. (Moscow: Nauka, 1974–83). References to letters are taken from the twelve volumes of letters, indicating volume number and page, and are preceded by *P*.

STAGING EXISTENCE

Introduction

Anton Chekhov is universally regarded as a great innovator in the genres of the short story and drama. With each generation of readers, critics, stage directors, and actors, Chekhov has appeared in a new light: while some early critics found him talented but "insignificant," he emerged as an almost iconic figure for the Russian intelligentsia and, ultimately, as an internationally acclaimed playwright and modernizer of the short story. Chekhov's influence on the modern short story and modern drama was unmatched, and many twentieth-century Western authors eagerly recognized their indebtedness to Chekhov the artist. And yet there is something peculiar about the way we perceive Chekhov: universally recognized as a great artist, Chekhov is rarely seen as an important thinker. Compared to such Russian classics as Pushkin, Tolstoy, and Dostoevsky—who are often recognized not only as great writers but also as thinkers and philosophers—Chekhov may appear to be strangely "unphilosophical," or at least detached from metaphysical preoccupations. To some extent, this perception was deliberately cultivated by Chekhov himself. In his attempt to dissociate himself from every ideological and philosophical movement of his era, Chekhov at times seems to vehemently attack philosophers, and even goes so far as to call into question philosophy itself. It is hardly surprising, then, that Chekhov is rarely considered a philosophical writer of fiction and drama. Although scholarship devoted to the philosophical and religious dimensions of Chekhov's oeuvre certainly exists, its conclusions have been tentative. It is hard to speak about the philosophy of Chekhov and about Chekhov the thinker not only because he left no systematic philosophical account of his views and frequently mocked any kind of philosophizing, teaching, or preaching but also because his writings resist what Chekhov himself calls a "unifying idea." Trying to reassert the notion that Chekhov may be considered a philosopher, Vladimir Kataev uses terms that carefully avoid any direct reference to Chekhov's "philosophy" while focusing on the "philosophical basis" (*filosofskoe nachalo*) or "philosophical density" (*filosofskaia napolnennost'*) of his writings. He concludes: "Chekhov did not offer new ideas, but new ways of considering ideas and opinions."[1] Indeed, Chekhov seems not to have discovered new philosophical truths as perhaps Dostoevsky did, and he was also much less flamboyant than Tolstoy in his attacks on authorities; instead, he expresses a new sensibility of a person who is trapped in modernity, who undergoes a crisis of traditional religiosity that results in the new cultural paradigm of a thoroughgoing skepticism. For this reason, his "philosophy" is better understood by twentieth-century thinkers than by his contemporaries, who admired his art but objected to his "ideas" or apparent lack thereof. Chekhov's oeuvre as a whole reflects the agony of modernization as culture shifts to a secular humanism that displaces both political dogma and older sacred paradigms. One could even say that if there is any philosophy in Chekhov it is to be found precisely in his unphilosophical stance.

In many respects, Chekhov is unique in Russian culture of the period in that he recoiled from the metaphysical binaries deeply ingrained in Russian consciousness and the intelligentsia's indulgence in behavioral extremes. He was distinct from the great majority of Russian cultural figures in his inimitable common sense and respect for the European middle class, which the Russian intelligentsia generally viewed with deep suspicion. Commenting on the peculiarities of Russian history, the nineteenth-century public intellectual, memoirist, and journalist Alexander Herzen once observed: "Russia will never be Protestant, Russia will never be the *juste-milieu.*"[2] By contrast, Chekhov appears to be curiously "un-Russian" in his emphasis on moderation and tolerance. His refusal to choose sides and adhere to any single ideology is the reason why he stood out as a lonely figure in the context of Russian culture. Chekhov's contemporaries easily misinterpreted Chekhov's common sense and his intellectual sobriety and reserve as expressions of a "lack of principle." They also misunderstood his refusal to associate with extreme positions at a time when multiple new social, political, and economic institutions were rapidly emerging, and they failed to recognize the novelty of Chekhov's underlying aesthetics of an unexpectedly expansive and heterogeneous middle ground.[3] Chekhov contemplated Russian cultural trends with anxiety and cast a critical eye on the tendency to indulge in extremes, a trend that seemed to usurp the contemporary stage and overtake other modes of theatrical expression.

Chekhov's refusal to adhere to the ideological extremes so prominent in Russian society of his time led not only to a more moderate and balanced worldview but also to the development of new literary practices based on a rejection of simplistic binaries and a deep suspicion of any ideologies and overarching "philosophies." An ironist and contextualist, Chekhov created his pioneering theater as a counterpart to Russian cultural and artistic polarities. As I argue in chapters 1 and 2 of this book, Chekhov's consciously and consistently disunified worldview and his philosophy of "neither/nor" represented, at least in part, Chekhov's reaction against Russian cultural maximalism; it led him to search for new forms of artistic representation, subverting traditional notions of plot, conflict, action, characterization, denouement, and symbolism. In the process of overcoming the extremes of Russian cultural self-expression, which thrived on overstatement, he developed an entirely new kind of theater based on the poetics of understatement, restraint, "nonexpression," or of hidden expression conveyed through silence, subtle transitions, and few suggestive details.

This book's ambition is to underscore the profound connection between Chekhov the thinker and Chekhov the artist. To what extent were Chekhov's innovations in the genre of drama a response to the new philosophical trends of his time and a consequence of his direct or indirect participation in these ideas? While critics have previously scrutinized Chekhov's artistic innovations and made several, albeit very cursory, attempts to discuss Chekhov's "philosophy," the chapters to come will attempt to integrate Chekhov's art and thought by placing his theatrical innovations in the context of his philosophical and artistic sensibility and by examining his engagement with Russian and European philosophical and literary traditions.[4] This book presents Chekhov as a writer who responded to major and rapidly changing political, economic, and social events in Russia and anticipated many of the trends we associate with modernism and existentialism.

I consider Chekhov's theater as a product of his modernist sense of reality, which questioned all kinds of existential certainties and the very possibility of ultimate knowledge or truth—a position that was gradually taking shape among the Western intellectuals at the end of the nineteenth century and beyond. Although Chekhov was often associated with naturalism in the theater, he rejected not only the old melodramatic conventions but also Konstantin Stanislavsky's attempts to make him more naturalistic. Similarly, although he might have some elements of symbolism in his plays, he subtly mocked symbolism and never was a truly symbolist playwright. Rather, his dramas were precursors to existentialist theater. He was interested not so much in conflicts *between* people as in the inherent tragedy (and comedy) of life. There is no question that Chekhov, similar to Maurice Maeterlinck, Henrik Ibsen, and August Strindberg, was responsive to the tragedy of the everyday. Yet the center of his attention is not the monotony of life per se, but the concept of being in time, and what constitutes the most authentic way of "being." Human existence itself is the main focus of his theater.

Chekhov's emphasis on existence—not on traditional conflicts between characters and explosive plot developments—leads him to a different concept of the theatrical event and a different approach to characterization. The event is conceived not as a "happening" but as an event of being, which he portrays as a drama of the human condition. This emphasis on the problem of being rather than on the conflicts between characters also gives rise to Chekhov's peculiar approach to characterization and his use of recurrent themes in his plays. In fact, his last four major plays seem to have over-lapping themes and leitmotifs, with characters grappling with major questions of human existence: What is the meaning of life? What is the meaning of work? What are the limits of human knowledge? What could be done to change the situation? Some of Chekhov's characters seem to repeat them-selves. Moreover, as Naum Berkovsky astutely observes, "characters move in Chekhov from play to play, although they change name and complexion in each. Chekhov sets store not in the personal idiosyncrasies of a character, but in the character's significance amidst the others in working out the gen-eral meaning of the play."[5] I further interpret this repetition not as a sim-ple redundancy on the author's part but as an empirically driven impulse to investigate a subject from a plurality of angles and contexts. Chekhov's last four plays emerge as a cycle that focuses on subtle variations of the charac-ters' experiences. Thus, the leitmotif of labor or work, for example, operates differently in each situation for a given character but is invariably linked to the question of being. This approach stems from Chekhov's "scientific" and medical training and also his diagnostically oriented insistence that every experience of a subject is unique, that every variation reveals a subject in a new light and contains the possibility of change and discovery. This cyclical representation of characters who, without losing their individuality, never-theless exhibit the same recurrent features was an essential phenomeno-logical tool in Chekhov's portrayal of human life. Chekhov rejects any kind of definitive "answer" to a character's predicament and instead tirelessly looks for various possible configurations of a life's trajectory. There is no conclusive treatment of any subject but instead an endless probing into the plurality of circumstances. Adamantly rejecting any "unified vision of the word" and any dominating "ideology," Chekhov strove to capture life's variability. His characters often emerge as building blocks in the construction of different models, with the result that one and the same piece or a character trait may acquire a different meaning in different contexts and configurations. Thus, another thesis that this book makes is that with his skepticism about the accessibility of the final truth, Chekhov develops a contextualist mode that expresses itself in cyclicality.

In the pages to come, I attempt to present Chekhov as a tireless contextualizer. Perhaps this is one of the reasons he never succeeded in writing a novel: that, he thought, required a more unified vision. By contrast, the power of his art stems from its plurality and variability. Chekhov's art thrives on isolated cases, whether they are presented in his short stories or plays, and indirectly raises larger questions of human nature and being in relation to time, work, and the meaning of life. What he tries to capture are not types (i.e., similarities among individuals), or exceptional individuals (i.e., unique characters), but how our similarity manifests itself differently under different circumstances. Chekhov views human nature, with all its vices and virtues, as raw material that everyone shares. Yet a particular situation or personality shapes that raw material in a variety of dynamic ways. In Chekhov's view, it is precisely this variability of the human within specific moments that should be the subject of artistic representation. With his relentless pursuit of experiential truth in his plays, Chekhov underscores that any larger truth always comprises an ensemble of individual cases.

Although a substantial corpus of criticism already deals with Chekhov's dramaturgy, this book considers his last four plays as part of Chekhov's modernist aesthetic and philosophical sensitivity and places them in the philosophical context of his time and beyond. Treating Chekhov as a playwright and thinker, this book places his thought and his artistic sensibility in a broad cultural context, establishing many previously untapped intertextual connections or links between Chekhov and various Russian and European writers and philosophers. I consider Chekhov's overlapping motifs not only in terms of the recurrent thematic material but also as part of Chekhov's unique poetics, analyzed here as a form of practical philosophy.

We might recall that in his essay on William Faulkner, Jean-Paul Sartre insisted that "[a] fictional technique always relates back to the novel's metaphysics."[6] Although Chekhov may have rejected metaphysics, his innovations in the poetics of drama issue from his philosophical or "anti-philosophical" sensibility. As a dramatist, Chekhov staged everyday life that was previously almost unknown to the stage—with no traditional tragic or comic resolutions or striking external events—only an abundance of seemingly meaningless and random lines. He created not only an ineffable mood (as Meyerhold and other stage directors perceived it) but life as a reflection of a dogmatic approach to the world. In order to fully understand Chekhov the playwright, we need to understand Chekhov the thinker. The main focus of this book, therefore, is the impact of his worldview on his poetics and approach to theater.

As suspicious as he was of all metaphysics, Chekhov consistently avoided systematic and even nonsystematic philosophy and recoiled from "philosophizing." The first chapter foregrounds Chekhov's thought in the context of Russian culture and discusses his "anti-philosophical" stance of "neither/nor." Examining Chekhov's position in comparison to that of the Russian existentialist philosopher Lev Shestov, I argue that both Chekhov and Shestov were iconoclasts who rejected theoretical and dogmatic thought. Looking at Chekhov through the prism of Shestov and later developments in existentialist philosophy helps us identify some important aspects of Chekhov's modern sensibility. I argue that Chekhov appears to both question the possibility of human knowledge and rebel against the limits of reason, but as opposed to Søren Kierkegaard, Lev Shestov, Albert Camus, and many other existential thinkers, he does not strive to find the truth in the absurd. Instead he insists that the task of the writer is only to describe actual experiences and be an "impartial witness." Chekhov is also aware that the kind of art that emerges from the modern individual's state of disbelief and confrontation with the absurd must be different from art familiar to us from centuries of literary and artistic traditions. I further argue that his anti-system sensibility and his deliberate avoidance of any kind of definite "outlook" or "conception of the world" (the lack of which he viewed as a "disease" of modernity) inevitably lead him to important innovations in prose and theater—that is, to a more fragmented and open-ended artistic production that is not goal- or end-oriented and that sees no need for the kind of "unified vision" that was characteristic of the great artists of previous centuries.

Closely connected to his overall rebellion against the Russian indulgence in extremes and his rejection of—or gesture of protest against—simplistically dualistic approaches to life is Chekhov's criticism of contemporary theater, particularly the conventions of melodrama and the "well-made play" discussed in chapter 2. Chekhov's anti-melodramatic imagination leads him to reconsider the role of plot, character, symbol, music, and sound. As an example of his attempt to reexamine the theatrical character, I consider Chekhov's first major play, *Ivanov*, which I regard as an experiment in anti-melodramatic thinking. In creating his protagonist Ivanov, who he insisted was new in Russian literature, Chekhov was emphasizing the destructive aspects of the binary mentality and paving the way for new principles in the construction of theatrical character and plot.

After the first two chapters, which serve as a bridge to a more detailed analysis of Chekhov's four major plays and his engagement with the major philosophical, aesthetic, and social issues of the time, I chart the formative stages of Chekhov's dramaturgy from *The Seagull* to *The Cherry Orchard*. Although the next six chapters are devoted to a thorough analysis of individual plays, each chapter addresses the relation of Chekhov's poetics to his general outlook. *The Seagull* undoubtedly plays a central role in the development of Chekhov's truly original voice as a playwright, and the chapter dedicated to this play gives a detailed analysis of Chekhov's views on art and his goals as an artist. Unlike many of his contemporaries, Chekhov never wrote artistic manifestos or articles on aesthetics with systematic poetic and aesthetic analyses. However, *The Seagull* is the most literary of all his plays, and it is closer to a literary manifesto than any of his other works. It is also probably the most metapoetical and metatheatrical play that had been written at the time. In particular, Chekhov is interested in the role of signs, symbols, and images in artistic production. Though Chekhov's images are open to being read as metaphoric, they often resist this kind of interpretation. Thoroughly purged of their symbolic significance, some of his key images defy the semiotic tyranny associated with melodramatic and metaphoric visions of the world. Ultimately, Chekhov's art represents a somewhat precarious balance between naturalism, symbolism, and realism, simultaneously sharing and rejecting the poetics of the play's two antagonist writers, Treplev and Trigorin.

While the question of art was always at the center of Chekhov's attention, he also indirectly addressed some questions related to epistemology and ontology, as discussed in chapters 4, 5, and 6. Although frequently viewed as an artist but not a profound thinker because of his apparent interest in the trivial and the mundane, Chekhov nevertheless responded to the major philosophical questions of his time, but in subtle and discreet ways. Examining Chekhov's hidden dialogue with Dostoevsky (and in part with

Tolstoy) elucidates Chekhov's existentialist sensibility and reveals his artistic response to the emerging nihilism and existential anxiety associated with the loss of traditional values and certainties. The comparative analysis of Chekhov's and Dostoevsky's thought fills a lacuna in Chekhov scholarship while also leading us to a better understanding of Chekhov's artistic practices. By comparing Chekhov's play *Uncle Vania* to Dostoevsky's *The Village of Stepanchikovo*, I not only identify multiple thematic overlaps between Dostoevsky and Chekhov but also examine how Chekhov develops certain narrative strategies that lead him to create a dramatic form characterized by dialogicality and open-endedness. My conclusion that Chekhov's theater embraces open-endedness is at variance with Bakhtin's assertion that theater is inherently monological. Many of the characteristics of the polyphonic novel described by Bakhtin—the lack of resolution and synthesis, a plurality and non-hierarchy of voices, internal dialogicality, and a nonlinear plot line—are concepts employed in Chekhov's theater. I suggest that Chekhov's rejection of binaries, rigid generic designations, and finalized worldviews leads him to a different type of artistic production—one that, as compared to traditional nineteenth-century theater, is more fragmented, amorphous, open-ended, pluralistic, and inherently dialogical. Rejecting the devices of classical comedy and melodrama, Chekhov also unexpectedly seems to appropriate a peculiar theatrical strategy of Dostoevsky—the verbal scandal. While Bakhtin argued that dramatic dialogue is in a sense monolithic because it is broken up into statement and response, we see that in Chekhov's plays this is often not the case.

The breadth and scope of Chekhov's engagement with contemporary social, philosophical, and political thought also manifests itself in his musings on the labor question and the existential role of work in human life. Chapter 5 discusses Chekhov's response to the pressing social and philosophical questions of the time by showing the centrality in Chekhov's plays of the theme of work as a possible means of finding meaning in existence. Almost every single character in *Uncle Vania*, *The Three Sisters*, and to some degree *The Cherry Orchard* comments on the significance of work for human fulfillment. I consider refractions of this theme in his major plays and how they are presented in the context of the contemporary polemics around work on the eve of the Russian revolution, a time of escalating forms of class conflict, mass protests, and the organized labor movement all over Europe. Delving into the role of work in human life, Chekhov links it to the problem of what it means to be human. I suggest that Chekhov is an important intermediary linking Dostoevsky to Camus in the way he considers possible responses to the absurdity of meaningless labor or of existence at large. Most of Chekhov's mature plays end with the characters' realization of the ultimate futility of their lives and their hard, incessant work, along with the absence of a higher meaning in their existence. Yet some of them resolve to persevere, even in the face of a world without transcendence or eternal values. Chekhov chooses his multiperspectival approach in dealing with larger social and philosophical questions and therefore treats the theme of work from a variety of different perspectives in several of his plays. His interest in work as an ontological problem also leads him to a different concept of eventfulness, a subject discussed in chapter 6, which focuses on *The Three Sisters*. This play in particular reveals Chekhov's interest in being as an event in its own right, in the human condition, and temporality. In this respect, Chekhov shares the field of interests of such twentieth-century philosophers as Shestov, Husserl, and Heidegger. I argue that many of Chekhov's dramaturgical innovations stem from his very modern concept of time, being, and event.

Finally, the final two chapters are devoted to Chekhov's last play, *The Cherry Orchard*, and focus on its central images, the nursery and the garden. While echoing themes and issues raised in *The Seagull*, *Uncle Vania*, and *The Three Sisters*, such as money, dispossession, industrialization, visions of the future, the perception of time, and the meaning of work, as well as the sense of existential abandonment, Chekhov's last play, more so than its antecedents, is preoccupied with the impact of modernization and social, economic, and political change taking place in Russia at the end of the nineteenth century. Through the images of the nursery and the orchard, Chekhov conveys his thoughts about Russia as it enters the twentieth century. Chekhov regarded the ineptitude of various classes in responding to change as a dangerous form of infantilism. The playwright's profound interest in the dynamics of the class structure and his concern for the responsibility of each class to preserve Russia's social well-being results in a highly ambiguous play and an elusive generic form that not only mixes the comic, the farcical, and the tragic but also emerges as a *conte philosophique* of sorts, or a *comedie philosophique*. By linking Chekhov's use of the garden to Voltaire's celebrated statement in Candide, "Il faut cultiver notre jardin," I suggest that for both Voltaire and Chekhov, the garden is not only a symbol but also a concrete plot of land that requires individual effort to be maintained. Chekhov clearly echoes here Voltaire's notion that it is our duty to cultivate our garden, but he places it in a modern context. All the characters in Chekhov's last play, although aware of human inequality and social stratification, tend to close their eyes to the necessity of change and the very real need for personal involvement and incessant work for the sake of universal well-being. Their passivity and acquiescence are presented by Chekhov as a form of a dangerous neglect leading to tragic consequences, both for particular individuals (e.g., Firs) and for entire classes of people (especially the Russian aristocracy). The words of Pangloss, uttered in response to Candide's revelation that "we must cultivate our garden," echo Chekhov's own ethics and emerge as a recurrent leitmotif not only in *The Cherry Orchard* but also in other Chekhov plays. Just as Voltaire's *Candide* is critical of Leibniz's metaphysics but seems to embrace the Lockean idea that our role in life is to work, even if this work may just be barely tolerable, Chekhov, in general, satirizes all kinds of "philosophizing" but believes in "separate individuals" and their work, even if this work may be as hard and sometimes seemingly as futile as that of Sisyphus (in Camus's interpretation). Like Voltaire, who was not a philosopher in the conventional sense, Chekhov never clearly articulated his philosophical views in the form of a comprehensive metaphysical blueprint. Instead he conveyed his philosophy as an affective gesture that possesses its own logic, expressing the possibility of a new kind of theater focusing on the drama of human existence.

In the conclusion, I consider Chekhov's "non-endings" as stemming from his quest for knowledge, while at the same time realizing that definitive knowledge is impossible. This realization led Chekhov to abandon standard conclusions and opt instead for a sense of non-ending, which is best conveyed by the literary trope of departure. What is the end of a play? What is the end of life? Chekhov sought to avoid "dramatic" moments and "dramatic" denouements in his art, as he did in his life. Before leaving for a health resort in Badenweiler, Germany, where he died on July 15, 1904, Chekhov told his friends that he was going there to die. The act of departure—his physical departure from Russia—clearly foreshadowed his final departure, his death. According to the recollections of his wife, Olga Knipper, "Anton Pavlovich quietly, calmly passed on into another world" (*otoshel v drugoi mir*). Emptying a glass of champagne, he "quietly lay down on his left side and soon fell silent forever." This quiet "departure" and "turning away" was Chekhov's last undramatic gesture, a gesture that he sought to turn into the basic principle of his theater.

1

Chekhov's (Anti-)Philosophy

There are nowadays professors of philosophy, but not philosophers. Yet it is admirable to profess because it was once admirable to live. To be a philosopher is not merely to have subtle thoughts, nor even to found a school, but so to love wisdom as to live according to its dictates, a life of simplicity, independence, magnanimity, and trust. It is to solve some of the problems of life, not only theoretically, but practically.

Henry David Thoreau, *Walden*

The Either/Or of Russian Culture

In 1909, writing about Turgenev's place within the Russian literary and cultural tradition and commenting on Russia's obsession with various binaries, Dmitry Merezhkovsky praised Turgenev's moderation and singled him out as a "genius of culture": "In Russia, in a land of every sort of maximalism, revolutionary and religious, a land of self-immolations, a land of the most frenzied excesses, Turgenev—after Pushkin—is almost the sole *genius of measure* and, therefore, a genius of culture."[1] Yet Chekhov was undoubtedly another striking exception to the Russian cultural practice of indulging in extreme or maximalist modalities and lifestyles. It is precisely Chekhov's ability to appreciate what Herzen referred to as *juste-milieu* (so alien to the dominant sensibility of the Russian cultural elite) that made him frequently misunderstood by the Russian reader, and by a Russian audience that was accustomed to extreme states of being. This criticism stemmed from a major misunderstanding of Chekhov's position vis-à-vis the "either/or" of Russian culture.

Chekhov was fully aware of the degree to which the aesthetics of excess were ingrained in Russian cultural history, and he openly objected to this "dramatization" of thought and experience, typical of both the Russian radical intelligentsia and mass or lowbrow culture. Chekhov's famous statement of religious belief, in which he associates the polarizing perception of reality with Russian national identity, is a classic expression of his refusal to commit to ideological or philosophical extremes:

> Between "God exists" and "God does not exist" lies a whole enormous field which a true sage crosses with great difficulty. A Russian, however, knows only one of these extremes, the middle ground between them does not interest him; that is why as a rule he knows either nothing or very little. (17:224)[2]

Chekhov clearly refers here to Russia's famous and explosive "philosophical" and "religious" debates, a good example of which is the celebrated exchange between Fyodor Karamazov and his two sons, Ivan and Alyosha, in Dostoevsky's *The Brothers Karamazov.*

Chekhov's reserved attitude toward Dostoevsky is well-known. A similar attitude informs Chekhov's fascination with, and criticism of, Tolstoy. Although Chekhov greatly admired Tolstoy, he is no less critical of his extreme positions than he is of Dostoevsky's. Reacting to Tolstoy's "Afterword to the *Kreutzer Sonata,*" Chekhov writes:

> The devil take the philosophy of the great ones of this world! All the great sages are as despotic as generals, and as ignorant and as indelicate as generals, because they are convinced they are safe from punishment. . . . And so, to hell with the philosophy of the great ones of this world. (P 3:11)

As much as he may have admired both Tolstoy and Dostoevsky as writers, when it came to the question of "philosophy," Chekhov viewed these otherwise very different artists as self-important "despotic generals."

Chekhov's frequently quoted letter to A. Pleshcheev, which articulates his artistic credo, also focuses on his anti-polarizing stand and his refusal to associate with "great sages" and literary generals:

> I am neither liberal nor conservative, nor monk nor indifferentist. I would like to be a free artist and nothing else. . . . Pharisaism, dull-wittedness and tyranny reign not only in merchants' houses and police stations. . . . I see them in science and literature among the younger generation. I look upon tags and labels as prejudices. My holy of holies is the human body, health, intelligence, talent, inspiration and the most absolute freedom imaginable, freedom from violence and lies, no matter what form the latter two take. (P 3:11)

Claiming that he wanted to be neither conservative nor liberal but merely a free artist, Chekhov resisted antipodal positions because he regarded them as forms of ideological tyranny. This artistic credo appears to be curiously "un-Russian" in its emphasis on the essentially classical Greek, and therefore pagan, ideal of mental and physical health, of equal respect for human intelligence and the beauty of body and soul.[3] Significantly, Chekhov frequently uses Englishmen, Germans, and Frenchmen as foils in his criticism of the Russians' lack of moderation, their indulgence in binaries, their militant "ethicism" at the expense of "aesthetics," and their inattention to mundane concerns.[4]

Chekhov's portrayal of Ivanov, in the play of that name, and of Laevsky in "The Duel," to take only a few examples, also emphasizes Russian excessiveness that results, as Chekhov sees it, in a depletion of cognitive—if not spiritual—resources. In his letter to A. S. Suvorin of December 30, 1888, he comments in detail on this Russian trait: "Thus, excessive irritability, a sense of guilt, and exhaustion are purely Russian qualities. The Germans never get overexcited, and that is why Germans are neither disillusioned, nor superfluous and exhausted" (P 3:115). In comparing Englishmen (as well as Germans and Frenchmen) to Russians, Chekhov often emphasizes their respect for form and their practicality. By no means isolated examples include the juxtaposition of English gentility with the Russian intelligentsia's disdain for form in *The Seagull* and the comparison of English practicality with perceived Russian ineptitude in *The Cherry Orchard*.[5] The opposition between ethics and aesthetics, the tendency toward ideological intolerance, and a lack of respect for or interest in the *juste-milieu* are only a few examples of Russian culture's indulgence in behavioral extremes. Chekhov contemplated these trends with anxiety and observed critically how Russian cultural indulgence in extremes also resulted in the popularity of certain modes of theatrical expression that seemed to usurp the contemporary stage.

Although Chekhov openly rebelled against "the philosophy of the great ones of this world," this does not mean that the characters in his plays and prose never engage in philosophical debates. Perhaps even the contrary is true: many of them raise the weightiest of philosophical questions. Yet almost invariably, Chekhov refers to these discussions as "philosophizing" and depicts them with detachment and irony. Chekhov's irony stems from his skepticism toward any overarching philosophy and unified vision of the world.

The Neither/Nor of Chekhov: Chekhov and Shestov

Chekhov's status among Russian writers is in many ways similar to the status among Russian philosophers of Lev Shestov, whose philosophy also offers no systematic unity or coherent set of propositions.[6] Shestov refuses to provide theoretical explanations of philosophical problems, engaging instead in an exercise in paradoxes and self-contradictions. Regardless of the fact that he later turned out to be an influential figure in the French existentialist movement and was viewed by some as one of the founding fathers of twentieth-century religious existentialism, he did not articulate a philosophy of his own until late in his life. Instead, he launched a powerful and passionate attack on the entire Western philosophical tradition. Both Chekhov and Shestov were iconoclasts who rejected theoretical and dogmatic thought, boldly questioning all accepted norms and "herd morality." Their skepticism about philosophical and artistic traditions extended even to the possibility of openly formulating their own programmatic positions. Both were outsiders to some extent and separated themselves from their own "soil." Neither of them belonged to any current or movement, and indeed, both made a point of scorning the possibility of such affiliations. Chekhov persistently refused to present himself under any label and avoided the seductiveness of any metaphysical, Nietzschean, or Marxist beliefs. Likewise, Shestov made it his life's task to debunk all systematic philosophy. Nikolai Berdiaev was undoubtedly right that Shestov's philosophy was, for the most part, one that was negative in the sense that it sought to call into question any comprehensive epistemology.[7] Nevertheless, both exerted profound influence on the development of their respective areas of creativity—Russian and Western prose and drama in the case of Chekhov, and Russian and (to a certain extent) Western philosophy in the case of Shestov.

It is not surprising, then, that Shestov finds in Chekhov a kindred spirit and is one of the first readers of Chekhov, along with Vasily Rozanov and Sergei Bulgakov, who sees in Chekhov not only a great artist, but also a philosopher, although a philosopher of a peculiar kind. Somewhat irritated (like Chekhov) by the demonstrably vatic pathos of Dostoevsky and Tolstoy, Shestov recognizes in Chekhov a bold and original thinker, a man who completely breaks with the Russian prophetic or didactic tradition. In his view, Chekhov is the only writer among Russian classics who does not actually possess a distinct "worldview" and who looks suspiciously at any kind of ideology or unified vision. Shestov senses in Chekhov a distinctive *Weltanschauung* that separates him from his predecessors and anticipates a movement that is gradually taking shape in Russia and Europe at that time. This outlook is theorized and articulated somewhat later and lays the foundation of the philosophical movements of existentialism and phenomenology. Looking at Chekhov through the prism of Shestov and the later developments within existentialist philosophy helps us to identify some important aspects of Chekhov's modern sensibility. As reductionist and idiosyncratic as Shestov's interpretation of Chekhov is, it elucidates some important aspects of Chekhov the thinker.

In his provocative essay on Chekhov titled "Creation from the Void" ("Tvorchestvo iz nichego," 1908), Shestov seemingly makes a number of grave accusations against Chekhov, notoriously calling him "the minstrel of hopelessness" and even a criminal ("what Chekhov was doing is called a crime and is subject to severe punishment").[8] But this charged statement is accusatory only on a surface level. Ivan Bunin recognizes this right away and observes that for all his seemingly negative evaluation, Shestov's essay is the most insightful piece written on Chekhov, for it points to something very important in Chekhov's oeuvre: as Shestov himself indicates in the essay, Chekhov the criminal only comes into view when regarded from the perspective of everyday or "ordinary" language.[9]

According to Shestov, Chekhov's "crime" consists first and foremost in his absolute honesty and courage in grappling with all accepted worldviews and received wisdoms that are generated by "the artificial habits of civilization." Chekhov does not bow to compromise and violates all ideological taboos in a manner that prompts Shestov to compare him figuratively to a man who "would prevent corpses from being buried, and would dig decaying bodies from the grave." While perverse in his contrarianism, such a man is not afraid to speak about what most writers and even philosophers attempt to conceal: namely, the utter disorientation of people in the midst of demanding yet often conflicting social clues that prevent them from being grounded. He claims: "More and more, Chekhov emancipates himself from old prejudices and goes—where? Were he asked, he himself could hardly answer. But he prefers to remain without an answer, rather than to accept any of the traditional answers."[10] Individuals in Chekhov's writings, according to Shestov, are always placed in situations of despair, and their desperate state is precisely what should be hidden from ordinary human eyes, for in a "normal and healthy mind" Chekhov's "ghastly occupation" of laying bare all human illusions should rouse "nothing but disgust and terror."

It is obvious, therefore, that what Shestov calls a "crime" is a crime only for philistines, including intellectual philistines and men of letters. In Shestov's own terms, Chekhov's refusal to participate in constructing conceptions of the world represents rather an extreme audacity of spirit. Likewise, when he claims that Chekhov "was killing human hope," he in fact means not so much optimism or the concept of hope as he does the seductive world of illusions: "Art, science, love, inspiration, ideals, the future—select all the words with which humanity is, or has been in the past, consoling or amusing itself—Chekhov has only to touch them and they instantly fade, wither, and die."[11] In other words, it is not that Chekhov demolishes "art, science, love, inspiration" per se. Nor does he destroy human hopes as such; rather, he questions the excessive emotional investment that humanity places in art, science, love, and inspiration, and he demonstrates that the perception of them as final truths is merely a dangerous illusion.

Chapters 3 and 5 of this book will focus in greater detail on Chekhov's critique of such ideals in *The Seagull* and *Uncle Vania*.[12] For now, it is enough to point out that Shestov is clearly attracted by the brazen liberty of Chekhov's critical spirit and undoubtedly shares Chekhov's antipathy to modes of thought that kill life by subordinating it to ideas, abstractions, and generalizations. He also relates to Chekhov's high esteem for the unique and unrepeatable individual who exists in a state of tragic solitude in the face of death and the world's apparent incomprehensibility. For Shestov, Chekhov is a "brother in arms" who struggles against the tyranny exercised by all kinds of ideology over human life. According to Shestov, Chekhov is "the irreconcilable foe of all kinds of philosophy": "Not one of his heroes philosophizes, or if he does, his philosophizing is unsuccessful, ridiculous, weak and unconvincing."[13]

Nevertheless, it would be a great simplification of both Chekhov and Shestov to say that they put store in the promise of a meaningful existence. Chekhov and Shestov struggled against totalitarian truth that claimed to have the last word. What concerned them was the possibility that utilitarian demands of the moment would flatten the subtle frequencies of experience. In his essay on Chekhov, Shestov claims that Chekhov's characters stand "before the fatal boundary which divides man from the eternal mystery" and that, forced to experience profound existential despair, they can only resort to "creating out of a void."[14] Shestov concludes that Chekhov's heroes "are faced with this abnormal and dreadful necessity. Before them always lies hopelessness, helplessness, the utter impossibility of any action whatsoever."[15] Yet it is obvious that this despair is the greatest virtue for Shestov, for it is the first step toward authentic existence. Shestov sees angst as the most genuinely human of all predicaments; he is therefore on the whole hostile to tranquility as a privileged cognitive modality. Anxiety, he insists, is a creative force that motivates human beings to discover new possibilities of existence and experience. For Shestov, a person living in the age of modernity can only experience revelation after first experiencing despair and a sense of utter abandonment in the search for God. This is precisely the state in which the Chekhovian protagonist finds himself, according to the Russian philosopher: "He has nothing, he must create everything himself. And this 'creation out of the void,' or more truly the possibility of the creation out of the void, is the only problem that can occupy and inspire Chekhov."[16] Shestov is one of the first readers to point out that Chekhov's characters experience existential crises, that they are alienated characters who struggle with hopelessness and absurdity. He also suggests that Chekhov, along with Dostoevsky, developed positions that were existentialists in all but name. As we shall see in chapter 4, though, the artistic embodiments of these ideas were drastically different in Dostoevsky's and Chekhov's works.

Shestov may be mistaken about reducing Chekhov to the philosophy of despair or of "creation from the void." It is obvious that some elements of Chekhov's *Weltanschauung* both annoyed and attracted Shestov. They attracted Shestov because he sensed the novelty of Chekhov's positions and ideas, but they annoyed him—as well as most of his contemporaries—because these ideas became more comprehensible only in the context of twentieth-century philosophy. Although Chekhov cannot be labeled existentialist and most likely would have rejected the label if it had been explained to him, there is no question that the human subject and its conditions of existence are his central concern. Both the brute fact of human existence and what it means to be human were indeed at the center of his work. Moreover, in his representation of the possibility of a radical freedom that would dispel the miasma of anxiety and perpetual state of uncertainty in which even the comfortable and privileged live, Chekhov anticipated many of Shestov's own philosophical positions, as well as those of other existential thinkers. It is also obvious that what Chekhov shares with Shestov, he shares with other representatives of existential thought—that is, a sense of alienation, disorientation, and confusion in the face of an apparently meaningless world; an awareness of the impossibility of rationally understanding the world; an appreciation of the exceptional value of individual human beings; a tragic sense of the finality of human existence; and a special interest in the problem of freedom of choice. Like most other existential thinkers and phenomenologists, Chekhov regarded traditional systematic or academic philosophy as too abstract and remote from concrete human experience. The point of departure for him was not a theory or an idea but an experience. This is why Chekhov's "gospel" or "holy of holies," as he puts it, is "the human body, health, intelligence, talent, inspiration, love, and the most absolute freedom." Rather than hypothesizing a human essence, he focused on the question of concrete human existence and the conditions of this existence. Shortly before his death, Chekhov writes in one of his letters to his wife (April 20, 1904): "You are asking what is life? This is the same as to ask: what is a carrot? A carrot is a carrot, we know nothing else" (P 12:93).

In other words, similar to phenomenologists in the Husserlian tradition, Chekhov is interested only in how things present themselves in actual experience rather than the dictates of some theory or system as to how they must be. There is no such thing as the carrot's essence apart from its concrete existence and apart from our perception of its existence. We cannot say what life is apart from the personal experience of life. Its meaning is to be found only in existence and in personal experience. As reflected in his prose, drama, and letters, this is a position that Chekhov takes consistently.

Many of the same ideas were formulated by various existential thinkers who also raised the question of knowledge and its limits. Thus, for example, Camus, in a book that was perhaps most typical of the period of emerging existentialist philosophy, wrote about the confrontation between the human need to know and the "unreasonable silence of the world":[17]

> This heart within me I can feel, and I judge that it exists. This world I can touch, and I likewise judge that it exists. There ends all my knowledge, and the rest is construction. . . . Aspects cannot be added up. This very head which is mine will forever remain indefinable to me. Between the certainty I have of my existence and the content I try to give to that assurance, the gap will never be filled.[18]

A carrot is a carrot, according to Chekhov. We know nothing else, or, in Camus's terms, "the rest is construction."

Chekhov's thought rejected systematic philosophy in favor of the individual personal experience, the individual's quest for truth, and emphasized the life of "flesh and bone," to use Miguel de Unamuno's terms, as opposed to abstract rationalism. In this sense, Chekhov is as much a "brother in arms" with Shestov as he is with predecessors of existentialism such as Søren Kierkegaard, Nietzsche, Unamuno, and later anti-rationalist philosophers, whom Camus in his *The Myth of Sisyphus* mentions as part of the same "family of minds" (e.g., Karl Jaspers, the phenomenologists, Martin Heidegger, and Max Scheler). It is no coincidence that Camus also includes Shestov in the group and believes the two of them had a lot in common regardless of their opposed methods and aims. A significant common thread was the notion of an indescribable universe "where contradiction, antinomy, anguish, or impotence reigns."[19] In his discussion of various authors who deal with the new "absurd man," Camus does not mention Chekhov, nor does he include Chekhov among those who, along with Dostoevsky, Nietzsche, and Ibsen, may have shaped Shestov's anti-rationalist thought. He acknowledges, however, Shestov's pivotal role in the development of the existentialist movement and existential line of thought, which undoubtedly also includes Chekhov.

The impossibility of knowing is a problem that concerned most existential thinkers. What distinguished them were the kinds of conclusions they drew from their discovery that the world is incomprehensible. Like Camus yet unlike Shestov, Chekhov values reason and wants the world to be rationally penetrable, but he finds that it is not. Chekhov laments the clash between the human need for understanding and the world's unintelligibility, what Camus calls "the unreasonable silence of the world." "There is no happiness if I cannot know," declares Camus. Chekhov's characters seem to complain about much the same thing. As some scholars have observed, the three sisters' "if only I could know" (esli by znat') and "I do not know" (ne znaiu) constitute a recurrent leitmotif in Chekhov's oeuvre.[20] Chekhov's position, however, is more radical than merely lamenting the lack of understanding. In fact, "those who know" are invariably portrayed in Chekhov in a more negative light than those who do not know or do not claim to understand the world. His most cherished thought is precisely the utter impenetrability of the world; not the exaltation of folly, as in the case of Shestov, but a sober acknowledgment of our inability to know the truth and yet at the same time the realization that, as Camus puts it, "there is nothing beyond reason." In his letter to Suvorin (May 30, 1888), he explains his views on epistemology and the task of writers, referring to his story "The Lights" ("Ogni"):

> Shcheglov-Leontiev blames me for finishing the story with the words, "There's no making sense of anything in this world." He thinks a writer who is a good

psychologist ought to be able to makes sense of things—that is what he is a psychologist for. But I don't agree with him. It is time that writers, especially those who are artists, recognize that there is no making anything out in this world, as once Socrates recognized it, and Voltaire, too. The mob thinks it knows and understands everything; and the more stupid it is the wider it imagines its horizons to be. And if a writer whom the mob believes in has the courage to declare that he does not understand anything of what he sees, that alone will constitute good knowledge in the realm of thought and a great step forward. (P 2:280–81)

Chekhov declines to explain the world and wants merely to give a description of actual experiences:

It seems to me it is not for writers of fiction to solve such questions as that of God or of pessimism, etc. The writer's business is simply to describe who has been speaking about God or about pessimism, how, and in what circumstances. The artist must be not the judge of his characters and of what they say, but merely an impartial witness. I [once] heard a confused conversation of two Russians about pessimism—a conversation which settles nothing—and I must convey that conversation as I heard it; it is up to the jury, that is, to the readers, to give it an evaluation. My business is merely to be talented, i.e., to know how to distinguish important statements from unimportant, how to throw light on the characters, and to speak their language. (P 2:280)

Chekhov appears to both question the possibility of human knowledge and to rebel against the limits of reason. In *The Three Sisters*, where the phrase "if only we could know" becomes a refrain—a refrain that also concludes the play—Masha articulates what may be viewed as Chekhov's challenge to traditional theodicy: "It seems to me, man ought to have faith or search for faith; otherwise his life is empty, empty . . . To live and not to know why cranes fly, why children are born, why stars are in the sky . . . Either you know why you live, or else nothing matters, all the same" (13:147). Masha's words seem to be an obvious reference to the Book of Job. For God questions Job precisely about his knowledge of the mystery of the creation of the universe. In response to Job's rebellion, God reminds him that he has no knowledge about the creation of the world and cannot, therefore, comprehend the meaning of the universe. This is why humans must accept suffering and death. Tuzenbach essentially embraces the traditional wisdom of the devout believer. Similar to Job's friends, he accepts life as it is, with its immutable laws, suffering, and death.

Masha's conclusion, however, that if one does not know why one lives, then "nothing matters, and everything is trivial piffle" (vse pustiaki, tryntrava) seems to be a curious modification of Ivan Karamazov's "if there is no God, then everything is permitted." While Dostoevsky places the questions of ethics into an ontological context, Chekhov is more interested in considering the ethical questions in the context of epistemology. As opposed to Dostoevsky and other thinkers who focus on the existence of evil in the world as the central question of theodicy, Chekhov fully accepts suffering, death, and evil as grim necessities. And yet, sadly, awareness of the laws of nature and necessity does not liberate the individual from despair. In his story "Terror" ("Strakh"), one of his characters, Silin, complains: "Our life and the other world are equally incomprehensible and terrifying. I don't understand life, my friend, and I am afraid of it.... When I lie on the grass and watch continuously an insect which was born just yesterday and which understands nothing, it seems to me that its life consists of nothing else but terror, and in it I see myself" (8:131). It is not suffering per se that Chekhov considers a challenge to religion but rather lack of knowledge. In Chekhov's work, the tragedy of the human condition consists in the fact that we never actually taste from the tree of knowledge, and that is why we suffer and our life is deprived of meaning. In his story "Terror," he directly links lack of knowledge and understanding of the meaning of life to the terror of being. Chekhov recognizes that Truth and God are inaccessible to thought. The tragedy of humanity is located precisely in the fruitless act of striving to transcend the limits of our knowledge and to penetrate the inaccessible realm of Truth. If Ivan Karamazov rebels against the idea of a divinely ordered universe because there is suffering in the world, Chekhov's heroes rebel because they do not know the meaning of the world. Yet unlike Ivan Karamazov, the Chekhovian protagonist does not juxtapose reason and science to faith, and he sees no inconsistency between scientific activity and the acceptance of mystery.

Chekhov was fully aware of the limitations of the so-called scientific method and was very skeptical about those who want to "embrace that which cannot be embraced scientifically."[21] In his letter to Suvorin (November 3, 1888), he gently mocks Merezhkovsky, who "has mastered the wisdom of the scientific method" and is vulnerable, therefore, to a number of "delightful temptations." Interestingly, quite in line with Husserl's famous assertion, "if we could contemplate clearly the exact laws of psychic processes, they would be seen to be likewise eternal and invariable, like the basic laws of theoretical natural science. Hence they would be valid even if there were no psychic process," Chekhov claims:

> Archimedes wanted to turn the earth upside-down, and present-day hotheads want to embrace that which cannot be embraced scientifically: they want to discover physical laws for creativity, they want to grasp the general law and the formulae by which the artist, who feels them instinctively, creates landscapes, novels, pieces of music and so on. These formulae probably do exist in nature. . . . Anyone who has a command of the scientific method senses intuitively that a piece of music and a tree have something in common and that both are created in accordance with identically regular and simple laws. Hence the question of what these laws are. Hence the temptation to write a physiology of creativity (Boborykin) and among the younger and more timid to refer to science and to the laws of nature (Merezhkovsky). A physiology of creativity probably does exist in nature, but all dreams of it must be abandoned at the outset. . . . It's always good to think scientifically, but the trouble is that that scientific thinking about art will inevitably be reduced to a search for the "cells" or "centers" in charge of creative ability. . . . For those who are haunted by the scientific method and whom God granted the rare talent of thinking scientifically, there is in my opinion only one way out—the philosophy of creativity. By gathering together all the best creations of artists through the ages and applying scientific method, we can grasp the common denominator that causes them to resemble one another and lies at the root of their value. That common denominator will then be law. (P 3:53–54)

Yet Chekhov himself was never interested in creating this kind of philosophy of creativity, which in his interpretation emerges as a rather utopian project—"gathering together all the best creations of artists through the ages." "The common denominator" in theory might exist (cf. Husserl's conditional statement about psychic processes, "if we could contemplate clearly the exact laws of psychic processes"), but it remains inaccessible to the human mind. Chekhov sought to avoid both irrationalism and overreliance on science in art, but he preferred to stay "within the limits of reason." He was a "materialist" only in the sense that he believed that the phenomenal realm is scientifically cognizable.[22] Moreover, as opposed to Shestov, who placed faith above knowledge and who believed that only faith may allow one to breach "the stone walls" of natural necessity ("only on the wings of faith may one fly over all the 'stone walls' and 'twice two is four,' erected and deified by reason and rational knowledge'"),[23] Chekhov aspired to reconcile faith to knowledge. The mystery of God, however, is not reducible for Chekhov to any accepted truth. In a letter to V. S. Miroliubov (December 17, 1901), Chekhov explains his attitude toward faith in detail and with biting irony and sarcasm tries to dissociate himself from any religious movement and religious philosophers of his time (including Rozanov and Merezhkovsky), referring to Merezhkovsky's "complete satiety" and calling Rozanov a "policeman":

> In regard to the questions that concern you, I will also say only that what is important are not the worn-out words, not idealism, but a consciousness of your own purity, that is, an absolute freedom of your soul from all kinds of forgotten and unforgotten words, from all kinds of idealism and other incomprehensible words. One must have faith in God, but if you have no faith, one must not replace it with fussiness [shumikha], but search, and search for it in loneliness, one-on-one with one's conscience. (P 10:142)

As opposed to Kierkegaard, Shestov, Camus, and many other existential thinkers, Chekhov does not strive to find the truth in the absurd. Instead, he confronts "absurd walls" in his own "quiet" way, without "fussiness" and in loneliness. Chekhov was an existential thinker *avant la lettre*, and to a degree that is seldom commented upon. This is why his philosophical—or rather, anti-philosophical—positions were not fully understood by his contemporaries and why the twentieth and twenty-first centuries found him more congenial. Shestov probably came closer than others to understanding Chekhov the thinker. Yet he, too, was somewhat irritated with Chekhov because to his taste Chekhov was never sufficiently enamored of folly and madness. He was slightly annoyed with Chekhov perhaps for the same reason that he disagreed with Husserl, who was too rationalistic for Shestov, for Husserl intended Reason to be an instrument for discovering absolute and eternal truths that would be valid for "men, monsters, angels, and gods."

To be sure, Chekhov does not use the terms of philosophy. But he intuitively distinguishes between the realm of experience and the realm of pure consciousness. For this reason, Chekhov objects to any "conjecture" of truth or surrogates of faith, whether they are those of Dostoevsky, of the "policeman" Rozanov, of the "most satisfied" Merezhkovsky, or of any other religious thinker. Their faiths are merely "truths of judgment," premature and stubborn assessments.

One could find multiple examples in Chekhov's texts that align him with philosophers of previous centuries, of his own time, or of our age. However, unlike, for example, Dostoevsky and Tolstoy, Chekhov is not known for his direct impact on any Western philosophers, nor is he known to have been directly influenced by contemporary Western philosophical thought. His own "philosophy" remains elusive, indeterminate, and irreducible to any of his characters' "judgments" or even his own. Chekhov consistently avoids systematic and even nonsystematic philosophy and recoils from all philosophy as "philosophizing." He juxtaposes philosophy not to another kind of philosophy or anti-philosophy but to life itself, the "meaning" of which is incomprehensible but could be described through artistic analysis of experience. Chekhov believes that "psychologists" and "artists" should not try to deal with the true meaning of reality because, as he puts it, "there is no making out anything in this world." We would be better off refraining from passing judgment upon the described universe. The task of the writer, as Chekhov insisted in his letter to Suvorin quoted earlier in this chapter, is not only to describe actual experiences and be an "impartial witness" but to suspend judgment regarding the true nature of reality (letter to Suvorin, May 30, 1888; P 2:280). This method of artistic reduction is best conveyed in Masha and Tuzenbach's exchange about the tension between the desire to know and the impossibility of complete knowledge:

> TUZENBACH: ... They [the birds of passage] fly and will keep on flying, whatever philosopher may emerge among them; and let them philosophize as they wish, so long as they keep on flying ...
>
> MASHA: But what's the meaning of it?
>
> TUZENBACH: Meaning ... Here, there's snow falling. What's the meaning of that? [*Pause*]. (13:147)

What is the meaning of snow? What is the meaning of life? What is a carrot? A carrot is a carrot, snow is snow, life is life. Our experience tells us only about what is but does not explain the meaning of what is. What we think or feel about snow, a carrot, and life could be rendered, however, through art. While artistic representation might not be used as a method for resolving philosophical problems, it may be used as a way of making us think about these problems, to struggle with the incomprehensible, and to search for truth "in loneliness and one-on-one with one's conscience."

Chekhov is also aware that the kind of art that emerges from the modern man's state of disbelief and his confrontation with the absurd must be different from that which comes to us from centuries of literary and artistic traditions. The lack of any kind of definite "outlook" or "conception of the world," which is a "disease" of the modern man, according to Chekhov, must inevitably lead to a more fragmented, amorphous, and open-ended artistic production, one that is not goal- or end-oriented and that lacks a "unity" and "unified vision" characteristic of the great artists of previous centuries:

> Keep in mind that the writers we consider eternal or simply good, who intoxicate us, have one very important trait in common: they are going in a certain direction and they induce you to follow, and you feel not only with your mind, but with your entire being that they have a certain goal. . . . Depending on their caliber, some have immediate goals—the abolition of serfdom, liberation of the motherland, politics, beauty or simply vodka, as in the case of Denis Davydov; the others have more remote goals—God, the afterlife, the happiness of humankind and so on. The best of them are realistic and describe life as it is, but because each line is saturated with the consciousness of their goal, as with juice, you feel life not only as it is, but also as it should be, and this captivates you. And what about us? Us! We describe life at it is and stop dead right there. . . . We have neither immediate nor remote goals, and our souls are completely empty. We have no politics, we don't believe in revolution, there is no God, we're not afraid of ghosts, and I personally am not even afraid of death and blindness. One who wants nothing, hopes for nothing, and fears nothing cannot be an artist. (letter to Suvorin, November 25, 1892; P 5:133–34)

The modern individuals experiencing a profound existential crisis must admit to having no knowledge of life, must feel empty and alienated, and therefore cannot be artists of a traditional sort. They must seek out not only "new forms," as does Treplev in *The Seagull*, but new modes of expression. Chekhov's dislike of any kind of definitive "outlook," his lack of a "unified vision" or "unified idea" (or "juice" saturating each line, in Chekhov's own terminology), and his experience of the state of uncertainty in which he as a modern man finds himself make him search for new literary paths.

Chekhov's originality was immediately acknowledged by his most discerning contemporaries, such as Tolstoy, who insisted that Chekhov created "new, absolutely new forms of writing" and had "his own unique manner of writing" that distinguished him from all previous writers.[24] Referring to Chekhov, Shestov perceptively observes that a man who rejects all accepted conceptions of the world must also reject the devices of routine. Indeed, Chekhov himself is fully aware that he is breaking new ground, creating new genres and new forms of artistic expression: "I am happy that I paved the way to the thick journals for many writers, and I am no less happy that thanks to me those same writers may now count on academic laurels. Everything written by me will be forgotten in five to ten years; but the paths I pioneered will remain intact—in this I see my only merit" (P 3:39). He did pioneer new paths not only in prose but also in drama. To a large extent, Chekhov's innovations in prose and drama are the result of his existentialist outlook, one that becomes distinct when we consider Chekhov in the context of the philosophical thought of his time.

2

Life without a Plot

The Drama of Being

FOCUSING ON THE MUNDANE

Many aspects of Chekhov's poetics derive from his "philosophical" outlook. Among the most important features of Chekhov's poetics that can be associated with his "philosophy" are his struggle with the traditional plot (which was thought to require a unified vision)—in both his prose and dramatic works—and his search for new kinds of beginnings and ends. It is noteworthy that Chekhov never managed to write a novel and preferred the genres of the short story and drama, which he modernized and which allowed him to grasp the fragments of existence that he believed could no longer be glued together into a coherent whole. In his 1944 essay on Chekhov, Boris Eikhenbaum observes that "the point is not that Chekhov introduced the genre of the short story into Russian literature, but that this brevity [*kratkost'*] was a matter of principle; as a new and more adequate method of describing reality it was a counterpart to the traditional genre of the novel and novella."[1] The novelistic genre—at least in the way that most of Chekhov's contemporaries, including Tolstoy, understood the novel—required a clearly defined "worldview." It is no coincidence, then, that Tolstoy, as much as he admired Chekhov's talent, objected to his lack of a "definite worldview" and "unifying thread," aspects he proudly located in his own architectonics, which privileged inner connections and "linkages" [*stseplenie*]. Tolstoy thus explains his position with respect to art and peculiarities of Chekhov's poetics:

> His artistry is of the highest caliber. I have greatly enjoyed rereading his stories.... But still, this is only a mosaic, you won't find here a truly unifying

inner thread. . . . Chekhov, as well as many of our current writers, has developed an extraordinary technique of realism. Everything is realistic in Chekhov, to the point of complete illusion; his works give the impression of a stereoscope. He throws words apparently without any order, but, like artists-impression-ists, he achieves great results with his brush strokes.[2]

Tolstoy's dislike of Chekhov's plays is well known. Tolstoy could understand and even appreciate the fragmented quality of Chekhov's prose, or Chekhov's "mosaic," insofar as such qualities were consistent with the pointillistic character of the short story as a genre. But Tolstoy failed to embrace the novelty of Chekhov's plays, which subverted all expectations of dramatic plot, characterization, and action, even though in his radical reconsideration of the dramatic structure, Chekhov demonstrated a certain affinity with Tolstoy, who waged a similar war against the structure of the novel. In fact, in the process of modernizing Russian drama, Chekhov altered traditional theatrical conventions on the same grounds on which Tolstoy modified or challenged traditional historiography. Tolstoy believed that in history "unheroic" figures such as Captain Tushin and numerous nameless Russian soldiers are no less important than Napoleon or Alexander, and that the truly important historical events are those that no one notices because, although they constitute the core of life, they are not dramatic. Similarly, Chekhov looked for drama not in theatrical and dramatic effects but in what is concealed. Chekhov insisted that the life of the people is more important and "intelligent" than what is presented on the modern stage. Criticizing Peter Alekseevich Sergeenko, he wrote: "Those stubborn peasants always try to pick up great subjects, because they are incapable of dealing with small things. . . . It is easier to write about Socrates than about a young girl or a cook" (letter to Suvorin, January 2, 1894; P 5:258).[3] For Tolstoy, history consisted of the tiny, barely perceptible acts of ordinary human beings, not of what were traditionally perceived as "events." To create his "counter-history," he wrote *War and Peace*, in which Napoleon and all the "historical" characters are relegated to the background and the seemingly amorphous lives of ordinary people with their daily occupations and concerns come to the fore. Likewise, for Chekhov, the drama consisted not of suicides, murders, and betrayals but of ordinary everyday affairs. "No one wants to love in us ordinary human beings," he complained to Suvorin (P 3:78). Life as it is portrayed on the stage, Chekhov argued, should consist of ordinary, undramatic, barely perceptible actions and events. This everyday life lacks teleology and is essentially unorganized:

"Life on the stage should be as complicated and at the same time as simple as in real life. People eat their dinner, just eat their dinner, and all the time their happiness is taking form, or their lives are being destroyed."[4] Tolstoy's and Chekhov's emphasis on the undramatic aspects of life leads both writers to many of the formal peculiarities that characterize their genres of choice—the novel and the play, respectively—such as the absence of a traditional plot, the lack of a traditional ending, a new approach to characterization, and the concept of heroism. As opposed to Tolstoy, however, who for all his attention to the "prosaics" of life was, nevertheless, infusing his works with a unified authorial vision, Chekhov withholds his authorial vision.[5] Instead, he strives for a more pluralistic and contextualized approach to artistic representation. He achieves this not only by making the author's "sympathies" and point of view imperceptible and somewhat diffused but also by treating the overlapping themes and leitmotifs in his plays from a plurality of angles and contexts. With his unique self-deprecating sense of humor, he sees the difference between the novelistic treatment of events (the historical or family novel of the Tolstoy type) and the depiction of life in the short story or drama—his genres of choice—as the difference between a palace and a birdhouse. A. N. Tikhonov (Serebrov) recalls his critique of Gorky's novel *Foma Gordeev*: "Only aristocrats knew how to write novels. But us, ordinary people of miscellaneous ranks can't handle a novel anymore. We are good at building birdhouses, that's what we are good at. . . . To build a novel, one must know well the law of symmetry and the equilibrium of the masses. The novel is a whole palace, and the reader must feel at home in it, not like in a museum where you are either surprised or bored."[6] The architecture of the novel—and the emerging view of historical processes—implies, according to Chekhov, a unified and tightly joined structure as opposed to the more fragmented, unstable, and discrete construction of "birdhouses." Although Chekhov was never interested in the genre of the history play, his theatrical experiments pay as much attention to history and society as historical novels do, but they present history not as it unfolds on the battlefield but as it manifests itself in how people "eat their dinners," "drink tea," and engage in mundane conversations—moments that Chekhov associated with more casual architectural structures such as "birdhouses" and more "democratic" literary genres such as the short story and modern drama. In his drama, Chekhov shared some of Tolstoy's "prosaic" impulses and his unorthodox treatment of plot without accepting Tolstoy's common moral denominator and epic vision—the features that later led Bakhtin to call Tolstoy's novels "monologic" and contrast them with Dostoevskian polyphony. As I will argue in chapter 4, Chekhov created a more dialogic theater than had been known before him—an experiment grounded in the quest he shared with both Tolstoy and Dostoevsky to create new forms.

Chekhov's path to innovation in the theater was not straightforward. In his early experiments he relied heavily on already existing conventions of popular drama.[7] However, early in his theatrical career Chekhov pushed against the dominant conventions of the so-called well-made play and melodrama in a manner that paralleled his renunciation of Russian binaries, excesses, and ideological fixations. In particular, he found the melodramatic mode, with its dualist narrative structure, moral certitude, and pervasive use of "labels" and "tags," too binding and constraining.

In his letter to Leontiev (Shcheglov) of November 7, 1888, Chekhov complains about the state of contemporary theater: "Everything good is being exaggerated to the skies, while everything base is being masked. . . . Contemporary theater is an eruption, a bad disease of the cities. One has to chase this disease away, but to like it is unhealthy" (P 3:60). In his criticism of E. P. Karpov's *Crocodile Tears* (*Krokodilovy slezy*) and similar popular plays, he continues to debunk contemporary theater with the same gusto: "Contemporary theater is the world of blockheads, Karpovs, stupidity, and windbags" (P 3:65–66). These harsh comments are not outliers in Chekhov's criticism of contemporary theater and cannot be dismissed merely as rhetorical flourishes. His statements about the theater, actors, playwrights, and the unenlightened audience range from pointed criticism to open disdain. In particular, Chekhov underscores the melodramatic conventions of *Crocodile Tears*: "The whole play, in addition to its crude naiveté, is a lie and calumny against life. . . . One of the heroines exclaims: 'And thus the vice is punished and the virtue is triumphant!' and with these words the play ends. . . . If I ever say or write anything similar, you have the right to hate me and have nothing to do with me" (P 3:67). No less savage are Chekhov's comments about the excessive scenery in popular entertainment and his opinions of the actresses who wring their hands or shed torrents of tears onstage. It is not theater per se that offends his artistic sensibility but the specific dominant practice of it on the contemporary stage. Chekhov singles out those aspects of contemporary theater that are traditionally associated with melodrama and a well-made play, such as unrealistic plots, exaggerated emotions, an underlying dualistic morality, a clear-cut division of characters into villains and their victims, and a stylized manner of acting.[8]

The contemporary theater's histrionic style of acting was associated with popular genres of urban entertainment and specifically melodrama: the genre relied heavily on nonverbal modes of expression and a stylized manner of acting that appealed to the bourgeois public's need for self-expression. Chekhov not only ridicules melodramatic characters and melodramatic behavior as a "calumny against life" and therefore a betrayal of realism in art; he also condemns them as a dangerous moral fallacy. It is worth noting that melodrama, as the genre most accessible to the bourgeoisie, was held in contempt by the intelligentsia. Yet, ironically, the intelligentsia itself, with its polarizing attitudes toward life and ethical intolerance, frequently ceded to the melodramatic mode of behavior. As a form of artistic expression, Chekhov too perceived melodrama as a distortion of realism and a dangerous theatricalization of life that distracted the audience from more mundane and realistic concerns. He was equally critical of the intelligentsia's melodramatic self-dramatization. He viewed melodramatic structure and melodramatic gesture as dangerous because of their potential to manipulate audiences for the sake of frequently questionable ends. Note that melodramatic behavior often figures in Chekhov's stories as a tool of manipulation and abuse of human kindness, or as a sign of a character's general foolishness.

Chekhov's dissatisfaction with contemporary theater, then, is primarily dissatisfaction with melodrama's "aesthetics of astonishment," to use Peter Brooks's term in his insightful study *The Melodramatic Imagination: Balzac, Henry James, Melodrama, and the Mode of Excess*. The Manichean duality that Brooks views as the central metaphysical system underlying melodramatic narrative structure and the conception of the world in terms of extremes were in general, as we have seen, quite alien to Chekhov's artistic imagination. Brooks argues: "The world according to melodrama is built on an irreducible Manichaeism, the conflict of good and evil as opposites not subject to compromise. Melodramatic dilemmas and choices are constructed on the either/or in its extreme form as the all-or-nothing. Polarization is both horizontal and vertical: characters represent extremes, and they undergo extremes, passing from heights to depths, or the reverse, almost instantaneously."[9] Melodrama was the genre that most consistently became the target in Chekhov's criticism of contemporary theater. What Peter Brooks identifies as "melodramatic imagination" was antagonistic to Chekhov's fundamental beliefs and artistic sensitivity. Moreover, Chekhov was aware of the degree to which the aesthetics of excess were ingrained in Russian cultural history, and he openly objected to this "melodramatization" of thought and experience, typical both of the Russian radical intelligentsia and of lowbrow culture. It is no coincidence that Dostoevsky, the most "melodramatic" of the Russian classics, is frequently satirized by Chekhov for portraying what Chekhov perceives as melodramatic suffering. Chekhov had reservations about Dostoevsky's dramatizations of human encounters and intense, excessive representations of life that reveal the essential conflicts in the realm of spiritual reality.

Russian melodramatic art, Chekhov felt, tended to reveal and was often confessional in nature. This applies not only to Dostoevsky but also to apparently more unlikely candidates, such as Tolstoy, who, as Gary Saul Morson persistently argued, advanced a "prosaic" approach to life as opposed to the dominant Russian trend of indulging in the exceptional and extreme. Yet while Chekhov shares Tolstoy's interest in the mundane, he is critical of Tolstoy's inflexible moralistic stance and his ideological tyranny. Significantly, Thomas Mann shows great insight and sensitivity when he singles out Chekhov's unusual talent and points out how he differs from other great Russian classics: "Until the end he has nothing of the literary grand seignor about him, still less of the prophet or the sage, unlike Tolstoy who looked down on Chekhov amicably and, according to Gorky, saw in him 'an excellent, quite, modest creature.'"[10] Chekhov develops a distinctly anti-melodramatic and, of course, anti-prophetic mode of expression that conceals emotions, avoids all the excesses of self-expression, and focuses on what is hidden. To a large extent, his drama is not only a "conversation of the deaf" (*razgovor glukhikh*), as has been pointed out, but also a drama of unspoken words (in which particular weight is given to silences, pauses, and transitions).[11] Significantly, when Chekhov offers a piece of advice to young aspiring writers, he always chastises them for melodramatic excesses in style and recommends restraint. Consider, for example, his advice to Gorky: "First of all, in my opinion, you lack restraint. You are like a spectator in a theater who is so unrestrained in the way he expresses his enthusiasm that he prevents himself and others from listening.... This is not breadth, not a bold stroke of the brush, but simply a lack of restraint" (P 7:352). Likewise, while objecting to the excessive expressiveness in acting, Chekhov insists on grace and restraint:

> The majority of people suffer, the minority experiences sharp pain, but where on the streets or at home do you see people rushing about, galloping, and snatching at one's head? One has to express sufferings the way they are expressed in life, that is, not with the help of ones' legs and arms, but with the tone

of voice and the expression of eyes, not with gesticulation, but with grace. . . .
You will say that such are the stage conventions. No stage conventions should
be an excuse for a lie. (January 2, 1900, to O. Knipper; P 9:7)[12]

Chekhov's famous statement of religious belief ("Between 'God exists' and
'God does not exist' . . ."), quoted earlier in chapter 1, which made the literary critic Alexander Chudakov identify Chekhov as a "man of the field,"[13]
clearly indicates Chekhov's skepticism about extremes. He viewed the polarizing perception of reality associated with Russian national identity as essentially the same problem as the surfeit of melodramatic reflexes: as Brooks
points out, the melodramatic mode excludes the middle condition. Chekhov's criticism of "the Russian man" is primarily a criticism of Russian
Manichaeism and its melodramatic sensibility that refuses to acknowledge
the existence and importance of "the huge field," or "the middle ground."
It is the middle ground, indeed, that becomes the focal point of Chekhov's
artistic representation.

I would suggest that to some degree, Chekhov's persistent struggle with
melodramatic conventions and the genre's "mode of excess," along with Russian "extremes" in general, is what led him to create his new theater, with its
reconceptualization of characterization, plot, use of sound, settings, speech,
and various theatrical effects. Like the Western European innovators of the
stage, such as Ibsen and Maeterlinck, with his revolutionary theory of "le
tragique quotidien," Chekhov forged his path to new theatrical forms *via
negativa*—that is, through the rejection of contemporary theater and its
"theatricality." Like Maeterlinck, who insisted that "there is a tragic of the
everyday which is more real, more profound, and more reflective of our true
being than the tragedy of great adventures,"[14] Chekhov wants to focus not
on the exceptional moments of life, which generate awe, sorrow, or intense
emotional response, but on the condition of life itself. The ways Chekhov
achieves these goals and attempts to show this essential tragedy of everyday
life, however, are significantly different from what emerged in Maeterlinck's
symbolist theater. Chekhov's response to melodrama and a well-made play
was not a "static theater" or replacement of action with inaction and dialogue with silence (although he adapted these strategies to his own plays
in a limited way) but destabilization of traditional dramatic structure and
hierarchy. Chekhov's plays do not lack action, as was frequently believed, but
reprioritize action—that is, reconsider what is important and what is less
important in human life and how the important things reveal themselves.

Moreover, Chekhov never rejected those "theatrical" elements that characterize vaudeville and farce; he freely indulged in slapstick and buffoonery in his theater, including in his later plays.

As a medical doctor with a firm grasp of contemporary practices of immunology, Chekhov was well aware of the need to introduce the virus of a disease into the body in order to prevent the illness.[15] In his mature plays, he introduces some elements of melodrama and uses some of its classical topoi (the enclosed garden, the space of innocence, the theme of the interrupted banquet, the devastated family nest) only to subvert the melodramatic responses that they tend to trigger.[16] We easily recognize his fabulae as hidden melodramas, such as, for example, the theme of dispossession in *The Three Sisters*, the abuse of virtue in *Uncle Vania*, and love triangles in *The Seagull*. But these melodramatic fabulae function precisely as an inoculation *against* the malaise of melodrama and reveal the prose of life as the main propelling movement of the plays. Even in *Ivanov*, which clearly relies on melodramatic coincidences and explosive scenes, Chekhov embarks on a demolition of melodrama, with its tunnel-vision understanding of human psychology.

Chekhov's mistrust of ideological extremes translated also into his deep mistrust of the artistic principles governing the contemporary stage. His aversion to any type of polarization and to contemporary theater's turning everything into ideological warfare made him reconsider the nature of dramatic character and action and the very core of conventional theater— the clash of characters, or conflict:

> Contemporary playwrights stuff their plays only with the angels, villains or buffoons—try to find these types in Russia! Well, you may find them but not in such extreme forms as these playwrights require. . . . I wanted to be original: I did not depict any single villain, or angel (although I could not refrain from buffoons), I did not condemn or justify anyone. (letter to his brother Alexander Chekhov, October 24, 1887; P 2:137)

Likewise, commenting on one of the characters in Gorky's play *The Philistines*, he gives Gorky the following advice: "But please, do not oppose him to Peter and Tatiana—let him be by himself, and them by themselves, they are all fine people independently from each other" (P 10:96).

While the characters in melodrama openly pronounce their moral judgments of the world, Chekhov ridicules characters who thrive on explicit self-expression and melodramatic rhetoric (Masha from *The Seagull*, Voinitsky and Sonia from *Uncle Vania*, Petia Trofimov from *The Cherry Orchard*, among many others). The typical example is Doctor Lvov from *Ivanov*, the so-called honest and straightforward man (*chestnyi i priamoi chelovek*) who stands onstage and utters the unspeakable: "Nikolai Alekseevich, I have listened to you and now I have to speak frankly, in plain terms. I cannot tell you, words fail me, but .. but I profoundly dislike you" (12:17). His melodramatic rhetoric is not only comical but is also presented by Chekhov as a moral fallacy as Lvov tries to impose his melodramatic vision of the world (he casts Sarah as a saint and Ivanov as a villain) on everyone around him. His histrionically moralistic rhetoric implicitly insists that the world is polarized, excluding any middle ground. Significantly, Lvov cannot understand—he can only overstate. This kind of pure self-expression is always ridiculed by Chekhov, who insists that a person cannot be understood in terms of set traits that lead him inevitably, deterministically to some kind of action. That is why Ivanov, who is caught in the web of melodrama, rebels against the tyranny of melodramatic vision: "No, Doctor. We all have too many cogs, wheels, and valves to judge each other by first impression or by outward appearance. I do not understand you, you do not understand me, and we do not understand ourselves" (12:54–56). The tragedy of Ivanov is that, being viewed as he is in melodramatic terms by everyone around him, he cannot escape the melodrama that is being imposed on him.[17] He fully realizes that Sasha's love is the result of this melodramatic distorted view of reality and tries to escape this trap: "So give me up! Just understand: you are prompted not by love, but by the stubbornness of your honest nature. You set yourself the goal of resurrecting the man in me, of saving me, come what may, and it flattered you that you are accomplishing a feat" (12:72). While struggling with melodramatic expectations and a melodramatic worldview that he finds oppressive, he commits the most melodramatic act—suicide—in the most melodramatic fashion—during his wedding in front of his bride. Thus, both the melodrama of life (histrionic behavior, acting, false theatrical aspirations, and viewing the world in terms of either/or) and melodramatic conventions (sudden discoveries, consumptive wives, suicide) explode in front of the audience as an inadequate answer to life's main challenge—the ordinariness of the daily life. Significantly, this truth is not expressed by any of the protagonists, but instead, as is often the case in Chekhov's plays, by a character who could hardly qualify as a central figure. In this instance it is Lebedev: "Look at things simply, the way other people do. Everything is simple in this world. Ceilings are white, boots are black, sugar is sweet" (12:73).

Chekhov's mature plays strive to depict this simple, ordinary life, which is the hardest to depict onstage. He is interested not in the "story" to tell, not in the kind of "real life" that is artificially presented onstage in terms of well-defined beginnings and endings, but in human existence itself, understood as unplotted and open. In a letter to Suvorin, he writes: "He who invents new endings for a play will start a new era. These nasty endings are so hard to manage! The hero either marries or shoots himself, there is no other way out" (P 5:72). Chekhov decides this dilemma by rejecting the traditional finale and focusing on human existence, on life unfolding. Life goes on, and there is no ending in a traditional sense—such are the denouements of *Uncle Vania*, *The Three Sisters*, and *The Cherry Orchard*. Even in *The Seagull* there is no sense that Treplev's suicide will bring a significant change in the lives of the characters.

While melodrama resolves conflicts by reaffirming the existing order and therefore can be interpreted as having conservative implications, Chekhov's plays are inconclusive and open to the future.[18] They never end with the restoration of the lost order. If melodrama urges toward harmony in the construction of its final moments, Chekhov's denouements lack reconciliation. But unlike tragedy, in which the hero moves from ignorance to knowledge at the moment of his downfall, Chekhov's heroes do not have a final downfall and gain only limited knowledge. The existing state of things almost invariably proves inadequate (as in *Uncle Vania*, *The Three Sisters*, *The Cherry Orchard*), and the audience is given the sense that there is no way back to the old order. At the same time, Chekhov is skeptical about the possibility of radical change and of the tragic vision associated with it. Thus, Sonia and Vania will continue to labor although their lives will never be the same; the three sisters may explore various options but most likely will not go to Moscow; the cherry orchard will be destroyed, but Ranevskaia will return to Paris. Chekhov's plays, therefore, are neither conservative nor radical in their ideological implications. Instead they present an ironical outlook that leads Chekhov to his most striking generic innovations, his subversions of traditional comic, tragic, and dramatic genres. Chekhov alludes to this aim in his complaint about how Stanislavsky made people cry at his plays: "I merely wanted to say to people honestly: 'Look at yourself, look at how bad and boring your lives are!' The important thing is that people understand this, and when they understand it, they will, without fail, create for themselves another better life. . . . What is there to cry about?"[19]

While relying heavily on unbelievable plots, coincidences, and inflated emotions, melodrama strove to locate and convey some hidden ontology.

Melodramatic representation therefore operated with signs that transferred significance into another context. Discussing the melodramatic mode in Balzac, Brooks argues that "the site of his drama, the ontology of his true subject, is not easily established. . . . We might say that the center of interest and the scene of the underlying drama reside within what we could call the 'moral occult,' the domain of operative spiritual values which is both indicated within and masked by the surface of reality."[20] Chekhov's vision, by contrast, recoils from hidden ontology and from metaphoric perception of reality in general. Instead, Chekhov's use of signs and symbols is both paradoxical and ironic. *The Seagull* is an interesting example of the reversal of melodramatic symbolization. As is demonstrated in chapter 3, which offers a detailed analysis of the play, the play's key metaphors seem to suggest melodramatic formulae. The dominant images of the lake and of the seagull have formulaic associations of innocence, purity, and freedom. The spectator's contemplation of innocence (Nina) should become the main "motor" of the action for the production and stimulation of the spectators' emotions. But the seduction by Trigorin, which takes place offstage, does not lead to the spectator's agitation. There is nothing that would enable enjoyment of conventional morality. Chekhov therefore does not simply reverse the traditional symbolic meaning of the lake and the seagull, but instead uses signs and symbols to parody signs and symbols, and the semiotic demands they make on us.[21] The metaphoric meaning exists only to the extent that the characters of the play, and possibly the audience, tend to interpret the world metaphorically. Treplev's suicide further shows that, like Ivanov, he cannot escape the melodramatic plot.

Just as he subverts the "moral occult" and melodramatic system of symbols, Chekhov also reverses the conventional melodramatic use of music and sound. In melodrama, music is used to emphasize dramatic moments, to mark entrances and exits, to delineate the emotional states of the personages, and to put the audience into a particular emotional mood. Music is an implement for the dramatization of life. In Chekhov's plays, however, sound and music are not employed to dramatize events and emphasize the characters' emotional disposition; they are not used as secondary acoustic effects, but rather have a function that is independent of characterization. Thus, the sounds of the military march in the end of *The Three Sisters* do not reflect the emotional condition of the heroines and do not even mark a particularly dramatic moment in the play. Instead they contrast with the emotional state of the sisters. In *The Seagull*, the sound of Treplev's gunshot is presented to the audience as a bursting bottle of ether, which clearly deflates the sense of tragedy. Various sounds that Chekhov uses in his plays are anti-melodramatic in their function since they do not intensify or create a mood in accordance with the devices drawn from the musicological doctrine of the eighteenth century. These sounds introduce into the action of the plays elements that are ironic, as if they run contrary to the emotions that are on display. Examples include the snatches of opera and sentimental songs sung by Dorn in *The Seagull*. Often the characters themselves assign symbolic value to various sounds and try to interpret them (as in *The Seagull* and *The Cherry Orchard*). The audience, however, is expected to keep an ironic distance from the characters' search for symbolic meaning. To be sure, the sound of a breaking string in *The Cherry Orchard* easily yields to symbolic interpretation, but it could just as well be an incidental sound of a bucket that, in Lopakhin's words, "must have broken loose." Once again, Chekhov's position oscillates between the two poles of reading: the sound could have symbolic meaning, but it is just as likely to have none. Chekhov plays with the audience's prowess at identifying symbols, engaging the audience in the game of deciphering symbols and establishing symbolic connections, only to show the futility of this project.

Chekhov's innovative aesthetics is an ambitious project not only because it goes against the grain of the popular and the accessible but also because it embodies a mode of perception that transcends traditional generic divisions. Chekhov's plays are neither comic nor tragic, neither melodramatic nor farcical, and they parody the Russian proclivity for self-dramatization and for dealing with the "accursed questions" of existence. Chekhov's revolution in the theater was a double-edged sword he used to expose the histrionics of Russian culture and to attack the theatricality of contemporary theater, which in his view was distorting real life. How could life and the stage be liberated from histrionics? The task seemed paradoxical: Chekhov used dramatic form to "un-dramatize" Russian culture and "de-dramatize" Russian theater. He started this project already with *Ivanov*, although this play—by all standards—is the most conventionally dramatic of Chekhov's mature plays.

FROM DON QUIXOTE TO HAMLET: IVANOV'S DRAMA

Although Chekhov's Ivanov was widely recognized as the heir to the Russian "superfluous man," Chekhov insisted that the play's protagonist represented essentially a new type. Indeed, what is new about Ivanov is not his inertia, his disillusionment, and his "superfluousness," but the fact that he is defeated and spiritually enervated because he sees everything in extremes and is unable to accept the mundane and the everyday. He vacillates between lofty aspirations and despair. In creating this type, Chekhov draws, to a large extent, on the typological dichotomies laid down by Ivan Turgenev in his seminal essay "Hamlet and Don Quixote" (originally a speech, delivered on January 10, 1860, at a public reading for the benefit of the Society for the Relief of Needy Writers and Scientists). Turgenev interpreted these two characters in terms of contrasting human types and their approaches to life: "These two types embody two fundamental, opposite aspects of human nature . . . . It seemed to us that all people belonged more or less to one of these two types; that almost anyone of us is either a Don Quixote or a Hamlet. True, in our time there are more Hamlets than Don Quixotes, but there are still Don Quixotes as well."[22] Chekhov is fascinated by both types and explores the implications of such characters for modern-day Russia in his drama *Ivanov*, a play that I see as his theatrical response to Turgenev's essay.

In this essay, Turgenev established a paradigm of the binary nature of man, viewing these two types as antithetical. Don Quixote embodies "first of all faith; faith in something eternal, stable, in truth; in a word, faith in the truth that is *outside* any particular man."[23] Turgenev argues that Don Quixote is an enthusiast and that his pursuit of altruism leads him to incessant activity. In contrast, Hamlet's preoccupation with his self and his rationality results in inaction. Hamlet embodies analysis, egoism, unbelief, and irony: "Analysis above all and selfishness, and therefore faithlessness. . . . In doubting everything, Hamlet, of course, does not spare himself; his mind is too developed to be satisfied with what he finds in himself: he is aware of his weakness, but all self-consciousness is strength; hence his irony, the opposite of Don Quixote's enthusiasm."[24] Turgenev concludes that this Shakespearean character represents an "element of negation" in human nature. However, neither type, according to Turgenev, is self-sufficient for life's purposes; both are interpreted by Turgenev as self-contradictory. Hamlet's skepticism and reflection are seen by him as a stumbling block to any activity. Hamlet is doomed to inaction as he does not believe in truth as such: "But we maintain that even if the truth itself appeared incarnated before his eyes, Hamlet would still not dare to guarantee that, indeed, this is it . . . the truth."[25] On the other hand, this very skepticism makes Hamlet an adherent of the truth he denies, for as a skeptic he uncompromisingly fights falsehood. As far as Don Quixote is concerned, he is the type who defends his ideal or his truth in spite of the evidence. But at the same time, while fighting for the truth,

Don Quixote undermines it by his acceptance of illusion. Turgenev views this dichotomy in terms of Hegelian dialectics: "Let us limit ourselves with an observation that in this separation, in this dualism to which we have referred, we must recognize the fundamental law of all human life; all this life is nothing else but the eternal reconciliation and eternal struggle of two incessantly separated and incessantly merging principles."[26] Turgenev concludes his essay with a suggestion that these dualistic attitudes are intrinsically limiting and that instead of leaning to these extremes it is important to balance them: "These are merely extreme expressions of two currents of thought, landmarks set up by the poets on their different paths. Life strives toward them without ever reaching them."[27]

Both types are almost literally embodied in the two phases of Ivanov's life: his past and his present. Chekhov viewed the problem of Russian identity as an inability to balance between these two poles. The modern Russian predicament, as he saw it, lay in an oscillation between quixotism and Hamletism. Whereas Turgenev considered Don Quixote and Hamlet as two distinct personality types, Chekhov presented his Ivanov not in terms of a dialectical struggle between the two principles in his character but as a tragic shift from one extreme to the other. Chekhov dramatized this polarity and revealed its destructive nature. It is clear that Turgenev's description of Hamlet and Don Quixote is typologically close to those two types of people (the inactive intellectual and the self-righteous active enthusiast) that captured Chekhov's imagination in many of his stories and plays. In *Ivanov*, this dichotomy is represented by the characters of Ivanov, who echoes this Russian Hamletian type, and Dr. Lvov, the Don Quixote type. However, the originality of Chekhov's drama lies not in creating Ivanov and Lvov as antagonists but in showing that the real drama takes place not between these antagonists but within Ivanov, who cannot reconcile these two extreme modes of being: his past is that of a Don Quixote, but his present is that of a Hamlet. When we meet him at the opening of the play, he appears to us as the Hamletian type of intellectual, disappointed in life, weak, passive, completely absorbed in introspection and self-criticism. (Note Turgenev's words about Hamlet: "Hamlet derives pleasure from excessive blaming himself, constantly observing himself, always looking into himself; he knows all his faults to the finest detail, despises them, despises himself—and at the same time, one might say, lives, feeds on this contempt.")[28] Although Ivanov has no active evil intentions, he lacks the will to oppose erroneous and dubious actions. It is his passivity that leads him to things that no decent person would do. However,

Ivanov's case is complex and ironical. He is apparently a Don Quixote turned into a Hamlet. It was his Don Quixote's idealist nature that led him to marry a Jewish girl and commit himself to social activism. Ivanov implicitly refers to his past as "quixotic" when he gives Dr. Lvov the following advice and speaks of the futility of "fighting windmills": "My dear friend, do not fight alone with thousands, do not fight with windmills, do not beat your forehead against the walls. . . . May God protect you from all kinds of rational farms, extraordinary schools, hot speeches" (12:16–17). He references "windmills" again in a confessional conversation with Lebedev at the end of the play: "I was young, spirited, sincere, intelligent; I loved, hated, and had beliefs different from everyone else's, worked and hoped for ten, fought windmills, banged my head against walls; without measuring my strength, without reasoning, not knowing life, I took on a burden that immediately made my back crunch and stretched my veins; I rushed to waste myself on youth alone, got drunk, got excited, worked; I knew no measure" (12:74). He consistently describes his past in terms similar to Turgenev's description of the Don Quixote type: "Not a year has passed since I was healthy and strong, vigorous, tireless, spirited, working with these very hands, speaking in a way that moved even the ignorant to tears, able to cry at the sight of grief, indignant at meeting with evil. I knew what inspiration was, I knew the beauty and poetry of quiet nights, when from dawn to dawn you sit at your desk or entertain your mind with dreams. I believed, I looked into the future as into my mother's eyes" (12:52–53).

But now Ivanov sees himself as a Russian Hamlet: "I am dying of shame at the thought that I, a healthy, strong man, have turned into either a Hamlet, or a Manfred, or a superfluous man . . . I don't know! There are pathetic people who are flattered to be called Hamlets or superfluous, but to me it's a shame!" (12:37; cf. Turgenev's observation, "everyone is flattered to be called Hamlet"). He repeatedly compares himself to a Hamlet. Consider his words to Sasha: "My whining inspires awe in you; you imagine that you have found in me a second Hamlet, while I think that my psychopathy, with all its accessories, can only serve as good material for laughter and nothing else!" (12:57–58); "I have played Hamlet, and you a high-minded maiden—and we've had enough of it" (12:70).

Clearly, Ivanov's situation is not that of a Turgenevian "superfluous man"—a man unable to find his place in society despite his education and talents. For him it is not a problem of society but a psychological and existential problem—a sudden transition from one extreme mode of existence to another. This is how he explains his breakdown: "It seems to me that I also overstrained myself. Gymnasium, university, then the farm, schools, projects . . . I believed differently than everybody else, I married differently than everybody else, I was spirited, I took risks, I threw money left and right, I was happy and I suffered like nobody else in the whole district. . . . I took the burden on my back, and my back cracked. At twenty we're all heroes, we can do anything, and by thirty, we're already worn out and good for nothing at all" (12:52). His breakdown is not the result of unfavorable social circumstances but of a problem inherent in the human type of Don Quixote—a man incapable of a measured approach to life and therefore overstretched ("I knew no measure"). He is destroyed by these ideological extremes. Behaving throughout the play as a Hamlet—and therefore unable to act in the proper sense of the world—at the end he declares that "youth has reawakened" in him and that now "the original Ivanov has found his voice." Ironically, if the original Ivanov is a Don Quixote, it is his quixotism that makes him finally act decisively, but this act leads to his suicide.

Ivanov is not a society melodrama about a scoundrel abandoning his dying wife—a plot Chekhov mocks. Rather, the play is a melodrama of the Russian intelligentsia, about its inability to sustain idealist impulses and achieve a balanced sense of identity. Chekhov laments that there is no middle ground between the dangerous extremes of blinkered zealotry of revolutionaries and the passivity of a tired liberal intelligentsia capable only of complaining. Ivanov tries to escape the entrapment of melodrama as a genre, of seeing the world in terms of a clash of villains and saints. He tries to resist the paradigms of trite fiction imposed on his life when he says to Sasha: "and our whole affair is a trite cliché: He was down in spirit and has lost his ground. She appeared, bold in spirit and strong, and gave him a helping hand. It's beautiful but true only in novels, not in life" (12:57). But ultimately he is unable to act in a measured, moderate way like an ordinary man. No one sees him as an ordinary man, either—except the author, who ironically gives him the most common name, Ivanov.

In one of his letters to Suvorin (December 30, 1888), Chekhov diagnoses Ivanov's malaise, a condition that points specifically to the Russian predilection for excess:

Russian excitability has one specific quality: it is quickly replaced by exhaustion. A man, just off the school bench, rashly takes on a burden beyond his powers . . . makes speeches, writes to the minister, struggles with evil, applauds the good, does not fall in love simply but inevitably with either bluestockings or psychopaths or Jewesses or even prostitutes whom he saves, etc. But hardly has he turned 30 or 35, he begins to feel weariness and boredom. ... Disillusion, apathy, nervous instability and exhaustion are the inevitable consequences of excessive excitability, and this excitability is characteristic of our young people to an extreme degree. (P 3:109–10)

The problem of Russian cultural identity, as Chekhov sees it, lies in its oscillation between extremes. It is no coincidence that Chekhov refers to Russian "excitability" as the key to the state of the Russian intelligentsia. Indeed, excitability is an important feature of literary characters, who in Russian cultural consciousness were associated not only with popular melodrama but also with Dostoevsky. Ivanov can rebel against the melodramatic plot imposed on him, but in the end he cannot free himself from it. His suicide is the final form of entrapment in melodramatic excess.

Reflecting on the generic peculiarities associated with fictional representations of the Hamlet and Don Quixote types, Turgenev notes: "We must not forget that just as in *Hamlet* the principle of analysis is brought to the level of tragedy, so in *Don Quixote* the principle of enthusiasm is brought to the order of comedy, but in reality one seldom meets the completely comic or tragic."[29] Chekhov adopted this lesson for his theater and explored both comic and tragic implications of the excesses of these types. Ivanov's tragedy and his comedy—his continuous self-dramatization—is the melodrama that Chekhov mocks. After *Ivanov*, his major plays subvert conventional notions of the tragic and the comic in ways that are even more thoroughgoing, if not radical.

3

A Seagull Is a Seagull Is a Seagull

Chekhov's What Is Art?

The Seagull is Chekhov's first truly "mature" play, a comedy in which he developed his own voice. Generating a formidable range of interpretations, the play became an emblem of Chekhovian theater, characterized by its elusive, dispersive, and centrifugal qualities as well as its ambiguity, opaqueness, and irony. The very opposite of the so-called well-made play, which was subordinated to a single organizing principle and unitary inner vision, Chekhov's comedy presents action that is scattered and diffuse, taking place on many levels and featuring themes that are compounded of heterogeneous elements, from art and love to generational and Oedipal conflicts. With no protagonist or even a central plotline, Chekhov's voice is at the same time nowhere and everywhere, and the play's purposeful violation of the conventional rules of dramatic art and multiple conflicts raise many questions that never receive conclusive answers. Its paramount symbol appears to be the titular seagull. But is it a symbol? If so, what does it symbolize? Chekhov calls the play a comedy in four acts. But is it a comedy? If so, what kind of comedy is it? Several deaths occur in the play—that of the seagull Konstantin shoots and presents to Nina, Nina's baby, and Konstantin (after a successful second attempt at suicide). The death of the owner of the estate, Sorin, also looms over the action—but no one, including the audience, seems much affected. We are left to imagine and speculate on the fallout from Treplev's suicide without experiencing any of the trappings that might normally accompany such a tragic turn of events, because some important components of tragedy are missing.[1]

THE INESCAPABLE ALLURE OF ART

Unlike many of his contemporaries, Chekhov never wrote a manifesto or programmatic essay on poetics and aesthetics. Perhaps precisely because of

46

his aversion to theorizing and attempting to fit the vast variety of experiences and ideas into an all-embracing system, he was never tempted by the rigidity of the monovision that a literary manifesto or literary criticism might imply. Chekhov chose instead to express his aesthetic ideas and views in the more mercurial genre of the play and in his correspondence with friends. Indeed, *The Seagull* is the most self-consciously literary of all his plays, and within his oeuvre it comes the closest to a statement of aesthetic principles. At the time of its writing, it may well have been the most metapoetical and metatheatrical play that ever existed. Robert Louis Jackson succinctly opens his discussion of *The Seagull* by zeroing in on its peculiar focus: "Everybody talks about art. Everybody embodies or lives out a concept of art. The problem of talent—what it takes and means to become an artist—is a fundamental theme of the play."[2] Indeed, the play deals not only with questions about writing and acting (two of its central characters are actresses and two are writers) but also with how we read, watch, listen, direct, stage a play and design a set, and respond as an audience. *The Seagull* presents a heated debate on the role of art and is saturated with multiple metapoetic devices: a play within the play, staging within staging, an audience observing the audience, actors playing actors that are playing parts in plays within a play, readers reading onstage, characters offering "subjects" for a short story or a play, and so forth. The play is also packed with literary allusions, including numerous references to Russian and European classics from Shakespeare, Goethe, and Maupassant to Turgenev, Dostoevsky, Tolstoy, and Vladimir Solovyov.[3] Claiming that Russian philosophical thought found its expression more in literature than in philosophy, the Russian philosopher Lev Shestov insisted that *The Seagull* represents a "challenge to all worldviews." Indeed, *The Seagull* is a challenge to most aesthetic thought and artistic systems—both in its form and in its implicit and explicit discussion of art and the artist's vocation. Similar to Chekhov's last play, *The Cherry Orchard*, which portrays Russian life on the eve of the 1905 revolution and anticipates the impending social revolutionary changes, *The Seagull* evokes the atmosphere of pervasive excitement about art and a need for artistic change. This chapter focuses on Chekhov's musings about art and artistic experimentation during the last decade of the nineteenth century, an exceptionally fertile period in Russian literature in which artists attempted to match philosophically ambitious content with innovation in genre and form. This period was also distinctive for its reevaluation of realism and naturalism and for the emergence of an exploratory modernism in early works by Silver Age poets such as Valery Briusov and Konstantin Balmont, who sought to break the barriers of symbolist conventions within which they had initially operated. Refusing to align himself with any movement, Chekhov freely drew on both tradition and experimentation, using different approaches to language, conflict, characterization, movement, mood, and theme. Although he shared the naturalists' faith in science, his largely modernist sensibility recoiled from an overextension of realist strategies and sought new forms of expression in a more flexible and more opaque use of artistic images.

While on the surface *The Seagull* deals with familiar tropes in presenting its "tons of love" (we may recall how Chekhov described his play in a letter to Suvorin on October 21, 1895: "A comedy, three female parts, six male parts, four acts, a landscape (a view opening to the lake); lots of conversations about literature, very little action, and tons of love [*piat' pudov liubvi*]"), the love triangles emerge as false leads of sorts, as tragicomic stories forming unending chains of unrequited feelings: Medvedenko loves Masha, Masha loves Treplev, Treplev loves Nina, Nina loves Trigorin, Trigorin loves to fish and has some feelings for both Arkadina and Nina, Arkadina loves mostly herself but professes to love Trigorin, Polina loves Dr. Dorn, Dr. Dorn loves many women, and so on ad infinitum (P 6:85).[4] Yet the real core and nerve of the play are problems of art and the love of art. *The Seagull* conjures an atmosphere of art idealization and the cult of art in fin-de-siècle Russia. The play's two writers (Trigorin and Treplev) and two actresses (Arkadina and Zarechnaia) are not the only characters making pronouncements about art. Practically all the characters express their opinions about the theater and literature and demonstrate a peculiar form of art worshiping. Even a pedestrian schoolteacher such as Medvedenko envies Treplev and Nina's creative collaboration and later suggests to Trigorin what he believes should be a good topic for the stage—"and you know, it would be good to write a play and get it produced about our friend the schoolteacher" (13:15). A strange obsession with seeing one's life as a work of fiction is a recurrent motif of the play: Arkadina refers to her love of Trigorin as "the last page" of her life (13:42); Masha tells Trigorin the story of her tragic and unrequited love for Treplev and suggests he should use this plot for his fiction (13:33). The estate's aged owner, Arkadina's brother Sorin, is convinced that theater is indispensable in life and confesses that he feels particular affection for men of letters and had all his life wanted only two things—to get married and to be a writer. "After all, it is very pleasant to be even an insignificant writer," he muses (13:9). Later on, he also initiates a "topic for a novella" that would be titled "The Man Who Wanted To" and translated in French as "L'homme qui a voulu"

(13:48). It would feature an unconventional plot about a clash between life expectations and reality, a theme that actually becomes one of the leitmotifs of *The Seagull*. The character Konstantin Treplev, an aspiring writer and the son of the renowned actress Arkadina, admits to his utmost humiliation and suffering at being a "nonentity" among famous writers, actors, and artists (13:8–9). Dr. Dorn, responding to the reproachful observation by Polina Andreevna (the wife of the manager of the estate) that everyone seems eager to bow down before actresses, notes: "If society loves actors and treats them differently from, say, the merchants, this is in the order of things. This is idealism" (13:11). Shortly afterward, he reveals his own idealized conception of art and his envy and veneration of creative individuals: "if I ever got a chance to experience the spiritual uplift artists feel during the creative process, I would despise my material trappings and all that they entail, and would be wafted far away from earth into the empyrean" (13:19). The manager of the estate, the retired lieutenant Shamraev, is singularly focused on opera and the theater and limits his conversation to various famous singers and actors of the bygone era. Nina Zarechnaia, a young aspiring actress from the nearby estate, discloses her exalted view of artists and her naïve belief that they are chosen individuals and high priests of art (13:28–30). Shamraev's daughter Masha falls in love with Treplev because of his poetic aura and his "manners of a poet" (13:23). The obsession with art is clearly ubiquitous.

Against this backdrop of ponderous idolatry of art, Chekhov poses questions about art's goals and tasks, its place in life, and its form in the context of various literary movements.[5] It has been said that the most important "events" of the play take place offstage (Nina's seduction, her abandonment by Trigorin, Treplev's suicide). These events, however, concern, for the most part, traditional conflicts, such as love interest, rivalry, and relationships between characters. The problem of art as such always remains at the center of the stage; it is the primary focus of most dialogues and monologues in the play. Apart from Treplev's play within the play and its performance by Nina, the dialogues and monologues that contain the greatest number of lines are those concerning Treplev's and Trigorin's views on art. By far the longest monologue is Trigorin's statement of his ideas about art and creativity. In general, the longest speeches in the play are dedicated to questions of art rather than interpersonal relationships. Even though these musings on art do not directly precipitate the events (understood as happenings) that unfold in the play, they nevertheless keep the audience focused on artistic concerns.

"The Maelstrom of Dreams and Images":
Treplev's Art Trap

To be sure, Trigorin and Treplev are antagonists not only because they share a love interest in Nina and compete for her attention, but also because they have rival and opposing views on art. In act 1, Treplev's play within a play sets the tone for an aesthetic confrontation that shapes the comedy's inner conflict. Trigorin and Treplev are frequently interpreted as representatives of, respectively, traditionalist and decadent art, and scholars have argued that both express some aspects of Chekhov's own views on art. Yet as Carol Apollonio argues, rather than trying to determine which artist is closer to Chekhov, it would be more fruitful "to note the fragmentation of the creative impulse into separate personalities of the play."[6] Without directly attributing the characters' views to the author, we should consider them on their own terms and assess the degree of their overlap with Chekhov's position with respect to fiction writing. Treplev's approach to art could be considered from three main points of view: (1) what he himself says about the theater, fiction, and their goals; (2) what he produces as an artist; and (3) how his artistic output is received by his audience.

Treplev's disparaging comments about the contemporary stage point to his attempt to find his own voice and what he calls the "new forms." In his criticism, he echoes Chekhov's own frequent pronouncements about the inadequacies of the modern theater. We may recall Chekhov's censure of thespian practices of his day in his letter to Leontiev (Shcheglov) of November 7, 1888, and his other negative remarks about the modern stage conventions. Treplev objects to modern theater's artificiality and dependence on clichés and worn-out devices of melodrama and popular drama, such as *La dame aux camélias*, by Alexandre Dumas fils (Arkadina's favorite repertory), and *Fumes of Life* (*Chad zhizni*), a popular play based on Boleslav Markevich's novel *The Abyss*, which Chekhov considered to be in poor taste.[7] While sharing his views on the theater with his uncle Sorin, Treplev vents his dissatisfaction with, and rebellion against, his mother, Arkadina, who embodies for him all that he detests in the modern theater:

> She also knows that I don't believe in the theater. She loves the theater; it seems to her that she's serving human kind, sacred art, but as far as I'm concerned, the modern theater is just a routine, a prejudice. When the curtain goes up in the room with three walls, lit by the evening lights, and these great talents, these priests of the sacred art, act out how people eat, drink, love,

walk, and wear their jackets; when from banal scenes and phrases they try to extract a moral—a petty moral, a convenient one and useful in their daily domestic life, when in a thousand different ways they present me with the same stuff, just the same, again and again—I run away and keep on running as Maupassant ran from the Eiffel tower, which was crushing his brain with its vulgarity. (13:8)

These caustic comments question not only the exaggerated role of art in contemporary Russian life but also its theatrical conventions—a traditional treatment of the stage with three walls and an imaginary fourth wall as a barrier separating the audience from the actors on the stage, along with a melodramatic concept of the world, with its trite and readily identifiable inherent morality. Although Chekhov may have shared this criticism, Treplev's disapproval of the theater portraying "how people eat, drink, love, walk, and wear their jackets" contrasts with both Chekhov's insistence that one should show life "as it is" and his famous musings on the necessity of new theatrical forms that would be truer to life:

In real life people don't spend every minute shooting each other, hanging themselves, or making declarations of love. They don't say intelligent things every minute either. They spend much more time eating, drinking, flirting, and saying foolish things—and that is what should be seen on the stage. One should write a play in which people come and go, dine, talk about the weather, and play cards, but not because the author needs it but because this is what happens in real life.[8]

In a statement that may be understood as an elaboration of these formulations about the indispensable presence of the prosaic or quotidian in dramaturgy (or "the tragic quotidian," in Maeterlinck's terms), Ilia Gurliand recalled Chekhov's words about how seemingly simple and quotidian activities might nevertheless acquire larger significance when presented onstage.[9]

Indeed, *The Seagull* is precisely this kind of play. But Treplev's play within a play is the very opposite. Although Treplev conceives of the stage as different from the conventional theater and chooses to incorporate the natural environment and destroy the artificiality of the four walls convention, his play does not become closer to life, and in fact, he does not want it to be. As he explains to Nina, he is not interested in portraying "living characters" or life as it is or should be. Instead he aims to show life "the way it appears in dreams" (13:11). In fact, in the opening of his play, Treplev announces that what follows should be understood as the audience's dream about the remote future: "O ye venerable and ancient shadows that hover above this lake at night, put us to sleep and let us dream of what is to be in two hundred thousand years!" (13:12–13). He is trying to engage the audience's senses and their subconscious by using not only human voice but also the natural environment and visual and olfactory stimulation. By contrast, Chekhov himself disliked sensory overstimulation in theater.[10] We may recall Vsevolod Meyerhold's story about Chekhov's conversation with the Moscow Art Theater actors and his objection to the overly naturalistic paraphernalia accompanying the production of *The Seagull*:

> One of the actors told A. P. Chekhov, who for the second time attended the rehearsal of *The Seagull* (September 11, 1898) in the Moscow Art Theater, that during the performance of *The Seagull* offstage frogs would be croaking, dragonflies crackling, and dogs barking.
> —What is it for?—asks Anton Pavlovich with dissatisfaction.
> —It's realistic,—the actor answers.
> —It's realistic? repeats A. P. with a grin, and after a short pause he says:
> —The stage is art. One of Kramskoy's genre paintings has beautifully depicted faces. What if you would cut a depicted nose out of one of the faces and instead insert a real one. The nose would be "real," but the painting would be destroyed.[11]

In fact, this is one of the key artistic strategies of Treplev, who is trying to accomplish precisely that—to substitute the depicted nose with the real one. He utilizes the natural environment of the lake and the moon, as well as the smell of sulfur, and combines these elements of reality with his imaginary creation—the symbolic image of the World Soul. We may recall that Chekhov was mocking the overdramatic "effects" in theater as early as in 1884, in his parody of the theater of Lentovsky and K. A. Tarnovsky's play *The Pure Ones and the Leprous*. In his biting satire *Impure Tragedians and Leprous Playwrights*, Chekhov fashions a grotesque version of describing Tarnovsky's overwrought dramaturgy: "on his shoulders, in place of a head, is a skull; sulfur is burning in his mouth; out of his nostrils jump little green devils ... He dips his pen—not into an inkwell—but into lava ... It's horrible" (2:319). Although Treplev's play is not a melodrama à la Tarnovsky, the "effects" are somewhat similar: sulfur, red eyes of the devil, and even the world soul's exclamation "horrible, horrible" that echoes Chekhov's satire of Tarnovsky. The point here is that Treplev's "effects" do not make his play more "real" and more "true to life." Nina complains that "there are no living characters" in it. And his mother is quick to identify these effects, and the play as a whole, as "decadent." Even when he becomes a published writer, Treplev apparently adheres to the same literary principles. In act 4, Trigorin repeats his earlier assessment of Treplev's work: "something strange, undefined, occasionally even similar to a delirium. Not a single live character" (13:54).

In his use of the natural environment and sensory effects, Treplev clearly juxtaposes himself both to realism and naturalism. It is no coincidence that when he speaks to his uncle about Trigorin's novels, Treplev compares his artistic rival (unfavorably) to Tolstoy and Zola, the two greatest writers associated with the realist and naturalist traditions, respectively. Trigorin himself also reveals that his fiction is routinely (and unflatteringly) compared to that of Tolstoy and Turgenev, the two Russian giants of realism. By raising questions that might have tormented Chekhov as well—how to write in the shadow of the great Russian realist tradition, emblematized by such towering figures as Turgenev and Tolstoy, on the one hand, and widely acclaimed representatives of naturalism and positivism, such as Zola, on the other—Treplev reveals his vulnerability to the pressures of literary movements of the time. As we know, Chekhov greatly admired Zola for his courageous and uncompromising defense of Alfred Dreyfus; he was also seriously interested in Zola's aesthetic ideas and his scientific approach to literature. Chekhov approved of the French author's disinclination to exclude the vulgar and raw material of life from the world of his fiction. Arguing with Maria V. Kiseleva for the need of a new movement within realism that would unhesitatingly acknowledge the sordid aspects of life, Chekhov echoes Zola's position about the role of the artist as an impartial scientific observer:

> Literature is called an art form because it depicts life as it really is. Its purpose is unconditional and honest truth.... To the chemists, there is nothing impure on this earth. The writer must be as objective as a chemist; he must renounce his everyday subjectivity and recognize that dung heaps play a dutiful role in the landscape, and that ignoble passions are as much a part of life as noble ones. (January 14, 1887; P 2:11–12)

Yet it would be a mistake to interpret this quotation as proof of Chekhov's realism as does Boris Eikhenbaum: "This is what distinguishes the realist 'sense of life' from any other sense of life, in that the realist is not conscious of an active element in creating what he calls 'reality,' and therefore may think that we see life 'as it is' and not as it seems to us.... Chekhov is a realist with a tendency toward naturalism."[12] Chekhov, as I have discussed earlier, was skeptical about the possibility of fully understanding reality and had no illusions about the active role of our consciousness in depicting this reality. But, like Zola, he argues for an honest approach to representation. It's worth recalling that Zola defined naturalism in novels and dramas as based on the commonplace contemporary subject, careful analysis of the world portrayed, and precise reproduction of nature—that is, on a scientific extension of realism. In his *Naturalism in the Theater* (*Le Naturalisme au Théâtre*, 1881), Zola thus explains his position:

> Naturalism in literature is both the return to nature and to man, direct observation, precise anatomy, the acceptance and the depiction of that which is. The writer and the scientist have the same task. Both have to replace abstractions with reality, empirical formulas with rigorous analysis. Thus, no more abstract characters in our works, no more false inventions, no more absolutes, but real characters.[13]

Insisting that writers should adopt a scientific approach in the analysis of facts, Zola called for merely registering those facts and "[avoiding] passing judgment and drawing conclusions":

> The novel writer should also only keep to the facts open to observation; thoroughly investigate nature and society if he does not want to get entangled in false conclusions. He thus disappears; he keeps for himself his own feelings and tells only what he saw. Here is reality; shiver or laugh, looking at it, draw a lesson from this site, but the author's only task is to present the true documents for your evaluation.... Thus, the naturalist writer, just as the scientist, never interferes.... They reproach us harshly for being immoral, because we stage scoundrels as well as honest men without passing judgment on them.... Our only guilt in all of this is that we accept nature as it is and do not want to correct what is with what has to be.[14]

The writer, then, according to Zola, only registers what he sees. In his May 30, 1888, letter to Suvorin, Chekhov seems to almost reiterate Zola's aesthetic program:

It seems to me that this is not up to the writers of fiction to decide questions like God, pessimism, etc. The writer's task is only to describe by whom, how, and under what circumstances something was said or thought about God and pessimism. The artist should not be a judge of his characters and of what they say, but only an impartial witness. I have overheard a confused and inconclusive conversation of two Russians about pessimism, and I must convey this conversation just as I heard it, but not to evaluate it, which is the task of the members of the jury, i.e. the readers. . . . Shcheglov-Leontiev faults me for ending the story with the phrase: "There is no understanding of anything in this world!" He believes that the artist-psychologist *must* understand—that's why he is a psychologist. But I disagree. It's high time for writers, especially for artists, to admit that we don't understand anything in this world, just as Socrates admitted in his time and as Voltaire did. The crowd thinks it knows and understands everything; the more stupid it is the broader their horizons seem to them. If the artist in whom the masses trust dares to declare that he understands nothing of what he sees then this by itself means great knowledge in the realm of thought and a big step forward. (P 2:280–81)

Although Chekhov himself may have subscribed to many of Zola's aesthetic principles, his views never coincided completely with the French writer's program.

Later in life, he dissociated his own artistic principles from those of Zola, although he always admired him as a human being. On September 18, 1902, Chekhov writes to his wife: "I feel melancholy today, for Zola passed away. This is so unexpected and seems untimely. I did not love him much as a writer, but I valued him highly as a human being during his later years, when the Dreyfus affair caused an uproar" (P 2:10–14).[15] In fact, already by 1892, Chekhov was skeptical of the naturalist method and lamented the limits of contemporary realism:

The works that we write today contain no alcohol that would inebriate and enslave us. . . . Tell me honestly, who among my contemporaries, that is between thirty and forty-five years of age, has given the world a single drop of alcohol? Are not Korolenko, Nadson and all the playwrights of today but lemonade? Have you ever been intoxicated with the paintings of Repin or Shishkin? It's nice and talented; you admire them and at the same time can never forget that you really want to smoke. It's a great moment for science and technology, but for people like us this time is lax, sour and dull, and we ourselves are sour and dull (letter to Suvorin, November 25, 1992). (P 5:132–33)

It is interesting that Chekhov juxtaposes here the new trends in science and literature, implicitly suggesting that scientific methods, yielding great results in science, are not as successful when applied to literary arts and may produce something that is "sour and boring."

Significantly, in reference to the present-day artists, Chekhov uses the bland and anodyne phrase "nice, talented" (*milo, talantlivo*) that Treplev will employ when evaluating Trigorin's writings ("Nice, talented … but … after Tolstoy and Zola you won't read Trigorin"; 13:9). In his conversation with Nina, Trigorin would also complain that the reading public refers to his art as "nice" and "talented," but not as good as Tolstoy or Turgenev. Implicitly Chekhov also suggests that a purely "scientific" approach to literature fails to lead to results that are as fruitful as those in the natural sciences. While admitting that he cannot and does not want to write differently, Chekhov nostalgically refers to the realist writers of the older generation whose art, according to him, was more powerful than both Zola's mere "protocol" and the indifferent "lemonade" of contemporary writers:

> You must remember that all those writers whom we call great or just good and who intoxicate us share one very important characteristic: they move in a specific direction and draw you along with them … they have a goal, like the ghost of Hamlet's father, which had a distinct purpose in coming and perturbing his imagination. Some of these writers … have immediate goals. … Others have more distant goals—God, life beyond the grave, the happiness of mankind, etc. The best of these writers are realists and depict life as it is, but because every line they write is like sap, saturated with a consciousness of their goal, you derive from them a sense not just of life as it is but of life as it should be, and it is this that captivates you. But what about us? Us! We describe life as it is, but stumble going any further. (P 5:133)

Dr. Dorn's advice to Treplev echoes this statement and sounds almost like a parody of Chekhov's own lament that contemporary writers lack a definite "goal." (Cf. also Chekhov's comments on the genre of the novel as a palace in contrast to the "birdhouses" of the modern short story writer, quoted in chapter 2.) Didactically insisting that the work of art should express "some kind of significant thought," Dorn delivers a sermon that Chekhov himself undoubtedly heard many times from his readers and critics: "Only the serious is really beautiful. . . . The work of art must express a clear and definite thought. You must know what it is you are writing for. Otherwise, if you go along that picturesque path without a definite aim, you will lose your way and your talent will destroy you" (13:19). Yet the lack of a definite aim clearly applies not only to those who take their subjects from the realm of abstract ideas, as does Treplev, but also to those who depict life as it is, as Trigorin does. Both Treplev and Trigorin therefore, regardless of their very divergent artistic principles, find themselves in the same dead end, without "alcohol" and in the state of "paralysis" that Chekhov complained about in his letter to Suvorin. The artistic principles of both writers, who to a limited degree bear autobiographical traits, reflect Chekhov's self-criticism as a writer and his acknowledgment that a new era and a new "worldview" inevitably lead to different poetics.

Regardless of its artistic merits or flaws, Treplev's play is a rebellion against naturalism's premises and its lack of potency, or "alcohol." It seems as if this young writer read Zola's "Naturalism in the Theater" and decided to turn the aesthetics it lays out on its head. Indeed, Treplev questions naturalism's aesthetic assumptions as well as its preferred subject matter. By rejecting the naturalists' worshipful stance toward material reality, he composes a play whose very subject matter is the struggle between matter and spirit, in which the former appears as a demonic and destructive force. The play opts not for the representation of the material world but for the presentation of abstract ideas (a major no-no for Zola). The only character onstage (aside from the devil whose red eyes glitter in darkness), the World's Soul, performed by Nina, is not conceived as a "true to life" personage. Neither does she speak as one—the World Soul's monologue is characterized by a highly stylized and poetic diction. Significantly, Treplev's audience immediately identifies his anti-materialist program. The schoolteacher Medvedenko, who is not very sensitive to the aesthetic aspects of art, points to its anti-materialist content: "No one has the basis for separating spirit from matter, because spirit itself is probably an agglomeration of material atoms" (13:15). Although Dr. Dorn seems to be emotionally affected by the play and acknowledges its "powerful impression" on him, he also observes that Treplev took "a subject from the realm of abstract ideas" and even expresses solidarity with Treplev's anti-materialism by declaring that he too "would have despised" his "material shell with all that it entails" and would have liked to "fly far away from earth into the empyrean," if he could experience artistic inspiration (13:19).

Scholars agree that Treplev's play reflects symbolist assumptions and aesthetics, but views diverge on how the audience is intended to interpret the performance. Is this strange play a parody of symbolism or a sympathetic portrayal of the new artistic trends? Significantly, Chekhov pre-empts the public and scholarly criticisms of Treplev's play by portraying an audience reaction to the artistic experiment, thereby anticipating the possibility of both dismissive and sympathetic responses. Arkadina rebuffs the play as "decadent gibberish," Trigorin fails to relate to it and admits he could not understand it, and Nina complains that it lacks living characters and love interest. Later she even dismisses it offhand as "uninteresting": "There's very little action in your play, only reading lines. And I believe a play must have a love intrigue" (13:11). By contrast, Dr. Dorn is more receptive to the play's innovations and praises the young writer for making a powerful "impression" on him with his "strange" work. Scholars largely echo Treplev's audience's disagreement about his play. We can safely say that although we have very limited information about Treplev's experiment based on the play's fragment—the World Soul's monologue—the play lacks a traditional plotline and realistic characters and is written in a symbolist vein. But as Robert Jackson cautions us, "though bad art—it is, paradoxically, full of Chekhov's art" and cannot be merely dismissed as "Chekhov's parody of a 'decadent' theatrical style."[16]

Analyzing the sources of Treplev's artistic inspiration, Elena Tolstaia identifies Konstantin Balmont, Fyodor Sologub, Alexander Dobroliubov, Vladimir Solovyov, Dmitry Merezhkovsky, and many others as literary sources for Treplev's opus; Tolstaia concludes that it is a parody of new artistic trends, and of symbolism specifically. She analyzes Treplev's "macaronic" text as essentially poetic rhythmic prose that produces a comic effect through its awkward use of poetic diction incongruously combined with various philosophical and literary sources. Tolstaia concludes—following scholarly consensus—that Treplev is an inept writer, lacking talent and taste. "Chekhov constructed for himself a convenient victim: Chekhov's text pitilessly and unconditionally characterizes Treplev as a bad writer. Treplev's play, therefore, is a biting parody of the consciously misunderstood and purposefully perverted themes of the authors of *The Northern Herald*, an example of cacophony."[17] Yet she also admits that Treplev's "new art" in Chekhov's play emerges in an ambiguous light. Other scholars and critics are more merciful and more sympathetic to Treplev's poetic experiment. In her thoroughly researched article "Treplev the 'Decadent' and the Pale Moon," Alla

Golovacheva also discusses multiple sources that may have shaped Chekhov's view of symbolism and decadence as a "new art," including Briusov, Balmont, Solovyov, and Merezhkovsky as well as European writers, especially Gerhart Hauptmann and Maurice Maeterlinck. She traces the composite image of Treplev as a new decadent artist to P. D. Boborykin's critical essays about the new type of Russian writer. Identifying the origins of Treplev's audience's response to his monologue of the World Soul in specific texts of Chekhov's contemporary criticism, she observes that "in the published articles [of Chekhov's time], one can find the whole array of judgments anticipating the audience's comments about Treplev's play."[18] As opposed to Tolstaia, Golovacheva insists that Treplev's play "undoubtedly is not a parody, but it is not the authorial self-expression either. It would be more precise to call it an example of stylization."[19] In his essay "Chekhov and Philosophy," Sergei Bocharov expresses a legitimate concern: "The playwright Treplev composed an ultra-philosophical text—but how can we take it seriously as such? It is parodically overburdened with scratches from all kinds of world philosophy. All of them are mixed up here—without any order, chaotically, and absurdly." Bocharov further argues that if Treplev's play is a parody, one has to determine what it is that it parodies rather than dismissing it outright as a mocking condemnation of symbolism: "If this is a parody on the newly born decadence (as many have concluded), then this is a compassionate parody: Chekhov's raisonneur Dr. Dorn has his hands trembling from emotion, and he says that this is 'fresh, naïve.'"[20]

Regardless of whether or not Treplev's play is a parody of symbolism or a more sympathetic representation of it, Chekhov does not take sides in Treplev's artistic duel with Trigorin. Both writers, in fact, are presented in the play as successful and acclaimed in the eyes of contemporary audiences—Trigorin from the very opening of the play and Treplev by the play's end; both apparently even publish in the same literary journals. In act 4, Trigorin informs the audience that as a writer Treplev has many "admirers" in Moscow and St. Petersburg and brings him a copy of the magazine with both Treplev's and his own stories. Nina also admits that he matured into a real writer. Without passing judgment on symbolism and naturalism, as represented by Treplev and Trigorin, Chekhov merely ponders what may follow from their respective aesthetic assumptions and subtly distances himself from both.

Treplev's monodrama reflects the symbolist method and style of representation, with its replacement of scenic action with a state similar to a dream and with actors resembling marionettes embodying the author's idea. The play may indeed be what Bocharov and other scholars suggest, a partial parody of symbolist aesthetics grounded in the idealist philosophy of Vladimir Solovyov. We may recall that Solovyov believed that the highest goal of art is "creation of the universal spiritual organism" and that the work of art should be a representation of the object or event "in light of its future" (v svete budushchego mira). Thus the poet is a priest of sorts, and the artists communicate with the higher world by means of their creativity. In his work "The General Meaning of Art," Solovyov claims, "Every sensual representation of an object or event from the point of view of its final state, or in light of the future of the world, is a work of art."[21] Art "anticipates" or acquires an insight into the "light of the future world." Art's goal, according to Solovyov, is to be found not in repetition or imitation but in the continuation of the artistic task that is already undertaken by nature. Treplev appropriates this idea almost verbatim by claiming that "one must depict life not as it is and not as it should be, but as it appears in your dreams" (13:11). And he indeed attempts to depict the objects and events not as they are but as they appear in light of the future world. His play about the World Soul is inspired by this aesthetic assumption and the meaning of art from the point of view of the universal cosmic processes. Although Treplev himself may not be in full command of his art at the opening of *The Seagull*, his play as his theatrical manifesto is a subconscious, intuitive attempt to penetrate into hidden meanings that are accessible only to the creator himself. He not only expresses the metaphysics of symbolism but also employs symbolist verbal strategies such as rhythmic repetitions and musical composition. Whatever the sources of his play may be, Treplev palpably attempts to present his art as a forceful counterpoint or riposte to realist and naturalist poetics. But at the end of the play, Treplev himself recognizes that what ultimately matters in art are not the old or new forms but artistic freedom.

Treplev's play is clearly intended to challenge not only Trigorin's poetic principles but also his mother's theatrical practices. As Apollonio aptly puts it, *The Seagull* "is a drama in which two generations will struggle to the death on the battlefield of art."[22] The implied target of Treplev's artistic attack is framed with references to *Hamlet*, a tragedy that plays a crucial role in the thematic and metapoetic structure of *The Seagull*.[23] Right before the performance, Arkadina and her son exchange lines from Shakespeare's tragedy, establishing a context that invites the audience to consider Treplev's play within the play as a mousetrap of sorts. As we know, Hamlet's *Mousetrap* was not intended to impress the audience with its particular artistic merits but instead to unveil his uncle's suspected guilt in the death of his father by catching the conscience of his mother and uncle if the suspicion should prove correct. Even before the play starts, Arkadina seems to identify herself with Gertrude and her son with Hamlet when she quotes Gertrude's lines: "My son! Thou turn'st my eye into my very soul. And there I see such black and grained spots as will not leave their tinct!" Treplev's motivation, however, was to prove an aesthetic point rather than a moral one. His performance was undoubtedly planned to be a polemic that would catch the conscience of the "king and queen" in his audience—Arkadina and her lover Trigorin— but only in a purely aesthetic and artistic sense, by revealing their artistic flaws. Indeed, Treplev's play seems intended to question all manner of thespian practices, from acting styles (whether realistic, melodramatic, or symbolic) to the use of stage settings, props and machinery, costumes, diction, and entrances and exits.

Like *The Murder of Gonzago*, to which high literary value cannot be assigned, Treplev's play is stilted and artificial, but its audience immediately interprets it as aesthetically provocative. Arkadina at once identifies her son's purpose in the staging: "So he staged this show and fumigated us with his sulfur not as a joke, but as a demonstration ... He wanted to teach us how to write and what to act in" (13:15). The impact of Treplev's play on us as spectators may, in fact, be similar to the impact of *The Murder of Gonzago* on an Elizabethan audience, and this, I believe, elucidates Chekhov's shrewd design. A stylistically old-fashioned, bombastic tragedy structured like a morality play and filled with conventional and somewhat formulaic speeches, *The Murder of Gonzago* would not have impressed the audience of the Globe Theater. Familiar and trivial, with monotonous rhymes and ponderous rhetoric, the play would have struck Shakespeare's audience as a throwback whose intentionally archaic and artificial nature helped to convey the illusion of a stage play before the actors in the main stage play.

Chekhov's play within the play is designed to have a similar effect. Although not old-fashioned—perhaps even somewhat avant-garde—Treplev's play is similarly out of tune with the audience-with-the-audience's expectations (especially Arkadina's and Trigorin's) but also with our expectations as spectators of Chekhov's play. Like *The Murder of Gonzago*, Treplev's play has very limited artistic value in itself and creates a jarring effect in the context of Chekhov's own play. Its diction and tone contrast sharply not only with contemporary theatrical conventions alluded to by Arkadina—thereby making it incomprehensible to Treplev's audience—but also with the prosaic speeches of all the characters in Chekhov's play. These jarring differences make it difficult for Chekhov's own audience to take Treplev's play seriously. If Chekhov's play seems to have "tons of love" and deploys supple, flexible, colloquial language, Treplev's play does not contain anything that approaches realistic speech patterns, and it has no "love interest" and appears to be overly abstract and allegorical. While Chekhov, for the most part, utilizes a literary style that reflects the way ordinary people speak, relying on a style of acting that tries to recreate reality and avoid any special effects, Treplev strives to do the very opposite: he leans into a highly stylized manner of acting, visual and olfactory effects, and the absence of dramatic dialogue. Just as Shakespeare emphasizes the difference between his own tragedy and Hamlet's play and its artistic merits, so does Chekhov. Both playwrights deploy the play-within-a-play device to draw attention to the failings—whether moral or aesthetic—of the performance's targeted audience. When Gonzago is murdered in the play, the King rises in anger and makes his way quickly from the room. Calling for lights, the King rushes from the hall, but in Chekhov's play it is the director of the mousetrap, Treplev, not Trigorin, who abruptly ends the performance and runs away, exposing, therefore, not so much Trigorin and Arkadina but himself. Unable to endure the shame of his perceived failure, he falls into his own trap.

Unlike Claudius responding to *The Murder of Gonzago*, Trigorin seems unaffected and quietly dismisses Treplev's provocation by saying that he understood nothing in this show and quickly steering the conversation to the mundane pleasures of life: "But I love to fish. There's no greater pleasure for me than to sit on the shore towards evening and watch the bobber" (13:17). Arkadina, however, recognizes Treplev's intent, but instead of feeling shaken by the similarity between her actions and those portrayed onstage, she views the performance as an affront to her sense of purpose as an actress. Thus, the aim of both plays—Hamlet's and Treplev's—is essentially similar: to reveal the corruption (moral or artistic) of the audience. Treplev fully anticipated Arkadina's reaction as he understood that both his type of play and Nina's acting were incompatible with his mother's theatrical practices. The play, therefore, was intended to reveal to his mother her thespian inadequacies. Aware of his mother's jealousy and her artistic ambition and intolerance, Treplev confides to Sorin his premonitions of Arkadina's response: "She's jealous. She's already against me, against the performance, and against my play, because her writer may take a liking to Zarechnaia. She doesn't know my play, but she already hates it. . . . She's already annoyed that on this tiny stage success will belong to Zarechnaia and not to her" (13:7). He consciously attempts to aesthetically "trap" his self-satisfied mother and her novelist-lover, and this desire to entrap them reflects his Oedipal struggles.[24]

Treplev's unresolved Oedipal complex—his obsessive love of his mother and unconscious hatred of her lover who usurps the place of his father—is transformed in Chekhov's play into an aesthetic rebellion—his unconscious wish to destroy the authority of the dominant culture and of the artistic "law of the father." Although seemingly enamored with Nina, Treplev displays a bizarre, semi-incestuous attraction to his mother. During his fortune-telling on flower petals—an activity that traditionally presupposes young girls or men using flower petals to determine whether their love is requited—Treplev seeks confirmation of his mother's feelings toward him: "(*Tearing off the petals of a flower*). She loves me—she loves me not, she loves me—she loves me not, she loves me—she loves me not. (*Laughs.*) You see, my mother doesn't love me" (13:8). As his mother's thespian and maternal flaws merge in his consciousness, his frustrated sexual drives are sublimated into an aesthetic conflict and his rebellion against the conventional theater and the "priests of high art." Significantly, his rebellion against contemporary art goes hand in hand with his professed love for his mother: "New forms are what we need. We need new forms, and if there aren't any, then we'd be better off to have nothing at all. (*Looks at his watch.*) I love my mother, I love her deeply; but she smokes, drinks, and openly lives with that novelist" (13:8). He views her relationship to the theater as a threat and obstacle to his own full possession of his mother: "Sometimes I feel sorry that my mother is a famous actress, and it seems if she were an ordinary woman, I might be happier" (13:8). After his first unsuccessful attempt at suicide, when he enjoys being tended to by his mother and completely infantilized by her ("when I'm away, you won't do any more *click-click*?" asks his mother), Treplev again tries to eliminate or displace obstacles to his full possession of his mother's love and attention—in this case, her mother's lover: "Lately, in these past few days, I have loved you as tenderly and selflessly as in childhood. I have no one left now except you. Only why, why is this man standing between you and me?" (13:38).[25]

When his theatrical experiment fails to impress the "king and queen," he explicitly rebukes all those who take his mother from him, especially Trigorin: "I overlooked the fact that only a few chosen ones can write plays and act on the stage. I've violated a monopoly!" (13:14). In act 3, in the scene with Arkadina changing the bandage on his self-inflicted wound, Treplev verbally attacks Trigorin as a representative of the artistic "law of the father," venting his frustration with artistic authority figures: "You people with your narrow-minded, run-of-the-mill conventions have usurped the leadership in the arts today and consider to be legitimate and genuine only what you do yourselves; everything else you suppress and suffocate! I don't accept you! I just won't accept either you or him!" (13:40).

Treplev displaces his violent urge to kill Trigorin by first killing a seagull and then by attempting suicide. He does not kill Trigorin but only threatens to challenge him to a duel, yet he finally succeeds in killing himself. His failure to successfully resolve his Oedipal conflict leads not only to failure in his personal life but also to his inability to find his voice as an artist. His fixation on his mother and his inability to move beyond the rivalry with her lover both prevent him from developing his own literary language. Recognizing his own artistic vulnerability, he struggles with his failure to escape clichés and feels he is slipping into a literary rut: "the white face, framed by dark hair," "the tremulous light," "the soft glimmer of the stars," "the faraway sounds of a piano dying off in the calm, fragrant air" (13:55). Without his own path and "aim," as Dr. Dorn points out, he cannot achieve full subjectivity. The mere rebellion against the old forms of art and the authority of the dominant culture are no more productive than rebellion against the father: "I'm still drifting in a maelstrom of dreams and images, without knowing why it has to be or for whose sake" (13:59). Trying to set an artistic "trap" for his mother and authoritative writers such as Trigorin, Treplev finds himself trapped in the dead end of "dreams and images." Moreover, his unresolved fixation on his mother leads to his final regression into childhood. Significantly, Treplev's last words before his suicide concern his mother. He is worried that someone might meet Nina in the garden and tell his mother about her visit: "It won't be good if someone runs into her in the garden and tells Mama. It might upset Mama" (13:59). One can only wonder why he does not worry that his suicide might "upset Mama." His focus appears to be on the prospect of Nina provoking Arkadina's jealousy and therefore intensifying her attention to Trigorin. His suicide, by contrast, will finally make his mother think about *him*. Treplev's quest for new forms is presented by Chekhov through the prism of his Oedipal conflict and emerges as an unresolved rebellion against tradition that ultimately leads to his downfall as a lover, a son, and an artist.

Chekhov manipulates theatrical conventions and depicts a young symbolist artist's experimental play to help us understand his own view of the theater and its goals. Just as *The Murder of Gonzago* contrasts with Shakespeare's play as a whole, so does Treplev's play contrast with Chekhov's. Chekhov, however, may be sympathetic to Treplev's criticism of modern theater and even, to some extent, to the poetic qualities of his play's imagery, although its metaphysics are clearly at odds with Chekhov's comedy. In contrast to Treplev, Chekhov created most dramatic illusion through simple activities and dialogues, and a few props. By depicting the very opposite of his own playwriting—Treplev's overly symbolic experiment—Chekhov indirectly defends the need for a more natural performance.

TRIGORIN'S LITERARY PANTRY AND THE EVIDENTIAL PARADIGM OF MODERNISM

Does this mean that Trigorin's aesthetic principles do a better job than Treplev's of saturating art with the "alcohol" Chekhov values so much in the Russian classics? Even though there is no direct confrontation between Treplev and Trigorin onstage and their unrealized "duel" is assumed to be about their rivalry for Nina, the real duel is an aesthetic one. Not only is Treplev vexed that Trigorin corrupts Nina's innocence and interferes with his bonding with his mother, but he explicitly states that he dislikes Trigorin's art. We do not know, however, if he has read Trigorin closely, for at the beginning of the play he proclaims to Nina that he has not. Yet to Sorin's question about Trigorin as a writer and person, Treplev unhesitatingly replies: "nice, talented . . . but . . . after Tolstoy and Zola you would not like to read Trigorin" (13:9).

Trigorin's naturalist approach to fiction writing seems to be confirmed at the end of the play, when he reveals his practice of writing based on observed reality: "By the way, I have to look around the garden and the place, where—remember?—your play was performed. I've developed a theme; I just have to refresh my memory on the setting of the action" (13:52). He also confesses that he does not have enough imagination to envision how a young girl may think and feel and that his young female characters are, for the most part, inauthentic and stilted because he only infrequently meets them in real life. While Treplev has no interest in portraying life as it is, Trigorin's writings stem from the notion that the duty of the novelist is to present as accurate a picture of life as possible. Like the writers of the naturalist school, he believes this is best accomplished by presenting material as objectively as possible, relying on observation and notebooks. He acknowledges that his creativity is stimulated by direct observation and that describing nature is the only thing he does well: "I love the water over there, the trees, sky, I have a feeling for nature, I feel passionate about it and it inspires me with the irresistible desire to write" (13:30). However, he feels that being a landscape writer and merely true to nature is insufficient for a successful artist, and therefore he must also "speak about the people and their suffering, about their future, discuss science, human rights et cetera, et cetera" (13:30). Yet in trying to attach ideology to his descriptive method, Trigorin betrays his genuine talent and as a result is forced to admit that, in fact, he only knows how to write about landscapes, and everything else he composes is "phony, and phony to the core" (13:31). We may recall that Chekhov himself repeatedly objected to literature with an ideological or didactic function and took issue with the pressure on him "to write seriously."[26] Trigorin's predicament echoes Chekhov's own concerns as outlined in his letter to Suvorin of November 25, 1892, about the generation of writers who are doomed to offer their readers only "lemonade" without any "alcohol" because they lack authentic goals and worldviews, have no distinct political opinions and religion, and henceforth are stuck and paralyzed with their emptiness. "Those who want nothing, who have no hopes and are afraid of nothing, cannot be artists," concludes Chekhov, viewing this lack of beliefs and foundations as a disease of his time that inevitably affects artistic practices (P 5:133–34). Trigorin is clearly a writer of these modern times whose fiction is "nice" and shows "talent" but ultimately amounts to no more than "lemonade." Significantly, Chekhov describes Trigorin's and the modern writer's continuous but fruitless compulsion to write in similar terms. Mocking his own unquenchable urge to write, Trigorin grumbles: "I've barely finished one story, when already for some reason I have to write another, then a third, after the third a fourth.... I write nonstop as the pony express, and cannot do otherwise" (13:29). These words reverberate with Chekhov's comments about the writers of his generation: "We write mechanically, only submitting to the old accepted order, according to which some engage in civil service, others in trade, and still others in writing" (P 5:134).

Although we have only, for the most part, indirect knowledge about Trigorin as a writer, we gain some insight into his creative laboratory and receive some information not only about his naturalist artistic inclinations but also about his fictional plots and his specific narrative strategies. As follows from

Treplev's remarks at the end of the play, he has read enough of Trigorin to recognize his particular literary devices and poetic principles: "Trigorin has worked out his own devices, it's easy for him. . . . He'd have the broken neck of a bottle glistening on the dike and the shadow of the mill wheel getting darker and darker—and there it is, the moonlit night all set" (13:55). As we know, Chekhov used this same image in his own story "The Wolf" and suggested it as a literary device to his brother Alexander in a letter of May 10, 1886.[27] Does this mean, then, that Chekhov fully aligns with Trigorin's artistic principles? While Trigorin's aesthetics are closer to Chekhov's than Treplev's, they still fall short of Chekhov's own. To be sure, many of Trigorin's literary strategies—in particular, the use of suggestive details evoking a larger picture and his metonymical strategy of conveying the whole through a part, such as the glistening on the broken neck of a bottle to covey the atmosphere of the moonlit night—may be congenial to Chekhov's own strategies, just as Treplev's criticism of the contemporary stage may echo Chekhov's disapproval of modern theatrical practices.

Yet as readers we have very little firsthand information about Trigorin's fiction. As in the case of Treplev's play, we have no text that would allow us to draw our own conclusions about his literary talent. In fact, the only sentence taken directly from Trigorin's works is a quotation from his novel *Days and Nights* that Nina has engraved on the medallion she gives him as a token of her affection: "If ever you have need of my life, come and take it" (13:40).[28] This quotation, which is, in fact, a line quoted from Dostoevsky's *Crime and Punishment*—Dunia's words to Raskolnikov—suggests a melodramatic plot that is quite at odds with Chekhov's own tastes.[29] Similarly melodramatic is the plot of a short story that he jots down in his notebook upon seeing a seagull killed by Treplev: "Subject for a short story: from her childhood, a young girl, just like you, lives on the shores of a lake; she loves the lake, like a seagull, is happy and free, like a seagull. But by chance a man came along, saw her and, having nothing better to do, destroyed her, just like this seagull here" (13:31–32). This plot is essentially a staple of sentimentalist fiction, reminiscent of Karamzin's *Poor Liza*. Just as the pastoral existence of Liza in Karamzin's celebrated story is destroyed by a bored nobleman who has nothing better to do, so the innocent girl of Trigorin's fancy is also ruined by a jaded outsider; both poor girls die as a result of their unhappy love—Liza throws herself into a pond, and Trigorin's poor girl perishes at the shores of the lake. Initially, Nina indeed adopts this melodramatic narrative for herself, only to discard it later. This unoriginal and even hackneyed plotline precludes any possibility of interpreting Trigorin as Chekhov's ideal writer.

Yet although Chekhov clearly distances himself from Trigorin as a writer, he has him share some of his own narrative strategies. We know that Trigorin has a reputation as an acclaimed writer and that the two women who are in love with him—Arkadina and Nina—highly praise his prose. As biased as Arkadina's praise of Trigorin may be—when she offers her evaluation of Trigorin's writing, she is chiefly motivated by her desire to flatter him. She therefore singles out those aspects of his prose that differ fundamentally from Treplev's: his "sincerity," "simplicity," "freshness," and "wholesome humor" (13:42). More importantly, she identifies the same "device" Treplev mentions in his assessment of Trigorin as writer—his ability to be concise and to deploy suggestive details to covey the whole picture: "With a single stroke you can convey the most essential feature significant in a person or a landscape; your characters are so alive" (13:42). Thus we may conclude that Trigorin indeed may be a master of suggestive details. This aspect of his creative method is further supported by his practice of taking notes and jotting down a few characteristic features that function as indexes—that is, as signs describing the connection between signifier and signified. A good example of Trigorin's use of a signifier as an index for the core aspects of someone's personality are his comments about Masha: "[She] takes snuff and drinks vodka . . . Always in black." He is not describing Masha's actions per se or the way she looks, but instead singles out elements of her character that underscore her self-dramatization and eccentricity. The description is not based on similarity but on contiguity. In his characterization of her, Trigorin refers to Masha's black dress not as a traditional symbol of mourning but as a detail pointing to her unhappiness and her desire to present herself as being in mourning. Her vodka-drinking and snuff-taking similarly indicate her impulse to violate conventions associated with a young girl's behavior and her estrangement from accepted social norms. These details direct our attention to her rebellious, unconventional manner, which implies certain key aspects of her personality. Masha's statement in the play's opening that she is "in mourning" for her life also functions as an index for her character. Chekhov subtly mocks her sentimental "disillusionment" with life and her self-portrayal as someone older than she is—the traits that were rendered ironically already by writers of the romantic era, such as Pushkin. (Cf. Pushkin's portrayal of Vladimir Lensky in *Eugene Onegin*: "He sung of lifetime's fading bloom, when not quite eighteen years of age" [Он пел поблеклый жизни цвет / Без малого в осьмнадцать лет].) A few details about Masha's character registered by Trigorin and bespeaking her penchant for self-dramatization are later confirmed by her other melodramatic gestures. Not only does Masha cast herself consistently as an angry young woman who dresses in black, drinks vodka, takes snuff, and is unhappy in love and prematurely disillusioned with life, but she also histrionically emphasizes her uprootedness and "superfluousness," evoking what was by then a hackneyed Russian nineteenth-century literary type. When she asks Trigorin to send her his books, she tells him to autograph them with the following extravagant and overdramatic words: "To Maria, who does not remember her origins, who doesn't know why she is living on this earth" (13:34). Thus, she casts herself as the proverbial "Ivan who does not remember his origins"—that is, a vagabond or a runaway criminal who pretends not to remember his name or renounces his family ties, traditions, and national history.[30] Indeed, Trigorin incisively captures her character with only a few suggestive details.

In the play's longest speech—during Trigorin's conversation with Nina—Arkadina's lover further reveals the aesthetics underlying his artistic practices. Describing his compulsive need to write, he highlights his creative strategy of selecting a few suggestive details that allude to a larger picture: "There is a smell of heliotrope here. And I quickly take note: a saccharine smell, the widow's color, I should mention this in a description of a summer evening. I catch you and myself at every phrase, every word and I hurry as fast as I can to lock up all these words and phrases in my literary pantry—they might become useful one day!" (13:29). The smell and color of heliotrope are important not in themselves but as indexes for a person wearing those scents—a widow. They therefore convey a sense of loss and the suffocating feel of a summer evening.

It is probably no coincidence that this technique of characterization echoes what the Italian historian Carlo Ginzburg refers to as the "evidential paradigm." In his influential study *Clues, Myths, and the Historic Method*, Ginzburg suggests that by the end of the nineteenth century a new epistemological model, the "presumptive" or "evidential" paradigm, emerged in the area of humanities. Observing some inherent similarities between the so-called Morelli method in the area of art criticism, the sleuthing methods of Sherlock Holmes, and Sigmund Freud's psychoanalysis, Ginzburg outlines the key principles of Morelli's method of identification and attribution of paintings. This approach pays particular attention to the least conspicuous aspects of a painting and seemingly insignificant details, such as the shape of a figure's earlobes or fingernails in a portrait. He maintains that these inconspicuous details reveal the artist's individual manner and idiosyncratic style more than the obvious and prominent elements of a painting because, viewing them as less significant, artists frequently paint them with the least amount of care. As a result, these details are less affected by the influence of a concrete artistic movement and school and can serve as the artist's "finger prints." Linking Giovanni Morelli's approach to painting identification to the emerging evidential paradigm of the end of the nineteenth century, Ginzburg points out that the detective discovers the criminal on the basis of clues and evidence that may be barely noticeable to everyone else. Similarly, the psychoanalytical method focuses on the interpretation of unconscious gestures, on details that appear insignificant and hidden to the common observer, on inadvertent verbal slips and neurotic symptoms—namely, everything marginal that reveals something about the subconscious. In formulating his own empirical approach to diagnostics, Freud acknowledged an affinity to Morelli's interpretive method, which has a lot in common with Sherlock Holmes's detective work. Connecting them to a particular type of visual perception typical of modernism, Ginzburg emphasizes that all three methods of interpretation lead to a deeper understanding of reality: "In each case, infinitesimal traces permit the comprehension of a deeper, otherwise unattainable reality: traces—more precisely, symptoms (in the case of Freud), clues (in the case of Sherlock Holmes), pictorial marks (in the case of Morelli)."[31] Not coincidentally, all three "investigators" discussed by Ginzburg—Freud, Morelli, and Conan Doyle—passed through a regimen of medical training that came to dominate clinical practice in nineteenth-century Europe. According to this methodology, the proper diagnosis of a malady can only proceed when a *Gestalt* of observed symptoms is achieved through the observation of immediate symptoms together with quirky physical details that would not seem to fit into any conventional medical assessment.

The model of medical semiotics described by Ginzburg must have been congenial to Chekhov in his capacity as a physician, as someone who relied on diagnosis of diseases inaccessible to direct observation based on superficial symptoms and adopted this strategy to his literary method. Chekhov's attention to all sorts of symptoms, insignificant details, and things below the surface connects him to Morelli, Conan Doyle, and Freud, who were his contemporaries. Marginal details, or "trifles of life" (to use the title of one of his stories), are endowed in Chekhov's texts with increased semiotic value. To a large extent, Chekhov's poetics is based on careful selection of details, phrases, gestures, clues, and signs that in themselves carry no symbolic significance but are used by the author as indexes for meanings that Chekhov's characters and the text itself may keep hidden. Through slips of the tongue and seemingly insignificant or trivial features, deeper meanings are revealed, as if unintentionally. Chekhov relies on the reader to act as a detective or psychoanalyst of sorts, identifying elements of the text that serve as "clues" or "symptoms." As Chekhov puts it in the letter to Suvorin quoted above, he sees his reader as being analogous to a member of a jury or a detective, drawing on the "clues" the writer has left but coming to independent conclusions.

Chekhov frequently emphasizes the active role of the reader and the task of the writer as a gatherer of suggestive details:

> You censure me for objectivity, calling it indifference to good and evil, lack of ideals, ideas, and so on. . . . Let the jury judge them [Chekhov's characters]; my task is simply to show what sort of people they are. . . . Of course it would be pleasant to combine art with a sermon, but for me personally it is extremely difficult and almost impossible owing to the conditions of technique. . . . When I write, I entirely rely on the reader to add for himself the subjective elements that are lacking in the story. (letter to Suvorin, April 1, 1890; P 4:54)

Even before the publication of Conan Doyle's stories about Sherlock Holmes, Chekhov was interested in the genre of the crime short story and the detective method. (See, for example, his story "The Swedish Match" ["Shvedskaia spichka"].)[32] Every detail, according to Chekhov, can potentially be used as a "clue." Indeed, in Chekhov's prose and theater, those marginal and insignificant details—symptoms and clues—lead to a deeper understanding of reality. The insignificant turns out to be significant and vice versa, and the function and meaning of those details may diverge from what is expected in the beginning. Chekhov's contemporaries noted his use of the "detective" method without naming it as such. For example, we find this indication of Chekhov's observational techniques: "He regularly attended school openings in the vicinity of Melikhovo, and by a few trifling details in a schoolteacher's apartment he could draw a conclusion about the degree of his culturedness [*intelligentnosti*]. Chekhov would give an infallible characterization of the apartment's owner only on the basis of how and where he kept his papers and books, how he arranged furniture and decorated the walls."[33] Chekhov's poetics is characterized by an "evidential" approach to reality in terms of his own narrative style and his characters' ways of "reading" and interpreting the world around them. For this reason Chekhov calls special attention to tiny details such as scents, colors, and the manner of speech. For example, to convey a class tension between landowners and their servants, he makes his characters register particular smells and scents. In *The Cherry Orchard*, Gaev notices that Yasha "smells of chicken" or of "patchouli," and Ranevskaia is disgusted by the smell of his "repulsive cigars." Smells have semiotic significance because their evaluation is rooted in specific historical and social contexts. Chekhov's reference to patchouli in the characterization of Yasha can only be fully understood if we know how his contemporaries perceived its smell: by the end of the nineteenth century, the smell of patchouli, which used to be fashionable in earlier decades, was no longer considered pleasant. As Olga Vainshtein observed in her book *Dendi: Moda, literatura, stil' zhizni* (Dandy: Fashion, literature, lifestyle), "Patchouli were out-of-date in the olfactory landscape of the second half of the nineteenth century and were perceived as a sign of bad taste."[34] Chekhov's gaze is directed toward those semiotically charged details—dresses, manner of speech, scents, furniture—all that functions as symptoms or clues and carries semiotic connotations that must be deciphered by a careful observer. The meanings of colors and smells for Chekhov are not universal and symbolic but contextual and historicist. The smell of patchouli or the oriental perfumes of Anna Sergeevna from "Lady with the Lapdog" or the green color of Natasha's belt in *The Three Sisters* are not vulgar in and of themselves but only in specific social and historical contexts of shifting trends in couture and taste.

In his plays, Chekhov fully discloses the psychoanalytical aspects of the evidential details in his poetics. His characters reveal or expose themselves through accidentally spoken phrases, verbal tics, blunders, silences (or even, as in the case of Lopakhin from *The Cherry Orchard*, through bleating and neurotic outbursts), and small errors—all that served as the most important material for Dr. Freud. Chekhov wrote his plays for a new type of acting, as Stanislavsky sensed. The key aspect of Stanislavsky's Method stems from his conviction that actors must know more about the characters they play than the characters know about themselves. There was a clear synergy, therefore, between Chekhov's poetics and Stanislavsky's theory of acting. Chekhov's character is a "patient" of sorts, both for the actor and for the audience. The character hides what the actor reveals for us. Inadvertently and subconsciously, the character may reveal some hidden thoughts and personality traits through tiny "clues" and "symptoms." That is why it is so important to consider the clash between what the characters say on stage and what they mean or think in reality. Very often Chekhov's characters seem to say something meaningless and containing very little information about themselves. But these meaningless phrases reveal their hidden anxieties and concerns. Chekhov explicitly refers to his narrative strategy as the description of symptoms rather than specific ideas. "Is it that you value all kind of opinions so much that you concentrate only on them as centers of gravity, without taking into consideration the manner in which they are expressed, where they come from, and so on?"—he writes to Suvorin in connection with his story "The Boring Story" ("Skuchnaia istoriia"): "For me as a writer, these opinions have no value whatsoever in themselves. It is not the content [*sushchnost'*] of these opinions that is important—their content is neither fixed nor new. The whole point lies in the nature of the opinions, their dependence on external influences, and so on. They should be scrutinized as objects, as symptoms, completely objectively, without trying to prove or disprove them" (P 3:266). Trying to explain his thought about the nature of discourse in his works, Chekhov emphasizes the symptomatic, psychoanalytical, and evidential aspects of his poetics (P 3:271). The characters' words may not have any meaning in themselves, but they emerge as symptoms of the "malaise" the author is trying to depict.

Trigorin uses an "evidential paradigm" similar to Chekhov's. Like Sherlock Holmes, who enjoyed compiling information in his index and solved his cases using reasoning, scientific observation, logic, and deduction, Trigorin identifies "clues" and "incriminating" details, storing them in his "literary pantry" (literaturnaia kladovaia) for future use (13:29). His characterization of Masha through smell, taste, and color reveals Masha's somewhat ridiculous pretensions, which are incompatible with her age. Trigorin shares Chekhov's own strategy of using signs as indexes for characterization and emphasizing the significance of inconspicuous details.

But despite these similarities, neither Trigorin's "lemonade" nor Treplev's "maelstrom of dreams and images" emerges in Chekhov's play as a model of writing. Trigorin's narrative methods may be closer to Chekhov's than Treplev's unrestrained symbolism, which seems divorced from life, but Chekhov is far from identifying with Trigorin's melodramatic plots and his failure to draw on the imagination and memory. Chekhov's own position is hidden. The task of the writer, according to him, is not to choose between two opposing views and not to simply find the middle ground but to make us think. Both Trigorin and Treplev express some of Chekhov's ideas about art. In his memoirs about his meeting with Chekhov in July 1889 in Yalta, D. Gorodetsky recalls that Chekhov's guests once asked Chekhov about his insistence that one needs to write a play in which people simply dine and play cards and in which everything happens as in real life: "So then should this be naturalism in the spirit of Zola?" Chekhov objected: "One needs neither naturalism nor realism. One should not try to fit in into any framework. Life must be depicted as it is, and people as they are, not following any formulae."[35] Treplev shares this discovery at the end of the play.

To further consider how Chekhov partakes in his protagonists' views but also navigates between their extremes, we will consider the use of the image of the seagull—the title image of the play.

THE SEAGULL'S METAMORPHOSES

From a flying, warm-blooded vertebrate to the lifeless creature that has been shot and placed at Nina's feet, to Nina's assumed pen name, to the stuffed bird in Shamraev's cupboard, the image of the seagull undergoes a dizzying range of transformations in Chekhov's play.[36] The play's title designates not only a particular image or association; it also points to the very process of image making and the way the word itself functions in discourse. What is a "seagull"? Is it a word that designates an object—that is, a particular kind of bird? If so, what are its attributes? Is it a metaphor or a symbol of innocence, freedom, or high aspirations? Or is it a personal symbol that each character invests with his or her own meaning? Does Chekhov use this image as Treplev or Trigorin does, or does he employ it in a different way?

At the play's opening, Chekhov introduces a problem of artistic image and its formation but does so through a character—the schoolteacher Medvedenko. Even though Medvedenko himself is very distant from literary creativity, as a teacher he is accustomed to operating with literary categories and terms. Returning from a walk with Masha, whom he woos without hope, Medvedenko grudgingly complains about the sad lot of schoolteachers and compares his failure to win Masha's heart with Treplev and Nina's fortunate union: "They're in love, and today their souls will merge in an attempt to create a joint artistic image. But my soul and yours have no mutual points of convergence" (13:5). This first mentioning of the "artistic image" is ironic and typical of Chekhov's strategy of initially introducing important concepts in a low key, parodically and ironically. Yet Medvedenko's awkward remark draws the audience's attention to some of the central semiotic concerns of the play—the very process of image-making and various types of signs generated by an artistic thought process. Each character in the play seems to have his or her own aesthetic framework that reveals itself in the way the character's consciousness conceptualizes individual or disparate objects.

The problem of the artistic image and what constitutes an image was part of late nineteenth-century literary debates. In the nineties, Chekhov also intensely reflected on the nature of language and the function of artistic images. In one of his letters he refers to "the nature of language" and interrelationships between language and thought, as well as between language and nations.[37] The latter interest, as suggested by one scholar, may have been influenced by Chekhov's possible reading of the celebrated Russian and Ukrainian philologist and linguist of the time Alexander A. Potebnja and his ideas about language as a means by which the mind orders the influx of impressions and stimuli. In the poetic word and in the poetic work as a whole, Potebnja distinguishes three components: outer, or external, form (sound); content, or idea (semantics); and inner form (image, or modality by which the word's content is conveyed, which he essentially identifies with the closest etymological meaning). The internal form is rooted in myth and acts as a bridge between language and national folklore, which contains its own unique worldview. The concept of "inner form"—through which the objective world is subjectivized—offers an analogy to the way Chekhov conceived of the image of the seagull. The inner form, according to Potebnja, represents the means of comprehending something new by the correlation of new impressions with a preexisting image: "The inner form, apart from the actual unity of the image also imparts the awareness of this unity; it is not an image of the object, but an image of the image, that is, *representation*."[38] According to Potebnja, an artistic image does not reflect the world, which exists independently from our consciousness; this world is not accessible and signifies only a part of the subjective world of the artist. The subjective world of the artist in turn is unknowable to others and is not expressed but merely signified by an artistic image. An image, then, is a symbol, an allegory; individuals invest it with their own subjective content. That is why mutual understanding is fundamentally impossible. The inner form is important only as a sign, as something that replaces the multifacetedness of the sensual image. But this sensual image is perceived differently by various individuals, depending on their prior experience. Thus, the word, according to Potebnja, is a continuously renewable sign that every person invests with subjective content.

Whether or not Chekhov was familiar with Potebnja's writings about the structure of the word, Potebnja's ideas may offer a theoretical basis of the Chekhovian dialogues of non-understanding, or mutual incomprehension. Furthermore, we could consider *The Seagull* as a linguistic experiment of sorts that reveals the way one creates images and how the words are endowed with meaning. Not accidently, the play contains a reference to Hamlet's famous "words, words, words"—Hamlet's provocative statement questioning the relationships between words and meaning, a problem Shakespeare was also profoundly interested in. "The word in a sense does not express the whole thought, taken as its content, but only its one attribute," wrote Potebnja. And so Potebnja distinguished between two types of content: the objective one (the one "closest etymologically"), which always contains only one attribute, and the subjective one, which may have "multiple attributes."[39] The way Chekhov's characters interpret the image of the seagull tracks with Potebnja's idea of subjective content. For each character in the play, the seagull signifies something subjective, depending on their personal associations and aesthetic positions. Chekhov employs the same strategy of an open artistic image in his use of the images of Moscow in *The Three Sisters* and of the "broken string" and the orchard in *The Cherry Orchard*.

Apart from the play's title, the word "seagull" is introduced for the first time by Nina. Using it as a simple simile, she explains that she is drawn to Sorin's estate and the lake "like a gull" (13:10). Although the word "gull" can evoke many attributes, here it conveys only one meaning—a bird living near water. Yet in Chekhov's play, "the seagull" is not only a word and a sign but also a material object. When Treplev lays a slain gull at Nina's feet, the seagull is introduced as a material object, a "thing in itself" that in itself has no meaning. All its attributes—such as, for example, its size, shape, and color—are equally important for the gull as a material object, although as a material object the gull itself signifies nothing. However, through gesture, by an act of laying the bird at Nina's feet, Treplev creates an image of the seagull on the stage and semiotizes the material object. Now it is not merely a concrete material seagull but also an indexically symbolic marker. Nina tries to understand its meaning—that is, the content of this image: "What does this mean?" (13:27). The image of the seagull—created by Treplev's gesture—is part of the system of signification, whereas the material gull may exist only as a thing in itself without participating in any symbolic system. But the image of the seagull, as opposed to the material seagull, is not stable, for it depends on the consciousness that generates it. It is clear that signification is relative and depends on various other factors, including aesthetic ones. In *The Seagull*, the characters' consciousness creates images that are based on their particular aesthetic orientation.

We could say, therefore, that Chekhov's play raises the problem of signification and the relationship between a thing and a sign. While Treplev creates a symbol, Chekhov himself wryly uses the image of the slain bird as a clue for the characterization of Treplev. If we view the slain seagull as a "clue" to Treplev's character, it will reveal an important aspect of Treplev's personality: his capability of a senseless murder and ultimately another senseless murder—suicide. Chekhov's interest in the nature of language is not accidental. The slain seagull, "this seagull" ("I was mean enough today to kill this seagull. I lay it at your feet") becomes not only an image of a particular bird customarily associated with water but also a sign of something Nina cannot or does not want to understand (13:27). In fact, Nina's "what does this mean?" is a central leitmotif of the play. The play repeatedly draws our attention to the objects' signification. "Why do you always wear black?"—Medvedenko's question, which opens the play, forces the audience to think about the significance of Masha's black dress—that is, to pay attention not to the color black as a concrete attribute of a concrete object (signifying nothing in itself) but as a sign of something else. Likewise, "this seagull" initially is only a sign-index. But gradually the seagull is endowed with various subjective meanings by each character. At the moment when Nina is looking at the slain seagull as an object not signifying anything ("What's wrong with you? [*Picks up the seagull and stares at it.*]"), Treplev explains: "Soon I'll kill myself in this same way" (13:27). Treplev shifts the emphasis from the seagull as an object to his own act of killing. Assigning a particular significance to the dead seagull as an object, Treplev too selects only a single attribute—the fact that it is slain—and produces a transparent image revealing a different and purely subjective meaning of the seagull as a victim. In creating a purely subjective content that has nothing to do with objectifying the thing by means of a word, Treplev invests the sign with an untraditional aspect. Nina responds with bewilderment: "You do not express yourself clearly, but in symbols of some kind. And this seagull is obviously a symbol too, but forgive me, I don't understand it ... (*She puts the seagull on the bench.*) I'm too unsophisticated to understand you" (13:27). Through her gesture of putting the seagull on the bench, Nina creates a contrast between a thing in itself and a thing for us or a thing for Treplev. A symbol requires an interpretation and explanation, but an object (the concrete seagull placed on the bench) remains a thing in itself and means nothing. Instead of simple naming, which Potebnja describes as simple speech, used in its authentic, nonfigurative way, Treplev utilizes complex figurative images. Nina, however, insists that her nature is "unsophisticated" or "simple" (prosta) and rejects these obscure meanings. The semiotic communication between Nina and Treplev becomes impossible because they approach the process of signification differently. For Treplev, signification is symbolization, and he uses an image to convey an emotional and figurative meaning. By putting the seagull on the bench, Nina rejects Treplev's symbolization and breaks the spell of his symbolic placement of the bird at her feet. She tries to return the object to itself, to a thing in itself that signifies nothing. Yet this idea of signifying nothing is ripe with possibilities for meaning. Nina's straightforward observation of things calls for a fresh perception of reality, unhindered by tradition or myth.

The way Treplev and other characters in the play use signs reflects their respective aesthetic codes. Treplev and Trigorin are juxtaposed in terms of how they think as artists and how they semiotize the image of the seagull. Treplev's metaphoric self-expression contrasts with Trigorin's metonymic mode of characterization. The two approaches are consistent with their symbolist and realist aesthetic codes, respectively. It's worth recalling here Roman Jakobson's insights about metaphor and metonymy as two polar types of discourse in the unified "symbolic process." As Jakobson observes, various styles in verbal art emerge as a result of the preference for one over the other (romanticism and symbolism are characterized by the primacy of the metaphorical process, whereas realism relies on the predominance of metonymy). These two very different ways of perceiving the world lead to the formation of dissimilar cultural entities. The lack of understanding between Trigorin and Treplev and their mutual estrangement stem from their distinct and even polar opposite artistic assumptions. The artistic style of Trigorin is clearly metonymical, whereas that of Treplev is metaphorical. That is precisely why Treplev presents the seagull as a symbol, while for Trigorin the seagull is only an element of the atmosphere, of the broader picture and broader plot.[40]

Immediately following the scene of the symbolization of the seagull by Treplev, Trigorin appears on the stage and reveals to the audience his metonymical creative method by making notes in his notebook and pronouncing aloud: "She takes snuff and drinks vodka ... Always in black. A schoolteacher loves her." The details about tobacco and vodka are signs-indexes, based on the metonymical process of contiguity. These signs for Trigorin complement each other as attributes of the portrait of a young eccentric woman. As we discussed earlier, her black dress, vodka, and tobacco are symptoms pointing to the defiant style of behavior of the young woman trying to dramatize her life. Trigorin's particular attention to the settings and details of the environment—such as a cloud that looks like a grand piano—further reveals his metonymical way of thinking and perceiving reality. For Trigorin, the essence of an image lies not in comparisons, even when he compares a girl to a seagull (each comparison is subjective and arbitrary), but in the metonymical "condensation" that Jakobson attributes to the realist style. In his article "On Realism in Art," Jakobson comments on the narrative prose style that favors metonymy and calls it new "progressive" realism, or the realism of the new prose. What primarily characterizes this artistic movement is "the condensation of the narrative by means of images based on contiguity, that is, avoidance of the normal designative term in favor of metonymy and synecdoche. This 'condensation' is realized either in spite of the plot or by eliminating the plot entirely."[41] Therefore the type of prose that does not rely on the plot tends to be more metonymical. It is not a coincidence, then, that Trigorin mostly enjoys landscape descriptions. As Jakobson explains, "following the path of contiguous relationships, the Realist author metonymically digresses from the plot to the atmosphere and from the characters to the setting in space and time. He is fond of synecdochic details."[42] The atmosphere and the setting appear to be the chief stimuli of Trigorin's creativity. Those details of the setting come to embody his entire impression, and therefore take on a synecdochical character.

In line with his realist orientation, Trigorin does not favor metaphors. He undercuts Nina's inflated rhetoric by rejecting her metaphor:

> NINA: If I were a writer, like you, I would give away my whole life to the crowd, but I'd realize that their only happiness lay in being brought up to my level, and they would carry me in a chariot.
> TRIGORIN: Well, well, in a chariot . . . Am I Agamemnon or something?"
> (13:31).

Consistently with his metonymical realist aesthetic code, he also refuses to semiotize the seagull as a metaphor or symbol. Upon seeing a slain seagull, he merely asks, "What is it?" instead of Nina's "What does it mean?" or Treplev's emphasis on its symbolic function. For Trigorin the dead seagull is not a symbol or metaphor but simply an object requiring naming, a "beautiful bird" metonymically associated with the lake. Although he intends to utilize the image of the seagull for his "subject of a short story," it serves him as part of the general atmosphere; his comparison of Nina to a seagull only registers various associations that a lovely white bird evokes, but this simile never evolves into a full-fledged metaphor or a symbol. Even though he associates certain aspects of Nina with the seagull—white bird/Nina's white dress; beautiful bird/beautiful girl; free flight of the bird/Nina's closeness to nature—it remains for him a thing, an object, a detail of the larger landscape ("We were having a long walk … and something else, there was a white seagull lying on the bench"). This explains why at the end of the play, Trigorin refuses to see any additional figurative meaning in the stuffed seagull that Shamraev shows him and does not even remember the circumstances (or pretends not to remember, which from an aesthetic point of view is the same thing), which led to his strange order to stuff the bird. The stuffed seagull in the end of the play appears as an ominous sign of the deadening symbolization, mummification of life and art. Significantly, it is at the very moment when Shamraev takes a stuffed seagull out of the cupboard and shows it to Trigorin that Treplev kills himself. Trigorin does not remember when or why he ordered the bird to be stuffed, but Treplev's fatal shot reminds the audience of his promise to kill himself just as he killed the seagull. And his act of killing himself reenacts the killing of the bird. Treplev's identification with the seagull—whether it is a symbol of himself as a victim or of his unrequited love or of life in general—becomes complete. Scenically, the simultaneity of Treplev's shot with Shamraev's indication of the bird specimen as a "thing" ("Here is that thing I was talking about before … [*Gets a stuffed seagull out of the cupboard.*] You ordered it.") produces a powerful and jarring effect of the "realization" of the symbol.

While Trigorin and Treplev are predisposed to the two opposite stylistic poles—metonymical and metaphorical ones—Nina does not exhibit stylistic consistency. Her stylistic orientation is more complex. Her use of tropes reflects her growth and maturity. In the beginning of the play, she refuses to see the seagull as a symbol and explains her refusal by her naïveté and simplicity. Yet under the influence of her infatuation with Trigorin, she transforms Trigorin's simile into a metaphor. When she signs her letters "Seagull," she fully appropriates Trigorin's "subject for a short story" and applies it to her fate. The seagull becomes for her a metaphor for a life reduced to that of a slain bird, destroyed by a man who has "nothing better to do." Curiously, she appropriates Treplev's symbol but applies it to the story composed by Trigorin. Not only does she submit to Trigorin's "plot" of a young woman who is destroyed by a man like a slain bird, but she also tells Treplev that she deserves being killed. At the end of the play, however, she liberates herself from this gripping but destructive metaphor: "I am a seagull. No, that's not right." At this point she is making a conscious aesthetic choice rather than naïvely struggling to decipher a complex image. The rejection of metaphor marks Nina's true liberation and her awareness of her role in life and her vocation: "I am an actress." The connection of the seagull with Nina turns to be a "false clue."

Chekhov's play invites us to see various ways of conceptualizing the seagull and its function as an image. The seagull means something different for Treplev, Trigorin, and Nina. What, then, does it mean for the author? The play starts with its title, which expresses only an objective meaning and appears only as an "external form," in Potebnja's terms. The characters of the play invest the word "the seagull" with their subjective meanings, which reflect their aesthetic orientations, and which Chekhov uses as a form of characterization. But the artistic image of the author does not coincide with the images of the seagull created by the play's characters and is not only a sum total of various meanings that other characters invest in it. Chekhov's artistic image is structured to generate meanings. The work of art, according to Potebnja, similar to a word, "is not so much an expression but a means of creation of thought"; its goal, similar to that of a word, is "to generate a certain subjective mood" in the creator and in the reader/audience. Therefore the work of art, according to Potebnja, is not static but "continuously evolving." The seagull in Chekhov's comedy serves as an image of an image, a means of sequential thought generation. But even though Chekhov suggests that we have to appreciate things for what they are without a surplus of mythological or literary meaning (i.e., "a carrot is a carrot and we know nothing else"), he is also aware that things are not accessible in themselves but only through their perception and therefore inevitably have a multiplicity of meanings. A seagull for Chekhov is a consciously open image with a variable semantic potentiality. The meaning, therefore, is both recovered and created. Chekhov expands the limits of interpretation, inviting his audience/reader to take part in the process of filling this image with intersubjective content. This turns *The Seagull* as a work of art into a dynamic process.

Chekhov's approach to an artistic image, therefore, reflects his understanding of language and discourse as process, and thus the generation of thought, as subject to continuous renewal and becoming.

Echoing Trigorin's conviction that "there is room enough for everyone; new and old—What's the point of shoving?" Treplev also later realizes that "the point isn't old or new forms." Chekhov seems to suggest there is room for metaphors and metonymies, for symbolism and realism, for symptoms and clues, and ultimately for a seagull be a seagull. The title of the play uses the name of a thing and by doing so invokes the imagery and emotions associated with it, but the play as a whole deploys the word "seagull" as a direct relationship to an actual seagull; as a trope, used variously by the play's characters; and as a mean of characterization, a clue. The characters "stuff" the seagull both literarily and figuratively. The stuffed seagull in Shamraev's cupboard is both a material thing and an image of a thing; finally, it emerges as an image of a stuffed image, a representation of symbolic meaning as a catastrophic attainment that mortifies the object it refers to.

Chekhov uses signs and symbols to parody signs and symbols, thereby disarming them of their portentousness and overblown semiotic urgency, but at the same time he plays with symbolic potentials. He achieves this by juxtaposing or setting off versions of the same sign against each other and playing with the audience's expectations of those signs, demonstrating how those expectations diverge from the meanings some of the play's characters are trying to invest them with. The metaphoric meaning exists only to the extent that the characters of the play, and possibly the audience, tend to interpret the world metaphorically. Thus, though Chekhov's images are open to metaphoric readings, they also resist them. Some of his key images—such as the seagull and the lake—hold out against the semiotic tyranny associated with melodramatic and metaphoric visions of the world. Chekhov questions not only the symbolic totalitarianism of Treplev but also the prosaic naturalism of Trigorin. Ultimately for Chekhov, being true to life does not mean following a realist, naturalist, symbolist, or other poetics, adhering to a prescribed formula, but rather unlocking the polyvalence of meaning. The image of the seagull as a central component of the plays' structure is elusive and evolving. It includes commonly shared, relatively stable, and objectively given representations of reality, but it also exceeds them as a cluster of potentialities and linguistic indeterminacy.

Chekhov's play is animated by many of the modernists' linguistic concerns, particularly the desire to create new forms of art by refreshing the ways in which language and artistic images are used. Many modernist writers and poets shared the notion that the word is a continuously renewable sign (cf. Potebnja's ideas) and wanted to free language from the deadness that accrues through the continuous figurative use of it. Is it possible to name things without adding extraneous layers of metaphorical meaning? In his memoirs about Chekhov, Ivan Bunin recalls how Chekhov admired the unforced simplicity of children's perception of the world and the way they name things: "It's very difficult to describe the sea. Do you know what description of the sea I read recently in one student's notebook? 'The sea was big.' That's all. In my opinion, it's wonderful."[43] The American modernist Gertrude Stein would go even further in her quest for liberation of the word from excessive symbolization or signification, in trying to revitalize poetry by "unusing" the names, or finding a way for the word to be new each time it occurs. In "Poetry and Grammar," Stein explains her understanding of nouns as proper names that have become impoverished, as words that have been stripped of their initial inner form through overuse:

> Now actual given names of people are more lively than nouns which are the
> name of anything and I suppose this is because after all the name is only given
> to that person when they are born, there is at least the element of choice even
> the element of change and anybody can be pretty well able to do what they
> like, they may be born Walter and become Hub, in such a way they are not like
> a noun. A noun has been the name of something for such a very long time.[44]

After words have been used for a long time, they lose their "liveliness." "Rose is a rose" is an attempt to name an object or a person anew. Referring to her famous lines about the rose, used for the first time in her poem "The Sacred Family" (1913), Gertrude Stein said: "Now listen! I'm no fool. I know that in daily life we don't go around saying is a . . . is a . . . is a . . . Yes, I'm no fool; but I think that in that line the rose is red for the first time in English poetry for a hundred years."[45]

Russian Acmeists, as well as other modernists, launched a similar fight against "dead words" (Nikolai Gumilev's term) in their campaign to liberate words from "utilitarianism." Osip Mandelshtam echoes Stein's aesthetic imperative as he writes: "Acmeism arose from the resistance: 'Away from symbolism, long live the living rose!'" Mandelshtam explains his point in "About the Nature of the Word": "In essence, there is no difference between a word and an image. . . . The word is already a sealed image: it cannot be touched. But, on the other hand, the sealed, exempted image is hostile to man, it is in its own way a stuffed animal, a scarecrow." He argues with the symbolists who diminish the value of an image in its own terms and approach it only through the prism of "correspondence":

> For the Symbolist none of these images is interesting in itself, but the rose is the likeness of the sun, the sun is the likeness of the rose, the dove is the likeness of the girl, and the girl is the likeness of the dove. The images are gutted like stuffed animals and stuffed with alien content. Instead of a symbolic 'forest of correspondences' there is a stuffed animal workshop. This is where professional symbolism leads. Perception is demoralized. Nothing real, authentic. A terrible counterdance of "correspondences" nodding at each other. The eternal winking. Not a single clear word, only hints, understatements. The rose nods to the girl, the girl to the rose. No one wants to be themselves.[46]

Both Stein and Mandelshtam refer nostalgically to the ancient Greek models (Homer) for their ability to name things so that the word would coincide with the image.[47] Without engaging in philosophical or theoretical discussions about language, Chekhov was also interested in the nature of the artistic word and did not want to reduce the image to a symbol. Chekhov's stuffed seagull at the end of the play is a reminder of how literary symbolization sets into motion an evisceration of content or meaning, culminating in what Mandelshtam describes as the image becoming "stuffed with alien content." The titular avian of *The Seagull* is not Shamraev's stuffed bird, nor is it the name Nina signs her letters with. These are all false "correspondences": between Nina and the seagull, Treplev and the seagull, a girl by the lake and the seagull, and so forth. Although those meanings lurk behind the image of the stuffed bird, the play invites the audience to discover the noun constituting the title as a revitalized name, as both a perpetually renewed reference and an autonomous entity. Even if Chekhov's seagull is an image abundant in meaning and cultural weight, it is always in *statu nascendi*. When Nina asks Treplev "What is this?" when he lays the dead gull at her feet, we have no reason to think that she does not see the object and does not understand that it is a bird. A seagull is a seagull. Her question underscores the naming function of language and sets in motion the polyvalence of meaning by requesting a new naming of the object. Like some modernist thinkers, Chekhov is concerned with the dynamics of meaning deceptively obscured by the repetition of the same word. At the same time, his artistic use of the word is not simply a return to some obscured but fixed original meaning. Mandelshtam later referred to such fixed connections as "serfdom" and insisted that "it is most convenient and scientifically correct to consider the word as an image, that is, a verbal representation." For Chekhov, the inner form of the word is ripe with different, or multivalent, possibilities for growth. Each reiteration of "seagull" can mean something different from its previous one, for it constitutes a new verbal representation—the seagull is a seagull is a seagull is a seagull.

4

Dostoevsky's Graft

"Ward Six," *The Wedding, The Three Sisters,*
and *Uncle Vania*

"Good but Immodest":
Chekhov's Irritation with Dostoevsky

Before we proceed to a discussion of Dostoevsky's "presence" in *Uncle Vania,*
we should address the question of Chekhov's overall response to the celebrated Russian writer. As Chekhov's plays, short stories, and other texts are
saturated with literary allusions and the names of various authors, it is in most
cases futile and counterproductive to speak about particular "influences"
on Chekhov. Although Chekhov was certainly not writing in a vacuum, his
dealings with the cultural heritage of the world reveal not only intellectual and artistic independence but also engagement with various authors
he occasionally deployed as peculiar generic "transplants" in his innovative
approaches to the short story and drama. What Tolstoy and Dostoevsky
treat as a subject for a novel, for example, Chekhov uses as "a subject for a
short story" (to use Trigorin's words) or a play; likewise, Chekhov adopts
devices used by novelists in their prose for his theatrical works. As scholars
such as Andrei Stepanov have noted, during the second half of the nineteenth century, "novelization" affected not only smaller prose genres but also
dramaturgy.[1] In this process of literary genetic engineering, Chekhov significantly modifies the existing genres of drama and the short story.

Chekhov's engagement with Russian and European classics was never
straightforward. In his texts we find literary references and allusions to
Homer, Socrates, Marcus Aurelius, Voltaire, Pushkin, Gogol, Turgenev, Tolstoy, Maupassant, Zola, and Ibsen, among others. These references offer ample
material for intertextual analysis and comparative poetics.[2]

86

Certain affinities with and connections to the Russian classics such as Pushkin, Gogol, Turgenev, and Tolstoy are immediately apparent and have been widely discussed. Chekhov's response to Dostoevsky is much more elusive, contradictory, and complex, even though it, too, has attracted the extensive attention of scholars.[3] In his 1914 essay on Chekhov, Boris Eikhenbaum simply rejected any possible connection between Dostoevsky and Chekhov ("It's characteristic that Dostoevsky was completely alien to Chekhov").[4] In his seminal book *Literaturnye sviazi Chekhova* (Chekhov's literary connections), Vladimir Kataev barely mentions Dostoevsky, although in his later book *Chekhov plius . . . Predshestvenniki, sovremenniki, preemniki* (Chekhov plus: Predecessors, contemporaries, and followers), he addresses the theme of guilt, a prominent topic in Russian literature, by comparing its treatment in the works of Dostoevsky, Tolstoy, and Chekhov. But even here, he touches upon the theme only in the most general terms. In his article "Dostoevskii i Chekhov: Preemstvennost' i parodiia" (Dostoevsky and Chekhov: Continuity and parody), Roman Nazirov analyzes in great detail Chekhov's novella "Drama on the Hunt" ("Drama na okhote"), a text saturated with Dostoevskian motifs and other allusions to Russia's great novelist.[5] Elaborating upon Nazirov's analysis of "Drama on the Hunt," and supplementing it with his analysis of *Ivanov* as a continuation of Chekhov's polemic with Dostoevsky, Sergei Kibalnik also addresses Chekhov's complex and polemical attitude toward Dostoevsky.[6] Most scholars, however, as a rule consider Chekhov's allusions to Dostoevsky as nothing more than opportunities for parodying the novelist. Yet the presence of Dostoevsky in Chekhov's works runs deeper than it may seem at first sight.

In fact, Chekhov's response to Dostoevsky may be as complex as that of Nabokov, who not only explicitly disavowed Dostoevsky's influence on his own writing but considered Dostoevsky a secondary writer and made him the frequent target of sarcastic comments and attacks. While in his criticism of Dostoevsky, Chekhov is more reserved than Nabokov, it is obvious that he is far from being in awe of the famed Russian author. Scholars have observed Chekhov's restrained comments about Dostoevsky in his letter to Suvorin of March 5, 1889: "I've bought some of Dostoevsky's works in your store and now am reading him. It's good, but well too lengthy and immodest. Too pretentious" (P 3:169). It is important to emphasize that in these comments Chekhov questions not so much what Dostoevsky has to say as his *mode of expression* ("immodest," "too pretentious"). Curiously, as different as Chekhov and Nabokov are in their temperament and their poetics, both writers respond negatively to the same aspects of Dostoevsky's art, a fact pointing to a certain affinity in their worldviews. While Nabokov criticized, often caustically, many classics of both Russian and world literature, he not only specifically praised Chekhov and referred to him as his "predecessor" but even confessed that if he were to travel to another planet he would take with him none other than Chekhov's works.[7] The affinity between Chekhov and Nabokov is reflected, to an extent, in their literary antipathies. Of course, neither of them viewed Dostoevsky as their literary "enemy," yet both writers found themselves quite irritated by certain aspects of Dostoevsky's poetics that they tried to suppress very hard in their own writing, if not always successfully. Thus, if we consider what it is that irritates Chekhov and Nabokov so much in Dostoevsky's writings, and how this irritation is refracted in their own poetics, we may acquire a better understanding of their artistic philosophies.

Both Chekhov and Nabokov recoil from Dostoevsky's virtuous prostitutes and noble murderers (both writers dismissively and ironically commented on Raskolnikov) and from what they considered to be stylistic devices of lowbrow detective novels. Both rejected Dostoevsky's psychology of extremes, his intense psychologism in general, and his indulgence in improbable coincidences, scandals, and dramatic effects. In other words, both rejected the melodramatic core of Dostoevsky's poetics (putting aside whether it is correct to interpret melodrama as a central aspect of Dostoevsky's works). Indeed, while Mikhail Bakhtin may have recognized these same aspects of Dostoevsky's poetics as elements of Menippean satire and carnivalized literature, many readers and scholars of Dostoevsky (e.g., Peter Brooks) instead interpreted these elements as melodrama. Both Chekhov and Nabokov mercilessly parodied these aspects of Dostoevsky. Nabokov often directly attacked him for his melodramatic tastes, such as in his review of Jean-Paul Sartre's *Nausea* (translated into English by Lloyd Alexander), in which Nabokov deems Sartre a second-rate writer and chastises him for following Dostoevsky "at his worst." Dostoevsky, according to him, was in turn a follower of Eugène Sue, to "whom the melodramatic Russian owes so much."[8] Georges Nivat points out that Nabokov's novel *Despair* reveals an obvious parody of "dark dostoevskivism" and plays with the conventions of Russian literature.[9] Analogous parodies can be found in Chekhov, not only in his "Drama on the Hunt" but even in his earlier stories, many of them published in *Splinters*, such as "Words, Words, and Words" ("Slova, slova, i slova," 1883) and "A Mysterious Nature" ("Zagadochnaia natura," 1883).

Let's consider how this irritation with Dostoevsky impacts Chekhov's poetics.[10] Long before expressing his skepticism toward Dostoevsky's works in his letter to Suvorin and writing his parodic "Drama on the Hunt," Chekhov explicitly conveyed his ironic attitude in regard to Dostoevsky in his 1883 story "A Mysterious Nature." It is especially important to consider this story because of its portrayal of a particular type of behavior and mode of expression as well as certain thematic motifs, all of which Chekhov associates with Dostoevsky. In this story a young and eccentric lady (an obvious nod to Dostoevsky's famous eccentrics) complains of her suffering to a young, inexperienced writer, advising him to depict her "soul" and her "mysterious nature" in his own literary creations. Chekhov directs his irony against the melodramatic suffering of the lady and in general against any attempt (in real life or in literature) to present life's conflicts exclusively through the prism of spirituality. The "mysteriousness" of the Russian soul, with its eternal struggle between good and evil, turbulent passions, psychological lacerations, and perpetual suffering, forms the network of familiar clichés in Dostoevsky's novels, the poetics of which were shaped, according to Peter Brooks, by a "moral occult" and "modus of extremes" characteristic of melodrama. Brooks detects this type of "melodramatic imagination" not only in Balzac's prose but also in Dostoevsky. The melodramatic clichés and excessiveness of Dostoevsky's writing constitute the main target of Chekhov's parody.

The eccentric lady in "A Mysterious Nature," while describing her life with all the standard attributes of melodrama (she is the daughter of a poor clerk, her father was kind in heart but also a drunkard and a gambler, she has been crushed by poverty—"My mother . . . ah, why say more! Poverty, the struggle for a piece of bread, the consciousness of insignificance"), directly refers to Dostoevsky: "My life has been so full, so varied, so multi-colored . . . But above all—I have been unhappy! I am a sufferer in the taste of Dostoevsky. Reveal my soul to the world, Voldemar, reveal that poor soul! You are a psychologist" (2:90–91). The young writer manages to "comprehend" or "fathom" her soul ("O, ia postigaiu Vas!") and its "broad nature," which has undergone the turmoil of "doubt" and "the pains of the emerging disbelief in life": "Your sensitive, your responsive soul is seeking for an escape from this maze ... Yes! This is a terrific, horrifying struggle, but ... do not despair!" He responds to her unbearable sufferings by kissing her hand, just near the bracelet, and, appropriately, does not forget to mention Raskolnikov: "'My wondrous woman!' murmurs the writer, kissing her hand near the bracelet. 'It's not you I am kissing, oh wondrous one, I am kissing human suffering! Do you remember Raskolnikov? This is how he kissed'" (2:90–91). Actions and mode of behavior "in the taste of Dostoevsky" will remain a common target of Chekhov's irony in his later works as well. Thus, in his story "Neighbors" ("Sosedi," 1892), Chekhov describes "this strange marriage in the taste of Dostoevsky" between the liberal and high-minded Vlasich and the girl whom he "rescues," only to later find her to be far from an innocent victim. The story includes another phrase taken from Dostoevsky's novel, "If you ever need my life, come and take it." This phrase, as has been noted by M. Gromov, may have its source in several of Dostoevsky's texts, including *The Village of Stepanchikovo* and *Crime and Punishment*.[11] Chekhov frequently mocks "borrowed" feelings, "borrowed" words and melodramatic gestures, inserting them in his stories and plays in the most unexpected of configurations. Thus, for example, when Nina Zarechnaia from *The Seagull* gives Trigorin her medallion with a purported quote from one of his texts ("If you ever need my life, come and take it"), she is repeating the Dostoevsky reference employed in Chekhov's "Neighbors" while also echoing Dunia Raskolnikova's words ("Now I have only come to say ... that if you happen to need me or need ... all my life, or anything ... you should call me, I will come").[12] As Chekhov "plagiarizes" this episode with the medallion and the quote inserted in it from his personal experience with Lidia Avilova, who had sent him her own medallion with reference to that passage from his story "Neighbors," this same quotation in *The Seagull* becomes a double or even triple borrowing. Avilova's borrowing from Chekhov (who used this line in his story as a reference to Dostoevsky) and her conscious or subconscious imitation of Dostoevskian gestures turns in *The Seagull* into Chekhov's borrowing of Avilova's borrowing of someone else's borrowing, and his mockery of it.[13]

To be sure, Chekhov's "A Mysterious Nature" conveys more than his mockery of the stereotypes of the melodramatic imagination (which he frequently ridicules in many of his other texts, as noted by Stepanov[14]) and his profound suspicion of all the so-called spiritual abysses, lacerations, noble murderers, prostitutes, and various sufferers filling the pages of Dostoevsky's novels. Here Chekhov clearly has a polemic of his own in regard to the very notion of realism and what constitutes it. While Dostoevsky seeks realism in the "excesses" of behavior and in eccentric characters that, according to him, better convey the spirit of the "idea," Chekhov strives to depict life "as it is" and how it is reflected in everyday activity and its simplest manifestations. Scholars frequently cite Chekhov's words about the need to present people "eating, drinking, flirting, and saying stupidities" onstage as an informal artistic manifesto.[15] To be sure, these words represent not only Chekhov's own artistic creed but also his hidden anti-manifesto against Dostoevsky, for Dostoevsky was doing precisely the opposite of what Chekhov aspired to: his heroes say strikingly intelligent things nearly every minute, and they find themselves in the most eccentric and "improbable" of situations. While Dostoevsky's novels are saturated with drama and tragedy (it is not a coincidence that Viacheslav Ivanov refers to them as "novel-tragedies"), Chekhov is trying to do the very opposite: to avoid drama and tragedy not only in his prose but also in his theater. At the same time, Chekhov's struggle with melodramatic conventions and his strategy of avoiding overly dramatic action and discourse do not mean that his works are devoid of profound inner drama and tragedy. In fact, quite the opposite is true.

Dostoevsky's and Chekhov's very different approaches to their craft may be fruitfully illuminated by a comparison of their texts, in which Chekhov, rather than turning to direct quotations or allusions to Dostoevsky, finds himself tackling potentially similar plots and collisions. Although in many of his works, such as "In the Ravine" and "The Peasants," Chekhov depicts the darkest aspects of Russian peasant life, he recoils from what he sees as melodramatic suffering and recasts the plots of classical Russian literature based on the never-ending suffering of the Russian people into ambiguous and frequently ironic narratives. In this process of "grafting" the tragic literary plots of Russian classics on to his own story lines, he develops his own artistic philosophy based on understatement; a reduction of dramatic effects; the rejection of a dualistic view of body and soul; and the abandonment of any kind of polarization, excesses, or unambiguously tragic denouements. The tragic is instead shifted into the mundane, as is the case in his story "The Trifle of Life," for example, which depicts a young boy's first discovery of the poisonous impact of lies. The tragic lurks in the drudgery of everyday life and work (e.g., in *Uncle Vania* and *The Three Sisters*), or even in the most trivial, banal, and "hidden tears" shed by those living routine, married lives, as in Chekhov's humorous and ironic 1884 story "Tears Invisible to the World."

Forms of Rapprochement: Dostoevsky's "The Dream of a Ridiculous Man" and Chekhov's "Ward Six"

> As for the obstinate, he must be plunged into fire, since fire and non-fire are identical. Let him be beaten, since suffering and not suffering are the same. Let him be deprived of food and drink, since eating and drinking are identical to abstaining.
>
> Avicenna, *Metaphysics*

The fact that Chekhov recoiled from Dostoevsky's artistic principles should not be confused for a lack of interest in the profound philosophical questions at the heart of Dostoevsky's concerns. Nor does it mean that Chekhov, because of his reserved attitude toward the "ultimate questions" of Dostoevsky—regarding faith, religion, and God—simply bracketed them as irrelevant to everyday life. This is quite visible in Chekhov's letter to Diaghilev (December 30, 1902), in which he reveals his radical ideas about the relationship between faith and knowledge and mentions Dostoevsky, who was widely viewed as the greatest literary authority in regard to such "ultimate questions." Ironically, in the context of Chekhov's mention of Dostoevsky— "not to seek it [the truth of the real God] in Dostoevsky … but … know it clearly, as one knows that twice two is four"—his expression "twice two is four" may be interpreted as a reference to the attack on rationalism by Dostoevsky's Underground Man.[16] But it is not Dostoevsky Chekhov rejects; rather, it is the truth found *in* Dostoevsky—or, readers' attempts to interpret Dostoevsky's philosophy as a final and unquestionable truth.

It would be a great oversimplification to consider Dostoevsky and Chekhov as antipodes of Russian literature—religious versus secular, Slavophile versus Westernizer, politically engaged versus indifferent, nationalist and conservative versus liberal, and so forth—as the comparison has often been framed. Dostoevsky's religious doubts were just as pronounced as Chekhov's skepticism, and Chekhov's search for God, whether or not he eventually found Him, was no less intense than Dostoevsky's struggle with his faith. The two writers, as dissimilar as they may be in their artistic temperaments, meet in what they understood to be a ceaseless quest for truth. It is no coincidence that the Russian philosopher Lev Shestov, who took acute interest in the works of both Dostoevsky and Chekhov, did not view them as antagonists. He considered both Dostoevsky and Chekhov as representatives of the specifically "Russian idea" and Russian "thought," represented by the Russian literary tradition from Pushkin onward.[17] Significantly, Shestov views Chekhov as essentially a brother in arms with Dostoevsky and describes both writers as "treasure-seekers" or "treasure-diggers." He links them in their quest for ultimate and forbidden truths.[18] As different as they may seem, these writers have one important thing in common: a bold ability to look into the abyss.

Shestov argues that Chekhov leads his characters to extreme despair and unsolvable problems without any fear of the ultimate questions. Moreover, Shestov includes both writers within an anti-tradition of great writers and philosophers who engage, as he does, in a "struggle" against the absolute supremacy of logic and reason, and therefore against the acceptance of necessity. He viewed Dostoevsky and Chekhov as his hidden allies. In Shestov's assessment, all great minds ultimately reach a state of despair, although their responses to despair may be quite different. Those who are on the side of Jerusalem—a tradition that he juxtaposes with the domineering Western tradition of Athens—respond with something "beyond reason and knowledge": Plotinus with his ecstasies and the "cult of groundlessness," Kierkegaard with a recognition of the Absurd that leads him to a leap of faith, Dostoevsky with Underground Man's "two times two is five," and Chekhov, Shestov argues, with his "beating one's head against the wall." Shestov conceives of struggle as both a method and the very substance of philosophical inquiry, stemming from the acceptance of groundlessness. Shestov believed that both Dostoevsky and Chekhov reached a state of revelation and extreme alertness or wakefulness, which forced them "to doubt the self-evidences and to start a struggle against them, which is completely ungrounded."[19]

Indeed, although Chekhov may have rejected Dostoevsky's *mode of expression*, which he found "immodest" and "pretentious," he took a dialogical, rather than polemical and antagonistic, approach to Dostoevsky's profound and intense philosophical questions. Chekhov has some surprising commonalities with Dostoevsky, whose resonances—never borrowings—lead Chekhov in new directions and inform his texts, sometimes leading to quite unexpected results.

Consider, for example, how Chekhov deploys and reworks one of Dostoevsky's recurrent concepts central to his critique of nihilism: "it's all the same," or "nothing matters." Although most scholars in their analysis of "Dream of a Ridiculous Man" (1877) focus on the dreamer's dream, his image of "the Golden Age" and his utopian or anti-utopian discourse, the notion of "it's all the same," another of the story's major and far-reaching philosophical motifs, is strangely overlooked.[20] The story opens with a detailed description of what preceded the narrator's dream and what triggered it—that is, the conviction that "nothing mattered in the whole world."[21] In Dostoevsky's text, the phrase "nothing matters" or "it's all the same" (*vsio ravno*) is italicized. Indeed, "it's all the same," or "nothing matters," is both the starting point and the main leitmotif of the story; it represents the Ridiculous Man's principle philosophical position and constitutes his fundamental "crime," the crime of indifference. It is the idea that "everything is the same" (*vsio ravno*) that leads him to his suicidal thoughts and to his refusal to assist the poor girl pleading for help whom he meets on the street. In the first five pages of the story, the expression "it's all the same" is used seventeen times, only to completely disappear from the following chapters, once the Ridiculous Man is cured of his affliction by his mysterious revelation. The pervasiveness of this expression dominates the beginning of the story.

The corrosive effects of the Ridiculous Man's moral nihilism encompass not only the destruction of all values (and thus his indifference toward human suffering) but also an extreme pessimism that ultimately condemns and questions existence itself. With religious convictions crumbling (Dostoevsky refers to his protagonist as a "progressivist" who does not believe in immortality), the Ridiculous Man is logically led to thoughts of suicide (similar to the "logical suicide" of the Ridiculous Man's predecessor, Kirillov from *The Devils*, who embraces the theory of "nothing matters").[22] Only when the Ridiculous Man realizes that it is not "all the same" to him and when, by accepting responsibility for all the evils of the world (which also, at least in part, stem from the philosophy of "all is the same" and "nothing matters"), he modifies his actions in accordance with his new moral vision, does he reawaken to a new life. He recovers from his moral nihilism and indifference when he acknowledges his own guilt. Dostoevsky acutely sensed the significance of the doctrine that "nothing matters" for modernity; he observed with anxiety the various forms of nihilism, regarding them as a malaise within Western culture and a fundamental threat to morality.[23]

The phrase *vsio ravno*, which undoubtedly stems from Dostoevsky's use of it in *The Devils* and in "The Dream of a Ridiculous Man," is also a recurrent motif in many of Chekhov's texts, especially "Ward Six" and his drama *The Three Sisters*. In "Ward Six," *vsio ravno* is used ten times, and its variant "there is no difference" (*raznitsy net*) another four times. It is therefore surprising that even such a fine reader of Chekhov as Andrew Durkin, in his article "Chekhov's Response to Dostoevskii: The Case of *Ward Six*," which discussed the text's numerous allusions to *The Brothers Karamazov*, completely overlooks another text that constitutes the ideological kernel of the story, "The Dream of a Ridiculous Man."[24] Scholars frequently point out that in "Ward Six," Chekhov spars with the Stoics and, in part, with Tolstoy.[25] The Stoics' subtexts are indeed crucial to the reader's understanding of the story, even if Chekhov's doctor, Andrei Efimych Ragin, may have misinterpreted them. Based on his misinterpretation of the philosophy of the Stoics, Dr. Ragin refuses to recognize any distinctions and differences in the world around him and advocates indifference toward suffering.[26] Similar to the Ridiculous Man, he attempts to reject the world's objective reality and accepts only the reality of his mind—his consciousness, feelings, and subjective perceptions. However, Chekhov not only argues against the misconceived indifference of the Stoics (who were in fact far from advocating for such indifference) but also considers the moral consequences of the belief that "nothing matters," the very same concept that Dostoevsky dealt with in deploying his recurrent phrase *vsio ravno*.[27] Dostoevsky, however, connected the belief that "nothing matters" not with the Stoics' quest for equanimity and self-control but with the nihilistic tendencies of his time that resulted in the rejection of responsibility for the world's evils (or so he felt).

Chekhov's "Ward Six" builds upon many of the motifs present in Dostoevsky's story: perceived insanity, suicidal thoughts, the challenge of pain (physical and emotional), and, most importantly, a testing of the idea that "nothing matters." The Ridiculous Man and Dr. Ragin, two characters who both enjoy ruminating at night and ultimately lose their interest in life, connect their philosophy of "nothing matters" to their disbelief. The Ridiculous Man imagines that the world will completely disappear in the moment of his suicide. He does not believe in the "other world," or immortality: "What angered me was my conclusion that if I had really decided to commit suicide this very night, then everything in this world should have felt the same to me now more than ever."[28] Dr. Ragin imagines a cold earth some millions of years after his own death and similarly rejects the idea of immortality: "Oh, why is not man immortal? He thinks. Why these brain centers and their convolutions, why vision, speech, feeling, genius, if all this is destined to go into the ground, ultimately to grow cold together with the earth's crust, and then for millions of years to whirl with the earth around the sun without aim or reason?" (8:90). It is from the perspective of materialism, the complete annihilation of existence and feelings of nothingness, that both characters conclude that "nothing matters." Significantly, the rejection of immortality forms one of Dr. Ragin's fundamental beliefs and figures prominently in his discussions with Mikhail Averianovich and Gromov. It is hardly a coincidence that Dostoevsky's name appears during Dr. Ragin's and Gromov's discussion of immortality: "'And immortality?' 'Oh, come on now!' 'You don't believe in it; well, I do. Someone from Dostoevsky's works, or maybe from Voltaire's, said that if there were no God, man would have invented Him. And I firmly believe that if there is no immortality, sooner or later the great human mind will invent it.' 'Well said,' observed Andrei Iefimych, smiling with pleasure. 'It's good that you believe. With such faith one may live happily even sealed up in a wall'" (8:97).

Both characters at points contemplate suicide: the Ridiculous Man in the beginning of the story, before his redemptive dream, and Dr. Ragin in the end of the story, before his final demise. Both are proclaimed insane. The people corrupted by the Ridiculous Man in his dream threaten to put him in a psychiatric prison.[29] In response to his preaching of the newly discovered "truth," upon waking from the dream, the people around him also "call him a madman now." In Chekhov's story, Dr. Ragin "actualizes" what for the Ridiculous Man remains only a threat: he is indeed proclaimed insane and is locked up in a psychiatric ward. Drawing on Dostoevsky, Chekhov shows the practical insolvency of the doctrine "nothing matters" and refutes it through the reality of physical pain. In Dostoevsky's *The Devils*, Kirillov considers physical pain as one of the two main challenges to his philosophy of suicide stemming from his nihilistic belief that nothing matters (the other challenge being the potential existence of the "other world"): "'I ... I still know very little ... only two prejudices stop me, two things: only two; one of them is very small, the other one is very big. But the small one is also quite big.' 'So which is the small one?' 'Pain.'"[30] The Ridiculous Man also contends that physical pain may represent a serious challenge to the philosophy of "it's all the same": "You see, though nothing mattered to me, I could still feel pain, for instance. If someone hit me, I would have felt pain. It is the same in the moral sense: should anything really pitiful have happened, I should have felt pity, just as I used to do at the time when in my life things still mattered to me."[31]

The theme of pain is prominent in Dostoevsky's story. Describing his suicidal dream, the Ridiculous Man says that though at first he did not experience any pain, after his "death" he suddenly sensed an intense physical pain, when he was not supposed to be feeling anything, being "dead" and even "buried": "Suddenly deep indignation blazed up in my heart, and I suddenly felt physical pain in it. 'That's my wound,' I thought, 'It's the shot. There's a bullet there . . .'"[32] While the Ridiculous Man philosophizes about pain, sensing it only in his dream, Dr. Ragin "actualizes" the motif of pain just as he "actualizes" the Ridiculous Man's insanity. Although he originally tries to reject the significance of pain by referring to the philosophy of Marcus Aurelius, when he experiences actual physical pain, he is forced to reconsider his ability to not feel it through mental effort.[33] Chekhov thus turns the Ridiculous Man's and Kirillov's hypotheses about physical pain into a practical experiment. Dr. Ragin's "philosophy" is challenged first and foremost by his most basic and primitive physical needs—his desire to smoke and to have some beer—and then by the fists of the victorious guard Nikita, symbolizing brutal elemental force.[34]

Chekhov depicts the catastrophic consequences of the philosophy of "it's all the same," which leads to physical and moral chaos, entropy and death. When Dr. Ragin decided that "nothing matters," much like the Ridiculous Man, he stopped regularly going in to work at the hospital. In both cases the philosophy of "nothing matters" leads to a lack of concern for others—the Ridiculous Man rejects the poor little girl on the street, and Dr. Ragin betrays his duty as a doctor, neglecting his patients and arriving at the terrible conclusion that there is no difference between his drab hospital and the best Viennese clinic: "Thus, it is all futile, senseless, and there is no essential difference between the best Viennese clinic and my hospital" (8:126). The notion that "nothing matters" leads both characters to immorality and crime, as this "idea" absolves them of personal responsibility. Only when the Ridiculous Man acknowledges such personal responsibility during his mysterious dream—that is, when he begins to see himself as a second Adam responsible for the fall ("I only know that I was the cause of the fall")—does he realize that not everything on earth is "all the same." At that point he resolves to save the girl and other people. This idea is fundamental to Dostoevsky's view of sin and responsibility and his idea of the mutual sharing of guilt.

Unlike the Ridiculous Man, Chekhov's Dr. Ragin does not have the good fortune of having a "second chance" at life after his fantastic revelatory dream of paradise and moral regeneration. Chekhov instead replaces Dostoevsky's motif of the happy awakening and the recovery of "truth" with a somber and sober image of the eternal, final sleep. Dr. Ragin's extinguishing consciousness registers only several disjointed images imprinted in his brain by personal experiences and memories: "A herd of reindeer, extraordinarily beautiful and graceful, about which he had been reading yesterday, ran past him; then a peasant woman stretched out her hand to him with a registered letter . . . Mikhail Averianych said something . . . Then everything disappeared, and Andrei Efimych plunged into the eternal sleep" (8:126). Far from being mysterious and revelatory, Dr. Ragin's dream is but a neurological function of his brain, a reflection of bodily stimuli: the beautiful reindeer of his last dream are not even a fruit of his fantasy, but an image shaped by his reading the day before. Chekhov dedicates the last paragraph of his story to a detailed description of Dr. Ragin's bodily perceptions. His dream represents a staggering contrast to the Ridiculous Man's paradisiacal vision. Chekhov denies his hero a happy ending, a final conversion or recovery of the Truth. In fact, not only does Dr. Ragin not wake up from his dream, but he experiences no real remorse, no guilt, no repentance for his philosophy of "nothing matters." He feels only brief pangs of conscience, realizing that he has ignored the reality of human pain and has done nothing to alleviate the human suffering around him.

Dostoevsky's Ridiculous Man ultimately discovers the "truth" for the sake of which he is prepared to struggle: "'The consciousness of life is higher than life, the knowledge of the laws of happiness is higher than happiness'— that is what one has to fight against!"[35] In other words, the Ridiculous Man accepts the supreme value of life rather than its rationalization.[36] Dr. Ragin, in contrast, considers the "comprehension" (urazumenie) of existence to be more important than existence itself: "Freedom and profound thought that strives for the comprehension of life and complete contempt for the world's silly vanity—these are two of the highest goods man has ever known" (8:97). However, life as he experiences it—not as he understands it—ultimately triumphs over his philosophizing and his speculation. Dr. Ragin is destroyed, physically and psychologically, precisely by that very same real life he tries to reject as unimportant. It is only at this moment, a moment of extreme physical pain and humiliation, that he briefly thinks about suicide. Understating and undermining suicide's grandeur, drama, and tragedy, Chekhov, in a literary gesture typical of his art, deprives his hero of such drama— Dr. Ragin is prevented from suicide by his physical incapacity. While the Ridiculous Man contemplates suicide as a logical extension of his philosophical nihilism, Dr. Ragin thinks about it only at a moment of weakness, when he realizes that his physical suffering challenges his philosophy of "nothing matters." He quickly reverts to his *vsio ravno* in a desperate attempt to adhere to his doctrine: "But now he felt it was all the same [*vsio ravno*] to him. . . . 'It doesn't matter . . . [*vsio ravno*],' he thought, when he was questioned. 'I won't answer . . . It doesn't matter [*vsio ravno*]'" (8:125–26).

The universe of Chekhov's story contains nothing beyond the empirical realm of human physiological experience. There are no hints at any kind of metaphysical reality. Dostoevsky, on the other hand, maintains a high degree of ambiguity on this score, even calling the story "fantastic" to imply the existence of a nonempirical realm. Although the Ridiculous Man's dream may be interpreted as stemming from his guilt and subconscious desire for redemption (i.e., nothing more than an extension of his consciousness, shaped by myths of the Fall and redemption that are available in our culture), this dream also emerges as a revelation of a higher reality. This utopian vision, the description of paradise and a new Fall, serves to reverse his philosophy of indifference. Now he has to admit that life matters, people matter, mistakes matter, and actions matter. Dostoevsky's story offers a vision of an "ideal" and explores the theological meaning of sin and the Fall, which make the Ridiculous Man renounce his moral nihilism. In his dream, Dr. Ragin's brain registers nothing but random images of the material world. Moreover, not only does he not discover a higher meaning of life or regain a belief in immortality, but he continues to actively reject any prospect of immortality even at the brink of extinction: "Andrei Iefimych realized that the end had come and remembered that Ivan Dmitrich, Mikhail Averianych, and millions of others believed in immortality. And what if there were immortality? But he felt no desire for immortality, and he thought about it only for a moment" (8:126). The final image of the story—Dr. Ragin's dead body lying on the table in the chapel with its eyes open, lit by the moon—is an emblem of materiality, excluding any possibility of metaphysics. The story also mentions a very unusual but significant detail: although it was customary to close the eyelids of the dead immediately after death, Dr. Ragin's corpse's eyes remain open for the whole night ("Peasants came, picked him up by arms and legs, and carried him to the chapel. There he lay on a table, with his eyes open, lit by the moon through the night. In the morning Sergei Sergeich came, prayed piously before the crucifix, and closed the eyes of his former chief" [8:126]). This detail, of course, points to the hospital attendants' neglectful attitude, but it also has a symbolic meaning: rather than "sleeping peacefully," Dr. Ragin stares into the void. The image of a dead man facing an unresponsive eternity provides a grim resolution to the story, raising the question of whether we bear responsibility for our actions in the face of a godless universe with no hope for immortality.

While the Ridiculous Man's conversion is contingent on his discovery of a higher reality that forces him to reconsider his nihilism and to find the little girl he has rejected, in Chekhov's story the dualism of body and soul is replaced with the identity of body and consciousness.[37] Questioning the metaphysical split between mind and body acknowledged at least since the seventeenth century, Chekhov's story seems to suggest that there is nothing beyond the body. Although Dr. Ragin theorizes that intellectual experiences and pleasures of the mind are more important than bodily perceptions, he is ultimately forced to experience his body as subject and accept the primacy of body and perception. He is compelled to recognize his own body not only as a thing, a potential object of study, but as a permanent condition of experience. Although Dr. Ragin recognizes his defeat, the acknowledgment of this defeat is triggered not by a revelation of a higher reality and a metaphysical experience, but by his suffering body. Considering one's rational function to be primary in the definition of what it means to be human, Ragin underestimates the corporeality of perception until he is forced to acknowledge his body as both a subject and object of perception. The Ridiculous Man errs by ignoring the existence of a higher reality and learns only by accessing it; Dr. Ragin learns from nothing but his own body, which he has so forcefully tried to ignore.

Chekhov engages seriously with Dostoevsky's philosophical concerns and does not shy away from his "ultimate questions." Although Dr. Ragin's behavior is presented as immoral, Chekhov does not lead his protagonists to repentance—Chekhov's doctor does not completely renounce his views, suddenly embrace immortality, or even entirely renounce his philosophy. It is the reader, not the hero of the story, who is expected to see the danger of nihilism. Significantly, in the first part of the story Chekhov adopts a narrative voice fairly uncommon in fiction (though notably used by Tolstoy in his *Sebastopol Sketches* to implicate the reader): the second-person point of view.[38] Dostoevsky's preaching madman and Chekhov's doctor-turned-psychiatric patient begin with the same doctrine of "nothing matters," but their end points are radically different, with the Ridiculous Man preaching love and paradise on earth and Dr. Ragin facing the void. Chekhov omitted what constituted the largest part of Dostoevsky's story, the Ridiculous Man's dream, and focused almost entirely on the concept presented by Dostoevsky in the story's exposition, the philosophy of "it's all the same" and its implications. Even prior to Dr. Ragin "theorizing" the problem of "nothing matters," Chekhov subtly introduces the consequences of this worldview by providing a description of the hospital and its surroundings as an image of chaos and neglect. The story opens with a picture of the hospital yard, overgrown by "a whole forest of burdock, nettle, and wild hemp," an image of rot with its pile of rubbish in which, in fact, "everything is the same" (8:72). At the story's end, Dr. Ragin, locked in the psychiatric ward, sees the hospital's surroundings as an emblem of reality at large, a prison and a "bone-black plant" where everything disintegrates:

> Not far from the hospital fence, some two hundred yards, not more, stood a tall white building surrounded by a stone wall. It was the prison. "So this is reality!" thought Andrei Iefimych, and he became terrified. The moon was terrifying, and the prison, and the spikes in the fence, and the distant flames in the bone-black plant. . . . Andrei Iefimych assured himself that . . . in time everything would rot and turn into clay, but he was suddenly overwhelmed with despair, and he clutched the iron grill of the window with both hands and shook it with all his might. (8:121–22)

Ragin's theoretical speculations that "everything is the same" are put into new perspective here, with physical images of life turned into unified matter: the image of the bone-black plant in the background (a plant that literally turns all animal debris into "the same" organic matter) and everything eventually rotting and turning into mud. The story's stark ending offers no hope, no exit from this prison, this "reality," and no anticipation of a supernatural or fantastic revelation. There is only the grim reality of life as rotting matter, an image of hell. This hell, however, is the creation of those who embrace the philosophy of "nothing matters" and on that basis refuse to resist life's entropy.

It would be a mistake to conclude that Chekhov simply condemns Dr. Ragin's philosophy and refutes it by making him experience physical pain. Pain, humiliation, and privations "prove" only one thing to Dr. Ragin, that he is not strong enough to subordinate his senses to his mind (8:122). After he endures the guard Nikita's heavy blows, he feels again that "nothing matters" and "everything is the same," but this time not as a "theory" that does not account for pain and for the difference between "being beaten and not being beaten," but as a matter of fact: "He was not ashamed of remembering his weakness the day before. Yesterday he had been cowardly, frightened even of the moon, and he had frankly expressed thoughts and feelings he had never suspected in himself. For instance, his thoughts about the lack of satisfaction among the philosophizing lightweights. But now he felt it was all the same to him" (8:125). It is therefore truly surprising that Shestov, who offered such a provocative analysis of Chekhov's "The Boring Story" as an example of his "creation from the void," completely misunderstood "Ward Six," which he interpreted as Chekhov's concession to the critics who had chastised the writer for not advancing a unified and comfortable "worldview." Commenting on Dr. Ragin's philosophy of indifference, Shestov claims that the doctor renounces his ideas as soon as he endures physical pain and therefore that Chekhov dismisses his philosophy and advances a socially useful "idea" by condemning his hero: "Chekhov had openly repented and renounced the theory of non-resistance. And, so it seems, 'Ward Six' was met with a sympathetic reception at the time. In passing let's note that the doctor dies very beautifully: in his last moments he sees a herd of reindeer, etc."[39] Not only does Dr. Ragin not die beautifully, but he dies without renouncing his philosophy and without accepting a belief in immortality. Additionally, as discussed earlier, his vision of the herd of reindeer is nothing but a random image from his reading the day before. Furthermore, Shestov did not recognize in the story Chekhov's portrayal of a most extreme and sober confrontation with the void by a character driven to the very brink of existential despair. Shestov concludes: "Chekhov wished to make a concession and he made a concession. He had come to feel how intolerable was hopelessness, how impossible the creation from a void."[40] "Ward Six," however, does not glorify the "idea" and does not embrace "idealism." As opposed to the conversion to "truth" and promotion of the "idea" of Dostoevsky's Ridiculous Man, revealed to him through his otherworldly experience, Chekhov's hero is left with no "truth," no "idea," no belief in immortality, and not even an indisputable rejection of his nihilism, even when he acknowledges the immorality of his indifference. While the protagonist of Chekhov's story is not saved, the story does implicitly question whether there is anything that can make humanity abandon moral nihilism and try to make a difference, large or small. What could prompt humankind to act morally in a world that has lost its faith in immortality? Although Dr. Ragin's hostile interlocutor Gromov claims that physical pain demonstrates the unsustainability of the philosophy of indifference ("and if you get your finger pinched by a door, you'll scream at the top of your lungs!" [8:103]), Chekhov suggests that even pain by itself does not refute nihilism. In his final thoughts, Dr. Ragin clings to his philosophy of *vsio ravno* and rejects the idea of immortality. The readers, then, are not offered any solution or way out of the hero's hopeless situation but are invited instead to search for a solution on their own. Chekhov comes close to an existentialist evaluation of nihilism, with its emphasis on personal responsibility as an alternative to the absurdity of the world. Chekhov leads both his characters and his audience to the question of how to face a world that may appear absurd. Indeed, many of Chekhov's characters are compelled to confront the apparent meaninglessness of the world and its frightening absurdity. In chapter 5, we will explore how some of them, striving to ascertain the purpose of human existence in a world that seems devoid of meaning, find it only in perseverance and perpetual struggle that resembles the hopeless labor of Sisyphus.

From "Nothing Matters" to Tarara-boom-dey-a and *Renyxa* (Ченыxa): *The Three Sisters* and the Absurd

Dostoevsky's invisible presence in Chekhov's *The Three Sisters* elucidates the plays' philosophical undercurrents. In this play, Chekhov uses the expression *vsio ravno* thirty-one times.[41] In Chekhov's play the problem of the Ridiculous Man's moral nihilism grows into a terrifying ontological and epistemological nihilism that threatens to turn all of life into the absurd. The Ridiculous Man to some extent anticipates this ontological nihilism but does not go beyond the idea of solipsism as an extension of the philosophy of "nothing matters":

> It might almost be said that the world now seems to be created for me alone: if I were to shoot myself, the world would cease to exist, at least for me. To say nothing of the possibility that nothing would in fact exist for anyone after me and the whole world would become extinct as soon as my consciousness became extinct, would disappear instantaneously like a phantom, like an integral part of my own consciousness, and will be annulled, for all this world and all these people are perhaps only me myself alone.[42]

The Ridiculous Man is also an epistemological solipsist, for he believes that he is the only being in the universe capable of knowledge: "they do not know the truth, whereas I know it. Oh, how hard it is to be the only one to know the truth!"[43] In *The Three Sisters*, epistemological solipsism grows into epistemological nihilism as all characters are paralyzed by their lack of knowledge. Furthermore, metaphysical solipsism grows into ontological nihilism as one of the characters, Chebutykin, not only suggests that there may be nothing outside of his mind but goes so far as to question all existence, including his own.

The loss of meaning, the impossibility of understanding why people live and suffer, is a recurrent motif in the play. While in Dostoevsky's prose and Chekhov's "Ward Six" the motif of "nothing matters" or "there is no difference" is connected with the protagonists' worldviews, in Chekhov's play the leitmotif of "nothing matters" becomes ubiquitous, growing into a web enveloping the entire life of the provincial city and its inhabitants. It is no longer a predicament of one character who has lost his sense of life's meaning, be it the Ridiculous Man, who recovers this meaning through a mysterious revelation, or Dr. Ragin, who dies facing the void. In *The Three Sisters*, "nothing matters" engulfs the entirety of society's state of being; it becomes an ominous symptom of being in general, existence that is devoid of any foundations or firm beliefs.

As the play begins, the characters announce their profound dissatisfaction with life, and the sisters' naïve dreams of returning to Moscow to escape their senseless lives are dismissed as fantasy from the start. Chekhov cuts short Olga's nostalgic hope ("I began to long passionately to return to my hometown") with a series of laconic rebukes:

OLGA: I began to long passionately to return to my hometown.
CHEBUTYKIN: Like hell, you will!
TUZENBACH: Sure, it's nonsense.
(*Masha, brooding over her book, quietly whistles a tune.*) (13:120)

Masha, the smartest of the sisters, is clearly bored with her sisters' fantasies and Irina's and Tuzenbach's pointless chatter about the importance of work; she does not hide her impatience with their idle conversations. Masha's resentment toward her life taints the seemingly festive atmosphere of the first act: "'Oh yes, it's easy to say 'don't go' . . . This damn unbearable life" (13:134). Responding to life's frustrations and lack of meaning, the characters of the play either resort to utopian philosophizing about the salvific quality of work or plunge into numbing indifference. The notion that "nothing matters" or "it's all the same" is thus one of the central leitmotifs of *The Three Sisters*. All the main characters of the play use this phrase in various contexts: Irina, Olga, Masha, Natasha, Andrei, Tuzenbach, Solyonyi, Vershinin, and especially Chebutykin, who emerges as the main ideologue of the philosophy of "nothing matters." Let's consider how the motif of *vsio ravno* unfolds in the course of the play's four acts. Depending on the context, *vsio ravno* could be translated as "anyway," "there's no difference," "it doesn't matter," "all the same" and "never mind," among other analogous phrases. To give a sense of the pervasiveness of this phrase, an extensive citing is in order:

IRINA: "Brother most likely will become a professor. He won't go on living here <u>anyway</u> [*vsio ravno*]." (13:120)

MASHA: "<u>It doesn't matter</u> [*vsio ravno*] . . . I'll be back this evening." (13:124)

CHEBUTYKIN: "It's been two years since I stopped drinking for days on end. (*Impatiently.*) Anyway, lady, <u>what difference does it make!</u> [*ne vsio li ravno!*]" (13:134)

NATASHA: "I'll have to tell her, meanwhile she can share a room with Olga . . . She's not home during the day <u>anyway</u> [*vsio ravno*], only spends the nights here." (13:140)

ANDREI: "Never mind. (*Examining the book.*) Tomorrow's Friday, we have a day off, but I'll go there <u>all the same</u> [*vsio ravno*] . . . I'll find something to do, it's boring at home." (13:141)

VERSHININ: "Yes, ma'am . . . But I <u>don't think it matters</u> [*vsio ravno*] much whether they are civilian or military, they're equally uninteresting, at least, in this town. <u>It doesn't matter!</u> [*vsio ravno!*]" (13:143)

MASHA: "But OK, go on, do talk, <u>it doesn't matter</u> to me [*mne vsio ravno*] . . . (*Hides her face with her hands.*) It's <u>all the same to me</u> [*mne vsio ravno*]." (13:144)

IRINA: "I think <u>it doesn't matter</u> to her [*ei vsio ravno*]." (13:145)

TUZENBACH: "<u>It doesn't matter</u> [*vsio ravno*]. (*Gets up.*) I'm not good-looking, what kind of military man am I? Besides, <u>it doesn't matter</u>, anyway . . . [*vsio ravno*]." (13:147)

ANDREI: "In a word, I don't know, it's positively <u>all the same to me</u> [*vsio ravno*]." (13:152)

CHEBUTYKIN: "Although, essentially . . . of course, <u>it doesn't matter</u> at all! [*vsio ravno!*]" (13:153).

SOLYONYI: "Well, it <u>doesn't matter</u> [*vsio ravno*]. You can't force someone to love." (13:154)

SOLYONYI: "It <u>doesn't matter</u> to me [*vsio ravno*]. Good-bye!" (13:154)

OLGA: "Whoever would propose, I'd marry him <u>all the same</u> [*vsio ravno*], so long that he is a decent man. I would even marry an old man." (13:168)

OLGA: "(*Goes behind her screen.*) Stop it. I don't hear you <u>anyway</u> [*vsio ravno*]. Whatever silly things you may say, it <u>doesn't matter</u> [*vsio ravno*], I am not listening." (13:169)

KULYGIN: "Nobody likes it but it <u>doesn't matter</u> to me [*vsio ravno*]. I'm
content. With moustache or without it, I'm just as content." (13:174)
CHEBUTYKIN: "What happened? Nothing. Trivialities. (*Reads the newspaper.*) It <u>doesn't matter</u>! [*vsio ravno!*]" (13:174)
CHEBUTYKIN: "I don't know. Perhaps, I'll be back in a year. Who the hell
knows, though . . . <u>Doesn't matter</u> . . . [*vsio ravno*]." (13:177)
CHEBUTYKIN: "The Baron is a good man, but one baron more or less—
<u>does it really matter</u>? (ne vsio li ravno) Let it be! It <u>doesn't matter</u>! [*vsio
ravno!*]" (13:178)
CHEBUTYKIN: "There's nothing in the world, we aren't here, we don't exist,
but it only seems that we exist . . . And what <u>does it matter</u>? [*ne vsio li
ravno?*]" (13:178)
MASHA: "Life's a failure . . . I don't need anything now . . . I'll calm down
right now . . . <u>Doesn't matter</u> [*vsio ravno*]." (13:185)
CHEBUTYKIN: "Yes . . . something came up . . . I'm tired, exhausted, I don't
want to talk . . . (*Annoyed.*) Anyway, <u>it doesn't matter</u>! [*vsio ravno!*]"
(13:187)
CHEBUTYKIN: "(*Pulls a newspaper out of his pocket.*) Let them cry . . .
(*Hums quietly.*) Ta-ra-ra-boom-de-ay . . . I'm sitting on a curbstone . . .
<u>What does it matter</u>! [*ne vsio li ravno!*]" (13:188)
CHEBUTYKIN: "(*Sings quietly.*) Tara . . . ra . . . boom-de-ay . . . I'm sitting on
a curbstone . . . (*Reads the newspaper.*) <u>Doesn't matter! Doesn't matter!</u>
[*vsio ravno!*]" (13:188)

The overwhelming frequency with which the characters express their emotions in terms of "nothing matters" points to the centrality of this motif in
the play. The bacillus of "nothing matters" infects the entire town. Yet it is
Chebutykin who becomes the most ominous figure of them all, especially
because he, being a doctor much like Dr. Ragin, is particularly accountable
and responsible for the consequences of his indifference, ignorance, and
non-interference. We learn that one of Chebutykin's patients died because
of his incompetence and medical mistakes. We are likewise informed that
he has forgotten all his medical knowledge and spends his time reading
nothing but newspapers of questionable quality. As will be shown in more
detail in chapter 6, his refusal to actively participate in life and his immersion in "newspaper time" instead of authentic temporality leads him to moral
relativism and the avoidance of responsibility. Chebutykin is clearly responsible for not preventing Tuzenbach's and Solyonyi's duel, which results in

the murder of Irina's fiancé. Not only does he turn out to be liable for Tuzenbach's death, but he consciously professes his moral nihilism, completely denying the value of human life: "The Baron is a good man, but one baron more or less—does it really matter? Let it be! It doesn't matter!" (13:178).

While *vsio ravno* seems innocuous at the beginning of the play, it acquires increasingly ominous overtones in the course of the four acts. Tuzenbach uses this expression when he decides to leave the army, get married, and start "working." We realize, however, that he is in fact driven by despair: "The die is cast. You know, Maria Sergeevna, I'm resigning. ... It doesn't matter ... (*Gets up.*) I'm not good-looking, what kind of military man am I? Besides, it doesn't matter, anyway ... I'll be working. If only one day in my life to work so much that when I return back home at night, I would collapse on my bed exhausted, and fall asleep in an instant" (13:147–48). Tuzenbach's *vsio ravno* clearly points here to his extreme disillusionment with life. His determination to work "if only for one day" is nothing more than the desire "to fall asleep"—that is, to withdraw from life and escape his misery. In the same act Andrei also repeats this phrase at a turning point in his own life, a moment signifying his retreat from his ideals and his complete submission to Natasha's manipulations, including her gradual eviction of the sisters from their home: "Bobik isn't very well, and so ... In a word, I don't know, it doesn't matter to me in the least" (13:152). Andrei's extreme disillusionment and adoption of the dangerous mantra "nothing matters" leads him to gambling, eventually resulting in his own financial ruin as well as that of his sisters.

Chebutykin echoes Andrei's words with his own *vsio ravno* when he complains to him about his solitude and lost life: "However you philosophize, loneliness is a terrible thing, my friend ... Although, essentially ... of course, it doesn't matter at all!" (13:153). In both cases "it does not matter" signifies resignation, a withdrawal from life. By act 4, the phrase becomes increasingly menacing. When at the end of the play Vershinin leaves and Masha has to reconcile herself to their separation, she tries to console herself with the same idea she uses to express her frustration with life—that "nothing matters" (13:185). To Irina's question about Tuzenbach's quarrel with Solyonyi, Chebutykin replies, "What happened? Nothing. Trivialities [*pustiaki*]. (*Reads the newspaper.*) Does not matter." When Kulygin comments on the potential seriousness of this quarrel, Chebutykin adds, "I don't know. It's all nonsense [*chepukha*]" (13:174). Thus, "nothing important," "trivialities" (*pustiaki*), "it's all the same" (*vsio ravno*), and "nonsense" (*chepukha*) become words of the same order signifying the utter absurdity of existence as seen by Chebutykin. Chekhov masterfully underscores this absurdism with another absurd word employed by Kulygin in response to Chebutykin's dismissal of the events as "nonsense" (*chepukha*). Kulygin tells a story of the misreading of the Russian word for "nonsense," "chepukha" (чепуха in Cyrillic), as a nonexistent Latin word, *renyxa*, thus delineating its nonsensical aspect: "In a seminary a teacher once wrote 'nonsense' [чепуха] on a student's paper, and the student read it as *renyxa*, thinking it was written in Latin. (*Laughs.*)" (13:174). The Cyrillic script of the Russian word for nonsense (чепуха), once read as if it were written in Latin letters, therefore becomes an incomprehensible and nonexistent *renyxa*. The absurd word "renyxa" grows into a symbol of life for Chebutykin. Significantly, he comes to repeat this ridiculous word again when Irina mentions her premonitions about the fate of her fiancé: "Renyxa. Nonsense" (Реникса. Чепуха) (13:176).

The doubly absurd word *renyxa*—a word signifying both the absurd (чепуха) and its incomprehensible Latin reading—merges with Chebutykin's other leitmotif phrases—"nothing matters" (*vse ravno*) and "Ta-ra-ra-boom-dey-a" (*Тара-ра . . . бумбия*), a popular music hall tune that Chebutykin sings several times. Similar to *renyxa*, "Ta-ra-ra-boom-dey-a" is completely devoid of meaning. The first time he sings this tune is in response to Irina's advice that he needs to change his life: "Yes. I feel it myself. (*Sings quietly.*) Tarara . . . boom-dey-a . . . I'm sitting on a curbstone" (Да. Чувствую. (*Тихо напевает.*) Тарара . . . бумбия . . . сижу на тумбе я" (13:174). While waiting for the fatal duel between Solyonyi and Tuzenbach to take place and indulging in his favorite pastime, reading a newspaper, he repeats this musical leitmotif again: "(*Reads the newspaper and sings quietly.*) Tarara . . . boom-dey-a . . . I'm sitting on a curbstone" (13:176). Finally, after reporting the tragic news to Olga and proclaiming in his typical manner that it does not matter to him ("anyway, it doesn't matter"), he also announces to Irina the death of her fiancé, resuming his favorite tune: "(*Sits on a bench far upstage.*) I'm exhausted . . . (*Takes a newspaper out of his pocket.*) Let them cry . . . (*Sings quietly.*) Ta-ra-ra-boom-dey-a . . . I'm sitting on a curbstone . . . What does it matter!" (13:187). This same tune also concludes the play: "(*Sings quietly.*) Tara . . . ra . . . boom-dey-a . . . I'm sitting on a curbstone . . . (*Reads the newspaper.*) Doesn't matter! Doesn't matter!" (13:188). The choice of tune is significant. "Ta-ra-ra Boom-de-ay" was a signature tune of Lottie Collins in its London version and was known as "Tha-ma-ra-boum-di-hé" in the French, itself a major hit in Folies Bergères. In the classical Lottie Collins tune, a "good girl," "a papa's daughter," tells a playful and teasingly erotic story about her "innocence" and then dances a kick dance to the boisterous but unintelligible refrain "Ta-ra-ra Boom-de-ay." The cheerful and provocative song, along with its buoyant cancan refrain, is glaringly incompatible with the tragic events that occur at the end of *The Three Sisters*.

There is, however, another twist to Chebutykin's compulsive singing of this tune. The Russian rendering of the song's text is drastically modified from both the English and French cabaret versions. The Russian text mysteriously changed the part sung by a female singer, from a female point of view, to a male part, sung by a drunkard sitting on a street curbstone (tumba). This text is not only comic but also pathetically sad, with distinct overtones of existential anxiety:

Та-ра-ра-бумбия,
Сижу на тумбе я,
И горько плачу я,
Что мало значу я.
Сижу невесел я
И ножки свесил я.
Та-ра-ра-бумбия,
Сижу на тумбе я …

Tara … ra … boom-de-ay …
I'm sitting on a curbstone,
Bitterly crying,
Because I am so insignificant.
I'm sitting sadly,
Hanging my legs.
Tara … ra … boom-de-ay …
I'm sitting on a curbstone …

Chebutykin clearly recalls not only the nonsensical and bouncy refrain "Ta-ra-ra-boom-dey-a" but also the pathetically comic Russian lines about the drunken man's grief and awareness of his insignificance. After all, Chebutykin himself is a drunkard and a man painfully aware of his own insignificance and ignorance: "I will be sixty years old soon, I am on old man, a lonely, insignificant old man" (*nichtozhnyi starik*) (13:125–26). As he sits on the bench, singing the lines about a drunkard sitting on a curbstone, his words echo his own movements and predicament. "Tara-ra-boom-dey-a," an incomprehensible and nonsensical refrain, becomes a fitting expression of Chebutykin's existential anxiety. The logical outcome of his philosophy of "nothing matters" is an abracadabra, *renyxa* and "tara-ra-boom-dey-a."[44] It is no coincidence that Chebutykin's "Tara-ra-boom-dey-a" and "nothing maters" (*vsio ravno*) conclude the play along with Olga's expression of nostalgic yearning. At the curtain's fall Olga's words convey her existential uncertainty about the meaning of life and human suffering ("Just a little while longer, and we shall know why we live, why we suffer … If only we knew, if only we knew!" [13:188]). Although in the end of the play the sisters seem to accept life as it is and try to convince themselves to persevere and go on living, the audience would recall Masha's words earlier in the play, insisting that "you have to know why you live, or else it's all nonsense, devil-may-care" (*Ili znat', dlia chego zhivesh', ili zhe vsio pustiaki, tryn-trava* [13:147]). Masha uses the idiomatic expression "tryn-trava," which is itself more or less equivalent to "nothing matters." Although by the end of the play the sisters still reach for hope, Chebutykin's sinister *vsio ravno* and the absurd "Tara-ra-boom-dey-a" create a somber dissonance, not only with the receding sounds of the cheerful military march but also with their emotional state, their desperate longing for life and knowledge.

In the context of the play the attitude "nothing matters" is associated not only with irresponsibility, leading to misery and even death, but also with an extreme existential anxiety and the sense of the absurdity of life. Some of the most profound philosophical questions of the play—those of the meaning of life and human agency—are directly linked to the notion of the absurd through the character of Chebutykin. Like the Ridiculous Man and Dr. Ragin, Chebutykin loses his sense of life's meaningfulness and slips into the indifferentism of "nothing matters." There is a significant difference, however, between Chekhov's portrayal of Chebutykin and Dostoevsky's portrayal of his nihilist the Ridiculous Man. Similar to the Ridiculous Man and Dr. Ragin, Chebutykin withdraws from life. His nihilism, however, is of a more ominous variety as it grows into an ontological position. He doubts his own existence and even yearns for complete nonexistence: "Nothing … My head's empty, my soul's cold. Maybe, I'm not even a human being, but only pretend to have arms and legs … and a head; maybe I don't even exist at all, but it just seems to me that I walk, eat, and sleep. (*Weeps.*) Oh, if only I didn't exist!" (13:160). Again and again Chebutykin questions not only the meaning of life but existence altogether, a step forward in his nihilism beyond the limits of the Ridiculous Man and Dr. Ragin: "Maybe it just seems to us that we exist, but in fact we don't" (13:162). When Andrei challenges him on the immorality and irresponsibility of not having prevented the duel and agreeing to be present at it in his capacity as a doctor, Chebutykin muses: "It only seems that way . . . Nothing exists in the world, we aren't here, we don't exist, but it only seems that we exist . . . And what does it matter?" (13:178). Significantly, however, although Chebutykin is miserable and disoriented, he does not contemplate suicide. Suicide becomes in a way superfluous as his ontological nihilism denies the basis of existence itself. Neither is Chebutykin tormented by the grand questions of God's existence or immortality; he sees all human existence as nonexistence, an illusion or complete nonsense—*renyxa*, "Tarara-boom-dey-a." It is not surprising, then, that all his activities and most of his words convey such a sense of absurdity (such as, for example, his discussion of naphthalene dissolved in alcohol as a recipe for hair loss or his non sequitur about Balzac marrying in Berdichevo).

As opposed to the Ridiculous Man, the characters of *The Three Sisters* do not discover the Truth and a higher meaning of reality. Whenever they have dreams about the ideal world of the future, Chekhov presents this idealization in a highly ironic light. Vershinin's utopian vision of the future thus appears as a humorous counterpart to the Ridiculous Man's vision of the Golden Age and earthly paradise: "In two hundred or three hundred years life on earth will be inexpressibly beautiful, stupendous. Man needs a life like that, and if it isn't here and now yet, he must anticipate it, wait, dream, get prepared for it; to do so, he must see and know more than his father and grandfather saw and knew" (13:131).[45] With his exceptional passion for "philosophizing," Vershinin places the Golden Age in the remote future (13:145–46). Masha only laughs in response. Although Vershinin (with his vaudeville-like last name, formed from the Russian word "summit," *vershina*) preaches lofty ideas, it is obvious that Chekhov does not take him seriously and gently pokes fun at his "lofty way of thinking."

Chekhov structures his play (as well as "Ward Six") in such a way that it is the reader and the audience rather than the characters themselves who are tasked with realizing the deadly aspect of the philosophy of "nothing matters." As opposed to the Ridiculous Man, Chekhov's heroes, aside from lame philosophers such as Vershinin, preach nothing. Chekhov reveals to his audience and his readers a profound affinity with the philosophical ideas of Dostoevsky. Yet while Dostoevsky criticizes nihilism from religious and moral perspectives, Chekhov focuses more on its existential aspects. His characters confront the tragic incomprehensibility of a world that often generates angst and despair, but they do not discover any meaning outside of human perception. In the face of the absurd they attempt to create meaning, often unsuccessfully, through indefinite struggle and perseverance. As we will see in chapter 5, all of Chekhov's major plays problematize human existence as potentially devoid of meaning unless humanity undertakes to endow it with meaning through work, creativity, and active engagement, defying the philosophy of "nothing matters" with personal involvement and responsibility.

Uncle Vania: Chekhov Reading Molière and Dostoevsky

In much the same manner in which he engages with the ideas of the Stoics—in part, through the prism of Dostoevsky—Chekhov responds to other themes, plots, and motifs of world literature through intermediaries, refracting and contaminating them with other sources. Chekhov's allusions to Molière's *Tartuffe* via Dostoevsky's *The Village of Stepanchikovo and Its Inhabitants* is a good example of this technique of contamination and the use of intermediaries. *Uncle Vania's* connection to *Tartuffe* is quite explicit. In the eyes of Voinitsky, Professor Serebriakov appears as a real Tartuffe, while he himself subconsciously assumes the role of the naïve and trustworthy Orgon. Maria Vasilievna, mother of the Professor's first wife, is in many ways similar to Orgon's mother, Madame Pernelle, who idealizes the impostor and hypocrite Tartuffe. Chekhov makes use of an archetypal comic plot, such as the motif of the family's eviction from their estate, but this similarity is limited to the skeleton of the plot. What the scholarship on the play has overlooked is the fact that its connection to *Tartuffe* passes through an intermediary text, Dostoevsky's novella *The Village of Stepanchikovo.*[46]

At the time Chekhov was writing *Uncle Vania*, Stanislavsky's 1891 production at the Society of Art and Literature of a play titled *Foma*, adapted from Dostoevsky's *Village of Stepanchikovo*, significantly popularized Dostoevsky's novella and made it highly visible. The refraction of Molière's comic plot through the prism of this work by Dostoevsky, and then further transformed in Chekhov's play, elucidates salient aspects of Chekhov's dramaturgy.

K. V. Mochulsky pointed out that Dostoevsky's novella was in fact at least partially inspired by *Tartuffe*, observing that *The Village of Stepanchikovo* is structured according to the rules of classical comedy and draws on the plot line of *Tartuffe*.[47] Moreover, in his letter to Apollon Maikov in January 1856,

Dostoevsky confided that he had started writing a comedy but, being carried away by the adventures of his hero, had rejected the genre of comedy in favor of a comic novel. Dostoevsky's widow, Anna Grigorievna Dostoevskaia, also confirmed in her conversation with Stanislavsky that Dostoevsky originally conceived his *Village of Stepanchikovo* as a play, not a novella. Despite an obvious connection with *Tartuffe*, Dostoevsky believed he had created a purely Russian type in his "comic novel." Indeed, in addition to the plotline's similarity to *Tartuffe*, his characterization of Foma Fomich Opiskin has multiple Russian sources of inspiration, amply discussed by critics who considered Opiskin a parody of Gogol and even Belinsky.[48]

Here I trace the transformation in Chekhov's play of two of the main characters of Molière's comedy—Tartuffe and Orgon—via Dostoevsky's characters Opiskin and Colonel Rostanev. This transformation illuminates some important aspects of Chekhov's poetics and dramaturgy. Chekhov enters into a very complex cultural and generic dialogue with his famous predecessors: drawing on the "novelized" comedic plot of Dostoevsky, Chekhov distills and identifies the theatrical kernel of Dostoevsky's text and grafts Dostoevsky's text on to the plot of his play.

Let's first consider some of the more plainly obvious parallels. In the play, Chekhov chooses a peculiar point of view, the perspective of the "uncle," so that the events are presented through the prism of Voinitsky's relations with his niece Sonia and their perception of the world around them. A similar family dynamic is present in Dostoevsky's novella, that of Sergei Aleksandrovich and his uncle, Colonel Egor Iliich Rostanev. In fact, *The Village of Stepanchikovo* begins with the "uncle" (the very first word of the novella, used in reference to Colonel Rostanev), whose story is narrated by his nephew. Chekhov moves the word "uncle" to the title of his play.[49] Both Dostoevsky's novella and Chekhov's play are in a way "scenes from country life" (also the subtitle of Chekhov's play). The "approximately forty-year-old" Colonel Rostanev is close in age to Voinitsky, who is forty-seven. Having inherited an estate after the death of his wife, Colonel Rostanev settles in the country. Although in Chekhov's play the "uncle" does not receive an inheritance, he lives on an estate belonging to his late sister and by law passed on to his niece, Sonia (this estate having been purchased by Voinitsky's father as a dowry for Vania's sister). However, Voinitsky is entitled to a share in this estate as well: "This estate would not be purchased if I hadn't relinquished an inheritance in favor of my sister, whom I loved deeply. Moreover, for ten years I labored like an ox and paid off the whole debt" (13:101).

Both Dostoevsky and Chekhov follow Molière in their use of the motif of the mother who idealizes an impostor. Similar to the widow of General Krakhotkin (called маменька [Mommy]) in Dostoevsky's novella, in Chekhov's play Maria Vasilievna, the widow of a privy councilor and Voinitsky's mother, continuously reproaches her son for his lack of reverence even as he dedicates his entire life to providing for those who abuse his kindness and generosity. Dostoevsky's narrator, we recall, comments on the self-sacrificing work of Colonel Rostanev: "Carriages, lackeys, and armchairs were paid for by the disrespectful son, sending his mother his last savings, mortgaging and remortgaging his estate, limiting himself with all the necessities, plunging in debt, almost unpayable with his means at the time."[50] Both Colonel Rostanev and Voinitsky worship intellect, erudition, and the assumed moral virtues of their domestic version of Molière's Tartuffe. After a Russian Tartuffe (be it Opiskin or Serebriakov) settles into the same house with his benefactors, the habitual lifestyle of the owners of the estate changes completely. Dostoevsky's narrator notices this change: "Soon the uncle's house was like Noah's ark."[51] Similarly, Voinitsky laments: "Ever since the professor and his spouse have been living here, our life's been out of joint" (13:64).

It's possible to identify many other parallels. Let us consider for the most part only how Molière's characters of Orgon and Tartuffe are transformed in both Dostoevsky and Chekhov. Molière's Tartuffe is not only a hypocrite, dissembler, and manipulator but also a crook who violates the law; he tries to get hold of Orgon's property and is ultimately put in prison for this felony. To a very large extent the foregrounded collision of Molière's comedy is based on the struggle for property. As opposed to Molière's impostor, the Russian Tartuffe of Dostoevsky, Foma Fomich Opiskin, behaves in a much more irrational way; he does not transgress the law and does not even pursue distinctly mercenary goals. While Tartuffe manages to make Orgon hand over the deed to his estate and all his property, the Russian Tartuffe refuses to accept money offered to him by Colonel Rostanev (even if there may be a degree of manipulation in this refusal). Molière's protagonist is a calculating villain. Opiskin is an improviser of manipulation; he is closer to Gogol's characters of the type of Khlestakov, who gets carried away with his lies to such an extent that he starts believing in them himself. He does not have a premeditated plan of action. Yet Opiskin is not as simple-minded as Khlestakov. Striving to compensate for his humiliating position, he looks for self-affirmation at the expense of others and derives pleasure from his tyranny and the exertion of psychological power over those closest to him.

His main impulse is not so much greed as the desire to dominate and suppress those around him. Although Opiskin makes use of pious religious rhetoric as skillfully as Tartuffe, his presumed piety is not the main virtue that blinds Colonel Rostanev and his mother. In addition to his fake godliness, Dostoevsky endows his character with an aura of refinement, erudition, and wisdom. Opiskin allegedly "once studied literature in Moscow." He pledges to write something grand. As the narrator puts it, Foma was a "man of letters" but was "ill-treated and did not get recognition," although, the narrator further explains, this "genius determined to become famous." The Russian Tartuffe of Dostoevsky is not an unambiguous crook and a villain. In the eyes of Mme. Krakhotkin and Colonel Rostanev, he is not only a virtuous person but a scholar and unrecognized genius, although in fact he is neither a scholar nor a writer. Thus Dostoevsky complicates the plotline and characters of Molière by introducing a theme that is very prominent in Russian culture—that of worshiping a genius.

Chekhov further develops the theme of the cult of the genius outlined by Dostoevsky. Professor Serebriakov, Chekhov's Tartuffe, is indeed a professor, and although Voinitsky ironically refers to him as a writing *perpetuum mobile* and censures him for being such a nonentity, it is obvious that Serebriakov could not have achieved such a high status and attain a professor's chair if he did not have sufficient knowledge and qualifications. While Opiskin only pretends to be writing something as he secludes himself in his room, Serebriakov indeed continues his scholarly work: "Dear friends, could you please send me some tea to my study. I need to write something today" (13:66). Regardless of the quality and quantity of his actual work and regardless of Voinitsky's doubts about the worth of his scholarship, the audience/readers do not have sufficient evidence of Serebriakov's poor scholarship to assume that he is merely a fraud. Opiskin only comically demands that Colonel Rostanev call him "your Excellency." Professor Serebriakov indeed achieves this status of being called "your Excellency." The resentful Vania cannot restrain his mocking indignation of the professor's achievements: "The son of a common deacon, a student in the religious seminary, he's obtained academic degrees and a professor's chair, became Your Excellency and son-in-law of a senator and so on and so forth" (13:67). As opposed to Tartuffe and Opiskin, Professor Serebriakov does not appeal to the religious feelings of his victims and does not manipulate their sense of morality. They become his victims completely voluntarily. He is not a villain and not even a manipulator; he is simply a self-centered egoist, absorbed with his own interests.

As his wife, Elena, justly observes: "There's nothing to hate Alexander for, he's the same as anybody else. No worse than you" (13:73).

Thus, it seems that Chekhov "purges" his Tartuffe of any law-breaking, fraud, and conscious tyranny. By doing so he refocuses our attention from the "villain" to his "victims." Why and how does Voinitsky become a "victim" of Serebriakov's assumed tyranny, if Chekhov's "Tartuffe" can be blamed only for being an ordinary egoist? Chekhov, in fact, is more interested in the character of Uncle Vania than in the image of the potential victimizer, Serebriakov/Opiskin/Tartuffe. How, then, is the character of Molière's victim, Orgon, transformed into Voinitsky via Dostoevsky's Colonel Rostanev? Molière clearly focuses his satire on the extreme piety and religious hypocrisy of the society in which he lived. Orgon is enchanted with Tartuffe only because of his assumed "saintliness." Orgon is kind, loyal, and trustful, although naïve and excessive in his impulsiveness. Molière mocks Orgon's blindness and his extreme piety but on the whole is less interested in the phenomenon of the victim than are Dostoevsky and Chekhov. Orgon is a purely comic figure by virtue of his naïveté and lack of common sense.

Dostoevsky's Colonel Rostanev in many ways follows the image of Orgon. He is trusting, kind, and generous. As opposed to Orgon, however, he is fascinated not only with Opiskin's piety but with his learning. He becomes excited at the very mention of the words "scholarship" and "science." While at the end of Molière's comedy Orgon realizes that Tartuffe is a crook— this much is revealed to him before his very eyes—Colonel Rostanev rebels against Opiskin only for a brief moment. The novella ends as a farce, with a "happy" ending and the enthroning of Opiskin as an absolute authority among the grateful and respectful family of Colonel Rostanev. Common sense triumphs in Molière's play, but in Dostoevsky's novella the masks are never completely stripped away. In fact, Opiskin's influence even intensifies by the end: not only are the retired colonel and his mother under his spell, but so are many more characters, such as Nastenka, Rostanev's future wife. The character of Opiskin is obviously at the center of Dostoevsky's attention, but in the character of Colonel Rostanev, Dostoevsky also mocks the enigmatic Russian predilection for creating idols, a practice that was often evident among the intelligentsia: "To sacrifice oneself for other people's interest is their vocation. Someone would call him a pushover, lacking character, a weakling."[52]

Chekhov further develops this theme of the spineless Russian intelligentsia creating idols for themselves in his elaboration and transformation of the character of Orgon/Rostanev. Voinitsky's character, however, is not merely comic. Chekhov playfully and humorously refers to Dostoevsky in his characterization of Voinitsky: in his desperation, Uncle Vania claims that he could have been a Schopenhauer or Dostoevsky. Chekhov places Dostoevsky's critique of the progressive Russian intelligentsia's strange aptitude for creating idols in a broader philosophical and existential context. In Chekhov's play the conflict is not based on the intrusion of a crook, fraud, or nonentity such as Tartuffe or Foma Fomich. Professor Serebriakov is not a malefactor or a scheming intruder; he is Voinitsky's own creation. The question is only why and how these Serebriakovs are being created and who is responsible for allowing a Tartuffe to have such power and influence over other people's lives. The external conflict of the intruder and the victim becomes internalized in Chekhov's play. For Voinitsky, Professor Serebriakov is a scapegoat on whom he can place the blame for his own failed life. Chekhov's character is no longer a purely comic personage, a victim of deceit and manipulation. Rather than being a victim of a calculating and conniving villain or of unfavorable circumstances, Voinitsky is a victim of his own ideology, typical of the Russian liberal intelligentsia of the time. Lamenting his contemporary Russian life, Chekhov observes bitterly: "How much people enjoy being deceived, how much they like prophets and preachers, what a herd they are" (17:82). "Nowhere does authority suppress man as much as it does in Russia, humiliated by centuries of serfdom and fearing freedom" (17:68). Uncle Vania's conundrum is caused by his internal lack of freedom. Voinitsky's tragedy stems from his worship of authority figures and his loss of his own identity in the process, so much so that he becomes known as Sonia's uncle rather than as himself.

Chekhov's play does not have a comic resolution like those of Molière's comedy and Dostoevsky's novella. He recasts the hero-ideologue's psychological makeup not only in a comic light but also in an almost tragic one. Yet Vania's tragic aspect reveals itself not when he attempts to shoot the professor or poison himself but when he realizes the futility of his hopes and expectations that have stemmed from his idea of service to higher ideals and his inability to resolve the conflict between reality and his wishful thinking. Molière's play culminates with a traditional plot resolution of comedy—a *deus ex machina*. The happy ending of Dostoevsky's novella endows it with farcical overtones. Chekhov, in contrast, leaves his comic character facing an existential tragedy.

Molière exposes hypocrisy and bigotry. Dostoevsky explains the peculiar phenomenon of the impostor Opiskin by way of his low self-esteem and injured pride. Chekhov exposes no one and does not explain anything. He is raising questions: Why and how are these various Tartuffes being created? Who is to blame for the resurfacing of this type? Indeed, Chekhov's dramaturgical goals become more apparent through a comparison of the counterparts of Molière and Dostoevsky. Not only does he reject a plot based on conflict between the villains and the virtuous and renounce a happy ending or even any resolution to the conflict; he shows the comic aspect of the tragic and the tragic aspect of the comic. Vania's attempts at murder and suicide (traditionally a tragic action) appear in a comic light. But the comic reconciliation is not without tragic overtones. Both Tartuffe and Opiskin are grotesque comedic characters. Chekhov's "Tartuffe" Serebriakov is no more than an ordinary egoist. The kindhearted and naïve character of Colonel Rostanev belongs to farce, but the ridiculous and pathetic Voinitsky emerges as a hero of the existential drama of being.

SCANDALS ON THE STAGE

Now that we have identified multiple thematic overlaps between Dostoevsky and Chekhov, we should consider how Chekhov's poetics could also be viewed as "grafting" Dostoevsky's narrative strategies on to the "tree trunk" of drama and comedy. In particular, I would like to consider Chekhov's original use of scandalous scenes and dialogue.

Dostoevsky's inherent theatricality has been substantially discussed in the scholarly literature, and his interest in theater is well documented. The connection between his novels and the form of tragedy was especially strong. Thus, V. Ivanov has argued that Dostoevsky's works fundamentally follow the narrative structure of classical tragedies, including the ultimate catharsis of the novel's conclusion.[53] Despite planning several times to write a comedy, Dostoevsky wrote no plays, comedies or tragedies, and there must have been reasons for his choice of the novel form and not theatrical works. There have been, however, many successful stage productions of Dostoevsky's works, and stage directors have found that Dostoevsky's texts lend themselves easily to dramatic form—at least in part because his novels are dialogue-heavy and full of explosive "scenes." Dostoevsky's characters talk and express themselves through conversations abundantly, even if these conversations are self-directed. These features, theater directors have often assumed, invite dramatization.

Yet a difficulty arises once we consider the nature of dialogue (and, we could add, of scandal) in the dramatic form as compared to its function in the novel. Dostoevsky himself claimed that his theatricality was inherent in the genre of the novel but was not, in fact, an element of "drama." In response to Varvara Dmitrievna Obolenskaia's interest in staging *Crime and Punishment*, Dostoevsky shares his views on the connection between the work's "idea" and its generic form in his letter to her of January 20, 1872:

> As regards your intent to extract a drama from my novel, I of course fully agree, and have made it a rule never to hinder such attempts; I have to note, however, that almost all such attempts have been unsuccessful, at least not quite successful. There is some mystery of art according to which the epic form will never be able to find its counterpart in the dramatic one. I am even convinced that series of artistic forms correspond to series of poetic ideas, so that one and the same idea cannot be expressed in the form that is not inherent to it.[54]

Dostoevsky's observations about the inextricable link between form and content have been further theorized by Mikhail Bakhtin, who also insisted that it is impossible to adapt Dostoevsky's novels for the stage. Arguing that drama is in fact a monological form, as opposed to Dostoevsky's polyphonic novel, Bakhtin also emphasized that in contrast to polyphonic dialogue, dramatic dialogue works within the framework of a monological form. Maintaining that scandal scenes and explosive dialogues in Dostoevsky represent only a superficial theatricality ("authentically dramatic dialogue can play only a very secondary role in Dostoevsky's polyphonic novel"),[55] Bakhtin analyzes the polyphonic aspect of the novel and its inherent dialogicality, claiming that it is different from the way dialogue functions in the theater.

Although Dostoevsky's inherent theatricality has been observed by many of his readers, there was no agreement on how to interpret the dramatic element of Dostoevsky's art.[56] While Viacheslav Ivanov, for example, viewed Dostoevsky's novels as "novel-tragedies" and Leonid Grossman detected in them a dramatic form that he interpreted as the mystery play, Bakhtin adamantly denied the prominence of purely dramatic dialogue in Dostoevsky, although dialogue may be frequently associated with the dramatic form or philosophical discourse. Bakhtin argues that Dostoevsky's dialogue is of a different kind. As opposed to Grossman's interpretation of dialogue in Dostoevsky as a dramatic form, Bakhtin insists that the dramatic dialogue in drama is characterized by a monologic framework, in contrast to the complex dialogicality of Dostoevsky's novels. Viewing dialogue in dramatic form as inherently monological, Bakhtin claims:

> In drama the world must be made from a single piece. Any weakening of this
> monolithic quality leads to a weakening of dramatic effect. The characters
> come together dialogically in the unified field of vision of author, director, and
> audience, against the clearly defined background on a single-tiered world. A
> true multiplicity of levels would destroy drama, because dramatic action, rely-
> ing as it does upon the unity of the world, could not link those levels together
> or resolve them. In drama, it is impossible to combine several integral fields
> of vision in a unity that encompasses and stands above them all, because the
> structure of drama offers no support for such a unity. For this reason, authen-
> tically dramatic dialogue can play only a very secondary role in Dostoevsky's
> polyphonic novel.[57]

Bakhtin undoubtedly made a profound insight into the nature of Dostoevsky's dialogical form, opposing it to "ordinary dialogic form" and detect-
ing in it "ultimate dialogicality" or a "dialogicality of the ultimate whole."
He seems, however, to have completely overlooked the possibility for a dramatic form characterized by dialogicality and open-endedness. Unsurpris-
ingly, Bakhtin had little interest in Chekhov and barely mentioned him in
his works.[58] This omission may in part be due to the fact that Bakhtin's
conception of the theater was limited: he did not write on modern theater,
and, so it seems, underappreciated Chekhov's innovations in the dramatic
genre as well as his contributions to modernism and a new modernist worldview. Yet Bakhtin's ideas about the antithetical relationship between the novel
and the classical drama may help to elucidate how similar techniques used
in different genres led Dostoevsky and Chekhov to their innovations in the
novel and dramatic forms, respectively.

Many of the characteristics of the polyphonic novel described by Bakhtin
—the lack of resolution and synthesis, a plurality and non-hierarchy of voices,
internal dialogicality and a nonlinear plot line—are concepts employed in
Chekhov's theater. Chekhov, to be sure, was not interested in the "adaptation"
of Dostoevsky's or anyone else's novel and did not attempt to utilize the novelistic plot for theatrical needs. He instead deployed some of the very same
theatrical devices that Dostoevsky effectively "novelized" in his novels—
verbal action and scandals—and in the process created a new dramatic form.
By returning Dostoevsky's "novelized" devices to theater, Chekhov completely changes not only Dostoevsky's "poetic idea" but also the function of
these artistic devices. Bakhtin argued that the novel gives "no firm support outside the rapture-prone world of dialogue for a third, monologically

all-encompassing consciousness."[59] But the lack of an "all-encompassing consciousness" is a salient feature of the Chekhovian play as well. Chekhov himself, in fact, lamented the lack of a unified vision and a singular point of view in his fiction but considered it to be a prominent aspect of modern consciousness leading the modern artist to a more open-ended and pluralistic artistic production. In fact, in his letter to Suvorin of November 25, 1892 (quoted in chapter 1), he rejects what Bakhtin refers to as a monological worldview, but he does so almost apologetically (P 5:133–34). There, Chekhov speaks precisely of his inability to create monologically with an encompassing consciousness of the "third voice."

Nor does Chekhov believe in completeness or the possibility of a resolution of the plurality of points of view. In an earlier letter to Suvorin (May 30, 1888), he insists on his poetic principle of nonresolution in his embodied dialogues and noninclusion of this third voice: "The artist must be not the judge of his characters and of what they say, but merely an impartial witness.... It is up to the jury, that is, to the readers, to give an evaluation" (P 2:280). Thus, both in his prose and in his theater, Chekhov avoids a kind of dramatic action that Bakhtin, following the Aristotelian tradition, attributes to drama, one that resolves all dialogic oppositions. Chekhov, however, does precisely what Bakhtin believes is impossible in drama—he gives no priority to any particular point of view and is not afraid of the "weakening of dramatic effect" by destroying the monolithic quality of his work. Chekhov constructs his plays in such a way that it becomes impossible to detect "the whole of a single consciousness"; neither does he offer any "unity of the world" or "the point of view of a nonparticipating 'third person.'"

It could thus be said that while Chekhov extracts from Dostoevsky's prose a dramatic kernel, which he appropriates for his theatrical needs, much like the great novelist he refrains from offering monological resolutions. Dostoevsky's *Village of Stepanchikovo*, for example, as well as many of his later novels, is very theatrical and "dramatic" in the sense that it contains a number of almost thespian dialogues. Bakhtin refers to this theatrical aspect of Dostoevsky as "carnivalization" and considers Foma Fomich Opiskin a "carnival king." Maintaining that the life portrayed in the novella is a "life that has left its normal rut," Bakhtin interprets its scandalous elements as the carnivalesque: "The entire action of the tale is an uninterrupted series of scandals, eccentric escapades, mystifications, decrownings and crownings."[60] Bakhtin, however, does not mention Molière's *Tartuffe* as the intermediary of this "carnivalized" tale. Even if, as Bakhtin argues, the more archaic roots of Dostoevsky's poetics may be connected with Menippean satire and "carnivalized" literature, the more immediate source is obviously Molière's comedy. Chekhov, in turn, responds to the comedy and farce of Dostoevsky's novella and recognizes its inherent theatricality.[61] In fact, Chekhov appropriates a peculiar aspect of Dostoevsky's poetics—his use of scandal scenes. While Dostoevsky's contemporaries frequently criticized this element of Dostoevsky's poetics for being improbable and aimed at external effects, Bakhtin believed it constituted the very core of Dostoevsky's art.[62] The main "drama" in Dostoevsky's *Village of Stepanchikovo* comes out not through characters' actions but through conversations and verbal scandals, which is to say through verbal action.

A similar kind of verbal action takes place in Chekhov's plays. Although Chekhov, as we have pointed out earlier, responded negatively to what he perceived as Dostoevsky's melodramatic poetics, including his improbable scandals and extraordinary plot situations, he adopted those same elements for his comedic and satirical goals. The explosive scandals of Dostoevsky that lead to revelations and exposures of the characters' inner essences and to major consequences for the plot are replaced in Chekhov by comic and frequently inconsequential scandals. Many critics have claimed that Chekhov's plays are uneventful, lack external conflicts, and do not amount to much more than the flow of everyday life. Chekhov's plays, however, contain a surprising number of verbal scandals.[63] Many important events of his plays are indeed not those generated by external action but "scandals in a drawing room"; they are stirred not by what characters do but by what they say. Whatever "happens" reaches us through words more than action, or often by a clash between words and actions. Rejecting the devices of classical comedy and melodrama (Chekhov does not expose villains with the traditional machinery of comedy, such as hiding under a chair and eavesdropping), Chekhov nevertheless unexpectedly seems to appropriate a peculiar theatrical strategy of Dostoevsky—the verbal scandal. Most of Chekhov's major plays have scenes that clearly qualify as scandals, when characters say something that would be inconceivable in the normal course of life. These scandalous elements appear not only in *Ivanov*, the most "melodramatic" of his plays. (Recall how Dr. Lvov, trying to expose Ivanov, whom he accidentally names "a Tartuffe," tells him things unacceptable in polite society and by the end of the play consciously tries to "set a scandal," publicly calling him "a scoundrel.") This occurs in the later plays as well. Thus, in act 3 of *The Seagull* an exchange full of insults between Arkadina and Treplev appears as a perfect "scandal scene," yet it turns out to be almost a farce and leads to no significant change in the characters' lives:

> TREPLEV: ... I don't believe in any of you! I don't believe in you or him!
>
> ARKADINA: You decadent!
>
> TREPLEV: Go back to your darling theater and act there in pathetic, talent-less plays!
>
> ARKADINA: I have never acted in such plays. Leave me alone! You are incapable of writing even a miserable vaudeville. You petty bourgeois from Kiev! You sponger!
>
> TREPLEV: You miser!
>
> ARKADINA: You pauper! (*Treplev sits down and weeps quietly.*) You nobody!" (13:40)

A similarly farcical scandal takes place in act 3 of *Uncle Vania,* when the professor proposes to sell the estate:

> VOINITSKY: All your works, which I so much appreciated, aren't worth a dam! You duped us! ... Wait, I haven't finished! You ruined my life! I haven't lived, I haven't lived! Because of you I have wasted, destroyed the best years of my life! You are my worst enemy! ...
>
> SEREBRIAKOV: What do you want from me? What right do you have to talk to me in such manner? A nonentity! If the estate belongs to you, then take it, I don't need it!
>
> ELENA ANDREEVNA: I am getting out of this hell this very minute! (*Screams*) I can no longer stand it!
>
> VOINITSKY: My life is wasted. I'm talented, intelligent, brave ... If I had had a normal life, I might have become a Schopenhauer, a Dostoevsky ... I have messed up! I am going mad ... Mother, I'm in despair! Mother! ...
>
> SEREBRIAKOV: A real nonentity! ...
>
> (*Offstage a gunshot; we hear Elena Andreevna scream; Sonia shudders*) ...
>
> SEREBRIAKOV (Runs in, stumbling in fear.): Restrain him! Restrain him! He's gone out of his mind!
>
> (*Elena Andreevna and Voinitsky are struggling in the doorway.*)
>
> ELENA ANDREEVNA (trying to wrest the revolver away from him.): Give it to me! Give it to me, I tell you!
>
> VOINITSKY: Let me go, Hélène! Let go of me! (*Liberating himself, he runs in and looks around for Serebriakov.*) Where is he? Ah, there he is! (*Shoots

> *at him.*) Bang! (*Pause.*) Missed him? Missed him again?! (*Angrily.*) Ah,
> damn it, damn it … damn it to hell … (*Throws the revolver on the floor
> and sits exhausted on a chair.*) (13:102–4)

We have here a most outrageous scandal scene, containing unexpected behavior, insults, accusations, tears, intense emotions, kneeling, fears, despair, and even gunshots. But the outcome of this highly theatrical moment is more comic than tragic, and Voinitsky's scandalous behavior has no consequences and resolves nothing. As in Dostoevsky's novels, Chekhov's scandals take place in "drawing rooms" and doorways. But as opposed to Dostoevsky's scandals, Chekhov's are not turning points that reveal previously hidden information or change the characters' lives and decisions. Rather, these are comic, farcical scandals that nevertheless lack comic resolution. Thus, Chekhov returns from the novel to the theater what Dostoevsky adapted from the theater to his prose, that which he "novelized," to use Bakhtin's term.

Another interesting example of Chekhov's re-theatricalization of Dostoevsky and his dramatization of scandal scenes can be found in his one-act play *The Wedding*, which is connected with more or less the same class conflict explored by Dostoevsky in his "A Nasty Story" ("Skvernyi anekdot," 1862).[64] Regardless of whether or not Chekhov was familiar with this story of Dostoevsky's, the way the two writers treat similar subjects is illuminating. Although Chekhov first dealt with this subject in prose (his story "A Wedding with a General," 1884, among several others), he did not leave unnoticed Dostoevsky's inherent theatricality and satire and adapted it to his own theatrical experiments. He recasts the plot of the general's visit to the petty official's wedding and the theme of the arranged marriage in dramatic terms, extracting from it its theatrical aspects. Although Aleksei Remizov, for example, in his essay included in *The Fire of Things* (1954) and dedicated to Dostoevsky's underappreciated "A Nasty Story," claims that "Dostoevsky is outside theater, and any theatrical attempt to present him is like plucking a bird," he nevertheless discusses Dostoevsky's story in theatrical terms: "In 'A Nasty Story' there is only one act, a single scene: the wedding in the Mlekopitaev house."[65] Curiously, Chekhov is doing precisely this: he writes a one-act play dedicated to the wedding celebration of the daughter of a retired petty civil servant. The scene that Remizov identifies as an "one-act play" in Dostoevsky's story begins with General Pralinsky walking home and incidentally overhearing the music and sounds of a quadrille from a wedding celebration that turns out to be that of his subordinate official, Pseldonimov. Chekhov's play begins at this very moment and with the following stage instructions: "Offstage, a band is playing the last figure of a quadrille." Chekhov truncates the part of the story concerned with the ideological motivation of the liberal and "enlightened" General Pralinsky, which led him to his unfortunate experiment, and focuses instead entirely on the general's visit. As opposed to Dostoevsky's real general, who appears at the wedding of his inferior uninvited and who is motivated only by his liberal ideas, stimulated by his intoxication, in Chekhov's play at the request of the groom, the parents of the bride delegate their friend to hire a general to attend the wedding and add prestige to the celebration. He brings instead, however, only a retired, semi-deaf naval captain to pass off as "the General."

Both Dostoevsky and Chekhov use conventional devices of comedy such as "talking names," comic misunderstandings, and slapstick humor, but they conclude their texts with something that is more horrifying than comic. A conventional farce-vaudeville (Dostoevsky's "nasty story," sometimes translated as "unpleasant incident") grows into a truly demonic cosmic vaudeville. In both cases the result of the marriage of convenience and the visit of "the General" develops into a scandal that leads to a grotesque climax and biting social satire. The drunken general of Dostoevsky and the deaf pseudo-general of Chekhov both generate the most extreme commotion and discord. In both cases, the general and the pseudo-general's visit strips the other characters of their masks and reveals their hidden motivations. Briefly comparing the two texts in her book *Chekhov and the Vaudeville*, Vera Gottlieb quotes a useful passage from Ruben Simonov's book about Evgenii Vakhtangov that compares Dostoevsky's story with Chekhov's play.[66] In doing so, however, she misleadingly draws on an erroneous translation of Simonov's text and refers to Dostoevsky's story as a play.

Indeed, it is no coincidence that the resemblance of the plots of Dostoevsky's story and Chekhov's one-act play was noticed by the renowned Soviet actor and director Simonov. In his book *With Vakhtangov* (*С Вахтанговым*, 1959), Simonov comments on similarity in fabulae and glaring difference in artistic principles between the two texts:

There are two texts, written by two great Russian writers, Chekhov and Dostoevsky, *The Wedding* and "A Nasty Story," on the same theme—"a General at a wedding." Their plots are similar, but how different these works are in their

main ideas, their mode and manner of expression! *The Wedding* is imbued
with a subtle and, at times, bitter humor; "A Nasty Story" is written with a cruel,
sarcastic, and merciless pen.... With his usual consistency, Dostoevsky unfolds
the gradual downfall of the General from the "height" of his grandeur.... The
result is a hopeless and grim picture of human degradation. ... If "A Nasty
Story" were a play, one would have to find for its scenic embodiment an especially sharp and grotesque form, analogous to the art of Goya. In the beginning
of this chapter, we have observed that a remarkable Russian painter, Fedotov,
is the closest to Chekhov's dramaturgy in his artistic peculiarities.[67]

Simonov's thoughts on the two texts' generic distinctions are insightful,
but in fact miss the horrifying, grotesque aspect of Chekhov's play. Although Simonov believes that the pictorial analogue of Chekhov's dramaturgy would be the works of the Russian painter Pavel Fedotov, a genre
painter known for his satire, realism, and tragic minimalism, Chekhov's
one-act play is in fact sharp and grotesque and even develops into a "devil's
vaudeville," to use Kirillov's words from Dostoevsky's *The Devils*. Chekhov
undoubtedly sensed what Bakhtin identified as a "carnivalized Menippean
satire" in "The Nasty Story." Bakhtin writes: "This *deeply carnivalized* story
is also close to the menippea (but of the Varronian type)."[68] Chekhov appropriates this Menippean kernel of Dostoevsky's story for his own cosmic
vaudeville, depicting an upside-down world that ultimately culminates in
a jumble of absurdity and cacophony. *The Wedding* is indeed a staged carnival. A person in Dostoevsky's works, Bakhtin argues, is always depicted on the
threshold and in a state of crisis—a feature that made many of Dostoevsky's
readers interpret his novels as melodramatic. Chekhov brings the crisis and
scandal scenes back to the stage, yet as opposed to the traditional theatrical
treatment of a crisis, culminating in a resolution, Chekhov leaves his characters in a state of perplexity and does not resolve their tensions. Neither
does Dostoevsky, who, according to Remizov, turns his story into a "universal nasty incident" (*vselenskii skvernyi anekdot*). Dostoevsky's satire is aimed
both at the liberal discourse of pre-reform Russia and at the petty bourgeois
customs of lower officials. He mocks both the liberal General's vanity and
his "humanitarian" experiment and the nest of "mammals" (the name of host,
Mlekopitaev, is derived from Russian word for "mammal"). Chekhov's *The
Wedding* is also a satire, but a satire of humanity at large. At his exit, Chekhov's
poor, humiliated, offended pseudo-general, Revunov-Karaulov, utters a series
of lines suggesting a much larger symbolic meaning:

How revolting! What baseness! To insult an old man this way, a navy man, a distinguished officer! . . . If this were a respectable society, I could challenge someone to a duel, but now what can I do? (*Disoriented.*) Where's the door? What direction should I go? Waiter, show me the way out! Waiter! (*Going out.*) What baseness! How revolting! (*Exits.*). (12:122)

Clearly these words are addressed not only to the hosts and their guests but also to humanity at large. The Russian word for "waiter," *chelovek*, also means human being and allows the moment to take on a larger symbolic meaning ("Человек, выведи меня! Человек!"): this is an appeal to the humanity of a man who sees no exit. No one responds to his plea; no one even seems to hear his words. With its lack of comic reconciliation, *The Wedding* appears to be strangely open-ended. If satire might have an implied standard, Chekhov's ending is more absurdist and calls into question the very possibility of a meaningful resolution in the absurd world of the play. Dostoevsky's story ends with Pralinsky's recognition of the fiasco of his "humanitarian" experiment and with a frightening image of a man losing his face, as Remizov aptly observes in his essay dedicated to the story: "He looked into the mirror and could not see his face." Remizov defines Dostoevsky's "hidden idea" in this story in the following way: "The story's theme is this: a man to man is a wedge, but at the same time a man to man is a crossover" (человек человеку—подтычка, и в то же время человек человеку—поперек). In his idiosyncratic interpretation of the story, Remizov suggests "The Nasty Story" anticipates Svidrigailov's vision of eternity as a "bathhouse full of spiders": "From the house of Mlekopitaev, this spiders' nest, he [Dostoevsky] will lead me to the bathhouse of Svidrigailov (*Crime and Punishment*, 1866): the bathhouse full of spiders—this is 'eternity.'"[69] Whether or not Chekhov read Dostoevsky's story, his *Wedding* shares its somber vision of humanity losing both its collective face and its most essential human faculty—communication. The state of the world as complete incommunicability culminates in the image of the world as hell. The dark nature of the play is intensified by its peculiar non-dialogues, which frequently have been referred to as "conversations-of-the-deaf," that is, a type of discourse in which real communication does not take place. Sometimes miscommunication is caused by real physical impediments, such as deafness and external interfering noises, but just as often the cause is simply characters' inability to engage with each other. Chekhov theatricalizes the lack of what is both the most essentially human and the most "dramatic" activity by stripping the dialogue of its most indispensable component—interaction with the other.

Bakhtin argued that dramatic dialogue is in a sense monolithic because it is broken up into statement and response. We see, however, that in Chekhov's plays this is often not the case. Chekhov either creates the non-dialogue of non-communication (a distinct departure from nineteenth-century drama and melodrama) or constructs a very complex type of dialogue characterized by internal dialogization. Consider, for example, how in *The Three Sisters* Olga shares her thoughts about her life with her sisters:

> I got older, became much thinner, this must be because I get angry at my school students. But today I am free, I am at home, I no longer have a headache and feel younger than yesterday. I'm twenty-eight years old, but ... Everything is good, everything is God's will, but it seems to me, it would have been better if I have married and spent the entire day at home. (*Pause.*) I would have loved my husband. (13:120–22)

Everything about this disclosure is highly unusual. First of all, it is not clear to whom Olga's words are addressed. There is no reason for her to inform her sisters that she is at home and that she is twenty-eight years old. This statement would be completely superfluous if it were addressed to them. Her words, therefore, are directed to an invisible interlocutor (an imaginary opponent or perhaps the audience) and to herself. One of her imaginary "opponents" reminds her of her age and the fact that women of her age are usually married. She uses the conjunction "but" right after mentioning her age, yet significantly, she does not complete the sentence, for at this very moment her other "voice" tells her something that people frequently say to console those who are upset over their lot: "Everything is good, everything is God's will." Her first "voice" responds with another clause beginning with "but" that contrasts with these words of consolation: "but it seems to me, it would have been better if I have married and spent the entire day at home." This inner dialogue does not end here, however. Chekhov uses the stage direction "a pause" to further develop it. The strategy of internal dialogue is further theatricalized by Chekhov: the pause as a theatrical, nonnovelistic device calls the audience's attention to the clash of Olga's contradictory thoughts and impulses. The onstage pause is no longer truly silent but is a theatrical way to interrogate a statement, in this case Olga's stated motives for wanting to be married. As if responding to the interrogating pause, Olga hastily explains: "I would have loved my husband." Her inner doubts about marrying simply to be able to stay home and avoid work at school lead her to try to convince her other "voice" that she would have married for love, not mere comfort. This is a good example of that which Bakhtin would refer to as an internally dialogized speech, but in Chekhov this internal dialogization is also theatricalized. Chekhov further complicates this dialogized discourse by using another theatrical device available on the stage: visual and audial synchronous participation in a discourse of other characters. At the very same moment in which Olga ruminates about her marriage, Tuzenbach enters the room and we hear his words, addressed to Solyonyi but also sounding as if they were a response to Olga's assurance that she "would have loved" her husband: "Tuzenbach. (*To Solyonyi.*) What nonsense you are saying, I am tired of listening to it. (*Entering the living room.*)" (13:22). Thus a very complex, nonmonological but nonetheless very theatrical dialogue is being created, one that includes not only the internally dialogized speech of Olga but also a peculiar kind of dialogue that engages the audience, who are able to consider together both Olga's remarks and Tuzenbach's words.

Chekhov's plays embody this internal dialogization—a feature Bakhtin attributes exclusively to the novel, Dostoevsky's especially. Although Bakhtin juxtaposes the single and closed dialogue of drama to the plural and open dialogism of the novel, Chekhov clearly creates a new form of theatrical dialogism. Even if some contemporaries blamed Chekhov (just as they did Dostoevsky) for not presenting a coherent whole in his works and not offering a solution, this was a constituent element of Chekhov's achievements in both prose and drama. Not only does Chekhov not identify with any of his characters, but he also does not offer a third, synthesized point of view. Although Bakhtin argues that drama cannot support the coexistence of voices without a finalizing viewpoint, this is precisely what happens in Chekhov's plays. Chekhov's theater challenges Bakhtin's argument that drama is a closed genre, as opposed to the open-ended novel. Chekhov, to be sure, does not "borrow" this polyphonic strategy from Dostoevsky, but he shares his non-monologic model of the world. Although Chekhov had reservations about Dostoevsky's fiction—he recoiled from what could be easily mistaken as melodrama, prophetism, and religious zeal—he enters not so much into a polemic against Dostoevsky but a dialogue that endeavors to return Dostoevsky's theatricality to the theater.

5

Homo Laborans

The Ontology of Work in *Uncle Vania* and *The Three Sisters*

Chekhov had no relationship with the working class and never studied Marx. No working-class poet in the mold of Gorky, he was nevertheless a poet of labor. [*Tschechow hatte sur Arbeiterklasse gar kein Verhältnis, und Marx hatte er auch nicht studiert. Ein Arbeiterdichter, wie Gorki, war er nicht, wenn auch ein Dichter der Arbeit.*]

THOMAS MANN, *Essays*

THE CATCHER OF SUNBEAMS

In his *Fragments from My Diary: Memoirs*, Maxim Gorky remarks that when people think they are alone and unobserved, they can seem mad, talking to their own reflections and addressing animals, invisible apparitions, or even objects; they can engage in all sorts of vain and absurd pursuits, such as listening to see if a cotton ball makes any noise when landing on a porcelain dish. He recalls a very telling scene starring none other than Chekhov:

I saw A. Chekhov, seated in his garden, try to catch a sunbeam with his hat and—completely in vain—put it on his head along with his hat; and I could see that this failure irritated the sunbeam catcher,—his face grew angrier and angrier. Finally, slapping his hat on his knee despondently, he jammed it briskly on his head, impatiently shoved his dog Tuzik away with his foot, and, screwing up his eyes and squinting skyward, went toward the house. But when he noticed me on the porch, he said with a grin:

—Good day! Have you read Balmont's "The Sun Smells of Grass"? It's silly. In Russia, the sun smells of Kazan soap, and here it smells of Tartar sweat . . .

It was Chekhov, too, who tried long and hard to poke a thick red pencil into the neck of a tiny pharmacy vial. This was clearly a desire to break a certain law of physics. Chekhov devoted himself to this pursuit steadily, with the obstinate perseverance of an experimenter.[1]

This sketch vividly illustrates Chekhov's intriguing existential position. What could be more absurd than trying to catch sunbeams? Gorky does not elaborate on Chekhov's eccentric behavior, but this story captures a very important aspect of Chekhov's personality and artistic sensibility: his interest in activities that seem completely futile and even nonsensical. There is much more to Chekhov's strangely pointless endeavors than appears at first glance: his squinting skyward seems to suggest a metaphysical rebellion and a heroic challenge to fate, a challenge to the laws of nature and to the gods, and a struggle with the incomprehensibility and absurdity of being, which nevertheless cannot destroy man. His actions essentially exemplify this struggle with the impossible. The story also reveals Chekhov's humble desire to hide his defiance with understatement and to deflate pathos ("the sun smells of Tartar sweat"). In his art, Chekhov remained a catcher of both sunbeams and the ever-elusive truth—engaging in tasks that were hopeless but beautiful in their impossibility.

Gorky does not attempt to explain the phenomenon he describes, people undertaking activities that appear hopeless, useless, irrational, and often ridiculous. All the examples Gorky gives, including his striking story about Chekhov's attempt to catch sunbeams with his hat, point to people's bizarre fascination with the absurd—their full awareness of the irrationality of their behavior combined with a simultaneous desire to engage in a completely futile activity, stubbornly and defiantly. Although Gorky does not address the notion of the absurd or the absurdity of existence, an issue that would come to plague the imagination of later generations of writers, this sketch lends itself well to the concept of the absurd man as later articulated by Albert Camus. Chekhov's pointless activity is of course quite distinct from the labor of Sisyphus, condemned by the gods to eternally push his boulder to the top of a hill, only to see it roll back down the slope. However, even if Chekhov's undertaking is completely voluntary, as opposed to that of Sisyphus, it reflects a similar awareness of its futility and meaninglessness, along with a defiant determination to accomplish the task despite its impossibility. Catching the sunrays, much like pushing a boulder toward the top of the hill knowing that it will roll back down, may not be "work" in the sense of purposeful labor; it is an absurd activity but it still involves mental and physical effort.

It is no coincidence that Camus discusses absurdity using the example of the mythological laborer. Work and its meaning are for Camus directly connected to questions about the meaning of life and human existence in general. His concept of the absurd, which became the central theme of his philosophy, advances a staggering image of human fate embodied in Sisyphus laboring in vain. His exercise in futility is an emblem of human existence that has no meaning but begs for answers. If work has no fundamental purpose or meaning that reason can articulate, then life itself becomes senseless, and the only way to endow it with meaning is through rebelling against our mortality and the universe's incoherence. Camus articulated a problem that captivated the imagination of many other writers and thinkers of the existentialist orientation, but he chose to frame it in the language of philosophy and myth.

In the Russian context the question of what work is and how it relates to meaningful existence—that is, work as not only a sociological but also as an ontological concept—had notably attracted the attention of nineteenth-century Russian writers from Dostoevsky in his *Notes from the House of the Dead* (1860–62) onward. The semi-autobiographical novel published upon Dostoevsky's return from prison and exile raises the issue of the meaning of work and its ontological significance. He describes many of the horrifying experiences he witnessed while in prison, focusing on the convicts' work and various types of forced labor in the camp. Dostoevsky's narrator, Aleksandr Petrovich Gorianchikov, describes how work in the House of the Dead inflicted its greatest pain not through hard labor itself but through the uselessness of the tasks it required of the prisoners. The narrator also emphasizes that what makes the work in the camp so hard is not the work itself but the fact that it is punitive and forced, without "a reasonable purpose."[2] Gorianchikov condemns the punitive aspect of subjecting the convicts to completely useless hard labor: "The thought once occurred to me that to completely crush a man, to destroy him utterly and subject him to the most terrible punishment so that even the worst murderer would tremble in fear, shrinking from it in advance, all one would have to do would be to make his work utterly and absolutely useless and absurd."[3] Dostoevsky then offers examples of this senseless and absurd labor: "But if, for example, he [a convict] were forced to pour water from one tub to another and then back again, or to grind sand or carry a heap of soil back and forth again and again, I think that such a convict would hang himself within a few days or commit a thousand crimes to even die but escape from such degradation, shame, and torment."[4]

Although Dostoevsky does not mention Sisyphus's boulder as an example, the nature of the futile and absurd work he describes conveys the meaning of the myth of Sisyphus in all but name. He adds, "undoubtedly, such a punishment would turn into torture, a form of revenge, and would be senseless because it would serve no reasonable purpose."[5] Dostoevsky sees this senseless labor much the same way that Camus did in the twentieth century, as the cruelest of punishments and a form of senseless torture that could lead one to experience the absurdity of existence and perhaps even resort to suicide. However, like Camus's Sisyphus, Dostoevsky's narrator Gorianchikov resolves to find meaning in his labor: "I had a feeling that work may save me, strengthen my health and my body.... But I paid no attention to anyone, and would resolutely go off somewhere, even, for instance, to bake and pound alabaster, one of the first jobs I learned."[6] Gorianchikov also observes an unusual determination among some convicts condemned to their hopeless labor to accomplish their tasks at any cost.[7]

Notes from the House of the Dead raises a problem that would later concern both Chekhov and Camus: the question of how to face the unbearable suffering of senseless work and the effects of its absurdity on psychological well-being. The convict's awareness of the absurdity of his work could lead him either to desire to "hang himself" or to consciously embrace his lot and the decision to perform his task in the best possible way, even in view of the complete hopelessness of the enterprise.

Although in his discussion of the absurd Camus recognizes Dostoevsky as an important predecessor, referring in particular to Dostoevsky's Kirillov from *The Devils*, he does not mention this passage from *Notes from the House of the Dead*. In his essay "The Myth of Sisyphus," however, he develops a concept of the absurd through the example of meaningless labor. "Probably no one so much as Dostoevsky," he writes, "has managed to give the absurd world such familiar and tormenting charms." While Dostoevsky does not consider the convicts' existence to be a metaphor for the human predicament in general, Camus sees Sisyphus's labor as emblematic of the absurdity of existence itself. Even if Dostoevsky, as opposed to Camus, seeks solutions through transcendence and "eternal values," both writers suggest that suicide is not the only way to respond to the absurdity of the human experience. Gorianchikov's affirmation "I want to live and will live" and his embrace of his punitive labor despite its absurdity anticipated Camus's conclusion formulated in the preface to his "The Myth of Sisyphus": "Although 'The Myth of Sisyphus' poses mortal problems, it sums itself up for me as a lucid invitation to live and to create, in the very midst of the desert."[8]

Aside from Dostoevsky, Chekhov is the great Russian writer who came closest to the existentialist sensibility, which raised the question of the meaninglessness of human existence in conjunction with the concept of work. In writers' conceptualizations of possible responses to the absurdity of meaningless labor or of existence altogether, Chekhov is an important link between Dostoevsky and Camus. Work is not only a question of political economy and a social problem for Chekhov but an ontological problem closely connected with the meaning of human existence. The role labor plays in Chekhov's concept of being elucidates his views on life and its purpose as well as on humanity's ability to conduct a meaningful existence and experience a sense of reality. Chekhov's approach to the meaning of work—a question of critical social and ideological significance at the end of the nineteenth century in Russia—anticipates the later concerns of writers with an existentialist orientation.[9]

I consider Chekhov's "drama of being" not in the narrow sense of an interest in life's tragedy or the drama and dramatic events of life but as an ontological concept that positions his interest in the problems of being in the context of his proto-existentialist philosophical worldview. What is being? What is the meaning of human existence? Work is one aspect of this ontological problem.

Work and Idleness: Russian Debates

Before analyzing the ontology of work in *Uncle Vania* and *The Three Sisters*, it will be beneficial to briefly outline a general context of the contemporaneous Russian debates on work.[10] In Russia the question of work as it relates to the problem of being has a long history. Much as Europe was a battleground for competing conceptions of work from the Reformation to the Industrial Revolution, so too was Russia, even if it lacked the Reformation and joined the Industrial Revolution belatedly. Work became an increasingly important sociological and ideological concept in the emerging Russian capitalist society. Nineteenth-century Russian literature intensely engaged with these themes. Many nineteenth-century writers—from Gogol to Turgenev, Goncharov, Dostoevsky, Aleksei Tolstoy, and Lev Tolstoy—responded passionately to the problem of "work" in both their artistic and nonfictional writings. By the end of the nineteenth century, many artists—in both the West and Russia—began depicting "scenes" from modern life widely addressing the subject of labor.

Although questions of work and its meaning have always figured prominently in Europe, during the nineteenth century, with the impact of the Industrial Revolution on the workers and the rise of the Marxian theory of labor, they acquired particular urgency and reconsideration. As labor activities and labor movements increased throughout Europe along with industrial development, the position of workers and their conditions of life became a central societal issue. Marx's ideas of workers' alienation contrasted with the idealization of labor since the Reformation, when Luther's concept of work as an inherently dignified and valuable activity held sway. While Luther insisted that any person's labor serves humankind and pleases God, Marx argued that human alienation is intrinsically linked to workers' separation from their own labor. When a worker experiences this alienation, "he does not affirm himself but denies himself, does not feel content but unhappy, does not develop freely his physical and mental energy but mortifies his body and ruins his mind. The worker therefore only feels himself outside his work, and in his work feels outside himself. He feels at home when he is not working, and when he is working he does not feel at home. His labor is therefore not voluntary, but coerced; it is *forced labor*."[11] Thus, two competing interpretations of work—all work as a divine calling (a position especially advocated since the Reformation), and work as a concept distinct from religion and in some forms dehumanizing, as theorized by Marx—coexisted for some time in the European debates on work.

Although the Russian polemic on work was inspired to a very large extent by Western democratic movements and social thought, the Russian attitude toward work continued to remain distinct from that of the West. In the Protestant West, Luther had proclaimed work to be the best way to serve God. Calvin went even further, insisting that it was one's responsibility to seek out the kind of work that would maximize one's profits. It was Calvin who, according to Weber, provided an interpretation of work as a calling that was essential to the development of capitalism and symbolized "the Protestant work ethic." Wealth became associated with salvation and righteousness, while poverty was connected with damnation and vice. This philosophy generated a new type of individual, one who was hard-working, strong-willed, abstemious, and goal oriented. Work was associated with the progress and well-being of humankind. As Michael Walzer points out in his book *The Revolution of the Saints: A Study in the Origins of Radical Politics*:

> The new view of work and the rhetorical violence of the accompanying critique of idleness formed the concrete basis of the Puritan repudiation of the old order. God honored men as he honored angels: in proportion to their "serviceableness"—that is, to their zealous application, their skill, and their effectiveness. And he organized men as he organized angels: through a division of labor, in chain of command. All men must work, gentlemen and commoners alike.[12]

Protestant ideals began to penetrate Russia in the 1860s and 1870s, wielding particular influence among the radicals and populists who were to launch a violent attack on idleness. Work acquired special significance in the aftermath of emancipation. Nikolai Mikhailovsky considered work an important tool of individuation as well as a social duty. The influence of Stundism on Tolstoy has likewise been acknowledged.[13] Yet Western Protestant ideas were never completely assimilated into Russian consciousness. Even Russian radicals such as Alexander Herzen questioned the mystification involved in the ideology of work as both duty and goal in and of itself. In his polemical response to Pierre-Joseph Proudhon's ideas of labor, justice, and family, Herzen, who overall greatly admired Proudhon, describes Proudhon's ideal this way:

> Feeling is banished, everything is frozen, the colors have vanished, only the exhausting, dull, inescapable toil of the modern-day proletarian is left. . . .
> Man is doomed to labor, he must labor till his hand drops . . .
> "But what are we wearing ourselves out for?"
> "For the triumph of justice," Proudhon will tell him.
> And the new Cain will reply:
> "But who charged me with the triumph of justice?" . . . "Justice is not my vocation; work is not a duty but a necessity."[14]

The notion that work is "not a duty but a necessity" will be echoed by many Russian writers, including Tolstoy. As the Protestant Reformation completely bypassed Russia, Russia never developed what came to be known as the "Protestant work ethic," with its conception of work as a calling, a life-task set by God. As much as Tolstoy insisted on the importance of manual labor, he too questioned the idealization of work characteristic of Western societies. In his 1893 essay "Non-Activity" ("Nedelanie"), written in response to Émile Zola's speech and Alexandre Dumas fils's letter about the meaning of work, and published in the French press, he considers work as a formative and intrinsic aspect of human existence but dismisses its inherently positive value: "Besides, I have always been amazed by the opinion that became especially firmly ingrained in Western Europe that work is something like virtue in itself.... For only an ant in a fable, as a creature deprived of reason and aspirations to do good, could think that work is a virtue and could be proud of it."[15] Regardless of his incessant preaching of the ethical responsibility of all people to be engaged in manual labor, Tolstoy, much like Herzen, considers work not as a panacea against all life's complications but as a basic necessity, responsibility, and a condition of life: "Work can be just as little virtue as food. Work is a need, denial of which constitutes suffering, but by no means is it a virtue. Elevating work to the status of virtue is just as ugly as elevating man's nourishment to the status of goodness and virtue."[16] Work, Tolstoy observes, can be also stupefying and dehumanizing.

Tolstoy also passionately lashes out against private property, capitalism, and the division of labor. The title of his treatise, "What Then Shall We Do?" ("Tak chto zhe nam delat'?," 1886), is openly polemical and dialogical. As he admits himself, Tolstoy is responding to the widely discussed issue of poverty and exploitation by underlining the moral necessity of individual work in order to abolish this exploitation.[17] Tolstoy's treatise as well as his other articles on the subject of poverty, social inequality, work, and private property had a great impact on both the Russian and European intelligentsia and generated intense debates. Tolstoy's ideas regarding the moral value of work in his fiction as well as in his nonfictional works generated passionate responses on the part of the Russian intelligentsia, Chekhov included. Although Tolstoy's pronouncements about work were highly contradictory—and although he actually rejected the unconditional value of labor as a moral virtue—most Russian (as well as Western) readers saw him as a prophet of manual labor. Thus, the young French writer Romain Rolland wrote Tolstoy a letter asking him to clarify his views on the relationship between manual and intellectual work. In his response to Romain Rolland (October 3?, 1887), Tolstoy explains,

I have never considered manual labor as a stand-alone principle but as the most simple and natural application of moral principle.... Manual labor in

our corrupt society (the society of the so-called educated people) is manda-
tory for us at least because the chief fault of this society was and still is in
liberating itself from labor and in profiting, without any reciprocity, from the
work of poor, ignorant, unfortunate classes, who are slaves just like the slaves
of the ancient world.[18]

Tolstoy's ambiguous and contradictory attitude toward the question of work
reflects a larger Russian cultural ambiguity with respect to these questions.
Possession and wealth were not considered in Russia to be something un-
questionably and unconditionally positive. Neither was success, which was
frequently regarded with suspicion. In fact, beggars enjoyed a mysterious
respect in Russia. Chekhov comments on this peculiar aspect of Russian
character in his essay "Our Poverty" ("Nashe nishchenstvo," 1888), written in
response to Tolstoy's book "What Then Shall We Do?":

> A Russian, for example is very shy when it comes to lending and offering, but
> he loves and knows how to borrow and to take, and this even became his habit
> and constitutes one of his fundamental traits.... Lower classes have developed
> and cultivated for centuries passion for pauperism, beggary, and parasitism
> (prizhival'stvo); the middle class and upper classes—passion for all kinds of
> favors, gratuities, benefits, borrowings, concessions, discounts, and allowances.
> (16:238)

Chekhov laments the Russian inability to respect another person's work:
"Worst of all, the carelessness and artistic disorder that rein over the Russian's attitude toward someone else's property, beggary, and passion for getting things undeservedly and for free cultivated in our society a nasty habit
of not respecting someone else's work" (16:241). The key to social change,
Chekhov maintains, is to learn how "to respect someone else's labor and
someone else's money" (16:241).

This peculiar phenomenon of living in a family as a dependent, or a
sponger, designated using the word *prizhival* or *nakhlebnik*, attracted the
attention of many Russian writers who chose as their subject life on Russian
country estates, where wealthy landowners would host multiple "freeloaders,"
often from the impoverished gentry. From Turgenev (in his plays *The Sponger*
[*Nakhlebnik*], *A Companion* [*Kompan'onka*], *A Month in the Country* [*Mesiats
v derevne*], *It Tears Where It Is Thinnest* [*Gde tonko, tam i rvetsia*]) to Ostrov-
sky, Dostoevsky, and Chekhov, the figure of the sponger figures prominently

in Russian literature. The character of the impoverished nobleman became a prominent feature of post-reform Russia, leading to major social displacements of both the Russian nobility and peasantry. The humiliating position of a sponger was an especially noticeable theme in the works of Dostoevsky, whose novels depicted multiple "spongers," from Foma Fomich Opiskin to Stepan Trofimovich Verkhovensky and even Ivan Karamazov's devil. Chekhov, too, found himself preoccupied by this phenomenon. In one form or another, "spongers" appear in all of Chekhov's major plays.[19]

In nineteenth-century Russia the contemplative life was often considered superior to hard labor. This explains Goncharov's sympathetic portrayal of Oblomov and the Russian intelligentsia's refusal to accept the active and hard-working Stolz, with his Protestant work ethic, as a positive hero. Stolz advances his notion of work as a goal in itself, but it is incomprehensible to the Russian Oblomovs, who see leisure and contemplation as a final goal.[20] Significantly, even Chekhov, who criticizes the Russian phenomenon of "spongers" and "freeloaders" and the ensuing disrespect for work, never fully accepted Goncharov's Stolz as an ideal character and called him an "utter scoundrel [*produvnaia bestiia*] who thinks of himself very highly and is self-satisfied" (P 3:201). While Chekhov criticized the phenomenon of beggary and dependency, he was more ambivalent about the unconditional value of work and expressed sympathy, sometimes playfully, for contemplative idleness. In his letter to Suvorin of May 9, 1894, Chekhov writes: "I think proximity to nature and idleness constitute the indispensable elements of happiness; without them happiness is impossible" (P 5:296). He insists again and again that his "ideal of happiness" is idleness and leisure: "I am of the opinion that true happiness is impossible without idleness. This is my ideal: to be idle and to love a full-bodied girl. The height of delight for me is to walk or to sit and do nothing: my favorite occupation is to collect that which is not needed (leaves, straw, etc.) and to do that which is useless" (P 5:281; P 5:310). Chekhov's appreciation of leisure and its link to human happiness was of course not a new idea; the concept goes back at least as far as the classical Aristotelian view of happiness as requiring leisure and being associated with freedom. Apollonio offers a nuanced analysis of Chekhov's balanced and subtle approach to the problem of work versus idleness, arguing that this contrast may suggest an opposition between prosaic and poetic views of the world, but that both are key to Chekhov's creative process.[21]

By the end of the nineteenth century, however, recriminations on the basis of "idleness" (*prazdnost'*) became a constant feature of both liberal and conservative contemporary discourses. From Vissarion Belinsky's call for "activity," Goncharov's problematization of the work-idleness dichotomy in *Oblomov*, Chernyshevsky's novel *What Is to Be Done?*, the publication of the progressive democratic journal *Deed* (*Delo*, 1866–84), the populists' debates on specialization and the division of labor and their insistence that the intelligentsia had a moral obligation to work for a social and economic revolution—to the polemic around the gulf between lofty rhetoric and "minor deeds" (*malye dela*) in the 1880s—Russian intellectuals exhibited what practically amounted to an obsession with concepts of work and action. Under the influence of Belinsky, who absorbed Hegelian ideas about labor as both economically productive and constituting a key element in the laborer's self-conscious existence, work was being conceived as paramount to leading a meaningful life, while idleness was demonized as a source of injustice. The Hegelian notion that labor plays an important role in both personal and social development was emphasized in the populist movement. Thus Nikolai Dobroliubov delivered the diagnosis of "Oblomovism" to the Russian gentry in his essay "What Is Oblomovism?"

By the end of the nineteenth century, questions around work and the conditions and moral dimensions of labor acquired more and more urgency. The increased social mobility generated by the Great Reforms pushed various strata of the population into the workforce, including the impoverished gentry. The years leading up the 1905 Revolution were, in particular, characterized by rising social stratification and elite alienation from society. Discussions of labor focused not only on work's necessity for a meaningful life and sense of fulfillment but also on problems of isolation and alienation. The late 1880s and early 1890s brought the issue of social injustice front and center, and writers and artists turned with new urgency to the role of work in human life. The Marxist idea that individual fulfillment is tied to being reunited with the product of one's labor was gaining momentum among both the Western and Russian radical intelligentsia.

In the Russian context, however, we see that the glorification of work for its own sake was often received with suspicion. Thus, for example, although Tolstoy's own attitude toward work was in fact much more complex and ambiguous than was often thought by his contemporaries, he was nonetheless criticized for his supposed "deification" of labor. Significantly, a contemporary of Tolstoy, the Russian poet and critic Innokenty Annensky in his *Second Book of Reflections* (*Vtoraia kniga otrazhenii*, 1909), refers to Tolstoy's preaching of the necessity of physical work as a form of glorification of

Sisyphean labor. Annensky seems to overlook Tolstoy's rejection of the unconditional merit of labor; he instead considers Tolstoy's concept of work in terms of Sisyphus's absurd efforts.

> For his Buddhism, Tolstoy could not have invented a symbol more horrifying and hopeless than his *work*. Aesthetically, this *work*, which *is deified by him*, is nothing else but *the black rock of Sisyphus*. People, keep pushing this rock, tirelessly till you are exhausted. Procreate if you wish, but procreate only so you can roll your rock more successfully, that is, hopelessly.... But why do you want us, oh our prophet, to both worship the black rock of Sisyphus and roll it incessantly?[22]

Chekhov actively participated in these debates through his portrayal of members of the Russian intelligentsia rhapsodizing about the moral obligation to work. "Work" (*trud, rabota*) and "action" (*delo*) were clearly the catchphrases of the time, and Chekhov's characters participate in this discourse on the page and on the stage. Work is a central leitmotif of his major plays and fills the pages of his stories. In particular, the moral obligation to work and the value of engaging in physical labor are discussed at length in his programmatic novella *My Life* (1896). Many of Chekhov's characters have idealistic views regarding physical labor but those who actually work are frequently portrayed as exhausted, dispirited, and disillusioned. The theme of never-ending, Sisyphean work is prominent in Chekhov's fiction. With its link to the larger problem of human existence, it stands out as a central motif in *Uncle Vania* and *The Three Sisters*.

"Sisyphus's Silent Joy": *Uncle Vania*

In his "Myth of Sisyphus," Camus deploys the analogy of the Greek myth to do more than simply demonstrate the futility of human efforts and Sisyphus's work. The author instead presents the never-ending and meaningless labor of Sisyphus as a metaphor of modern existence in general. But as he will insist in the preface to a later publication of this essay, "this book declares that even within the limits of nihilism it is possible to find the means to proceed beyond nihilism."[23] For Camus, as well as for Chekhov, this sense of the absurd is the intellectual predicament of modern humanity. Ultimately Sisyphus finds meaning and purpose in his task simply by continually applying himself to it. Camus is less interested in the absurd itself than he is in it as a starting point of his discussion of tragedy and suicide. Camus claims, "there is but one truly serious philosophical problem, and that is suicide." As he suggests, the mind, "when it reaches its limits, must make judgment and choose its conclusions. This is where suicide and the reply stand."[24] Thus, there are two possible responses to the absurd, according to Camus—either suicide or recovery. The question that concerned him is what makes life worth living in the face of the absurd and the absence of "eternal values."

An existentialist *avant la lettre*, Chekhov asked similar questions, even though he never framed them in terms of Greek myth or the language of philosophy. In one of his letters to Suvorin (November 25, 1892), he speaks about the particular malaise of his time, which is essentially close to what Camus would later identify as "absurd sensitivity" (*sensibilité absurde*). He observes that what distinguishes modern writers from those of previous generations is the lack of goals and purpose connected with the modern loss of faith in God and with it, any sense of coherence in the universe. The great writers of the past, he insists, "march somewhere and call you along with them," "they have some kind of a goal" (P 5:133). What characterizes modern sensibility according to Chekhov, however, is a sense of disorientation and of the void, resulting from the lack of purpose and beliefs:

> We have neither near nor remote goals, and our souls are completely empty. We have no politics, we don't believe in revolution, we have no God, we are not afraid of ghosts, and I personally am not afraid even of death and blindness. One who wants nothing, who hopes for nothing and is afraid of nothing, cannot be an artist. . . . You and Grigorovich believe I am clever. Yes, I'm clever at least to the extent not to hide from myself my malaise and not to lie to myself and not to cover my own emptiness with someone else's rags like ideas of the sixties, etc. I won't throw myself down the stairwell, as did Garshin, but I won't delude myself with hopes for a better future either. (P 5:133–34)

Despite his awareness of the hopelessness and pointlessness of existence, Chekhov rejects suicide and resolves to live and to create, even if he believes it is impossible to be an artist with such a worldview. The question of how to cope with the realization of the void is Chekhov's primary concern. Although Chekhov acknowledges that modern thought has reached its confines (has come up against its boundaries), he rejects suicide as a way of dealing with this sense of emptiness. For Chekhov, as well as for Camus and many other existentialist thinkers, this recovery may be achieved only through unceasing struggle. Camus defines this struggle in terms that echo Chekhov:

"I must admit that that struggle implies a total absence of hope (which has nothing to do with despair), a continual rejection (which must not be confused with renunciation), and a conscious dissatisfaction (which must not be compared to immature unrest). . . . The absurd has meaning only in so far as it is not agreed to."[25] Chekhov frequently expresses similar sentiments: "I am far from deceiving myself, my dear friend, concerning the true state of affairs; I am not only bored and discontent, but am frequently convinced, even from a purely medical point of view—almost cynically—that one should expect from life nothing but bad—errors, losses, illnesses, weaknesses, and all sorts of nasty things" (P 5:117). In his November 13, 1898, letter to his sister, Chekhov once again emphasizes his stoic acceptance of the inevitability of human sufferings alongside his readiness to endure and carry on, regardless of the circumstances: "and one has to be prepared for anything and take everything as inevitably necessary, as sad as it may be. One only has to do one's duty as best one can, and nothing else" (P 7:327).

Shestov and others have noted that Chekhov brings his heroes to the verge of despair and face-to-face with the hopelessness of their existence. Still, Chekhov's affinities with Camus's "absurd sensibility" and heroic rebellion against it have received little attention. In his article "About the Meaning of Waiting (Chekhov's Dramaturgy and Beckett's *Waiting for Godot*)," Rolf-Dieter Kluge notes that "Chekhov of course was not an existentialist or absurdist; in his dramaturgy he avoids the consequences of nihilism and endows those characters who are inclined toward such an ideological position (Chebutykin, Dorn, Solyonyi) with ironic or comic traits and by doing so softens the ominous scope of their thought."[26] Nevertheless, Kluge connects Chekhov's skepticism, which he sees as "close to existentialism," with the later expression of these ideas in Camus's "The Myth of Sisyphus." He compares Chekhov's words from the letter to Suvorin on November 25, 1892 (quoted above) to what Camus writes on "the absurd man": "Pour l'homme absurde, il ne s'agit plus d'expliquer et de résoudre, mais d'éprouver et de décrire. Tout commence par l'indifférence clairvoyante. Décrire, telle est la dernière ambition d'une pensée absurde."[27]

Following Kluge's footsteps, Pyotr Dolzhenkov points out the possibility of comparing Chekhov's thoughts on the absurdity of the universe with Camus's ideas. Dolzhenkov points out that for Chekhov's characters, just as for Camus, the world is incomprehensible and meaningless, and this is the reason the two writers' characters strive for clarity and meaning. Discussing Chekhov's *Uncle Vania* with reference to Camus's ideas, he observes: "In *Uncle*

Vania we see those human reactions to the absurd about which the French philosopher would later write: an attempt at rebellion, then attempts of escape through suicide and through hope in its two variants: religion (we have in mind Sonia's last monologue) and the previous service to science."[28] Dolzhenkov concludes, however, that Chekhov and Camus resolve the problem of the absurd in drastically different ways: "While Camus sees the solution in rebellion, Chekhov believed that in the incomprehensible, meaningless, full of suffering life, man ought to fulfill his duty, despite everything."[29]

According to Camus, however, the absurd does not coincide with the world's incomprehensibility and meaninglessness. The absurd, Camus insists, emerges from the clash of man's need to know and the world's incomprehensibility: "I said that the world is absurd, but I was too hasty. This world in itself is not reasonable, that is all that can be said. But what is absurd is the confrontation of this irrational and the wild longing for clarity whose call echoes in the human heart. The absurd depends as much on man as on the world."[30] Dolzhenkov therefore seems to misinterpret Camus's notion of rebellion. The revolt Camus is talking about is not a goal in and of itself but a means of "recovery." Life "despite everything" is precisely the very foundation of Sisyphus's heroism, according to Camus. Discussing the sense of absurdity that characterizes modernity, Camus connects it to the contradiction between our need for knowledge and what he calls "the unreasonable silence of the world"; he reaches a paradoxical conclusion that "the absurd has meaning only in so far as it is not agreed to."[31] Thus, something that is absurd acquires meaning through rebellion. Rebellion, then, is a form of heroic signification. Chekhov's worldview is thus in fact close to this type of existentialist heroism.

Various philosophers and thinkers of the phenomenological and existentialist orientation who raised the issue of the impossibility of knowing the reality open to our senses formulated similar ideas to those discernable in Chekhov's works.[32] Camus dedicates a large portion of his book to the discussion of Shestov's irrationalism and the difference between his own philosophy of the absurd and that of Shestov. He read Shestov thoroughly, likely also reading his essay on Chekhov. Camus starts his discussion of the absurd with the same image of a wall with which Shestov concludes his essay on Chekhov: "One must beat one's head, beat one's head eternally against the wall. Where would it lead one to? And will it lead to anything at all? Is it a beginning or an end? Is it possible to see in it the warrant of a new and inhuman creation, a creation out of the void?"[33] The wall is an initial point of departure for both Chekhov, as he appears in Shestov's interpretation, and for Camus. Despair and awareness of the absurd may lead to heroic resistance and to "creation out of the void"—a creative way to endow the world with meaning. Both writers sought a heroic solution to this fundamental contradiction between the incomprehensibility of the universe and the desire to know; they found a response grounded in the resolve to endure and embrace life.

Referring to Sisyphus as an "absurd hero," Camus explains his heroism in terms of his simultaneous embrace of and resistance to his fate:

> His scorn of the gods, his hatred of death, and his passion for life won him that unspeakable penalty in which the whole being is exerted toward accomplishing nothing. ... Then Sisyphus watches the stone rush down in a few moments toward that lower world whence he will have to push it up again toward the summit. ... It is during that return, that pause, that Sisyphus interests me. ... I see that man going back down with a heavy yet measured step toward the torment of which he will never know the end. ... That is the hour of consciousness. At each of those moments when he leaves the heights and gradually sinks toward the lairs of gods, he is superior to his fate. He is stronger than his rock.[34]

Camus sees the tragedy of this myth and Sisyphus's heroism in the fact that he is endowed with full consciousness of his predicament. He compares Sisyphus's plight to that of modern workers:

> If this myth is tragic, that is because its hero is conscious. ... The workman of today works every day in his life at the same tasks, and this fate is no less absurd. But it is tragic only at the rare moments when it becomes conscious. Sisyphus, proletarian of the gods, powerless and rebellious, knows the whole extent of his wretched condition: it is what he thinks of during his descent. The lucidity that was to constitute his torture at the same time crowns his victory.[35]

The fact that the world is absurd and Sisyphus's labor is meaningless is only a starting point for Camus's development of his ideas about tragedy, which begins, according to him, with cognition. He finds the formula of the "absurd victory" in consciousness. Sisyphus's heroism stems from his conscious acceptance of his tragic and absurd fate and his ability to liberate himself from yearning for happiness: "If the descent is thus sometimes performed in sorrow, it can also take place in joy. . . . When the images of earth cling too tightly to memory, when the call of happiness becomes too insistent, it happens that melancholy rises in man's heart: this is the rock's victory, this is the rock itself. . . . But crushing truths perish from being acknowledged."[36] Tragedy and consciousness bring "victory" through the human ability to endorse and appreciate life, regardless of all its innumerable sufferings.

Camus thus quotes Oedipus's life-affirming words: "'Despite so many ordeals, my advanced age and the nobility of my soul make me conclude that all is well.' Sophocles' Oedipus, like Dostoevsky's Kirillov, thus gives the recipe for the absurd victory. Ancient wisdom confirms modern heroism."[37] What therefore makes both Sisyphus and the modern man heroic is the fact that despite their shared awareness of the absurdity of the universe and complete lack of hope, they nevertheless make the choice to see life as "good." Camus concludes:

> It teaches that all is not, has not been, exhausted. It makes of fate a human matter, which must be settled among men. All Sisyphus' silent joy is contained therein. His fate belongs to him. . . . The absurd man says yes and his effort will henceforth be unceasing. . . . I leave Sisyphus at the foot of the mountain! One always finds one's burden again. But Sisyphus teaches the highest fidelity that negates the gods and raises rocks. He too concludes that all is well. . . . The struggle itself toward the heights is enough to fill a man's heart. One must imagine Sisyphus happy.[38]

The same sensibility informs many of Chekhov's works, and especially his plays *Uncle Vania* and *The Three Sisters*. Vania, Sonia, and the three sisters' tragedy starts with the awakening of their consciousness—with their full awareness of the futility of their efforts, the inscrutability of life, the rejection of happiness, and the abandonment of all hopes and illusions. Their heroism commences with their conscious choice to endure, endorse, and appreciate life. Sonia's concluding monologue sums up her "absurd victory" very well, even if she uses rhetoric full of utopian and religious overtones.

> What can be done? We have to go on living! (*Pause.*)
>
> Uncle Vania, we shall live. We will live a long, long series of days, of long evenings; we will patiently bear the ordeals that fate will send us; we will labor for others now and in our old age, knowing no rest; but when our time comes, we will die humbly . . .

Poor, poor Uncle Vania, you're crying … (*Through tears.*) You've known
no joy in your life, but wait, Uncle Vania … We shall rest … (*Embraces him.*)
We shall rest! (13:115–16)

Sonia's references to the afterlife, angels, and "heaven in diamonds" could be
easily interpreted as the overblown religious rhetoric of a naïve young woman
whose exaggerated loftiness hinders the main thrust of her address to Vania
and the audience. However, Sonia is speaking the only language she knows,
using images available to her from her cultural environment. Even if she says
that she has faith and believes in a happy afterlife, these are evidently merely
words of consolation that she knows have nothing to do with reality. Sonia's
monologue is not about the promise of salvation in the afterlife. As far as reality is concerned, she has a lucid and sober view: there won't be happiness for
her or Vania; they will work with no end in sight; and instead of rest, they will
face suffering, tears, and bitterness. Stripped of all illusions, she nevertheless
says yes to life and instructs Vania to do the same. When she repeats her
incantation "we shall rest," she pronounces it in a "weary voice" and "through
tears," as Chekhov's stage directions indicate, while also wiping Vania's tears.

These stage directions make it impossible for the audience to take Sonia's
words at face value and believe that she believes in her own words about
rest. They can only trust in her determination to endure. Similar to Sisyphus,
who continues his struggle for the summit despite his knowledge that his
suffering has no end, Sonia finds purpose in her own perseverance and is
almost contented in her unhappiness. She even suggests that it is possible to
look at her present suffering with a smile. The quintessence of Sonia's concluding lines is not her despair and hopelessness, but her stoic affirmation
of life despite the futility of her efforts. As much as her rhetoric serves to
console and comfort, she insists that one must stand up and go on living. By
the end of the play, Vania and Sonia fully realize the futility of their work.
That is the moment in which their tragedy and their heroism begin.

The play's plot is centered on various attitudes toward work, and if it has
a peripetia, it has more to do with clashing understandings of labor than
with the narrative arcs of the characters' lives. Almost every dialogue in the
play deals with the problem of work versus idleness (although the weaker
motif of love is also present). On a superficial level, the characters are divided
into those who work (Sonia, Vania, Marina, and Astrov) and those who do
not. The two parties cannot live together and after an explosion must separate
and continue to live according to their own working habits. The play begins

with Voinitsky's crisis of belief, his realization that his labor has no meaning. Professor Serebriakov's visit serves specifically to reveal the meaninglessness of their work beyond tending to their daily needs. They can no longer deceive themselves with lofty ideals, "progressive thinking," "certain convictions," and the rhetoric of self-sacrifice. Vania's revolt is the result of his realization that he has lived in a state of perpetual illusion: "The past does not exist. It's been stupidly wasted on trifles, while the present is terrifying in its absurdity" (13:79). Serebriakov only lifts the veil and dispels these illusions. Both Sonia and Vania are profoundly unhappy and on the verge of despair, yet ultimately, much like Camus's Sisyphus, they find meaning in their work by applying themselves to it. Sonia thus admonishes Vania, trying to save him from suicide: "I may be just as unhappy as you are, but I don't give in to despair. I endure and will keep enduring until my life comes to an end on its own ... You must endure too" (13:109). She is trying to convince him to get up and continue pushing his own boulder up the mountain, regardless of the apparent absurdity and incomprehensibility of their existence. As discussed above, in "The Myth of Sisyphus," Camus claims "there is only one truly serious philosophical problem, and that is suicide." He suggests that the mind, "when it reaches its limits, must make judgment and choose its conclusions. This is where suicide and the reply stand."[39] Uncle Vania contemplates suicide precisely for this reason. Yet in this play, as elsewhere, Chekhov suggests a response to the absurd—the path of "recovery" through perseverance in spite of one's awareness of the void. Although the play's concluding scene creates a sense of absurdity, life nevertheless acquires meaning through the characters' efforts:

> VOINITSKY (Writes.): "February second vegetable oil twenty pounds ... February sixteenth another twenty pounds vegetable oil ... Buckwheat groats ..."
> (*Pause. The sound of harness bells.*)
> MARINA: He's gone!
> (*Pause.*)
> SONIA (*Returning, puts the candle on the table.*): He's gone ...
> VOINITSKY (*Checking over the accounts and making notations.*): Total ... fifteen ... twenty five ... (13:115)

Of course, there is nothing particularly uplifting or poetic about the monotony of their daily labor. This scene does not evoke a peaceful image of a prosaic paradise in which everyone is harmoniously engaged in work.[40] Voinitsky's work is mechanical and devoid of meaning. Undoubtedly, Voinitsky does not believe in any particular significance of "buckwheat groats" and "twenty pounds vegetable oil" even if taking care of his household is a necessity, and his disjointed registration in his notebook of dates and quantities intermingled with Sonia's and Marina's exclamations "He's gone!" creates a sense of sadness and absurdity for the audience. The play's concluding lines, "We shall rest," are no more convincing than the end of Sisyphus's suffering. Yet, in their perseverance through this endless and futile work, the characters ultimately find meaning and purpose. This purpose emerges precisely because they continue their work despite being conscious of its insignificance.

Everything seems as before in this last scene: all the characters return to their habitual activity—Telegin plays the guitar, Vania and Sonia check the accounts, Maria Vasilievna reads her progressive pamphlets, and Marina knits a stocking. The nurse Marina's comments in the beginning of act 4 suggest a return to "paradise lost": "We will live again, as it was, in the old way. Tea at eight o'clock in the morning, lunch at one o'clock, dinner in the evening; everything in its own order, as people do . . . in the Christian way" (13:106). In terms of external events, very little changes in the play—after a short, unsuccessful stay, the professor and his wife leave the estate, returning to their habitual lifestyle while life on the estate is as it was before—Vania and Sonia continue to work on the estate; Sonia is still in love with Astrov, who is still indifferent to her; Astrov continues his medical practice, plants trees, and drinks as before. The nature of change in the play is of a peculiar kind: it involves not only the loss of illusions but a shift in the concept of work. Not only is the ideology of work that motivated Voinitsky's service no longer tenable, but even traditional Christian attitudes toward work as a necessity, as exemplified by Marina, cannot satisfy the awakened consciousness of Vania and Sonia.

At the play's opening, we learn that Vania and Sonia view their labor as goal-oriented and work not only for simple sustenance but also as a form of service to a lofty idea. Voinitsky has been carried away by progressive ideas of the necessity of work and the concept of work and service as a calling. Significantly, his mother refers to his ideology-driven life as an example of progressivist thinking: "You were a man of certain convictions, an enlightened individual" (Ты был человеком определенных убеждений, светлой личностью; 13:70). As a member of the generation of the sixties, his mother completely absorbed the revolutionary and populist ideas about "activity" (*delo*) and female emancipation, worshipping the professor who inspired her with "sacred awe." Both the professor and Maria Vasilievna—the two characters inviting the least amount of sympathy from the audience—employ topical progressive rhetoric, emphasizing the superior value of *delo*, the motto of the liberal intelligentsia of the 1860s. Saying farewell to his hard-working relatives and the overworked country doctor, Astrov, the pompous Serebriakov gives them this piece of advice: "Gentlemen, one ought to commit to action" (Надо, господа, дело делать!; 13:112). Maria Vasilievna likewise dismisses Vania's complains about his wasted life and blames him for not "taking action": "You should've committed to action" (Нужно было дело делать; 13:70). Her reference to the "enlightened individual" or a "person of steadfast convictions" (*svetlaia lichnost'*) is a cliché of the time. In *The Devils*, Dostoevsky scathingly mocked these populist clichés, exposing their rhetoric as liberal sloganeering through his use of the expression *svetlaia lichnost'* in quotation marks and Pyotr Verkhovensky's reading of a notorious poem-pamphlet, with the phrase as its title.[41] Chekhov was very sensitive to these verbal clichés and used them to underscore the artificiality and unoriginality of Voinitsky's ideals. Voinitsky himself becomes irritated when this expression is applied to him. Moreover, Voinitsky embodies almost verbatim the dilemma outlined in Tolstoy's essay "Nedelanie," written some three years before Chekhov's play. In his response to Émile Zola's preaching of the unconditional value of science and work, Tolstoy formulates a predicament quite similar to that of Voinitsky in Chekhov's play:

> And therefore, wouldn't it be just as dangerous to follow the advice of Mr. Zola and to dedicate your life to serving that which in our time, in our world, is called science? What if I were to devote my life to the study of phenomena such as inheritance according to the teachings of Lombroso, or Koch's liquid, or fertilizing soil by means of worm activity, or Crookes's fourth state of matter etc., and all of a sudden I found out just before my death that what I had devoted my entire life to was silly, and perhaps even harmful, trivia, and I had only one life.[42]

Indeed, when he complains that he has been serving false ideas (not only false idols), Voinitsky also reveals that the ideology behind these ideas—not merely the fact that the professor did not meet his expectations of excellence—was itself misguided:

Now I'm forty-seven. Before last year, I was deliberately trying, just as you, to cloud my vision with this scholastics of yours, so as not to see real life,— and I thought was doing a good thing. And now, if you had the least idea! I don't sleep nights out of frustration, out of bitterness for having wasted my time so stupidly when I could have had everything that's being withheld from me now by my old age! (13:70)

This frustration of his arises from the fact that he has devoted his whole life to what he thought would serve knowledge: "Oh, how I've been cheated! I idolized that professor, that pathetic man with gout, I worked for him like an ox! . . . I was proud of him and his scholarship, I lived, I breathed for him! Everything he wrote and uttered seemed to me the words of genius . . . God, and now?" (13:80). This realization constitutes Vania's awakening and his return to consciousness as well as the main crisis that Chekhov puts onstage. Yet Vania still deludes himself into thinking that the professor, rather than his own misguided ideas about work and service, bears responsibility for his misery. He uses work as an escape, to avoid thinking about his own life. As previously discussed, in his essay "Non-Activity," whose title is an equally polemical reference to the liberal populist ideology of the 1860s, Tolstoy pointed out that work could sometimes be a form of escape, anesthetizing the pain of life: "in our wrongly organized society, [work] is primarily a morally anesthetic means, just like smoking or drinking wine, for hiding the wrongness and depravity of your life from yourself." For Vania work also seems to be a loophole through which one can avoid the pain of life. In his utter despair, when his idol has been stripped from its pedestal and when he begins to realize that it is up to him to decide how to live, that he must be his own master, he makes a last attempt to appeal to Astrov for help: "How can I live through those thirteen years? What will I do, how will I fill them? . . . To begin a new life . . . Tell me, how to begin . . . where to begin" (13:107–8). Astrov calmly advises him to discard all hope: "Ah, cut it out! What new life? Our condition, yours and mine, is hopeless" (13:108). Finally Vania is forced to acknowledge the hopelessness of his situation, but he also gives up on his plans for suicide. He returns to Sonia the poison he took from Astrov's medical kit and realizes that there is nothing for him to do but to continue his meaningless labor: "Here, take it! (*To Sonia.*) But we must start working quickly, do something quickly, or else I can't . . . I can't" (13:109).

Thus, what changes in the course of the play is the concept of work. Before the play's opening, work apparently seemed to Vania a meaningful and purposeful activity. For Sonia and Vania, taking care of the estate and sending the generated income to Professor Serebriakov and his wife was equivalent to serving the advancement of science. Through most of the play's action Vania rebels against what he now realizes was an illusion. Only at the very end of the play does he resign himself to his hopeless lot, fully aware of the meaninglessness of his work. "To do something"; "I have to quickly occupy myself with something . . . To work, to work!"—these phrases indicate that what matters for him is not the purpose of work but its process, which is what brings him solace. It is in this moment of lucidity that he becomes an "absurd hero" who has neither illusions nor hopes, but who is determined to work and to "push his boulder" forward, if only to see it roll back down the hill. For both Vania and Sonia, work becomes an unceasing and hopeless activity but one they choose voluntarily. "One always finds one's burden again," says Camus. Vania and Sonia will likewise find their burden again, find "something to do," as they put it. What may seem trivial from the outside—their preoccupation with twenty pounds of vegetable oil or buckwheat groats—now is filled with personal meaning for them, albeit without a higher purpose. Their work, stripped from any lofty goal, becomes absurd but also heroic. It also becomes tragic because, unlike the nurse Marina who is completely at peace with her daily travails, Sonia and Vania are fully conscious of the absurdity of their fate and their routine work. Marina's ideal of a working paradise, a healthy schedule and simple food, cannot be theirs. Vania's and Sonia's work is not a means to an end. Working on the estate is all they do and all they get to do. This has no intrinsic or extrinsic value for them, but they learn to embrace their purpose in life. Chekhov leaves his heroes "at the foot of the mountain," in the moment of their realization of the never-ending character of their efforts.

Most of Chekhov's mature plays end with what Camus calls "a lucid invitation to live and to create, in the very midst of the desert."[43] We find a similar sensibility informing the concluding scenes of *The Three Sisters*. Akin to Sisyphus, the sisters Prozorov are conscious of the absence of a higher meaning in their existence and the ultimate futility of their lives and their hard incessant work. Despite this, they nevertheless resolve to persevere. Life is still worth living for them on its own terms: "One ought to live . . . One ought to live. . . . one ought to live . . . one ought to work, only to work!" (13:187).

The Elusive Delights of the Brickworks: *The Three Sisters*

While many of Chekhov's plays deal with similar themes, they are replayed in different keys, thus creating a multifaceted treatment of larger philosophical and social problems through portrayals of individual fates and solutions. The cycle of his major plays emerges in segments of a larger dramatic whole. In *Uncle Vania*, Chekhov problematized the ideology of work as high service. In *The Three Sisters*, he addresses another aspect of the populist idealization of labor—a belief that work is good in and of itself, regardless of its type and its meaning—and shows that work separated from its ownership may lead to alienation.

Chekhov's *The Three Sisters*, along with some of his other plays and prose fiction, portrays the characters' craving for hard work and belief in its salvific power. They express many ideas that were catchphrases of the time, including Zola's appeal to work and the Russian progressivists' similarly passionate calls to join the labor force. At the opening of the play, the young Irina is exalted at the prospect of a life of hard labor. She naïvely and enthusiastically declares that she "knows how one must live" and has found an unexpected solution to life's mysteries—one must work as an ox to achieve happiness:

> Everything is clear to me in this world, I understand how one must live. Dear Ivan Romanych, I know everything. A person ought to work, to labor by the sweat of his brow, whoever he is, and only that constitutes the meaning and purpose of his life, his happiness, his ecstasy. How great it is to be a worker who gets up at the first signs of dawn and breaks stones on the road, or a shepherd, or a schoolteacher who teaches children, and a railway driver ... My God, it's even better not to be a human being, but be an ox, an ordinary horse, so long as you're working, rather than being a young woman who gets up at noon, drinks her coffee in bed, and then takes two hours to dress ... oh, how awful is this! (13:123)

Irina's ravings about the delights of hard work form a sharp contrast to Olga's opening remarks and complaints about work wearing her down. There is no doubt Chekhov does not intend for his audience to take Irina's words seriously, for a young woman's desire to be an ox or a horse cannot help but produce a comic effect. Moreover, she undermines the idea of conscious and meaningful work by referring to domestic animals as an enviable model, seemingly unaware that what distinguishes human work from animal work

is its purposefulness.[44] Evidently, she knows very little about the type of physical work she is craving; amusingly, she not only exalts hard labor but selects
the most laborious activities as her ideal, such as breaking stones or working at the railways. By expressing her unconditional admiration for working
in school, she also demonstrates a complete disregard for Olga's complaints
about the difficulties of being a schoolteacher. The audience, however, cannot miss these details. There are in fact two teachers in the play—Olga, who
teaches in a women's gymnasium, and Kulygin, Masha's husband. Neither of
them seems to particularly enjoy their jobs: both are exhausted, and Olga
laments her extreme fatigue throughout the play. Irina, however, continues
to rhapsodize about work as a solution to life's misery: "One ought to work,
to work. That's why we are unhappy, why we take such a dim view of life,
because we don't know what work is. We are born from people who despised
labor" (13:135). By act 2, Irina has assumed a position at a telegraph office
and become quickly disillusioned with her work, which renders her tired
and completely drained: "I'm so tired! . . . Finally, I'm home. . . . Have to rest.
I'm tired. . . . I'm tired. No, I don't like the telegraph office, I don't like it"
(13:144). Irina finds her job at the telegraph station dispiriting and dehumanizing. It has made her dramatically lose weight and caused her to become
insensitive and harsh to those around her. In one instance, she lashes out at
a woman seeking her help in sending a telegram and confesses that she was
rude to her for no reason. Although she believes that another position may
suit her better than working at the telegraph station, she confesses the need
for work that would not merely keep her busy but also engage her mind: "I
have to look for another job, this one's not for me. What I so wanted, what
I dreamt of is missing in this one. Work without poetry, without thought"
(13:114). In act 3 Irina becomes fully disillusioned with work. She not only
complains about work wearing her down but also views work as an alienating force stripping her of her identity and driving her to despair:

> I forget everything, every day I forget, and life goes on and won't ever, ever come
> back . . . Oh, I'm unhappy . . . I cannot work, I will not go on working. Enough,
> enough! I used to be a telegraph operator, now I work for the Town Council
> and I hate, despise whatever they give me to do . . . I've got nothing, nothing,
> no sort of satisfaction, while time marches on, and it seems I'm moving away
> from a genuine, beautiful life. . . . I'm desperate, I'm desperate! And why I'm still
> alive, why I haven't killed myself before now, I don't understand. . . . (13:166)

The alienating character of her work results in the loss of her sense of identity and genuine being. We do not need to interpret Irina's unhappiness in Marxian terms, as stemming from wage labor, which is frequently ungratifying, but Chekhov's critique is more tightly focused than Marx's: namely, work becomes a burden and leads to estrangement when it is devoid of personal meaning and purpose and lacks any element of creativity. Irina's confession is an indictment of the proletarian utopia that she shares with Tuzenbach. The idealization of hard work for its own sake is presented in the play as merely a naïve popular ideology embraced by the Russian liberal intelligentsia, an ideology completely detached from real life that does not consider the working conditions of the working class and the alienating forms of labor in contemporary capitalist society.

Significantly, the ideological aspect of Irina's fascination with work did not escape the attention of Chekhov's contemporaries. In his essay "Drama of Mood: *The Three Sisters*" (1905), from the collection *Kniga otrazhenii*, Innokenty Annensky insightfully observed this aspect of Irina, claiming that she is essentially in love with work:

> Irina is as pure and generous as her sisters, she is as touchingly noble, but she needs neither family as does Olga, nor love, that is, life, as does Masha; she needs, you see, *work*. . . . You see, this won't be simply work, from which one gets hollow cheeks and gray hair, and in addition to that gradually,—what a pleasure!—it will be some form of a perpetual sacrifice, a pink fire, on which Irina would burn down every day, but would get reborn at night in order to burn down again . . . Love! . . . However, you know, love, marriage—all of this is secondary. The main thing for her, Irina, will be work—not at the telegraph station, not at the City Council—pfui!—but necessarily in the school, and not in some kind silly gymnasium, where everything is so ordinary, blue and banal, but in a school that would be sort of a temple, where work is akin to ecstasy, to prayer, and to renunciation.[45]

Yet perhaps Irina is in fact not so much in love with work as she is with the idea of work.

Irina is not the only character in the play who idealizes hard manual labor. Her fiancé, Tuzenbach, engages in this same utopian and out-of-touch perception of work, telling Irina how much he longs to work. He passionately criticizes idleness and extols the value of hard work:

> The longing for work, oh God, how well I understand it! I've never worked
> in my life. I was born in St. Petersburg, cold and idle Petersburg, in a family
> that did not know work or hardship. . . . The time has come; there's a huge
> mass looming over us, there is a robust and powerful storm lying in wait, it's
> coming, it's already near, and soon it will blow all the laziness, indifference,
> prejudice against labor, rotten boredom out of our society. I shall work, and in
> some twenty-five or thirty years everyone will be working. Every single per-
> son! (13:123)

This paean to physical labor has distinct revolutionary overtones, alluding
to major social change and possibly even a proletarian revolution. Tuzenbach
evokes a socialist and democratic rhetoric, with its emphasis on economic
and political equality, the abolition of capitalist exploitation, the redistribu-
tion of wealth, and the reevaluation of labor practices. Tuzenbach may have
a naïve view of the inherent value of labor, which Chekhov subtly underscores
by mentioning that Tuzenbach has in fact never worked and therefore does
not really know what hard labor is. Yet he clearly expresses the radical intelligentsia's discontent with forms of social and economic exploitation that
characterized the newly industrializing Russia. He advances the populist
belief that wealth is created by the working classes and is wrongfully appro-
priated by the rich, who benefit disproportionately from underpaid labor.
He believes in the necessity of measures to carry out the reorganization of
society, making production serve the producers and hoping to bring about
a better society through the voluntary efforts of people of good will.

Yet for all his idealization of labor, Tuzenbach seems to be completely
oblivious to the often inhumane conditions of work in the new factories.
As is clear from Chekhov's prose and letters, the author himself was fully
aware of the nascent industrial sector's dark sides, including pollution, the
high mortality rate of workers, and the overall poor quality of life. He was
very concerned about the wretched conditions under which the new working class was laboring. Tuzenbach, however, articulates an ideology that Chekhov exposes as utopian and naïve, albeit without dismissing it outright.
Indeed, Tuzenbach's rhetoric, as well as that of Vershinin, is future oriented,
and his "philosophy" of work serves the goal of building an ideal life some-
time in the remote future: "Many years from now, you say, life on earth will
be beautiful, exquisite. That's true. But in order to take part in it now, even
from afar, one ought to prepare for it, one ought to work" (13:132). Even though
the characters in the play do not respond to his remark and Vershinin instead

speaks about the flowers in the room, Tuzenbach insists on his lofty idea of work: "Yes, one ought to work. Perhaps you are thinking: this German just got sentimental" (13:132). Tuzenbach probably hopes to be as effective and disciplined a worker as his German literary predecessor, Goncharov's Stolz, but he turns out to be only an idealistic dreamer. When Tuzenbach decides to quit his military service and start "working," it becomes apparent that work for him is a form of escape from life: "I'll be working. If only one day in my life to work so much that when I return back home at night, I would collapse on my bed exhausted, and fall asleep in an instant" (13:147–48). It seems strange that his ideal here is not fulfilling and productive work, but a numbing activity intended to wear him down physically so that he can fall asleep. That is why physically challenging work in particular appeals to him. Tuzenbach's pathos, however, is continuously undermined, either by the lack of attention on the part of other characters or by their humorously dismissive remarks. When he declares that after much deliberation he has finally come to the decision that he should work, Solyonyi responds with a reference to Pushkin's Byronic hero Aleko and Rachmaninov's opera: "Contain your wrath, Aleko . . . Forget, forget your dreams" (13:151). Tuzenbach's decision to engage in hard labor appears merely as a naïve, romantic dream. The absurdity of this dream is further underscored by the nonsensical conversation that follows his remarks—the non sequitur between Solyonyi and Chebutykin arguing about the difference between *cheremsha* (wild garlic) and *chekhartma* (a Caucasian lamb stew). Does Tuzenbach understand what work is any better that Chebutykin and Solyonyi understand each other or the difference between wild garlic and lamb stew?

Not only does Tuzenbach share Irina's naïve dreams about work; he also, like her, contemplates the most strenuous labor possible. Significantly, of all the possible options for a job, he chooses the hardest one, a brick factory: "I'm so tired, though . . . The brick factory . . . I'm not raving, as a matter of fact I'll be going to the brick factory soon, I'll start working there . . . There's been some talk about it already. . . . Oh, come away with me, come away to work together! (13:164). The brickworks, hardly the most romantic lure for a young woman, are the object of his strange obsession. In fact, factories and plants are recurrent background settings for Chekhov's plays and stories, pointing to the new, rapidly industrializing character of Russian life.[46] The brickworks were apparently quite economically profitable enterprises, and even Chekhov's own sister tried to convince him to invest in the Moscow brickworks (P 8:108, 439). Although Chekhov did not dismiss this potentially profitable investment, in his fiction these factories or plants in most cases evoked images of inhospitable work conditions and pollution, even when mentioned only in passing, as in "Gooseberries": "There was a river, but water in it was the color of coffee, because on the one side of the estate there was a brickworks, on the other—the bone-black plant" (10:60). Likewise, in "Steppe," Chekhov's reference to brickworks hardly evokes any romantic associations: "And beyond the cemetery the brickworks were smoking. Thick, black smoke came in large puffs from under the long reedy roofs, flattened to the ground, and lifted lazily upward. The sky above the factories and the cemetery was darkened, and large shadows from the puffs of smoke crept across the field and across the road. People and horses moved in the smoke near the rooftops, covered in red dust" (7:15). The brick factory also figures ominously at the end of "In the Ravine," as an emblem of incipient Russian capitalism and the ruthless exploitation of the peasants by unscrupulous predators, such as Aksinia: Aksinia's business prospers at the expense of poor peasant women who "cart the bricks to the station and load the wagons and earn a quarter-ruble a day for it," with their faces covered with "red brick dust" (8:9). Why, then, would Tuzenbach dream about going to the brickworks? Although financially advantageous, the brickworks certainly did not carry the reputation of a rewarding place of work. We might recall Dostoevsky's narrator from *The House of the Dead*, Gorianchikov, who specifically refers to the brickworks as the hardest form of labor.[47] It is therefore obvious that Tuzenbach is motivated not so much by the particular merits of working at the brickworks (nor do we get the sense that he is motivated by financial considerations) as by the ideology of hard labor. The brick factory stands as a symbol of this ideologically motivated labor for him. As discussed previously, Innokenty Annensky identified this symbolic aspect of the brickworks in the play, pointing out that it reflected a particular liberal ideology of the dreamy Russian intelligentsia. He thus paraphrases Tuzenbach's assumed stream of thought:

Oh, I'm so happy. I'm going to the brickworks ... Down with all this glitter ... Irina, aren't you going with me? You say you do not love me yet. But you already have trust in me, haven't you? ... Listen, you'll love not me but the brickworks ... No, not even the brickworks, this is nonsense, but the school—this is higher, more elegant than the brickworks—the school. ... But the school will be nearby, by the brickworks, and I'll be also there near you, you will allow it, won't you? Oh poor descendent of the knights of the Baron von Tuzenbach-Krone-Altschauer. He never was able to see what the brick-works were like.[48]

In his essay on *The Three Sisters*, Annensky further observes that Tuzenbach's dreams and his "philosophy" of work are in fact very Russian and quite typical of the Russian intelligentsia of the time: "But he should not have, this poor baron, so ardently tried to convince us that he was a real Russian and could not even speak German. What could be more Russian that these eternal brickworks, this salvific *tomorrow*. . . . Some people need Moscow, some need the brickworks. If only one could close one's eyes and not live."[49] Yet as much as Tuzenbach clings to his fantasy of hard work, it is obvious that he no longer fully believes in the "joys of hard labor." When he nostalgically recalls Irina's rhapsodizing over hard work, he admits that he views this dream differently now: "I look at you now and recall how once, a long time ago, on your name day, you were cheerful, happy and talked of the joys of hard labor ... And what a happy life flashed before me then! Where is it?" (13:165). Despite her disillusionment with hard work, the desperate Irina decides to join Tuzenbach at the brick factory (13:175). Accepting Tuzenbach's proposal even though she does not love him, Irina once again lulls herself into believing in her old illusions: "And suddenly, just as if my soul grew wings, I cheered up, I felt relieved and once again I started wanting to work, to work" (13:176). The play ends with Tuzenbach's death in a duel and Irina's resolution to go on working, even if she has to do it by herself: "one ought to live, one ought to work, nothing but work! Tomorrow I'll go away by myself, I'll teach in school and I'll give my whole life to those who may possibly need it. It's autumn now, soon there will be winter, everything will be covered up with snow, and I shall work, I shall work" (13:187).

The writer and translator Boris Zaitsev, a younger contemporary of Chekhov's, made a series of interesting comments about the enthusiasm for work displayed by Irina, Tuzenbach, and other like-minded characters in Chekhov's play:

Nevertheless there is something a bit overdone about *The Three Sisters*. Irina, Vershinin, and Tuzenbach are the most strained. All these "we shall work," "we shall start a new life, "in two or three hundred years" exist separately [from the rest of the play]. Chekhov, through his subordinates, expresses his own wishes, thoughts and observations ... sometimes they evoke a bitter chuckle now. ("Nowadays there are no tortures, no executions, no invasions"—in *those* times there were none indeed.) Chekhov did not turn out to be a prophet, and in general, Tuzenbach cannot be believed. Not one word of his belongs to him; similarly, it's impossible to believe Irina's excitement as she is about to move to a brick factory in order "to work" with a man she does not love.[50]

Although Zaitsev is mistaken in seeing the utopian ruminations of Tuzenbach, Irina, and Vershinin as Chekhov's own hidden wishes and ideals, he correctly identifies the artificiality in their rhetoric. Their ideas were in fact the popular slogans of the Russian liberal intelligentsia of the time. In many of his stories and novellas (especially "My Life"), Chekhov's characters discuss manual hard labor and the moral aspects of work. Capitalist exploitation, new forms of capitalist enslaving, social injustice in the distribution of labor and wages, the necessity of work for all classes (including the gentry), and the abolition of social privileges—all these topics inform many of the arguments and conversations of the Russian intelligentsia in Chekhov's works. Chekhov clearly responds not only to new social movements, including the intelligentsia's attempt to join the peasants and even the proletarians in their hard labor to correct social injustice, but also to the rhetorical and utopian aspects of these ideologies. Indeed, when at the end of the play Irina frames her incantation "I shall work, I shall work" in terms of the endless changing of seasons, it becomes clear that work for her is a form of resignation, which she views as a necessity rather than a lofty ideal. The audience has no reason to believe that Irina will find being a schoolteacher at the brickworks more fulfilling than her work as a telegraphist or her job in the Town Council, both of which drove her to despair. Thus, with its multiple characters who, on the one hand, crave work and indulge in utopian dreams about the meaningfulness and satisfaction of the working life and, on the other, are crushed by their work and as a result suffer from despair and the loss of identity, the play questions the meaning of hard work as a goal in and of itself. Alienation or separation from one's own work is a major problem that concerned Chekhov, who engaged with polemics about work's moral value and meaning in his sober and balanced way. Moreover, Irina's "I shall work, I shall work" appears as a form of Sisyphean labor, endless and meaningless. Chekhov's heroes ask the same question Camus's would later ask: if work has no meaning and life seems absurd, why live? The three sisters' "if only we could know" represents a passionate and desperate yearning for an answer to this question. Their quest for knowledge, combined with their awareness of the world's incomprehensibility, is the source of their drama.

Ultimately Irina, much like Sonia and Voinitsky before her and Camus's Sisyphus after, realizes the futility and endlessness of her sufferings. But the three sisters also stoically accept their lot, choosing to be masters of their fate: "One ought to live." The sisters do not know the meaning of their suffering and are aware of the repetitiveness and futility of their work and the work of those who would follow in their footsteps. Regardless, they resolve "to live." Irina's fiancé dies; Masha's lover leaves with the military battery, the sisters are stripped of any hopes of returning to Moscow and of their illusions of the salvific power of work. They stay alone "to begin … life anew" (13:187). Their predicament is indeed similar to Sisyphus descending the steep hill in order to begin his futile work again. They listen to the music of the military band playing in the distance and believe it to be cheerful and joyful.

Although Chekhov shows little sympathy for people who do nothing, as well as for those whose work is motivated by ideological considerations or delusions of grandeur (such as Serebriakov, who considers himself to be the only one who truly works), his hard workers do not necessarily achieve happiness through their labor, even if they invite respect and compassion. Moreover, they frequently appear dispirited, alienated, and even dehumanized. Thus, with all his dedication to his medical practice and admirable environmental work protecting the forests, Doctor Astrov confesses that he is unhappy, feels hopeless, and is unable to love anyone: "I work, as you know, as no one else in this district, fate beats me constantly, at times I suffer unbearably, but in the distance there is no light for me. I no longer expect anything for myself, I don't love people … For a long time now I've loved no one" (13:84). Although he blames Elena for idleness—"others work for her … Am I right? And a life of idleness cannot be pure" (13:83)—there is no evidence that his own life is any "purer." He is a drunkard, after all, and admits that his personality has changed, and that he has lost his true identity through hard work. We see the image of a man who is frustrated and even depressed, precisely as a result of his incessant work:

> In ten years I've turned into another man. And what's the reason? I've been working too hard, Nanny. … In all the time we've known one another, I haven't had a single day off. Why wouldn't I grow old? Besides, life itself is dull, silly, filthy … my feelings somehow became numb. There's nothing I want, nothing I need, no one I love. (13:63–64)

A simple opposition between "idlers" and "workers" turns out to be illusory and insufficient to answer questions about the role of work in human life. Chekhov's characters create themselves and their world through work—this is evident in the cases of Astrov, Sonia, and Vania from *Uncle Vania*; Nina Zarechnaia from *The Seagull*; and Olga and Irina from *The Three Sisters*. But if human work creates human beings, then it also destroys them. Chekhov's characters struggle to assert their identity through work, but often their work is only a palliative that makes life tolerable but cannot truly address their alienation. His most "heroic" characters—Nina Zarechnaia, Sonia, and the three sisters at the end of the play—are aware of their struggles in life and keep pushing through them, bringing about a form of existential "victory," even if this victory may seem more like resignation. Since most sources of alienation stemming from waged work and uncreative labor are ineradicable, they can do no more than lucidly confront them and stoically persevere through this somber state, trying to cope with it as best as they can. Although unhappy in her personal life, Nina Zarechnaia is perhaps the only character able to experience joy in her work, because for her work is a self-realization of her personality, a freely chosen vocation, not alienated labor.

While most of his characters engage in this discourse on work and participate in its polemic, for Chekhov ideas and theories matter less than experience. This is why he focuses not on how his characters resolve questions of the meaning and role of work in their conversations but on how work presents itself in actual experience, regardless of the theory or ideology of work the characters may adhere to. Just as we cannot say what life is apart from our own personal experience of it, we cannot identify the significance of work apart from personal experiences. That is why Chekhov chooses his multiperspectival approach in dealing with larger social and philosophical questions. He returns to these questions time and again in various contexts, forming clusters or cycles of texts unified by the same theme.

While acknowledging the fundamental role of work in humankind's moral development, Chekhov has no illusions regarding the unconditional value of labor. It may be a fact of life that the human being is a *homo laborans* and that work is a necessary precondition of existence. But work divorced from an understanding of the meaning of life, from its ontological foundations, becomes absurd, dehumanizing, and oppressive. Moreover, our humanness is shaped not only by incessant work, devoid of creativity, freedom, and ownership, which may turn the individual into an ox (as in Irina's naïve dream), but also by our ability to indulge in purposeless pursuits and pure play. In this sense, idleness appears not as a morally compromised state but as a humane and humanizing form of being, offering real freedom. As Chekhov wrote in a letter to Suvorin quoted earlier in this chapter, "my favorite occupation is to collect that which is not needed (leaves, straw, etc.) and to do that which is useless." The opposite of work, then, is not only idleness understood as passivity and non-activity,[51] but the more indolent pleasures of artistic creation and leisure involving non-goal-directed activity, such as a play. This navigation between *homo laborans* and *homo ludens*, between the realm of necessity and the realm of freedom, was Chekhov's way to assert his humanity—to be a doctor, a writer, and a "catcher of sunbeams."

6

The Three Sisters

Being as Event

Chekhov treats philosophy and philosophizing with recognizable irony in both his prose and dramatic works. As discussed in chapter 1, Chekhov was skeptical of the tendency among Russian authors (particularly Tolstoy and Dostoevsky) to use their literary works to engage in "theoretical" or "philosophical" discussions. This does not mean, however, that as an artist Chekhov distanced himself from the philosophical concerns of his time. Indeed, the opposite was true. Without trying to turn Chekhov into a philosopher, I propose that some aspects of his oeuvre are better understood or described through the prism of twentieth-century existentialist thought. To a large extent I see Chekhov as engaging philosophical ideas and inquiries that placed human existence, or *conditio humana*, at the center of attention.[1] Although it would be futile to draw any specific parallels between his philosophical views and any particular philosophy, Chekhov's play *The Three Sisters* undoubtedly reveals Chekhov's probing into the questions of being, the human condition, and temporality that will be at the center of twentieth-century thought, particularly as reflected in the ontology of Heidegger.

Although the terms "existential" or "existentialist" have been applied to Chekhov, the specifically existentialist aspects of his oeuvre have not been sufficiently explored.[2] I consider *The Three Sisters* to be a drama of human existence, or Dasein, to use Heidegger's term for a being that is capable of ontology, or of comprehending properties of the very fact of its own being.[3] Chekhov's interest in the question of being leads him to a particular concept of event as an unfolding of being in its temporality. Chekhov considers the temporal aspect of being and the ontological essence of time—that is, precisely the theme that would become the center of attention in the

164

existentialist philosophy of the twentieth century. The question of our being in the world, which I see as the central issue of the play, is presented by Chekhov with respect to time and temporality and results in a peculiar notion of event. Many of Chekhov's dramaturgical innovations stem from his very modern concept of time, being, and event. In my discussion of *The Three Sisters*, I use some of Heidegger's terms and categories as a convenient tool for describing Chekhov's implicit artistic philosophy.

Ontic and Ontological Events

In his dramaturgy, Chekhov avoided situations that in our common language we refer to as "events" (understood in the narrow sense of the word, as things taking place), such as murders, suicides, earthquakes, thunderstorms, hiccups, weddings, births, and so forth. However, it would be a mistake to claim that these sorts of events are absent in Chekhov's plays.[4] They are not, but they differ functionally from the way they are treated in classical drama.[5] People, as Chekhov insisted, do not shoot each other, make love declarations, or say intelligent things on a daily basis. Chekhov associated traditional "events" with mere "happenings" or "accidents" and as such treated them as detracting from a true understanding of human nature and the laws of life. Boris Zingerman makes a valid observation that "drama in Chekhov is to be found not so much in the event but in time, in that which takes place between the events." He further argues: "In ancient classical drama, time as a rule was measured by events, it revealed itself through events; if there were no events, then there was no sense of temporal movement . . . In Chekhov, by contrast, the movement of time is particularly perceptible in the area that normally was associated with stagnant immobility. . . . Pauses, as is well known, acquire special significance in Chekhov."[6] Zingerman then draws the radical conclusion that "being and event in Chekhov are worlds apart" (*bytie i sobytie u Chekhova razvedeny v raznye storony*).[7] It would be a simplification, however, to say that Chekhov merely prefers daily life to extraordinary events and the portrayal of the drudgery of monotonous quotidian existence to dramatic or heroic situations, as the Russian scholar seems to suggest. There is no question that Chekhov, like Maeterlinck, was responsive to the tragedy of the everyday. Yet the center of his attention is not the monotony of life per se but the question of what constitutes authentic being. It is for this reason, I believe, that he juxtaposes not so much the ordinary and the extraordinary but the *ontic* and the *ontological*. Concerned as he was with the central question of being and man's place in the world,

Chekhov differentiated between ontic events, or "plain facts," and an onto-logical event—that is, an event of being, which deals with the nature or properties of being.

Clearly, Chekhov rejected the notion of event that dominated the historical sciences, the idea that history comprises a multitude of events, of fragments of the past, or happenings, that deviate from normal everyday life and therefore belong to history. For Chekhov, these fragments of the past do occur, but they constitute "facts" that tell us little about the nature of our being. Chekhov's thought is more in line with the philosophical discourse of the twentieth century that reconsidered the notion of an event-happening as not having any ontological foundation and focused instead on the *event of being*—that is, the self-recognition of being in time.

Chekhov fully realized that most plots are constructed based on these sorts of event-happenings. But if the event is understood not as an excess (something violating the ordinary), not as a happening, but as an event of being, then the plot will have to be of a different sort. Fully aware of the fact that playwrights cannot dispense entirely with events in the narrow sense of the word (that is, as something that lies at the core of the fabula), Chekhov created an original dramatic form based on the interplay of the two types of events.

Chekhov scholars have pointed out that his plays seem to have a kind of double structure.[8] In his excellent analysis of *The Three Sisters*, Timothy Wiles has distinguished between the plot events (which take place for the most part offstage) and the action of the play, which emerges out of minor incidents from daily life that are not necessarily caused by plot events. He suggested that two large actions control the play's plot and that the events of both take place offstage, while the audience sees onstage only the results of these actions in characters' activities. These two actions form a tension between change and stasis. On the one hand, there is action that brings about change (such as Natasha's gradual eviction of the sisters from the house). On the other hand, through the workings of the other action, everything stays the same: the garrison comes and goes but leaves the lives of the sisters unchanged; Masha stays with her husband; Olga remains unmarried; and none of the sisters is any closer to Moscow at the end than at the beginning.[9] It has also been observed that Chekhov's plots often represent reworkings of stock melodrama plots.[10] Indeed, the external melodramatic structure of his plays is based on plots that depend on ontic events. However, the inner, ontological aspects of his plays are related to these external events only in an indirect way. The *factical* events—Tuzenbach's death in the duel, Serebriakov's departure, Treplev's suicide, the fire, the departure of the officers from the town—have little impact on the lives of the characters and are not even perceived by the characters themselves as significant events that lead to change.

The life of Irina in *The Three Sisters* and all her inner problems and torments are not connected with the loss of her fiancé, Tuzenbach. Furthermore, the fire in the town or even Natasha's eviction of the sisters from the house do not seem to change anything or to have any significance for the characters' inner lives. Neither the play's heroes nor its audience perceive these events as significant turning points leading to a denouement. The three sisters' most important concerns hardly depend on the external plot events at all.

If the event is understood as something that generates change, then these events—fire, duels, death—do not seem to generate change and are not, therefore, events in the ontological sense. The audience's interest in these factual events is also minimal. Chekhov juxtaposes these ontic events to the ontological event, or the event of being, which he portrays as the drama of the human condition.[11] I would like to focus in particular on Chekhov's portrayal of life as self-realization and to link his preoccupation with being and temporality to his existentialist ontology. The question of the understanding of being is inseparable from the way time is presented in the play and perceived by various characters. The meaning of being is intimately bound up with the phenomenon of temporality. In other words, the central question of the play—about how we understand the meaning of life—is presented in its temporality and relations to past, present, and future. Scholars have observed the importance of the theme of knowledge in Chekhov's play, on the one hand, and the theme of time, on the other, but they have not treated these themes as interconnected.[12] If viewed from the perspective of Heideggerian ontology, the play's preoccupation with the problem of time and understanding cohere into the central problem of human Dasein. I will focus now in particular on how the questions of understanding and knowledge are connected in Chekhov's play with the problem of the human condition and humanity, on the one hand, and time, on the other.

BEING AND UNDERSTANDING

An understanding of the meaning of being in its temporality and its potentiality is at the very center of *The Three Sisters*. The primary focus of the play is the problem of existence and human beings' understanding of their place in the universe and connection with others. The fundamental questions of human beings' being and authentic existence are not presented through external events but through a series of leitmotifs and philosophical debates that take place onstage. These problems are conveyed through the leitmotif of knowledge, emerging in various references to knowledge and understanding and the recurrent phrase "if only we knew."

Chekhov's characters should be viewed as "voices" in a choir creating a sense of profound dialogicality (see the discussion in chapter 4). No one individual can be interpreted as the "hero" of the play or the single representative of Chekhov's own ideas. Chekhov always retains an authorial distance from his characters. At the same time, almost all of them contribute to a search for truth and may express ideas that might be close to Chekhov's own. One and the same theme may be refracted in lines spoken by very different characters. Radislav Lapushin aptly refers to this peculiarity of Chekhov's characterization as "singlevoicedness of the protagonists that threatens to be monotonous" (*chrevatoe monotonnost'iu edinogolosie protagonistov*).[13] Indeed, Chekhov's characters are not necessarily juxtaposed to each other but flow into each other. Curiously, the three sisters almost merge into a kind of unity and are frequently referred to as "sisters" even when they speak about themselves.

Almost without exception and compulsively, the characters make statements about knowing or not knowing. I will skip most of the references to knowledge and understanding and mention only a few examples that explicitly endow the theme of understanding and knowledge with existential overtones. At the play's center of attention is existential understanding, an understanding of the ontological structures of existence. At the opening of the play, Irina claims that she knows everything: "When I woke up today, got out of bed and washed myself, it suddenly seemed to me that everything is clear in the world and that I know how one ought to live. My dear, Ivan Romanych, I know everything" (13:123). Her thoughts about knowledge and understanding are first presented in a seemingly insignificant way: "I don't know why my heart feels so light!" (13:120). A little later she repeats her question: "Tell me why am I so happy today? . . . Why is that? Why?" (13:122). It seems somewhat strange that a young girl would so obsessively repeat the question "why" with respect to her own emotions. But as the conversation continues, it becomes obvious that the problem of "why," of knowledge and understanding of the meaning of life and our place in the world, is not casual talk but something that lies at the very core of the sisters' preoccupations. After all, their own last name, Prozorov (*prozret'* means to gain insight), is symbolic of their striving for knowledge, for insight. The quest for knowledge and understanding is explicitly connected not with Irina's personal feelings and her personal happiness but with existential concerns, with the question of being in the world. Therefore, Irina speaks not about herself but about *chelovek* (human beings) in general:

> A person [*chelovek*] ought to work, to labor by the sweat of his brow, whoever he is, and only that constitutes the meaning and purpose of his life, his happiness, his ecstasy.... My God, it's even better not to be a human being, but be an ox, an ordinary horse, so long as you're working, rather than being a young woman who gets up at noon, drinks her coffee in bed, and then takes two hours to dress... oh, how awful is this! (13:123)

Irina discusses here what it means to be human and suggests that to be an idle young woman is worse than being an ox because an unenlightened, meaningless existence cannot be viewed as authentic. The leitmotif of being and understanding gradually acquires increasingly existential overtones.

The first time all the major characters get together they engage in a conversation about the meaning of life and the limits of knowledge, a conversation that is first introduced casually, in a low key, as a parody of the laws of logic—with reference to a train station. Significantly, the two characters don't consider the question about the absence of the train station in practical ethical terms—as a sign of Russian technological backwardness that needs to be acted upon—but as an abstract theoretical issue. To Vershinin's melancholic remark "only it is strange that the train station is twenty versts away... And nobody knows why that is," Solyonyi eagerly responds, "I know why that is. (*Everybody stares at him.*) Because if the train station were nearby, it wouldn't be far away, and if it is far away, that means it is not nearby. (*Awkward silence*)" (13:128). Solyonyi expresses here in a parodic way one of the fundamental laws of logic. Through Solyonyi, Chekhov parodies any attempt at resolving questions of human existence by way of logic alone. Vershinin tries to correct Solyonyi's reductionist approach to life and frames the conversation in existential terms:

> And the interesting thing is that now we have absolutely no way of knowing what will be considered lofty and important and what petty and ridiculous. Didn't the discoveries of Copernicus or, say, Columbus at first appear to be useless, ridiculous, while some inane nonsense written by a crank appeared

as the truth? And it may so happen that our current life with which we recon-cile ourselves now in time will seem strange, uncomfortable, unintelligent, insufficiently pure, and may be even sinful. (13:128–29)

Vershinin speaks here about the relativity of truth and the limits of knowl-edge. He links the notion of truth with an act of interpretation and an analysis of one's consciousness. An event acquires the status of event and an incident acquires the status of truth only through interpretation. The knowing sub-ject and the object of knowledge form a certain unity. Vershinin's story of the French minister who noticed birds only from the window of his prison further supports this notion of the unity of consciousness and being: "With what intoxication and excitement he recalls the birds he saw through the prison window, which he did not notice before when he was a minister. Of course, now that he is released and free, he no longer notices birds, just as before. Likewise, you won't notice Moscow once you are living there" (13:149). True being, or authentic existence, according to this position, can only be fully conscious being: "I often think: what if one could begin life anew, this time fully consciously? If one life, which has already been lived, were as if a rough draft, and the other one—a final copy!" (13:132). Once again, uncon-scious existence is differentiated from true being.

References to knowledge and understanding punctuate the entire play. In act 2, we first overhear Masha's words addressed to Vershinin. Her lines directly follow their entrance onstage: "I do not know. (*Pause*) I do not know. Of course, habit means a lot" (13:142). What starts as casual small talk grad-ually evolves into a conversation about the purpose of life and the problem of the meaninglessness of existence. Masha articulates the necessity of a link between human existence and understanding: "It seems to me, a man ought to have faith or search for faith; otherwise his life is empty, empty . . . To live and not to know why cranes fly, why children are born, why stars are in the sky . . . Either you know why you live, or else nothing matters, all the same" (13:147). Masha's words are spoken in response to Tuzenbach's acquiescent attitude toward the mystery of life. Tuzenbach accepts life as it is, with its immutable laws, with the mystery and unjustifiable suffering and death that come with life:

Not just in two or three hundred years, but even in a million years from now, life will remain the same as it has always been; it does not change, it remains constant, governed by its own laws, which are none of your business or, at least, which you will never know. Birds of passage, cranes, for instance, fly on and on, and whatever thought, lofty or petty, may drift in their heads, they will keep on flying and will never know what for or where to. They fly and will keep on flying, whatever philosopher may emerge among them; and let them philosophize as they wish, so long as they keep on flying. (13:147)

Tuzenbach includes human beings in the same realm as cranes or phenomena such as snow and does not, therefore, differentiate between beings and being in the ontological sense. Masha, however, concludes that if one does not know why one lives, then "nothing matters" (*vse pustiaki, tryn-trava*); she thereby connects questions of epistemology to ontology.

Chekhov's characters recognize that Truth may be inaccessible to thought. Yet the meaning of human life lies precisely in striving to transcend the limits of knowledge and penetrate the realm of Truth. The meaning of being is in conscious being.[14] Masha is preoccupied precisely with the being of human beings thinking about their being. That is why she dismisses Tuzenbach's refusal to differentiate between being as a state of having existence and individual human beings, as implied in his words: "Meaning ... Here, there is snow falling. What is the meaning of it?" (13:147). Snow does not think about its snow-ness, its existence, its being. But Masha insists on the need to understand. Understanding, thinking about one's being, is what makes us human—this thought penetrates the philosophical core of the play.

The ideas expressed in the above conversation and in *The Three Sisters* in general anticipate the way existentialist thought establishes a connection between being and understanding. Considering various modes of being (existentialia), Heidegger discusses human understanding, consciousness, and thinking as a person's being. The understanding discloses to the Dasein "for the sake of what" it exists. Things and persons and one's being in the world gain their significance from a dominant purpose or aim. We understand ourselves to exist only in respect to our understanding of the meaning of life. Human existence is meaningless unless we are capable of understanding its meaning.

This notion of being as conscious being is what connects Chekhov's philosophical outlook to Heideggerian ontology. Understanding as a mode of existing is a guiding concept for Heidegger. For Heidegger, "Understanding of being is itself a determination of the being of Dasein [*Seinsverständnis ist selbst eine Seinsbestimmtheit des Daseins*]. The ontic distinction of Dasein lies in the fact that it *is* ontological."[15]

The characters in *The Three Sisters* are preoccupied precisely with the problems of being and understanding of being. These problems constitute the inner skeleton of the play. The entire action of the play is subordinated to the characters' discussion of the search for the meaning of life and for an understanding of one's place in the universe. That is why the play culminates in Olga's words about the meaning of existence: "And it looks like just a little while longer and we shall know why we live, why we suffer . . . If only one could know, if only one could know!" Hers are also the final words of the play: "If only one could know, if only one could know! *Curtain*" (13:188).

The play seems to suggest that understanding of one's place in being is the truth of being. It is in this sense that *The Three Sisters* is a drama of Dasein. Being for Chekhov as well as for Heidegger is the being of humans thinking about their being. Significantly, in Chekhov's play, Natasha is the only character who is not concerned with the problem of being, for she is entirely immersed in the world of things. In a sense, she loses contact with true being. That is why Andrei refers to her not as human but as a human animal. His words about her may sound strangely harsh, but they point to the essential link between human being and consciousness: "A wife is a wife. She is honest, decent, and, oh well, kind, but at the same time there is something in her that degrades her to a petty, blind, and sort of bristly animal. In any case, she is not a human being" (13:178). According to Heidegger, understanding is itself an event in which being is revealed through Dasein. It is precisely this kind of ontological event that lies at the core of *The Three Sisters*. If being is understood as event, time is determined to be the horizon for the understanding of being.

TIME, TEMPORALITY, AND BEING

The problem of being in the play is inseparably connected with the problem of time. Even the title of the play makes a reference to temporality, if we recall Shakespeare's "Sisters Three," who prophecy the destinies of the main characters in *Macbeth*, or, of course, the Greek Moirae who span the thread of life—Clotho, Lachesis, and Antropos—who are also associated with present, past, and future.[16] Indeed, it is intriguing that all of the play's characters seem obsessed with time, and much of the dialogue emphasizes the relationship between meaningful existence and the passage of time. This preoccupation with time and the inability to respond properly to its flow is also characteristic of *The Cherry Orchard*. Not only do the characters onstage repeatedly complain about the passage of time and aging and discuss their past and future, but references to age and the time of the day or year punctuate the entire play, from its stage directions to stage props and the characters' conversations. The clock is ubiquitous from beginning to end. References to precise time in stage directions are especially striking.[17] The time of act 1 is noon; in act 2 it is "eight o'clock at night"; in act 3 it is "past two a.m."; and in act 4 it is "twelve noon." How can the stage be set to show eight o'clock at night as opposed simply evening, or "past two a.m." as opposed to nighttime, or twelve o'clock as opposed to simply daytime? Should a huge pendulum clock be installed onstage with hands showing the precise time? For the audience already attuned by the stage settings to paying attention to clock time, Kulygin's comparing the time on his watch with the wall clock, the characters' repeatedly inquiring about the time, Chebutykin's breaking of the sisters' porcelain clock, and finally Chebutykin's and Vershinin's incessantly looking at their watches at the end of the play—all these actions acquire a very special significance. Chekhov's inclusion of various clocks (the pendulum clock on the wall, the porcelain clock) and watches (Chebutykin's watch with the chime, Kulygin's watch, Vershinin's watch) onstage draws the audience's attention to the concept of mechanically measured time. Note that the opening lines of *The Cherry Orchard* also refer to the time on the clock ("The train has pulled in, thank God. What time is it?") and throughout the play references to the passage of time figure prominently, with Lopakhin being particularly dependent on the clock time.

Mechanical time has its counterpart in a conception of history as a mere mechanical accumulation of facts or incidents. Chekhov parodies the notion of history as mechanical accumulation of facts in Kulygin's obsession with chronology and his view of "history" as a "list of all the alumni of our high school for the past fifty years" (13:133). Kulygin writes his "history," but his utter lack of understanding of temporality is reflected in his lapses of memory or his inability to connect the past to the present. He gives the same gift—his history of his gymnasium for the past fifty years—to Irina twice. It is not surprising, then, that he is the one who pedantically observes that the sisters' clock is seven minutes fast. Time for him is mere chronology, mere numbers. Likewise, being for him is a mechanical world of things and objects, where love is placed next to curtains and rugs. His manner of speech reflects this mechanical temporality and represents a grotesque accumulation of incompatible objects and platitudes:

> Today, ladies and gentlemen, is Sunday, the day of rest; so let us rest and be
> merry, each according to his age and status. The rugs will have to be removed
> for summer and put away until winter . . . . With mothballs or naphthalene. . . .
> The Romans were healthy because they knew how to work and how to rest;
> they had *mens sana in corpore sano*. Their life flowed according to a set pat-
> tern. Our director says: in every life the most important thing is its pattern. . . .
> Whatever loses its pattern ceases to exist—and in our everyday life it is the
> same. (*Takes* Masha *around her waist, laughing*.) Masha loves me. My wife loves
> me. And the window curtains too along with the rugs. (13:133)

These lines reflect a concept of time that is completely mechanical and
therefore conceived in terms of patterns and external forms. The present
(*segodnia*) for Kulygin represents only a day of the week; merriment is measured by age and status; seasons are associated with "things" (rugs for winter, naphthalene for summer), and life itself is reduced to a pattern, a shape,
or a "form" devoid of any meaning. He understands being as outer form,
and therefore he claims that Masha loves him (which the audience knows
is not true), and he does not seem to distinguish between human feelings
and objects. ("My wife loves me. And the window curtains too along with
the rugs.")

Chekhov's critique of the mechanical notion of time and his particular
concern for human existence as it relates to time brings him close to Heidegger's interpretation of Dasein's temporality. Heidegger has repeatedly criticized the concept of time as an infinite succession of now-points. From
Being and Time to his later works, such as his lecture "Time and Being,"
he juxtaposes this commonplace, or inauthentic, calculated time to primordial, real time. In *Being and Time* the ordinary or "vulgar" conception of
time is conceived as *Vorhandenheit*, while the world-time is *Zuhandenheit*.
Dasein's temporality could be either inauthentic (*uneigentlich*) temporality
or authentic (*eigentlich*) temporality. As opposed to an unaware attitude
toward time, or the everyday mode of time lacking in some primordial quality, authentic temporality is realized when Dasein becomes aware of its own
finality. Dasein's temporality is oriented toward the future, and this futural
orientation regulates our concern by constantly realizing various possibilities. Temporality represents a dynamic structure of "a future which makes
present in the process of having been."[18] Heidegger calls the three moments
of temporality—the future, the present, and the past—the three ecstasies of
temporality.

In his 1962 lecture "Time and Being," Heidegger writes the following about the distinction between mechanical time and real time:

Time familiar to us as the succession in the sequence of nows is what we mean when measuring and calculating time. It seems that we have calculated time immediately and palpably before us when we pick up a watch or chronometer, look at the hands, and say: "Now it is eight-fifty (o'clock)." We say "now" and mean time. But time cannot be found anywhere in the watch that indicates time, neither on the dial nor in the mechanism, nor can it be found in modern technological chronometers. The assertion forces itself upon us: the more technological—the more exact and informative—the chronometer, the less occasion to give thought first of all to time's peculiar character.[19]

To this mechanical, calculated time and the notion of present as the "now," Heidegger juxtaposes a dynamic notion of temporality that reaches "ecstatically" into past, future, and present—that is, an authentic time understood as unity of past, present, and future, and present understood as presence. He explains:

However, the present in the sense of presence differs so vastly from the present in the sense of the now that the present as presence can in no way be determined in terms of the present as the now. ... Presence determines Being in a unified way as presencing and allowing-to-presence, that is, as unconcealing. ... Approaching, being not yet present, at the same time gives and brings about what is no longer present, the past, and conversely what has been offers future to itself. The reciprocal relation of both at the same time gives and brings about the present. We say "at the same time," and thus ascribe a time character to the mutual giving to one another of future, past and present, that is, to their own unity.

This procedure is obviously not in keeping with the matter, assuming that we must give the name "time" to the unity of reaching out and giving which we have now shown, to this unity alone. For time itself is nothing temporal, no more than it is something that is. It is thus inadmissible to say that the future, past and present are before us "at the same time." Yet they belong together in the way they offer themselves to one another. Their unifying unity can be determined only by what is their own; that they offer themselves to one another. ...

This unity of time's three dimensions consists in the interplay of each toward each. This interplay proves to be the true extending, playing in the very heart of time, the fourth dimension, so to speak—not only so to speak, but in the nature of the matter. True time is four-dimensional.[20]

Heidegger, therefore, characterizes time as this overarching, unified reaching of itself as four-dimensional. Our modern, new time, according to Heidegger, is characterized by calculation, a particular kind of attitude toward being and the world as an accumulation of things that does not allow us to focus on the most important thing that is given to us—being itself.

This opposition between mechanical, calculated time and time as presencing, as the mutual giving to one another of future, past, and present, is at the very core of *The Three Sisters*. The world of things, of the everyday (with its strollers, Bobiks, warm rooms, etc.), completely overshadows authentic being for Natasha or Kulygin, for whom time constitutes mere chronology and accumulation of things. It also weighs heavily on Andrei. Andrei's conversation with the deaf Ferapont—in other words, with himself (significantly, the etymology of his name means "manly")—reveals his profound preoccupation with authentic existence, with the meaning of time and being: "Oh, where is it, where has my past gone to, when I was young, merry, intelligent, when I dreamed and thought gracefully, when my present and my future glistened with hope?" (13:181). He laments the kind of present that receded for him to the past, a present as presence that has been open to the future. The present understood as merely "now" is revolting to him: "The present is repulsive, but when, on the other hand, I think of the future, I feel so good! I feel so light and so unconstrained; and a light begins to dawn in the distance, I see freedom, I see how my children and I are being liberated from idleness, from kvass, from goose with cabbage" (13:182). In other words his present is merely "now," and therefore, it merely represents the immersion in the world of things, such as the meaningless papers that Ferapont brings to him to sign. Significantly, he refers to this kind of existence that is not rooted in true being as the existence of dead men, an existence that is no different from animal existence, and therefore is inauthentic. When man does not think about himself as present in being, when he is not aware of his mortality, he becomes merely part of the world of things and is essentially dead:

Our town has already existed for two hundred years ... but there is not a single person who is not similar to all others ... not one even faintly remarkable man in it.... They only eat, drink, sleep, and then die ... others are born and they too eat, drink, sleep . . . and the divine spark in them flickers out, and they become the same pathetic, identical dead men as their fathers and mothers. (13:181–82)

Chebutykin's preoccupation with mechanical time is also reflective of his inauthentic existence. He is concerned with clock time and with history understood merely as a series of now-points, or curious occurrences taken out of context. That is why in the course of the play Chebutykin appears onstage either with a newspaper (most of the time) or a clock. He obsessively reads newspapers, reports about the here and now that reflect factical time, but he has no sense of real time or true being. His obsession with newspaper reading is a trait that is thoroughly emphasized in the play in stage directions and in Chebutykin's own words: "Ever since I left university, I have not lifted a finger, have not read even one book, nothing but newspapers . . . (*Takes out of his pocket a second newspaper.*) Here it is . . . I know by the newspapers that there was, let's say, Dobroliubov, but what he wrote—I don't know . . . God knows" (13:124). It is not surprising, then, that this newspaper-based "history" becomes an accumulation of absurdities, such as a recommendation to drink naphthalene dissolved in alcohol for hair loss or a non sequitur in which he asserts that Balzac got married in Berdichev. With all his obsession with "facts" and clock time, Chebutykin has no sense of time's unity and of his own place within history and tradition. Significantly, he has no memory of the past and no understanding of his place in being. His refrain is "I do not remember! . . . I do not know." "They think I am a doctor, know how to treat all sorts of illnesses, but I know absolutely nothing, I forgot all I knew, I remember nothing, nothing at all" (13:160). In Chekhov's last play, *The Cherry Orchard*, the motif "I do not know" is refracted in the character of Charlotta, who, like Chebutykin, also experiences an existential anxiety caused by her disconnection from both time and place.

Chebutykin's immersion in mechanical time is reflective of his inability to experience authentic being, resulting in a sense of disorientation and uncertainty about life itself. Without a genuine understanding of temporality, his existence is not a real existence, and so he experiences being as mere illusion:

I did know something twenty-five years ago or so, but now I remember nothing. Nothing at all . . . My head is empty, and my soul is cold. Perhaps, I am not

> even a human being, but only pretend that I have arms and legs … and a head; perhaps I do not even exist at all, and it just seems to me that I walk, eat, and sleep. (*Weeps.*) Oh, if only I didn't exist! (13:160)

Chebutykin obviously longs for being, but instead of authentic being he experiences only a meaningless existence and loses connection with true being.[21] The being of humans for him is no different from that of other beings or things, and therefore people for him simply exist as other objects, as things: "one Baron more, one Baron less—what the difference?" (13:178). It is symbolic that he breaks the clock. In his existential anxiety, trying to destroy the present understood as "now" and trying not to exist, Chebutykin wants to destroy time. Yet, in his rebellion against time, he finds that he can never actually destroy it. His smashing of a mechanical clock points neither to the past nor to the future but only to the "now." No wonder that this rebellion plunges him even deeper into existential uncertainty: "Maybe I did not break it, but it only seems like I did. Maybe it only seems to us that we exist, whereas, in fact, we do not. I don't know anything, nobody knows anything" (13:162). At the end of the play, Chebutykin reappears ominously with his watch again. Lack of knowledge and understanding, immersion into mechanical, calculated time ultimately leads him to moral relativity ("all the same") and rejection of responsibility. As has been shown in chapter 4, the phrase "all the same," which might have been derived from Dostoevsky's "The Dream of a Ridiculous Man," appears in many of Chekhov's works and is always associated with man's refusal to accept responsibility for the existence of evil in the world. The consequences of this moral relativism are not only dangerous but lead to entropy and death. Chebutykin's passivity in preventing Tuzenbach's death is a tragic outcome of this "philosophy," which subsequently affects almost all of the play's characters.[22]

The trappings of mechanical time prevent Chebutykin as well as other characters from experiencing what Heidegger would call Dasein. For Chekhov, as well as for Heidegger, it is a mistake to understand time as a linear series of past, present, and future. For a proper understanding of time, it is essential to see it in terms of its futural projections or potentialities. Human being, or Dasein, according to Heidegger, is cast as stretching out into the three ecstasies of time. Hence, Heidegger can characterize the future itself as a "coming-toward-us." Heidegger considers futurity as a direction toward the future that always contains the past—the has been. This is, according to him, a primary mode of Dasein's temporality.

Ultimately it is this notion of Dasein's temporality that informs *The Three Sisters*. Chekhov's characters may not fully experience this temporality, and they frequently fall into the inauthentic existence of calculated commonplace time, but in their best moments they are able to experience time in its unity (or ecstatic time, in Heidegger's terms) and are capable of casting themselves anew out of the situation in which they find themselves. Olga's final lines and the three sisters' symbolic embrace (it has been suggested that the sisters might be associated with the past, present, and future) convey the sense of Dasein's temporality:

> Time will pass, and we will be gone forever; people will forget us, they will forget our faces, voices, and how many of us there were, but our suffering will turn into joy for those who will live after us, happiness and peace will come into the world, and they will remember with a kind word and bless those who live now. Oh, dear sisters, our life is not over yet. Let us live! (13:187–88)

"Our life is not over yet" implies the present that contains the future (it will be over, but not yet) and also the past, because it will be over. Being is presented in precisely its ecstatic temporality. The present is described with reference to both past and future. Human temporality is presented here as overarching the past, present, and future. The language itself reveals that time is not linear. What is interesting here is not Olga's naïve faith in a happy future (which is similar to Sonia's naïve faith in the salvific role of work, as discussed in chapter 5 of this book) but the syntax of the sentence itself, in which time appears as reaching out and in which the future contains the past. In the future, which is future with respect to the present, the present will turn out to be the past. These syntactic structures are frequent in *The Three Sisters*. The notion of time's unity and its overarching is also expressed by Vershinin as early as act 2: "In two hundred or three hundred years, all right, a thousand years—the time's span is of no importance—a new and happy life will come into being. We are not going to take part in this life, of course, but we are living for it now, we work, oh and we suffer, we are creating it—and the purpose of our being and, if you like, our happiness is only in this" (13:146). Olga's words at the end of the play, as well as Vershinin's "philosophizing," suggest that the future and the past are present in the present. This kind of temporality is open to being and implies being as presence. The notion of temporality as interpenetration of past, present, and future informs the very structure of Chekhov's play. Rather than focusing on a series of "nows" supposedly comprising significant and meaningful moments in a person's life, Chekhov is interested in the temporality of human existence and one's belonging to being and time.

Chekhov's interest in human existence in its relation to time and being brings him close to the notion of event that Heidegger articulates. In his lecture "Time and Being," he writes:

> In the sending of the destiny of Being, in the extending of time, there becomes manifest a dedication, a delivering over into what is their own, namely of Being as presence and of time as the realm of the open. What determines both, time and Being, in their own, that is, in their belonging together, we shall call: *Ereignis*, the event of Appropriation....
>
> One should bear in mind, however, that "event" is not simply an occurrence, but that which makes any occurrence possible. What this word names can be thought now only in the light of what becomes manifest in our looking ahead toward Being and toward time as destiny and as extending, to which time and Being belong.[23]

Using the word "event" in the context of a discussion of being, Heidegger proposes to speak of the event of being: "For without Being, no being is capable of being as such. Accordingly, Being can be proffered as the highest, most significant event of all."[24] For Heidegger, event is not what is or what happens. Rather, it is that by means of which Dasein understands and relates itself to Being.

It is this kind of event that is at the center of *The Three Sisters*. The representation of being as event leads Chekhov to an original form of expression. An ontological approach to event and time may result in what often has been erroneously referred to as Chekhov's eventless dramas. In Chekhov's play we have what could be called a non-event of events, or an event of non-events (of Being). Chekhov's portrayal of man's being in his temporality onstage may have also led to a new form of acting.[25] Stanislavsky insisted that in building a character an actor must seek the character within himself; he theorized that "Chekhov's characters cannot be 'shown,' they can only be lived."[26] Drawing on his own emotions and experiences, therefore, the actor should "live" the character. In Chekhov's theater, which focuses on ontological rather than ontic events, life emerges not only as something narrated, as a narrative—which is always inadequate—but as life lived. The drama of Dasein, or of being-there, is also a drama of being there onstage. If Chekhov's characters strive toward present as presence, then the stage becomes a perfect medium for this presencing, as the actor appears before the audience as living/creating the self/character. That is why factical events for Chekhov only serve as outlines. Chekhov's actor performs not the story that he tells but an experience that he lives, an ontological event, which is not identical with narrative. Chekhov uses theater as a medium that incorporates a stage work that has an existence of its own and in which individuals can become conscious of their own Being and of the fundamental questions of their own Being. In other words, theater becomes the space for the realization of a practical philosophy.

7

The Temptations of the Nursery

One of the chief causes of the faults of our upper classes is the fact that it takes us so long to get accustomed to the thought that we are grown up. Our entire life till the age of 25 and sometimes even older contradicts this thought.

LEV TOLSTOY, Sobranie sochinenii v 22 tomakh

While echoing themes and issues raised in *The Seagull, Uncle Vania,* and *The Three Sisters* (e.g., money, dispossession, industrialization, visions of the future, the perception of time, and the problem of work), and evoking the same sense of existential abandonment and uprootedness, Chekhov's last play, *The Cherry Orchard,* focuses more than its antecedents on the impact of modernization and the social, economic, and political changes taking place in Russia at the end of the nineteenth century. Even though his other plays also thematize industrialization, the impoverishment of the landed gentry, general social disruption, and shifting class identities, *The Cherry Orchard* directly addresses the land question and the challenges faced by the upper classes in a rapidly changing social order. Chekhov's final comedy is even more decentered than his other mature plays. *The Seagull* is held together by the image of the seagull. In the *Three Sisters* the leitmotif of Moscow functions as a locus of hope for its central characters and its inevitable frustration. But in *The Cherry Orchard,* apart from the equal distribution of scenes in which the main characters are given prominence, the organizing principles are several dominant visual and audial images—the orchard, the nursery, and the sound of the breaking string (one could also add other important audial images, such as the sound of the shepherd's pipe and of the axes chopping down the cherry trees at the end of the play). Each of these motifs carries a "theme": the nursery exposes the characters' infantilism and underscores their lack of maturity; the orchard introduces the motif of paradise lost and the need to "tend" to one's garden; and the breaking string alludes to disruption and mortality as inevitable aspects of life, and thus the necessity of dealing with inevitable change. Through these images, Chekhov conveys his thoughts about Russia as it enters the twentieth century.

Both the first and the last act of the play take place in the nursery of Gaev and Ranevskaia's estate house, pointing to the centrality of the theme of childhood and suggesting the broken cycle of return to the nursery in act 1 and departure from it, now almost bare, in act 4. References to the cherry orchard are equally ubiquitous, encompassing the entire play and culminating in the sound of axes chopping down the cherry trees at the request of the estate's new owner, Lopakhin. I will focus on the significance of these two images and their role in conveying Chekhov's ideas about historical processes, his musings on the ineluctability of change and suffering and ways of coping with them, and his sense of the comic.

The French actor and director Jean-Louis Barrault summarizes the action of *The Cherry Orchard* in the following way: "In Act One, the cherry orchard is in danger of being sold, in Act Two it is on the verge of being sold, in Act Three it is sold, and in Act Four it has been sold."[1] This seemingly humorless plot was intended by Chekhov to be hilariously funny. And indeed, although we realize that losing one's estate and chopping down the cherry trees to clear space for vacationers' houses, not to mention abandoning and locking up old Firs, is hardly amusing, when staged properly, the play makes us smile, sigh, grin, laugh, smirk, or even giggle.

The confusion produced by the play is intensified by the history of the play's productions and by frequently conflicting literary interpretations. The Moscow Art Theater undoubtedly was responsible for some misinterpretations of the play from its inception, as became clear from Chekhov's long and painful altercations with its famous director. "This is not a comedy, not a farce, as you wrote," Stanislavsky stubbornly insisted to Chekhov, who was then exhausted by tuberculosis and already almost dying, "it is a tragedy, whatever outlet for a better life you may have offered in the last act. . . . I hear you saying: 'Wait a minute, but this is a farce . . .' No, for an ordinary person this is a tragedy."[2] Chekhov never agreed: "Why is it that my play is persistently called a 'drama' in the posters and newspaper advertisements? Nemirovich-Danchenko and Stanislavsky see in my play something completely different from what I have written, and I am ready to stake my word that neither of them has read my play through attentively even once" (P 12:81). In his much-quoted letter to Stanislavsky's wife (September 15, 1903), Chekhov insists somewhat defensively that his play is a comedy: "What has emerged from me is not a drama but a comedy—in certain places, even a farce" (P 11:248). His letter to Olga Knipper of September 21, 1903, echoes this sentiment: "The last act will be merry, and the whole play will be cheerful and light-hearted" (P 11:253). Chekhov was never able, however (at least not during his lifetime), to win the battle over his comedy. As Anna Linden convincingly demonstrates in her essay on Chekhov's relations with the Moscow Art Theater and Maxim Gorky, Chekhov's play was ruthlessly distorted by the joint efforts of Stanislavsky, Nemirovich-Danchenko, and Gorky, to the extent that even the latest academic edition of Chekhov's complete works still publishes *The Cherry Orchard* in the version "improved" by the very people who, according to Chekhov, completely misunderstood his play.[3]

Stanislavsky's own fame as a director and theoretician of the theater contributed to the long tradition of staging Chekhov's plays in terms of psychological realism with elegiac overtones and a naturalistic framework.[4] Yet it would be a mistake to conclude that Stanislavsky was insensitive to Chekhov's innovations. In fact, it could be said that his Method grew organically out of a Chekhov play. His approach to a deeper understanding of character and his emphasis on using the subconscious to reveal emotions and conducting "psychological research" was undoubtedly stimulated by his experience of staging Chekhov's plays, which were full of things unsaid, pauses, and gaps. How does one stage a thought that remains unspoken, a momentary lapse, an interruption of one character by another, a confusion? Chekhov frequently gives very detailed and very suggestive instructions about scenery (a narrative element in the otherwise dramatic form), but very often they point to the characters' perception of their surroundings rather than to anything specific that lends itself easily to a conventional set. For example, in act 4 of *Uncle Vania*, Chekhov's stage directions reference a map of Africa: "On the wall there hangs a map of Africa, clearly of no use to anyone here." But how does one stage this "of no use to anyone"? Or, as will be discussed in this chapter, *The Cherry Orchard*'s instructions refer to the nursery as "Room that is still called a nursery." How does one incorporate this "still" into the staging? Or consider the stage directions for act 2: "large slabs which were once, apparently, tombstones." Deciding what to make of this "apparently" is precisely the challenge of staging the intangible, ontological aspects of a Chekhov play that replace ontic events (see chapter 6 in this book). These are the kinds of challenges that prompted Stanislavsky to develop his Method, which called for actors to establish their own relationships with the characters and the environment and to supplement the director's and author's material with their own imaginations and psychological experience: "Bring to life what is hidden under words." Actors, then, become active collaborators, filling in the textual gaps, and the theater becomes inherently dialogical. Chekhov may have been unhappy with what could be considered Stanislavsky's project of the "death of the playwright," but in fact, these were peculiarities of Chekhovian theater that contributed to the most important acting theory of the twentieth century.

In his monumental study *The Chekhov Theater: A Century of the Plays in Performance*, Laurence Senelick chronicles the saga (or melodrama) of *The Cherry Orchard*'s stage productions from Stanislavsky and Nemirovich-Danchenko's production of 1904 to the 1994 Indiana Repertory Theater's version of the play. The play has been alternately interpreted as sentimental, cruel, comic, or farcical. Even though a number of critics and theater directors have tried to rescue Chekhov from the lachrymose nostalgia of the so-called Chekhovian mood, uncertainty about the comic status of the play persisted for a long time.[5] For as much as the critics deplored Stanislavsky's misinterpretation, and dutifully quoted Chekhov on his intentions to write a comedy, up to the 1990s directors were reluctant to accept the play as a comedy and frequently reverted instead to interpreting it in a somewhat tragic way. Thus, Maurice Valency argues that "it is inconceivable that Chekhov was insensible to the tragic implications of the situation he had created" and essentially concludes that Stanislavsky knew better: "It was precisely that blend of comedy and pathos with which, as it seemed to Chekhov, Stanislavsky was ruining his play, that gave *The Cherry Orchard* its originality and freshness."[6] *The Cherry Orchard*, according to Valency, is a "modern tragedy," "cosmic drama," or "cosmic vaudeville."[7] Likewise, J. L. Styan qualifies Chekhov's insistence that "the last act will be merry" with a reminder that "it will be the surface gaiety of desperation."[8] Moreover, even the first International Chekhov Festival held in Moscow in 1992 reopened, in Senelick's words, "all the old debates: is *The Cherry Orchard* a tragedy or a comedy? Does Chekhov need all that real-life impedimenta?"[9] At the same time, when stage directors in more recent years go to the opposite extreme, reducing Chekhov's play to a farce, they also make Chekhov "virtually unrecognizable."[10] It is true that *The Cherry Orchard* has more farcical elements and vaudeville-like scenes than his other major plays, but some of the postmodern farcical productions also fail to give full credit to the complexity of Chekhov's genre. There is no need for us to chronicle here all the productions of *The Cherry Orchard* in the course of the twentieth and twenty-first centuries—many of which have been very successful in achieving the balance between the comic, the potentially tragic, and the absurd (perhaps especially Peter Brook's 1981 production and Eimuntas Nekrošius's 2003 version of the play).

The nature of the comic in Chekhov's plays is a question that scholars and stage directors alike have already extensively tackled.[11] Clearly, its source lies not in the plays' fabulae or situations, not in *what* happens, but in *how* it happens, to whom it happens, and how the characters respond to what happens to them. The enigmatic, captivating, and almost mesmerizing effect that *The Cherry Orchard* continues to exert on its audience is to be found in its good-humored but foolish protagonists—both charming in their gullibility and pathetic in their utter confusion. But with the exception of several minor farcical characters, most of the play's characters cannot be classified as traditional comic types. Even the clumsy and incoherent bookkeeper Epikhodov, whose part largely draws on slapstick and who is appropriately nicknamed "Twenty-Two Misfortunes," shows some hidden tragic undertones while nevertheless making the audience laugh at his inner drama, which emerges as a parody of high tragedy: "I'm a cultured person, I read all kinds of remarkable books, but I can't figure out the direction [of his life], what I really want, to live or to shoot myself, but nevertheless I always carry a revolver with me. Here it is . . . (*Shows the revolver*)."[12]

As I will try to demonstrate in the remainder of this chapter, the play focuses on the universal childishness of Russian society. The comic nature of the play's characters furthermore stems to a large extent from their infantilism. Although infantilism is one of many features of the play that make it comic (including slapstick and farce), I am interested here primarily in how the comic features relate to the issue of infantilism. In *The Cherry Orchard*, Chekhov problematizes childishness as an almost all-embracing phenomenon of Russian life.

Even some of Chekhov's contemporaries recognized childish qualities in the characters of *The Cherry Orchard*. Although unduly harsh in his criticisms, Maxim Gorky was one of the first to point out the childlike characteristics of the play's chief protagonists: "Here they are, the weepy Ranevskaia and the other former masters of the Cherry Orchard, as egotistical as children and as flabby as senile old men."[13] Gorky was not the only one to observe the infantile nature of the careless and gullible characters of the play. Many of Chekhov's socially and more ideologically oriented readers followed in Gorky's footsteps in their somewhat crude reduction of the play to a social satire while almost completely disregarding the humorous aspects of the characters' infantile natures. Compare, for example, the following comment by V. Doroshevich: "These old children perish helplessly in front of our eyes" (13:508). Among later twentieth-century critics, Styan and Harvey Pitcher seem to be the most sensitive to Chekhov's representation of childishness in the play. Without either analyzing in depth the characters' infantilism or explaining the connection between their childishness and the nature of the comic in *The Cherry Orchard*, Styan provides a very astute interpretation of old Firs's final remark in the last act: "A final prick of comedy is felt in his irritation as he mutters under his breath, 'These young people. . . .' Time and his great age have reduced the whole family equally to the level of children who do not know what they are doing."[14] Some actors are even more sensitive to this aspect of Chekhov's characters than are literary critics. Maurice Benichou, the assistant director and Yasha in Peter Brook's 1981 production of *The Cherry Orchard*, explains why the play is neither sentimental nor tragic but pathetic and comic: "These characters are childish, excessive: when disasters occur, we cry with them; then we forget them, just as they do."[15] Indeed, the characters' childishness is in part responsible for their ambiguous portrayal as charming fools.

In this play, Chekhov weds the myth of the Golden Age (and the image of the garden as paradise) to the myth of childhood only to question both and to make a critical statement about the infantile nature of Russian society as it prepares to enter a new historical epoch.[16] Both the myth of the Golden Age and the myth of childhood are in turn connected with the tradition of the pastoral. While Paul Alpers may be right to argue that the historical pastoral is not necessarily connected with innocence and a childlike embrace of the world, he himself acknowledges that after Schiller's "On Naive and Sentimental Poetry," it became practically impossible for scholars and readers to separate the pastoral from such concepts as the Golden Age, innocence, and nostalgia.[17] The pastoral "method," in the broadest sense, is, according to Frank Kermode, "to exalt the naturalness and virtue of the simple man at the expense of the complicated one, whether the former be a shepherd, or a child, or a working-man."[18] Assuming that Andrew Durkin is correct in distinguishing three primary modes of pastoral perception within the Russian nineteenth-century tradition—spatial pastoral, social or political pastoral, and psychological pastoral—one could say that *The Cherry Orchard* launches a powerful attack on all aspects of the Russian pastoral: the pastoral view of nature, the pastoral idealization of the peasants and of the country estates, and the pastoral of childhood.[19] The pastoral harmony of nature, the gentry estates, and childhood is threatened by continuous intrusions from the outside world, be they the mysterious sounds of a breaking string, a row of telegraph poles and a faint outline of a large city against the idyllic landscape, debts, or death. The nursery—literally, "the children's room" (*detskaia*)—is the ultimate symbol of childhood as pastoral, and Chekhov uses it to present childishness as a malaise of contemporary Russian society.

Indeed, along with the orchard, the central emblem of Chekhov's comedy, the image of the nursery, is probably one of the most pervasive symbols of the play, one that appropriately introduces the cultural paradigm of childishness in its relation to the myth of childhood.

Significantly for Tolstoy and other writers who exalt childhood, the nursery is a locus of earthly paradise, a sacred place where the mysterious rituals of birth and nurturing take place. The goodness of Tolstoy's female heroines is measured by the amount of time they spend in the nursery (Natasha Rostova, Kitty, Dolly), which represents for Tolstoy the perfect unity of idyllic time and space. Similarly, this idyllic chronotope of the nursery is at the center of Chekhov's comedy *The Cherry Orchard*. Unlike Tolstoy's nurseries, however, Chekhov's is tempered with ironies and becomes the locus of his comic, rather than pastoral or epic, plot. From the outset, Chekhov links the myth of the Golden Age, or of paradise lost, to childhood as he combines two central images pertaining to both myths: the garden and the nursery. The perception of childhood as a golden age was typical of the myth of childhood in general,[20] but Chekhov makes this connection all the more explicit by simultaneously using the metaphors of the garden and the nursery.

In regard to the chronotope of the nursery space, we should remind ourselves that in dramaturgy the role of settings is infinitely more important than in prose fiction. Theatrical settings provide a visual and semiotic framework for a performed play. Thus, when act 1 opens in the "children's room" with windows facing the garden, the audience is immediately alerted to the semiotic potentials inherent in the images of the garden and the nursery. Yet, while most stage productions address the perennial question of how to show or not to show the orchard, the majority of them tend to ignore the significance of the stage directions concerning the nursery and the question of how the nursery should be portrayed. Giorgio Strehler's 1974 production of *The Cherry Orchard* was the first to emphasize the significance of the nursery as an emblem of childhood.[21] The suggestive power of the nursery, however, was lost in Peter Brook's 1981 production, whose minimalist stage sets may have worked well for the representation of the orchard as seen only by the characters onstage but provided almost no hints at the nursery aspect of the play.

Curiously, in his stage directions, Chekhov observes that "the room still goes by the name of the nursery." The author's "still" (*do sikh por*) may well be lost on the audience, but for the reader as well as the actors who are expected to follow Chekhov's script, "still" suggests a certain anomaly in the characters' perception of the room. Even though there are no more children on the estate, the room is still viewed as a "children's room"; this detail alerts the reader and the actors to the characters' refusal to separate themselves from their puerile past. The room's closed windows not only emphasize the sense of enclosure but suggest that the nursery is dysfunctional and remains merely a misplaced symbol of a lost childhood. Ironically, it is the daughter, Ania, who calls her mother's attention to the nursery: "Mamma, do you remember what room this is?" (13:199). Yet the mother remembers the nursery not as the place where she nursed her daughter but as where she herself used to sleep, as a child, and was doted upon by her late mother. Her brother, Gaev, has a similar fixation on his childhood experiences that he associates with the nursery: "There was a time, sister, when you and I used to sleep in this same room, and now I am already fifty-one years old, strange as it may seem" (13:203).

The depiction of the estate as a kind of paradise is further intensified at the end of act 1 with the stage directions alluding to a pastoral idyll: "A shepherd is heard playing on a reed pipe far beyond the orchard" (13:214). The images of the nursery and of the orchard merge in Ranevskaia's apostrophe to her childhood, which mutely echoes the beginning and end of a famous chapter from Tolstoy's *Childhood*:

> Oh, my childhood, my purity! I used to sleep in this nursery and look out into the orchard, happiness waked with me every morning, and then the orchard was just the same, nothing had changed. (*Laughs with joy.*) All, all white! Oh, my orchard! After the dark, rainy fall and the cold winter, you are young again, full of happiness; the heavenly angels have not deserted you . . . If only I could remove this heavy stone from my chest and my shoulders, if I could only forget my past! (13:210, ellipsis in the original)

Compare the passage with Tolstoy's text:

> Oh, the happy, happy time of childhood never to return! . . . Where is that finest gift—the pure tears of tenderness? A guardian angel flew in and wiped

those tears with a smile. . . . Can it be that life has left such heavy traces in my heart that those tears and that rapture have deserted me forever?[22]

Like Tolstoy's narrator, Ranevskaia endows the image of childhood with explicitly Edenic attributes: happiness; purity; and, of course, angels. The bliss of childhood is then contrasted to the heavy burden of postlapsarian and post-puerile adult life. Chekhov's allusion to Tolstoy, however, serves to subvert rather than to exalt Ranevskaia's nostalgic evocation of her childhood. Her vision of her late mother in a white dress, along with Ranevskaia's happy laughter and explicitly infantile behavior in the preceding scene, in which she contemplates jumping about and waving her arms like a child ("Can it be I who is sitting here? [*Laughs.*] I feel like jumping, waving my arms about. [*Covers her face with her hands.*] But what if I am just asleep!"), expose this monologue as patently ridiculous (13:204). The appearance of Trofimov, "dressed in a threadbare student's uniform," instead of her mother in a white dress brings comic relief. Ranevskaia's fetishization of her nursery seems to be a mocking allusion to Tolstoy's obsession with the image of the nursery:

> The nursery! My darling, wonderful room . . . I used to sleep here when I was a child [*kogda byla malen'koi*] . . . (*Cries.*) And now I am as a child [*kak malen'kaia*] . . . (*Kisses her brother, then Varia, then her brother again*) . . .
>
> I cannot sit still, I am unable to . . . (*Jumps up and walks about in violent agitation.*) I won't survive this joy . . . Laugh at me, I am silly . . . My darling little bookcase [*shkafik moi rodnoi*] . . . (*Kisses the bookcase.*) My little table [*stolik moi*]. (13:199, 204, ellipses in the original)

In childlike fashion, Ranevskaia pours out her love and affection not only on family members but also on inanimate objects. Her fifty-one-year-old brother intensifies the comic effect by addressing his own ridiculous paean to the same bookcase. It should be pointed out that the comic effect produced by the incongruity of Ranevskaia's infantile behavior with her age was originally supposed to be all the more poignant as Chekhov intended the role of Ranevskaia to be played by an older actress. Thus, for example, in his letter to Vera Kommisarzhevskaya of January 27, 1903, he maintains that "the central role in the play is that of an old woman" (P 11:134). In a letter of January 6, 1904, he repeats this reference to Ranevskaia's age and her inability to deal with the passage of time: "The central female role in the play is an old woman who lives entirely in the past and has nothing in the present"

(P 12:9). In his earlier notebooks, he even envisioned Ranevskaia as "a liberal old woman" who nevertheless "dresses up as a young girl" (13:479).

The timeless harmony of the nursery, as it is portrayed in Tolstoy, grows into an alarming symbol of human infantilism, ineptness, and inability to confront the reality of historical as opposed to cyclic time, the reality of change as opposed to the eternal return. Significantly, it is right after her Tolstoyesque apostrophe to childhood that Ranevskaia refuses to acknowledge the passage of time as she expresses her somewhat obtuse surprise at Trofimov's aging: "Why do you look so much worse now? Why have you aged so?" (13:211).

Similarly, Gaev counters the reality of death and change by retreating into his childlike habit of sucking caramels: "While you were away, the nurse died. . . . And Anastasy died too. Petrushka Kosoy has left me and now lives in town at the police inspector's. (*Takes a box of hard candies out of his pocket and sucks one*)" (13:204–5).[23] Moreover, the infantile and psychologically regressive nature of Gaev seems to come to the surface when he takes a box of caramels out of his pocket and starts sucking one immediately after announcing that the nurse (*niania*) died while Ranevskaia was away. This atavistic gesture speaks eloquently of his nostalgia for being nursed (sucking of the candy being a substitute for breastfeeding) and his resistance to being weaned away from the maternal breast. Lopakhin's remark "yes, time flies" falls literally on deaf ears. "Whom? [*Kogo?*]" is Gaev's only reply (13:203). It is not surprising, then, that he still cannot dress himself; pursues only adolescent occupations, such as playing billiards; and avoids the adult commitments of marriage and fatherhood. In act 1, Gaev recalls how he used to sleep in the nursery. In act 4, he retreats again to his childhood memories, as he bids farewell to the room of his childhood: "I remember when I was six years old sitting on that windowsill on the day of Holy Trinity, watching my father going to church" (13:252).

While the play begins and ends in the same location of the nursery, by the end any suggestion of a cyclical relation between these brackets is decisively broken. Not only is the nursery empty now, but Ranevskaia is finally forced to acknowledge that even the life of the cherry orchard, which had exemplified for her the timeless pastoral of nature and childhood, is threatened by the ultimate foe of every pastoral—mortality. It is thus highly symbolic that the play ends with two pending deaths: that of a man, old Firs, and that of the garden/nursery. The nursery will not only be abandoned but destroyed: "Farewell, my lovely home, my grandfather. Winter will pass, spring will come, and you will no longer be here, they will destroy you. How much these walls have seen!" (13:247). (Cf. Ranevskaia's words about the orchard in act 1: "After the dark, rainy fall and the cold winter, you are young again.") While brother and sister embrace each other and sob quietly, like two mistreated children, the audience hears the cheerful voices of Ania and Petia Trofimov, the younger generation being no less infantile in its merriment than the older one in its grief: "*Voice of* Ania *(gay and summoning)*: 'Mama!' *Voice of* Trofimov *(gay and excited)*: 'Halloo!' . . . *Voice of* Ania: 'Mama!' *Voice* of Trofimov: 'Halloo!'" (13:253).

Charlotta's "Mousetrap"

Charlotta's lullaby in the middle of act 4 is an appropriate requiem for the imminent destruction of the nursery. Her theatrical mini-performance emblematizes the action of the entire play and reveals the childish behavior of its characters for what it is: egotistical irresponsibility. Their childish self-centeredness and disregard for others has consequences that are not merely comic. As the stage directions indicate, Charlotta "picks up a bundle [*uzel*] which resembles a baby in swaddling clothes" and begins to sing:

> Bye, my little baby, bye . . .
> > *One hears a baby crying*: "Wah! Wah!" Hush, hush, my good darling little boy.
> "Wah! Wah"'"
> > I feel sorry for you! (*Throws the bundle down.*) So would you please find me a position? I can't go on like this. (13:248, ellipses in original)

Charlotta's performance is a sort of play within a play (Chekhov's appreciation of this device as is also evident from *The Seagull*) and has a function similar to Hamlet's "mousetrap," set to catch the conscience of the king: she reveals to her spectators what they have done to her and to each other. Their kindness and compassion are but empty words, as her gesture of throwing down the bundle right after she says "I feel sorry for you!" clearly indicates. This combination of affected care and neglect mirrors Ranevskaia's attitude toward most of the characters in the play, including herself and, of course, old Firs, but it especially parodies the mothering role at which she has failed so miserably in her life. For all her benevolence, the kind Ranevskaia, who gives alms to anyone who asks, takes the money designated for Ania by her grandmother and goes to Paris to squander it on her lover.

This scene also prefigures Lopakhin's final rejection of Varia. Lopakhin toys with the idea of marrying Varia but "throws the bundle down," so to speak, leaving Varia to cry like a neglected baby. Symbolically, the image of the "bundle" on the floor reappears in connection with Varia, after Lopakhin's failed proposal: "Varia sits on the floor and sobs quietly, her head on a bundle [*uzel*] of clothes" (13:249). Charlotta's words "I can't go on like this" suggest both her uneasiness in the role of surrogate mother figure, who cannot continue to "nurture" the grown-up children she serves (including Ranevskaia, Gaev, and Ania), and her dread of being abandoned herself as a neglected child. But in a typically Chekhovian twist, the people around her turn a deaf ear to the message. Only Gaev—the quintessential adult child, or the "eternal suckling," to use Freud's term—seems to identify subconsciously with Charlotta's abandoned "baby" as he says: "Everyone is abandoning us. Varia is leaving . . . We are suddenly no longer needed" (13:248). Gaev uses here the Russian verb "brosat'" (to abandon, to leave, to throw)—"Vse nas brosaiut"— the same verb Chekhov uses to describe Charlotta's gesture of throwing down the bundle she nurses in her arms like a baby.

Charlotta's "play" is not staged by Lopakhin, the hackneyed Hamlet of *The Cherry Orchard*, but is, in fact, addressed to him. In teasing Varia, Lopakhin quotes Hamlet's lines but consciously (so it seems) distorts Ophelia's name to the comic Okhmeliia, a name that brings to mind the Russian noun *pokhmel'e* (hangover) or the verbs *okhmelet'* (to get drunk) and *okhmeliat'* (to intoxicate): "Okhmeliia, get thee to a nunnery . . . Okhmeliia, oh nymph, in your orisons, remember me!" (13:564–65).[24] Ironically, however, the only moment when Lopakhin is actually intoxicated is when he returns to the estate after purchasing the orchard at auction. Lopakhin responds to Charlotta's request to find her a place: "Don't worry, Charlotta Ivanovna, we will find one for you" (13:248). But does he, who throughout the comedy plays the role of Hamlet with Varia, recognize that Charlotta's "mousetrap" is set to catch his own conscience? Is it a coincidence that to Lopakhin's comment "What a play I saw at the theater yesterday—very funny!" Ranevskaia suddenly replies: "And most likely there was nothing funny about it. Rather than going to see plays, you had better look at yourself more often" (13:220)? Lopakhin's Hamlet-like deliberation "to marry or not to marry" (cf. also Gogol's Podkolesin from his comedy *Marriage* [*Zhenit'ba*]) is exposed as the irresponsible self-indulgence of a child who plays with a toy and discards it a minute later. Appropriately, Lopakhin's failed proposal occurs in the children's room. To be sure, Chekhov builds here on a specifically Russian cultural tradition of interpreting Hamlet as an ineffectual and almost impotent individual doomed to inaction by his reflective nature.[25] The ironic portrayal of Lopakhin as a type of Russian Hamlet provides an original twist to an old theme: the alleged Hamletian inertia and inactivity is interpreted as a sign of infantilism and immaturity. In Chekhov's ironic version, the Russian Hamlet ceases to be a tragic hero; he may well have a noble soul and even suffer from indecisiveness in his personal life, but he successfully buys real estate and, after shedding a couple of tears at "our wretched, disordered life," leaves for a business trip to Kharkov. High tragedy is turned into a farce in Chekhov's sophisticated and ingenious parody of Russian Hamletism. One may say that Chekhov conflates here the theme of Russian Hamletism with the vaudeville theme of the indecisive suitor known to the Russian audience through Gogol's memorable treatment of the suitor's reluctance and hesitation in his two-act play *Marriage*.[26] Lopakhin's failed proposal to Varia represents, therefore, a culmination of a behavioral type that was long familiar to the Russian reader, and which Chernyshevsky deemed to be a characteristically Russian phenomenon. From Gogol's comically indecisive Podkolesin to Turgenev's ineffectual male characters in such works as "Faust," "Asya" and *Rudin*, to the painful marital deliberations of Goncharov's Oblomov, to Tolstoy's Koznyshev and Varenka, unable to verbalize their mutual attraction during the mushroomhunting scene in *Anna Karenina*, or Chekhov's own hesitant and evasive Alekhin in "About Love," Russian men in particular are perceived to exhibit a baffling indecisiveness and avoidance of commitment in matters of love.[27] In his influential essay "The Russian at the Rendez-vous," Chernyshevsky describes the indecisiveness of the Russian male as "a symptom of the epidemic disease rooted in our society" and specifically links it to childishness.[28] Chernyshevsky may well be mistaken in attributing the indecisiveness of the Russian male at the rendezvous to his Russianness. After all, the evasive bridegroom is an old and global comic trope. But what makes Chernyshevsky's analysis relevant to my purposes is his emphasis on the childishness of Russian society. His focus on this topic reflects the interest in infantilism in publicist writings of the time as a serious issue in Russia (as opposed to the more traditional, purely comic treatment of the trope of a suitor's evasiveness).

Lopakhin, who was intended by Chekhov to be the play's central character, is an ambitious and sensitive man, yet for all his practicality, he is peculiarly helpless in his relations with women. There have been numerous speculations about Lopakhin's inability to propose to Varia: he may be secretly in love with Ranevskaia or unwilling to breach the social structure by marrying a girl brought up in an aristocratic family, or he may simply not be interested in her.[29] Without probing the depth of Lopakhin's feeling, it seems clear that Lopakhin provides enough grounds to convince not only Varia but everyone around him that he is interested in her. Not only does he openly admit to Ranevskaia that he has nothing against marrying Varia, but he displays a kind of behavior toward Varia that traditionally has been interpreted as that of a wooer intending to marry. This is precisely why everyone congratulates Varia on her upcoming marriage with Lopakhin. Clearly, Lopakhin's torturous procrastination with the marriage proposal cannot be explained away by the degree of his interest in Varia. Rather, one may conclude that Lopakhin is yet another example of "the Russian at the rendez-vous" and that he too is affected by the disease described by Chernyshevsky in his essay. In his avoidance of marriage with Varia, Lopakhin is not cruel or sadistic, as some actors playing this role occasionally suggest, but merely awkward, careless, and childishly unaware of the implications of his frivolous games with Ranevskaia's adopted daughter. In the presence of his "Okhmeliia," our Russian Hamlet turns repeatedly to sophomoric pranks as, for example, in act 1, when he bleats like a calf: "(*Peeps in at the door and bleats.*) Meh-h-h. (*Disappears*)" (13:201).

Moreover, like most Russian indecisive male protagonists, Lopakhin seems to feel more comfortable with love that is motherly rather than purely sexual. It is noteworthy that Lopakhin reveals his longing for Ranevskaia's motherly affection precisely during the scene when the infantile Ranevskaia pours out her love for her "little cupboard" and her "little table": "I only want you to trust me as you used to, to look at me with your wonderful, touching eyes as you used to in times gone by. . . . I love you as family [*kak rodnuiu*] . . . even more [*bol'she, chem rodnuiu*]" (13:204, ellipsis in the original). A man of action in his business life, when it comes to his personal life, Lopakhin, nevertheless, regresses to nostalgic reminiscences of how he was "mothered" by Ranevskaia in the very same children's room where, predictably enough, he fails to propose to Varia three acts later: "Lyubov Andreevna, as I remember right now, who was still so young, so slim, led me over to the washstand here in this very room, the nursery. 'Don't cry, little peasant,' she says, 'it will heal before your wedding . . .'" (13:197, ellipsis in the original). To be sure, Chekhov fully exploits the irony of the situation. Lopakhin's "wound" does not heal and the promise of the wedding is not sustained. Lopakhin's longing for childhood is manifested in his attachment to the nursery and to his surrogate mother, Ranevskaia. As a site where he was, as a child, mothered and pampered by Ranevskaia, the nursery remains for him the place where he can act only in a childish manner, and where he fails, therefore, to respond to the sexual demands typically associated with adult age. As Karl Kramer duly notes, "in this play it is not the young who are determined to unite but rather the elders who insist on a unity which the young are incapable of consummating."[30]

Childishness, however, is an affliction that infects not only the older generation but the younger one as well. It is no coincidence that Chekhov points out that mother and daughter are almost identical. As soon as the conversation touches upon something serious (Lopakhin's proposal to Varia, for example), Ania retreats to her infantile experiences: "(*She goes to her room and speaks gaily like a child.*) And in Paris I flew in a balloon!" (13:201). Once again, in sending a list of casting notes to his wife, Chekhov insisted that "Ania is first and foremost a child, who is merry all the way through, who knows nothing of life, and does not cry once, except in Act II, and even then she only has tears in her eyes" (P 11:280). Clearly Chekhov wanted to stress Ania's childishness: "Ania can be played by anyone at all, even a completely unknown actress, as long as she is young and looks like a little girl and speaks in a youthful, vibrant voice" (P 11:293).

Ranevskaia herself draws our attention to Petia Trofimov's infantilism when she criticizes him for aging prematurely but, on the other hand, for his juvenile looks and immature actions: "I would gladly let you marry Ania, I swear I would, only, my dear, you must study and get your degree . . . And you must do something with your beard to make it grow somehow . . . (*Laughs.*) You are so ridiculous!" (13:234, ellipses in the original). Petia's worn-out student uniform and his status as an eternal student also suggest his immunity to the passage of time. Trofimov's age is indeed incongruous with his underdeveloped sexuality. "You are twenty-six or twenty-seven years old, but you are still a schoolboy! [*gimnazist vtorogo klassa*]," exclaims Ranevskaia with irritation. "You ought to be a man—at your age you ought to understand those who love. And you ought to be in love yourself . . . you should fall in love! . . . At your age not to have a mistress!" (13:234–35, ellipsis in the original). With the innocence of a child, however, Trofimov believes he is "above love" (13:233). This perpetual student may occasionally utter a word of truth in his high-minded sermons about social injustice in Russia, but he is absurd if not grotesque in his lofty rhetoric, in his sophomoric sexuality, and in his awkwardness that borders on slapstick.

It is hardly a coincidence that all three major male characters in the play—the "eternal suckling" Gaev, the "eternal student" Trofimov, and the "eternal suitor" Lopakhin—are not married and have no children. As different as these characters may be, they all cling to their puerile identities and refuse to confront the demands of the adult age. Although Lopakhin arguably may seem to be the only "realistic" and "adult" character who warns his friends about the necessity of confronting the change to come, his purchase of the estate reveals his fixation on childhood as well. After all, he buys the cherry orchard for neither aesthetic nor practical reasons. Rather, the purchase of the estate represents his desperate and misguided attempt to cope with his traumatic and deprived childhood and to resolve his Oedipus complex. It is to the male domineering figures of his father and grandfather that he ultimately addresses his drunken speech upon the purchase of the estate:

> The cherry orchard's mine now! Mine! (*Laughs.*) Lord! My God, the cherry orchard is mine! ... (*Stamps his feet.*) Don't laugh at me! If my father and my grandfather could rise from their graves and see everything that has happened—how their Yermolay, their often flogged and half-literate Yermolay, who used to run about barefoot in the winter, how that very Yermolay has bought the most magnificent estate in the world! I bought the estate where my father and grandfather were serfs, where they were not even admitted to the kitchen! I am asleep, I am only day-dreaming, I only imagine it. (13:580, ellipses in the original)

Is Lopakhin making his way in a real world or trying to fulfill his secret wishes and fantasies? As Lopakhin makes an attempt to regain what he had lost in childhood, he inadvertently plans a future on the pattern of the past. His compulsive repetition of the possessive pronoun "mine" turns possession into a childish obsession.

Whether idyllic or traumatic, childhood looms large in the imagination of the play's major characters.

Growing Up through Laughter

If the infantilism of Russian society lies at the center of *The Cherry Orchard*, it becomes clear why Chekhov understood his play as a comedy and kept insisting and reminding Stanislavsky that at times it is even a farce. It is surely funny when children behave like adults, just as it is ludicrous when adults behave like children. The characters' childishness, their short attention spans, impracticality, naïve self-centeredness, and inability to sustain a dialogue constitute some of the main sources of the comic in the play. To be sure, infantilism does not explain all the comedy and all the comic figures or situations in *The Cherry Orchard*. Chekhov is very sensitive to the many varieties of humor and incorporates many of them simultaneously in his plays. But the exposure of the characters' childishness is undoubtedly one of the means used to provoke laughter.

The view of Henri Bergson that the nature of the comic lies in human inflexibility may help us understand why we laugh at the characters of *The Cherry Orchard* when they fail to behave in an adaptive, context-sensitive way.[31] Thus Senelick, for example, explains the comic nature of the characters of Ranevskaia and Gaev by their resistance to the fluidity of lived experience.[32] In more general terms, one may argue that the characters' infantile behavior creates a kind of situation, first described by Immanuel Kant and then elaborated upon by Arthur Schopenhauer, that arouses laughter primarily because of the incongruity between what we expect and what we finally see.[33] But what makes Chekhov's humor so subtle is not the characters' inflexibility or the incongruity between what we expect and finally see but their ability to generate understanding and sometimes empathy rather than a sense of superiority. Although we may see the characters' behavior as incongruent with their age or position, we also experience a sense of enjoyment at recognizing their vulnerability and identifying this incongruity as a profoundly human one. While the characters of *The Cherry Orchard* become objects of laughter in part due to their infantile nature, it is precisely because they willingly allow us to laugh at them that they force upon us a perception of our kinship. When in her childlike happiness at seeing her nursery and her little old bookcase, Ranevskaia addresses her family and indirectly the audience—"Laugh at me, I am silly"—thereby disarming those of us who may be too ready to dismiss her outburst as mere farce, we laugh, but in a way that recognizes the characters' fundamental humanity and reflects, therefore, a condition that is also ours. Chekhov is critical of Russian immaturity and childishness, yet childishness may also be what makes the Chekhovian character so endearing and human. In this play, Chekhov combines comedy with satire by making us laugh both *at* and *with* his characters.

This is also why the reader or spectator may feel an admixture of sympathy and outrage toward the play's incorrigible children. The consequences of their childish behavior, however, are less than comic. Chekhov projects a certain psychological state or phenomenon—the nostalgia for childhood—

onto the whole nation. This is Chekhov's psychoanalysis of the nation and of Russian historical development. As not a single one of *The Cherry Orchard*'s characters (including Lopakhin) seems to be able to develop an adult personality, the problematics of the play go beyond the difficulty of inevitable social change and grow into a problem of the development of national selfhood. National and cultural nostalgia for the Golden Age and childhood, a longing for protection ensured by patriarchal relations and the comfort of the extended family, result in arrested national development, economic and otherwise. Maturation of the nation mimics the psychological development of its members.

Chekhov identifies the paradigm of childishness as an ailment of Russian culture (and possibly of contemporary society in general) and, true to his method, diagnoses the disease but suggests no cure.[34] Does this mean that the cherry orchard, as a symbol of both a golden age and the immaturity of its owners, has to be destroyed by Lopakhin's axes? Most certainly not. Chekhov always sought a middle ground. After all, maturity manifests itself not in the negation of the psychological, historical, or mythical past but in growth and the assimilation of it. Does the metamorphosis of the sound of the shepherd's pipe at the end of act 1 into the mysterious sound of a snapping string in act 2—and the ominous recurrence of this same sound combined with the sound of strokes of the ax against the cherry trees at the end of act 4—underscore the progression from idyll to the reality of the modern world, from the pastoral of childhood to the drama (or comedy!) of maturity? As Chekhov makes us laugh at his characters' childishness, he indirectly and subtly facilitates the process of growth in his audience. By laughing at the characters' lack of maturity, we become more mature ourselves, for, as was suggested by Freud in his discussion of the functions of humor, a good sense of humor is an essential component of maturity. If, as it has been demonstrated in research in the area of cognitive development, humor is a force in the process of maturity, then Chekhov's choice of the genre of comedy for the treatment of infantilism is truly a felicitous one and even therapeutic: not only is comedy the most amusing and enjoyable medium by which to discuss human weaknesses and society's flaws, but it is the most effective way of dealing with the subject of maturity and infantilism. By appreciating the play's comic nature, the reader or spectator grows in maturity—that is, responds to the comedy's criticism of infantilism in the most appropriate way.

While the orchard and the nursery might be symbols of paradise and childhood for the comedy's characters, in *The Cherry Orchard*, as well as in all his major plays, Chekhov consistently questions symbolization as a form of self-deception. "A carrot is a carrot." Likewise, the seagull is a seagull, Moscow is Moscow, the nursery is a nursery (that is, a place for children), and the cherry orchard is an orchard (that is, a place to grow and cultivate fruit). In the following chapter, I will consider other dimensions of the image of the orchard not as a symbol but as a concrete plot of land.

8

Back to the Cherry Orchard Itself

"Let Us Cultivate Our Garden"

Regardless of their realist, naturalist, or symbolist assumptions, Chekhov's audience and readers almost invariably interpreted the image of the cherry orchard in Chekhov's last play as symbolic. Some, such as Ivan Bunin, criticized Chekhov for the implausibility of his depiction of Gaev and Ranevskaia's estate and insisted that cherry orchards in which only cherries were grown did not even exist in Russia at all, and that orchards have never been planted near manor estates. Bunin also believed there was nothing particularly beautiful about cherry trees or remarkable about their blossoms. With his realist bias, Bunin disliked Chekhov's plays in general and viewed them as artificial and not true to life. In particular, he claimed that Chekhov, as a man who did not belong to the nobility, had a limited understanding of the nature of noble estates and their way of life. There is no reason, however, to expect that Chekhov should strictly adhere to realistic poetics and portray the orchard as it might be portrayed in realistic fiction. The accusation of "implausibility" merely points to Bunin's misunderstanding of Chekhov's innovative poetics, which freely combines elements of realism, naturalism, symbolism, and even the absurd. Moreover, there were indeed regions in Russia where mostly only cherry trees grew. As Dmitry A. Timiriazev states in his *Historical-Statistical Overview of Russia's Industry*, there were orchards that specifically specialized in cherry growing. Cherry trees were widely cultivated in the Kaluga and Kursk regions, and the city of Vladimir and its suburbs were especially famous for their cherry orchards.[1]

Bunin's blindness with respect to the role of the image of the cherry orchard in Chekhov's last play is indicative, however, of the general tendency of readers to interpret this image in purely symbolic terms. Most readers, stage directors, and scholars focus almost exclusively on its symbolic meaning—whether it is a poetic symbol of the nobility's way of life, their idyllic past or "lost paradise," the world at large, or beauty itself. In this chapter I will challenge this one-sided approach to Chekhov's play and examine the cherry orchard's commercial as well as symbolic potential.

In his memoirs, Konstantin S. Stanislavsky explains this poetic image in a way that became standard in interpretations of the play. Stanislavsky recalls how Chekhov once told him that he had found a beautiful title for his play—"The Cherry Orchard" (with the emphasis on the letter "ë" in the adjective *Вишнёвый*)—and that, by Chekhov's affectionate intonation, he realized that Chekhov was talking about something exceptionally beautiful and cherished. According to Stanislavsky, a few days later Chekhov announced again enthusiastically:

> "Listen, not *Вишневый*, but *Вишнёвый* sad" ... Anton Pavlovich continued to savor the title of the play, emphasizing the delicate sound *ë* in the word *вишнёвый* [cherry], as if trying with its help to caress the old, beautiful, but now unnecessary life, which he with tears destroyed in his play. This time I understood the subtlety: the *Vishnevyi sad* is a business, a commercial garden that generates income. Such a garden is needed now as well. But *Vishniovyi sad* does not bring any income; it keeps in itself and in its blossoming whiteness the poetry of the past noble life. Such a garden grows and blooms at whim, for the eyes of spoiled aesthetes. It is a pity to destroy it, but it is necessary, since the process of the country's economic development requires this.[2]

Apparently, Stanislavsky's underlying assumption was that the cherry orchard, no matter how beautiful it may be, is superfluous in its purely aesthetic function and should be destroyed for the sake of economic development. Stanislavsky thus set the paradigm for interpreting the image of the cherry orchard as purely symbolic—a symbol of the beauty and poetry of the aristocratic past.[3] The supposed inevitability and economic necessity of the destruction of the cherry orchard has become a staple in Chekhov scholarship.

Thus, a tradition was established of interpreting the orchard not as a concrete garden, but as a symbol of the nobility's way of life that had to be destroyed for the sake of necessary socio-economic and political changes. Emphasizing the purely symbolic function of the orchard, Donald Rayfield, for example, even concluded that the entire estate of Ranevskaia and Gaev was one enormous orchard. He calculated its size as follows: "Lopakhin's

figure of 25,000 roubles a year at twenty-five roubles per *desiatina* (a hect-
are) reveals to the numerate how hyperbolic the cherry orchard is. A cherry
orchard of a thousand hectares cannot exist. To a receptive audience, the
cherry orchard takes on from this point symbolic qualities: it is a dinosaur."[4]
However, there is no evidence in the text that the cherry orchard occupies
the entire 1,000-hectare estate. Moreover, Lopakhin specifically indicates
that his project requires the use not only of the cherry orchard, but also the
land along the river: "and if the cherry orchard and the land by the river are
divided into plots for vacationers, you'll have an income of at least twenty-
five thousand rubles a year" (13:205). He further explains his plan: "The location is marvelous, and the river is deep. Only one must, of course, to clean
up a little … for example, let's say, tear down all the old buildings and this
house here, which is no longer of any use, cut down the old cherry orchard"
(13:205). Obviously, the orchard is only part of the estate, and Lopakhin
emphasizes this several times, speaking of "both the cherry orchard and the
entire estate" (13:205). Granted, the orchard is large and famous, but there is
no reason to believe that it is as vast as Rayfield claims. The estate includes
land along "a beautiful deep river" and, apparently, an open field (the setting
of act 2), since we learn that the whole family gathers in the open fields behind
the house, at the edge of the cherry orchard. It is absolutely unfeasible to
imagine that all the characters in the play, including the old man Firs, walk
about 1,000 hectares of land (or 2471 acres of land) to reach the field if it
is located outside of the estate. Here Lopakhin reiterates his question, "Do
you agree to lease the land for dachas?" He uses the word "land" rather than
simply "cherry orchard": "It's necessary to lease both the cherry orchard and
the land to build dachas" (13:219).

I dwell on these details in order to reconsider the exaggeration of the
symbolic aspect of the orchard/garden at the expense of its realistic dimensions. If we evaluate the tension between *vishnevyi* and *vishniovyi* identified by Stanislavsky—the commercial garden versus the poetic symbol of the
gentry's life, depending on the stress on the first or penultimate syllable—
the play's problematic proves more complex and ambiguous than is frequently
thought. Could the orchard also potentially be a commercial garden? Since
Chekhov's play ends with the destruction of the old cherry orchard, the question inevitably arises: how are we to relate to the fate of the cherry trees under
Lopakhin's axes? Is the destruction of the orchard something inevitable that
the owners of the estate simply cannot accept? Are Lopakhin's axes the only
alternative to a homestead that no longer generates income? Should we trust

Lopakhin that this is the best and only solution? Most scholars and readers believe that it is. It is generally accepted that the play reflects a profound crisis in Russian society on the eve of the Russian revolution of 1905—not only an increase in social mobility but also drastic economic changes. The consensus seems to be that the demise of the cherry orchard was inevitable, and that the play problematizes the advent of a new industrial society along with the gradual disappearance of old patriarchal ways of life, and the crisis of agriculture. While the point about the need for change is undeniable, and while the play may indeed be "a theater-poem of the suffering of change," as Francis Fergusson labeled it, it is less obvious what concrete form this necessary change should take. This chapter offers an alternative interpretation and analyzes the image of the cherry orchard not only as a symbol but also as a real, concrete orchard—similar to the seagull in the play of the same name, which functions as both an object and an image of the object. Could the orchard in the play be interpreted as commercially profitable land? Or is it doomed to succumb to the threat of industrialization, which features prominently in the play in the form of background references to telegraph poles and the railroad?[5] Did modernization and industrialization, which were undoubtedly prominent aspects of life that Russia had to grapple with at the turn of the century, necessarily require the destruction of horticulture, including commercial gardening? In what follows, I will argue that they did not, but first I offer a brief outline of the state of commercial horticulture in Russia at the play's time of writing.

In the past, the old servant Firs reveals, the estate brought in substantial revenue because they knew how to cultivate the orchard and collect and transport cherries for sale to Moscow and Kharkov: "In times before, about forty or fifty years ago, the cherries were dried, soaked, marinated, and jam was made. . . . And it used to be they'd send cartloads of dried cherries off to Moscow and to Kharkov. We would have loads of money then!" (13:206). Lopakhin explains, however, that the cherry trees now bear fruit only every other year, and the market for cherries has dried up. He suggests that if leasers were willing to pay twenty-five rubles per tithe (*desiatina*), the estate would be able to generate twenty-five thousand in income. Lopakhin's idea of leasing the land to vacationers seems convincing and financially profitable, and so most readers accept his advice as sound and reasonable. Although Firs complains that the recipe for drying and preserving cherries has been mysteriously forgotten, it is hard to imagine that the commercial demand for cherries had also suddenly vanished. With the railroad running alongside the estate, transporting both dry and fresh cherries to Kharkov and Moscow would have been easier than ever before. Indeed, railroads substantially improved trade and commercial horticulture in late nineteenth-century Russia. Commercial gardening especially flourished after the construction of the railroad that connected Moscow to Nizhny Novgorod. New modes of agriculture were developing rapidly. Gardening and the cultivation of orchards were also on the rise. Timiriazev testifies, for example, that the small town of Maloiaroslavets in the Kaluga region, well-known for its cherries, sold thirty thousand rubles worth of cherries per season in good years, and peasants received two hundred rubles per tithe (a *desiatina* is equivalent to about 10,925 square meters). Gaev and Ranevskaia's orchard could potentially generate an income equal to, if not greater than, that proposed by Lopakhin in his plan to rent out the entire estate to vacationers. Moreover, in the second half of the nineteenth and early twentieth centuries, a whole group of prominent scientist-agriculturalists became engaged in the cultivation of gardens: M. V. Rytov, N. I Kichunov, I. V. Michurin, V. V. Pashkevich, and M. S. Balabanov, among others. Numerous magazines specializing in gardening were published and widely circulated (Chekhov himself subscribed to botanical magazines, ordered plants from catalogs, and thoroughly studied the art of designing parks and orchards), including the *Orcharder and Gardener* newspaper (*Sadovnik i ogorodnik*), the *Orchard and Garden* magazine (*Sad i ogorod*), and the *Bulletin of Horticulture* (*Vestnik sadovodstva, plodovodstva i ogorodnichestva*). The Russian Society of Fruit Gardening, focused on commercial horticulture, was established in 1891 and published the monthly *Pomiculture* (*Plodovodstvo*). Commercial fruit cultivation was especially developed by the end of the nineteenth century in the southern parts of the Russian Empire. The 1880s saw a great reawakening of public interest in gardening and the establishment of the first scientific centers and schools of gardening. By 1898, Russia boasted eighteen colleges and schools of horticulture. Horticultural schools and research institutions, such as the Nikitsky Botanical Garden, were widely known. Although after the Great Reforms the economic situation of the landed gentry's estates required reorganization, orcharding and gardening gradually became commercial and profitable. In 1887, there were 209,000 hectares of orchards in the nine Ukrainian provinces under Russian rule. The first significant contribution to scientific horticulture was made by the Symyrenko family and Vasyl Kashchenko. In addition to the famous Russian naturalist Ivan Michurin (who, as some scholars suggest, may have been the model for the gardener

Pesotsky in Chekhov's story "The Black Monk," 1893), M. S. Balabanov and his pomological nursery located on the border of Kursk and Kharkov governorates (*gubernii*) were particularly famous. His orchards were among the first commercial enterprises in Russia, and his name was known to all professional gardeners. Balabanov published his "Letters on Gardening" in the prominent periodical *Russian Gardening* and in other publications, describing the extensive orchards in the Korocha district and giving recommendations on fruit cultivation, including the commercial growing of cherries.[6] He participated in the first Russian Fruit Fair in 1892 and in the international symposium of pomologists in St. Petersburg in 1894.

This widespread interest in gardening and fruit cultivation was reflected both in Chekhov's own practice and in his fiction. Chekhov was a passionate gardener with a special fondness for fruit trees, including cherry trees.[7] He planted about eighty cherry trees on his estate in Melikhovo. Moreover, Chekhov seriously considered the commercial potential of his fruit orchard in Melikhovo. In his letter to Nikolai A. Leikin, he shows that he takes seriously the commercial aspect of growing cherries: "I ordered 100 lilac bushes and 50 trees of Vladimir cherry trees for the fall. In that place, which I have now fenced in with a solid fence and which serves as an extension of our garden, at least 700 trees will have to be planted. The orchard will be excellent, and in 8–10 years my heirs will have a good income from it" (P 5:76). Planting flowers and different varieties of trees in Yalta, he carefully selected rare plants (he kept a notebook called "The Garden"), ordered multiple books on gardening, and scrutinized *Flora of Gardening* (*Flora sadovodstva*), by P. P. Zolotarev. In his letters, he frequently emphasized his fondness for gardening and proudly declared to M. O. Menshikov: "If it were not for literature, I think I might have been a gardener" (P 9:58).[8] His story "The Black Monk," in particular, demonstrates Chekhov's familiarity not only with gardening but also with the scientific and technical aspects of horticulture. Pesotsky's garden is described as an exemplary, innovative, and successful commercial enterprise (its owner "made a fortune with his garden"), and the owner himself as a tireless toiler who rises before dawn and fumigates his fruit trees to protect them from frost. His orchard and garden are no less famous than the cherry orchard that Gaev is so fond of. "The garden is certainly fine, a model. It's not really a garden, but a regular institution, which is of the greatest public importance because it marks, so to say, a new era in Russian agriculture and Russian industry," Pesotsky says proudly. Pesotsky is also a dedicated pomologist and horticulturist who has published a variety of professional articles on the subject. The titles of his articles and pamphlets emphasize their specialized quality (8:237) and are proof of the existence of successful gardeners in late nineteenth-century Russia. Orcharding was far from obsolete, and the horticultural industry could indeed be profitable, as the growth of cities in central Russia in the late nineteenth century encouraged the expansion of market gardening and truck farming and the horticultural economy developed rapidly.

If we consider the scale of the development of commercial gardening in Russia by the end of the nineteenth century, as well as Chekhov's own expertise and great interest in gardening, it becomes less than obvious that Lopakhin's proposal to build vacation homes rather than cultivate the cherry orchard was the best solution to the estate's problems and that the land could not have been utilized otherwise. When Firs argues that the ways of growing, harvesting, and preserving cherries have been forgotten, there is no reason to believe that this was universal. It is more reasonable to conclude that if cherry trees are not bearing fruit, it only indicates that those who cultivate the orchard are inept workers who have no interest in maintaining it. As the successful gardener Pesotsky of "The Black Monk" explains, "The whole secret of success lies not in its being a big garden or a great number of laborers being employed in it, but in the fact that I love the work. . . . The whole secret lies in loving it—that is, in the sharp eye of the master" (8:236). Indeed, it is clear that Gaev's estate lacks skillful management and "the sharp eye of the master." If we consider the denouement of *The Cherry Orchard* in the context of Chekhov's other major plays, we see that although all four plays and *Ivanov* deal with financial pressures on their respective estates, these financial complications are resolved differently in each case. In the *Seagull*, for example, although Sorin lives on his country estate because the country lifestyle is more affordable than life in the city, he does not go bankrupt. In *Uncle Vania*, Serebriakov proposes to sell the estate to improve his financial situation, but Voinitsky and Sonia succeed in keeping it by their own labor. Only *The Cherry Orchard* ends with an image of destruction.

Why is this the case? If we consider the various solutions to the external pressures on the respective estates in Chekhov's four major plays, Lopakhin's plan to destroy the house and the garden appears problematic since leasing the estate is not necessarily the best or only solution to the problems that arise. Consider, for example, *The Seagull*. Although Sorin's estate does not bring in substantial revenue for its owner, who constantly complains about the inconveniences of country life, he manages to maintain a generally decent lifestyle, providing housing for his nephew, Konstantin Treplev, and hosting other family members, including Arkadina and her lover Trigorin, during their summer vacations. Sorin is no more adept at running the estate than are Ranevskaia and Gaev. Yet the main difference is that he has an estate manager, Shamraev, an authoritarian figure whom Sorin calls "a despot" and who may even take advantage of his master, but who nevertheless seems to manage the estate without ruining the financial well-being of its owner. All the characters in the play are annoyed with Shamraev and frustrated by his refusal to accommodate the demands of his master and his guests. We learn that Shamraev refuses to unleash the hauling dog because he wants to protect the millet in the storehouse from thieves. He also declines to give Arkadina the carriage horses for the trip to town because, as he explains, all the workers are busy hauling rye, and all the horses are being used in the fields. "You don't have any idea of what it means to manage the estate!" (13:25). They all blame Shamraev for his despotism and mismanagement, and Sorin complains that Shamraev leaves him penniless because he spends his entire pension on farming, raising cattle and tending bees. Although, according to Sorin, his money goes to waste because all the cows and bees die, and he is unable to use the horses when he needs them (13:36), it is unlikely that Shamraev is really such a poor manager. After all, Sorin is able to lead a relatively carefree life on his estate, drinking cherry wine, smoking cigars, doing nothing, enjoying good weather and fresh air with his guests, and supporting his nephew. There is no indication that he lives in debt or is pressured to sell the estate. For all the criticism Shamraev receives from other characters, there is no reason to believe that he runs the estate as a wasteful enterprise.

Uncle Vania offers an even more convincing model for the successful management of an estate. Thanks to Vania and Sonia's tireless hard work, the estate is completely paid off and generates a solid income, sufficient to support not only Sonia and Vania but also Professor Serebriakov and his wife. Although Professor Serebriakov is initially eager to sell the estate, it is ultimately preserved due to Sonia and Vania's diligence and devotion. The idea that one must work hard and that work makes life bearable and meaningful runs not only through this play but through Chekhov's entire oeuvre.

The motif of planting trees and cultivating land is central to Chekhov's prose and drama. Astrov's frequently quoted reasoning about the disastrous consequences of deforestation and the need to plant trees, rather than to cut them down, is a good example of this:

> Russian forests are cracking under the ax, millions of trees are perishing, the
> homes of the animals and birds are devastated, the rivers grow shallow and
> dry up, the marvelous landscapes are disappearing forever, and it's all because
> the lazy person doesn't have sense enough to bend down and pick up his fuel
> from the ground. . . . Only a thoughtless barbarian could burn beauty like this
> in his stove and destroy what we ourselves can't create. (13:72–73)

Astrov's agricultural enthusiasm, which is not limited to the problem of
ecology—he is also the proud owner of an "exemplary garden and a nursery" (13:71)—is not an isolated case in Chekhov's works. The destruction
of trees is repeatedly presented by Chekhov as barbaric and senseless. The
motif of cutting down trees also appears in *The Three Sisters*. Having a pre-
sentiment that he might be killed in a duel with Solyonyi, Tuzenbach admires
the nearby trees, which he associates with life and beauty: "It seems to me
as if I see these fir trees, maples, and birches for the first time in my life,
and everything seems to be looking at me, waiting with curiosity. What
beautiful trees, and what a beautiful life ought to be around them in reality!"
(13:181). When Natasha declares in the play's finale that she will cut down
the fir tree alley and the old maple ("I'll order first of all the alley of fir trees
cut down, then that maple there"), it becomes obvious that her pragmatism
and weak aesthetic sense are not the best alternative to the sisters' impracticality. Like Lopakhin, who wants to replace the cherry orchard with "happy,
rich, luxurious" plots for vacationers, Natasha, in her determination to eliminate the entire legacy of the estate's previous owners, is eager to replace the
alley of trees with "little flowers" (Chekhov uses the diminutive form "florets"
here [*tsvetochki*] to emphasize her petit bourgeois taste). The audience can
hardly be convinced by Natasha's "improvements," especially in the context
of Tuzenbach's praise of the beauty of these trees. Examples of the desola-
tion, neglect, and destruction of gardens and plants as signs of barbarism,
unculturedness, and degradation are numerous in Chekhov's fiction. Consider, for example, his story "The Reed Pipe" ("Svirel," 1887): "If a single tree
withers away, or let's say a single cow dies, it makes you feel sorry, but what
will it be, good man, if the whole world crumbles into dust?" (6:323). Like
The Cherry Orchard, *The Three Sisters* ends with the image of dispossession
as the sisters must leave their family home, but there is no reason to believe
that Natasha's control will lead to prosperity and beauty.

If we consider *The Cherry Orchard* not only in the context of the state
of agriculture and gardening in turn-of-the-century Russia but also in the

context of Chekhov's own works, it becomes clear that not so much a lack of commercial potential as mismanagement and irresponsibility lead to the sale and demise of the cherry orchard. The problem of mismanagement becomes particularly obvious when one recalls Petia Trofimov's lofty proclamation that "all Russia is our orchard." Petia's exaltation seems comical, for he expresses a utopian vision of Russia by suggesting the creation of a new paradise. But his words also seem to be an unconscious reference to A. K. Tolstoy's poem "History of the Russian State from Gostomysl to Timashev," with its famous line "Our land is abundant, it only lacks order" (Земля наша богата, / Порядка в ней лишь нет) and its epigraph from Nestor, "Our land is vast and abundant, but it has no order" (Вся земля наша велика и обильна, а наряда в ней нет.) After his reference to Russia as an orchard ("all Russia is our garden"), Petia's phrase "The land is vast and beautiful, there are many marvelous places within it" (Земля велика и прекрасна, есть на ней много чудесных мест), which echoes A. K. Tolstoy's "our land is vast and abundant," reminds us of what is missing—order and management (13:227). It is noteworthy that another poem by A. K. Tolstoy, "The Sinful Woman," is mentioned in act 3, which suggests that his poetry was widely known among the characters in the play. Indeed, idleness, lack of order, and lack of initiative are the scourges from which the owners of the estate suffer, as well as all the play's characters, including Petia himself. For all his high-mindedness and social conscience, Petia is as helpless as the awkward and inept bookkeeper Epikhodov. He rants about the necessity of labor ("What we ought to do is to work"; "The one thing we must do is to work, to help by all our means those who seek the truth"; "Here in Russia very few people work so far") but does nothing himself (13:223). His criticism of Russia's ignorance, lack of culture, and ineffective and hypocritical intelligentsia may be eloquent and sensible, but it comically points to the disparity between his own words and deeds (13:223).[9]

The play creates a picture of almost universal ineptitude: not only that of the landowners but also of servants, the student Petia, the clerk Epikhodov, and the governess Charlotta. All the characters, including the merchant Lopakhin, seem incapable of living productive lives and caring for the "orchard" of Russia. Gaev, in his own words, has "eaten up his fortune in lollypops." Ranevskaia has squandered everything she had on her Parisian lover. Neither Ranevskaia nor the "eternal student" Petia Trofimov, who worked as her son's tutor, could prevent the drowning of her little one in the river, a sign of neglect. Not only is Lopakhin unable to propose to Varia and arrange his personal life, but he constantly complains that they "all lead a foolish kind of life" (*zhizn' u nas duratskaia*) and, having bought the estate, laments "if only our unhappy and disorderly life could quickly change somehow" (13:241). Simeonov-Pishchik, the local landowner, lives in debt but has no qualms about asking Ranevskaia for money, even when he knows that she has none. Although he owns land, he does nothing with it but relies on his luck, which miraculously saves him from peril, at least for a while. He leases a plot of his land to English entrepreneurs who find white clay. The Englishmen, as opposed to the Russian landowner, know how to exploit the land. Simeonov-Pishchik, by contrast, simply continues to rely on serendipitous events: "Just as I think everything is lost, that's the end of me—lo and behold—they built a railroad right through my land . . . and they paid me for it. And then if not today, then tomorrow something else will happen . . . Dashenka may win two hundred thousand . . . She has a lottery ticket" (13:209). While the land may indeed be "vast and abundant," as A. K. Tolstoy puts it, the Russians in Chekhov's play dispose of their wealth and rely either on lottery tickets or the help of English entrepreneurs to manage their riches and establish "order." The figure who personifies this general ineptitude is the accident-prone clerk Epikhodov, nicknamed "Twenty-Two Misfortunes" for his incapacity, awkwardness, and lack of eloquence. Although he is obviously completely useless in his role as the estate's bookkeeper, the "practical" Lopakhin for some reason hires him and entrusts the estate to him in his absence. If all of Russia is an orchard, as Petia proclaims, then it is clearly an orchard that no one is able to tend to. It is either an orchard of the past or a utopian orchard of the future that has no place in the present. For Trofimov, the orchard is everywhere, which is the same as nowhere; for Ania, who jubilantly declares, "We will plant a new garden, more luxurious than this," it is an abstract garden, not attached to any specific place; and for Lopakhin, the garden's existence is predicated on its destruction—he oxymoronically proposes to "save" it by cutting it down: "one needs only . . . to cut the old cherry orchard. . . . In twenty years or so the vacationer will multiply to an extraordinary extent [Chekhov uses the term "vacationer" in the singular to suggest that the vacationer is a new kind of species] . . . and it may happen that on his ten hectares of land he will start up farming, and then *your cherry orchard* [emphasis mine] will become happy, abundant, and luxurious" (13:205–6).

Although Lopakhin prides himself on working from morning till night, the usefulness of his labor is also put into question. Destroying the orchard and the house and building cottages for vacationers in their place may be the fastest way to enrich Lopakhin, who is a capitalist interested in quick profits. But there is one detail that casts Lopakhin's enterprise in a different light: as much as he is eager to cut down the cherry orchard, he is not averse to commercial agriculture, for as he himself reveals, he sowed 1,000 hectares of poppies the previous spring (naming an amount of land that, incidentally, exactly matches the size of the Gaev estate) and earned forty thousand on its harvest (13:244). Why, then, is Lopakhin not interested in cultivating the land he purchases at auction? Why is cultivating poppies more profitable than cultivating cherries? Clearly, the destruction of the cherry orchard is not motivated purely by financial considerations. This fact is further emphasized by his impatience to cut down the trees while the former landowners are still there. This haste is not only insensitive but also makes no practical sense. We know that Lopakhin was leaving for Kharkov for the fall and winter and probably would not have been able to take up his reconstruction until spring. The only real motivation for Lopakhin to cut down the trees before Ranevskaia and Gaev left was not financial but psychological—to annihilate the memory of serfdom and the cherry orchard as a relic of that past. His desire to make everyone see the destruction of that past indicates resentment. Indeed, upon his return from the auction, the tipsy Lopakhin raves about the purchase of "the most beautiful spot in the world," proudly declaring "the cherry orchard is mine now." However, he must own it only to be able to destroy it: "Come on, all of you, to see Yermolai Lopakhin slash the cherry orchard with his ax, how the trees come crashing down!" (13:240). The destruction of the cherry orchard and the old house has symbolic rather than financial significance for him.

The demolition of the orchard is yet another act of "thoughtless barbarism," to use Dr. Astrov's words about the Russian disregard for tree preservation. Significantly, Petia Trofimov undermines the seeming practicality of the new capitalist Lopakhin with his ironic reference to Lopakhin's "useful labor" ("We're going away, and you will resume your useful labor"). He also expresses skepticism about Lopakhin's cottage-building enterprise: "Don't wave your arms around. And also when you count on building those summer cottages and count that the vacationers in time will turn out to be independent owners—that's just the same as waving your arms around" (13:243–44).

In conclusion, I would like to suggest that Chekhov's approach to the need for socioeconomic change was neither radical nor conservative but liberal, in the spirit of the European Enlightenment. Embracing industrialization and modernization, Chekhov hoped for reforms that would turn liberal ideas into reality, but he envisioned these changes as generated primarily through individual efforts and practical social, educational, and cultural work, both within the local self-government of the *zemstvo* institution and within the professions. His chief values and ideas were profoundly liberal, ethical, and practical: he believed in liberty, equality, and—above all—in human dignity and the value of individuality. He viewed the individual as an agent of change in improving the well-being of the people through constant labor, discipline, and cultivation (understood in both its literal and figurative senses, as cultivation of the land and the process of acquiring skills, education, and culture). For Chekhov, culture—in the tradition of the Enlightenment—is inextricably linked to the concepts of shaping, formation, cultivation, and education. It is no coincidence that he uses this word both in its original meaning associated with agriculture and in its second meaning related to human upbringing. In both cases, it is a constant struggle against wild nature and against barbarism, a struggle for civilization, construction, and cultivation in all senses of these words.

Culture implies the cultivation of a place—the cultivation of the land and habitats, and an attentive and careful attitude toward it. This is why Chekhov's works frequently make reference to "Asians," "Tartars," or "Pechenegs," ethnic groups that he associates with a nomadic way of life and hence a lack of "culture" (in the sense of agricultural prosperity and a comfortable, civilized lifestyle). Although he uses the terms "Tartars" and "Pechenegs" mostly in a pejorative sense, they do not refer to the real Tartars and Pechenegs. In his story titled "The Pecheneg," it is the Russian landowner who is called a "Pecheneg" because he is unable to keep his estate in order and "cultivate" his "place": "After they had driven approximately eight miles a low house and a backyard surrounded by a dark wattle fence came into view; the roof of the house is green, the plaster is peeling off, and the windows are small, narrow, like squinting eyes. The farmhouse stood completely exposed to the sun; neither trees nor water were visible anywhere near it. The neighboring landowners and peasants called it 'Pecheneg Grange'" (9:326). Chekhov's works often include critiques of those who consider themselves representatives of the nobility or the intelligentsia but who fail to "cultivate" their surroundings. Chekhov repeatedly observes a connection between culture and agriculture (this is why he values trees and gardens so much, for they signify culture for him). A case in point is the following passage from the story "My Life": "And how these people lived, it's a shame to say! No garden, no theater, no decent orchestra; the city and club libraries were visited only by teenage Jews, so magazines and new books lay uncut for months; the rich and intelligent slept in stuffy, cramped bedrooms, on wooden beds with bedbugs, children were kept in disgustingly dirty rooms called children's rooms, and servants, even old and respectable ones, slept in the kitchen on the floor and covered themselves with rags" (9:205). It follows from this description that culture, for Chekhov, is not only music, art, theater, and literature but also includes having a *garden*, comfortable and spacious premises, hygiene, comfort, and respect for human dignity.[10]

The ending of *The Cherry Orchard*, with the sound of axes against cherry trees, therefore challenges two of the most fundamental imperatives of Chekhov's life and work: the need for meaningful creative work and the notion of cultivation. Without disputing the scholarly tradition of allegorical readings of the garden in *The Cherry Orchard* as a Garden of Eden— among which Robert L. Jackson's essay "'What Time Is It? Where Are we Going?' Chekhov's *The Cherry Orchard*: The Story of a Verb" stands out as beautifully subtle interpretation of the theme of time in the play and also of the pervasive symbolism of the garden as "an innocent pre-fall world or Garden of Eden"—I propose to look in this chapter at the garden in its philosophical and pragmatic contexts.[11] Rather than alluding to a rosy utopian picture of Russia as a blooming paradise, Petia's notion that "All Russia is our garden" forces the audience to imagine a garden that needs cultivation. Perhaps it is no coincidence that these two concerns—the need to work and to cultivate one's garden, or orchard—find their classic representation in Voltaire's "philosophical tale" *Candide*. At the conclusion of *Candide*, the protagonist utters a phrase that has become widely and universally known: "Il faut cultiver notre jardin." As in Voltaire's tale, the symbolism of the garden is used extensively in *The Cherry Orchard*. However, for both Voltaire and Chekhov, the garden is not only a symbol but also a concrete plot of land that requires individual effort to be maintained. Inspired by the example of a happy, wise Turk working his plot of land, whom he meets at the end of his travails, Candide decides to do the same: "I know also," said Candide, "that we must cultivate our garden." Pangloss agrees with him and suggests that even the garden of Eden was not created for leisure but for cultivation: "for when man was placed in the garden of Eden, he was placed there *ut operaretur eum*—that he might work—which proves that man was not born to rest." Martin echoes this sentiment: "'Let's get down to work and stop all this philosophizing,' said Martin, 'It's the only way to make life bearable.'"[12]

The last statement sounds remarkably similar to the calls for labor that conclude *Uncle Vania* and *Three Sisters*: "we must work, only work." Like Voltaire, Chekhov was suspicious of lofty and all-resolving theories and advocated practical solutions. Similar to Voltaire, who questioned Leibniz's optimism and rational explanation of evil, Chekhov was skeptical of the philosophical pretensions of established philosophers and writers, and particularly of the overblown rhetoric of intellectuals and their utopian visions of the future. After all, we encounter the aging "eternal student" Petia, who is "above love" and full of "presentiments," and who indulges in philosophizing and preaches the necessity of labor but is himself incapable of any meaningful activity; the audience can only smile at his grandiose activist vision: "Forward! We are marching irresistibly toward the bright star, glowing there in the distance! Forward! Keep up, friends!" (13:227); "I'm a free man.... I'm strong and proud. Humanity is moving toward the highest truth, toward the highest happiness possible on earth, and I'm in the forefront!" (13:244).[13] Chekhov sneers at Trofimov's Panglossian rhetoric and naïve belief in marching forward toward "the highest truth" as much as Voltaire sneers at Pangloss's optimism. In lieu of Pangloss's Leibnizian mantra of "all is for the best in the best of all possible worlds" and Trofimov's call to march forward toward "the greatest happiness possible on earth," both authors offer a more prosaic and practical vision of reality. Both Voltaire, who was not a philosopher in the modern sense of the word, and Chekhov, with his distrust of philosophies and theories, mock idle philosophizing (cf. Dr. Ragin from "Ward Six" and Vershinin from *The Three Sisters*, among many other examples of philosophizers in Chekhov's works); both authors juxtapose philosophy with ordinary life, which involves work and perseverance, as a way to improve the welfare of humanity. Candide's motto, following Martin's advice to work without being distracted by theories and philosophies, promotes the idea of humble human efforts as an alternative to grandiose accomplishments.

These ideas certainly were congenial to Chekhov, who, like Voltaire, was a passionate gardener and knew in practice that careful planting and cultivation produce good fruit. Although Chekhov was more modest than Voltaire in his horticultural pursuits and could not match the scale of Voltaire's villa Les Délices and estate at Ferney, his enthusiasm for acquiring plots of land and ordering various cultivars for his garden bears some resemblance to the Ferneyan philosopher's passion for planting. Like Voltaire, he also was eager to play host to as many people as he could, whether at his estate in

Melikhovo, where he had a vegetable garden that his family members named the "South of France," or in Yalta. Both men certainly knew what it meant to cultivate a garden. Chekhov also believed in progress, conceived as hard-won advances based upon constant effort—in other words, gradual improvement rather than abrupt change. In Chekhov's notebooks we find a piece of oriental wisdom reminiscent of the wise Turk's advice in *Candide*: "Everyone is given the opportunity to leave a mark on the earth: dig a well, raise a man, or plant a tree." The necessity of real daily work—not just talking about work—is a refrain in most of Chekhov's plays, implying that labor only bears fruit when one constantly toils in one's "garden." *Candide's* ultimate conclusion that life is hard but bearable and that one must work without despair was close to Chekhov, many of whose characters in his plays—Sonia, Vania, Astrov, the sisters Prozorov, and Nina Zarechnaia—accept labor and perseverance as the only way to cope with life's hardships. Incidentally, the program of performing "small deeds," originally proposed in the Russian liberal-populist newspaper *The Week* (*Nedelia*) in the 1880s by the liberal-populist publicist Ia. V. Abramov, continued to be practiced in the 1890s. Rejecting revolutionism and any kind of violent improvement, proponents of the small deeds theory urged the intelligentsia to join local self-government institutions (*zemstvo*) and to work as teachers and doctors to improve the welfare of the people. Without openly aligning himself with any social movement, Chekhov was tirelessly engaged in a wide variety of "small" efforts—from building schools and assisting libraries to treating peasants and organizing aid during a cholera epidemic.

The Cherry Orchard need not be interpreted as a conscious reference to Voltaire's *Candide* in order to be placed in the context of Candide's motto "let us cultivate our garden," which was famous enough to be widely known. This context, however, adds an additional dimension to Chekhov's representation of Russia about a year before the revolution of 1905. Chekhov's position on the need for social change generally resembled Voltaire's liberal meliorism—he believed in gradual improvement but was skeptical of radical change. He also greatly admired Voltaire for his civic stance (especially his defense of Jean Calas) and for his ideals of responsible citizenship and enlightened democracy. Voltaire's example was on Chekhov's mind, especially during the notorious Dreyfus Affair, which started before Chekhov conceived *The Cherry Orchard* but ended only in 1906. In a letter to Suvorin from Nice on February 18, 1898, Chekhov uses the example of Voltaire as a model for "the best people, leading the nation": "Yes, Zola is not Voltaire, and we are all not Voltaires, but there are such circumstances in life when the reproach that we are not Voltaires is least appropriate" (P 7:167–68).

Chekhov also shared Voltaire's wit, gaiety, tolerance, aversion to prejudice, and taste for farce and satire. Voltaire's skepticism and his belief in the value of the skeptical position in its own right were particularly congenial to Chekhov, who insisted that "It is high time for people who write, especially artists, to admit that you cannot make out anything in this world, as Socrates once confessed and as did Voltaire" (P 2:281). It is no coincidence that Chekhov connected the figures of Voltaire and Socrates, both of whom rejected a systematic philosophical position as contradictory to their philosophical identity. Like Voltaire, Chekhov used satire and wit to undermine belief in the possibility of sophistic knowledge but at the same time showed respect for the power and value of empirical science. In his fiction, Chekhov frequently used the strategy that Voltaire employed in *Candide*—the testing and refutation of his characters' philosophizing by brute empirical facts and experience (cf. Chekhov's "Ward Six"). The events of Chekhov's last play— the loss of Gaev and Ranevskaia's estate, Varia's heartbreak, Charlotta's homelessness, the inevitable death of the abandoned Firs, Ranevskaia's doomed relationship with her lover and her uncertain future—are far from funny, but they are presented by Chekhov with the same gaiety, nonchalance, and matter-of-factness with which Voltaire describes even the far more terrible events that befall his protagonist.

Like Voltaire, Chekhov was above all an ironist, equally detached from all his characters, and treated serious historical and philosophical issues with humor: he was skeptical of the optimism of Lopakhin and Trofimov and their respective capitalist or socialist visions of a future "cherry orchard," but he mocked landowners who refused to adapt to new circumstances and were incapable of change. Similar to Voltaire, who favored gradual reform, Chekhov advocated meliorism, that is, a belief that the world can be made better through human effort and incessant work but not through violent revolution. Since the last sound of the play is the sound of an ax chopping down cherry trees, the finale emerges as an ironic inversion of Candide's motto, "let us cultivate our garden."

Although the cherry orchard as a symbol of an idyllic past or paradise is unviable, there are no reasons to believe that the orchard itself must be destroyed and cannot be made a commercial success (note Stanislavsky's verdict on the need to destroy the orchard, for "the process of the country's economic development requires this"). An orchard/garden is first and foremost a plot of land that must be cultivated. In his last play, as in his other major plays, Chekhov reveals the hidden dangers of a symbolic approach to life. Whenever the characters invest a particular object (the seagull in the play of that title) or place (Moscow in *The Three Sisters*) with symbolic meaning, the symbols prevent those characters from living productive and fruitful lives. Likewise, the characters in *The Cherry Orchard* describe and perceive the orchard not as it actually exists but as an abstract and symbolic entity. Whether a symbol of the past and childhood or serfdom and historical injustice, the particular garden, or the orchard, is abandoned and destroyed. The main target of Chekhov's satire is not only the inertia of the gentry class and the idle rhetoric of the intelligentsia, with its blind revolutionism and puerile enthusiasm for the future (Ania's "Hello, new life!"), but also the coarseness, near-sightedness, and self-righteousness of the capitalist, who is devoid of culture and incapable of cultivating the land. Behind the humorous and nostalgic façade hides a harsh critique of the lives of all classes in modern Russia. The play is a sharp critique of the social and political failure of Russia at the turn of the nineteenth century, when the intelligentsia seemed ineffective, the gentry parasitic, and the commoners ignorant. For both Voltaire and Chekhov, the garden is the better place to build with love, care, and local responsibility concentrated on immediate action. What Chekhov's Russia lacked, as shown in his last play, was the wisdom of Candide: the recognition that no matter how you choose to explain the world, the garden still needs cultivating.

Conclusion

Chekhov's Ironic Truth and the Sense of Non-ending

Perspectival seeing is the *only* kind of seeing there is, perspectival "knowing" the only kind of "knowing"; and the *more* feelings about a matter which we allow to come to expression, the *more* eyes, different eyes through which we are able to view this same matter, the more complete our "conception" of it, our "objectivity," will be.

Friedrich Nietzsche, On the Genealogy of Morals

The Irony of Not Knowing

"The truth about life which this author felt it his bounden duty to proclaim devalues the very ideas and opinions which he has his figures argue and fight about. That truth is by nature ironical." Thus writes Thomas Mann, characterizing Chekhov's art in his essay "The Stature of Anton Chekhov," published in 1955 in *The New Republic* magazine.[1] Mann admits that he developed his appreciation of Chekhov only later in life. In praising the great Russian short story writer and playwright, he concentrates mainly on his prose, almost entirely overlooking his plays. Nevertheless, he makes several valuable observations about the nature of Chekhov's art in general. In particular, he refers to "A Tedious Story" ("Skuchnaia istoriia," also translated in English as "A Boring Story" or "Dreary Story") as his favorite Chekhov work. Mann's fascination with this story echoes that of Lev Shestov, who was similarly captivated by this strange tale, which figures prominently in his interpretation of Chekhov's peculiar genius in his essay "Creation from the Void." Both the German writer and the Russian philosopher, who were personally acquainted, responded to the story's intense existential questioning and probing of the meaning of life. As Mann observes, the dying Professor Nikolai Stepanovich, the story's protagonist, feels that his life is devoid of any guiding idea, belief, or hope, that he "has always lacked a spiritual center, a 'central idea,' and that therefore at bottom it had been a life without sense and without hope." Both writers were enthralled with the way Chekhov portrayed the extreme despair of his main character, issuing from his honest assessment of his life and his helplessness in the face of approaching death. When Katya, a disoriented young girl and failed actress, turns to him for help and asks for advice on what to do with her life, the old professor has nothing to say to his ward except, "I don't know, Katya. Upon my honor, I don't know." Along with Shestov, Mann views this story as quintessentially Chekhovian. The professor's "I don't know" is also Chekhov's own, for, as Mann insightfully observes, the question of "what is to be done?" "haunts Chekhov's writings at every turn in a deliberately confused way." Yet we recall that drawing on the authority of Socrates and Voltaire, Chekhov insisted that the most he could do as a writer was simply to admit that we know nothing about the world (P 2:280–81). The ironic truth Mann speaks of is that the professor's "I don't know" in response to his ward's plea for advice is the only truth that even the smartest of his characters dares to offer. Indeed, the refusal to offer any "truth" other than the negative truth of "I don't know" is a recurrent theme in Chekhov's prose and theater. Like the professor in "The Tedious Story," Dr. Dorn in *The Seagull* also refuses to offer an answer to human suffering and fails to soothe Masha Shamraeva's desperate plea for help. His only response to the lovesick Masha's cry for help is: "but what can I do, my child? What? What?" (13:20). Mann argues that a writer who pursues this kind of "ironic truth" may appear to have no convictions or ideals: "If the truth about life is ironic by nature, then must not art be by nature nihilistic?"[2] Both Mann and Shestov note a distinct feature of Chekhov's art—his radical uncertainty and rejection of any definitive answers and solutions to the problems of human existence. Aware of the ultimate inadequacy of consciousness to fully comprehend the world, Chekhov treats human hopes, possibilities, and even truth with irony. This aspect of Chekhov's art and thought—that is, his refusal to commit to a monistic vision—was not immediately comprehensible to his contemporaries. Thus, he complained that his literary friends did not understand his new approach to the role of the definitive point of view and authorial position in fiction (2:280–81).[3]

Lack of knowledge is a pervasive theme in Chekhov's prose and theatrical works. Equally pervasive is Chekhov's ethical concern with education and the need to improve our practical knowledge. Many of Chekhov's characters and all of Chekhov's major plays reflect on the meaning of being. From Treplev's failure to understand why and for whom he writes, to Vania's despair over the meaning of life and work, to the three Prozorov sisters' nostalgia for knowledge and the characters' inability to grasp how they could change their lives in *The Cherry Orchard*, most characters in Chekhov's plays struggle with questions of being and knowledge. Each play challenges the idea that "knowing" is the primary way in which human beings experience the world. The lack of knowledge about why we live and suffer, the meaning of life in general, and how to "resolve" the human sense of disorientation and find a way to live meaningfully inform all of Chekhov's characters' concerns. Each play is an attempt to answer several key questions related to this ubiquitous and fundamental lack of knowledge in human life: How should we live? How should we write? What should we do? What is the meaning of work? His characters react to the loss of meaning in different ways: some stoically embrace perseverance and endurance (Nina, Vania, Sonia, Astrov, the sisters Prozorov), while others reveal their utter helplessness (Treplev, Gaev, Ranevskaia) or even demonstrate despair (Chebutykin, Charlotta). Others, like Dr. Dorn and Dr. Astrov, hide their existential uncertainty behind irony and skepticism. Significantly, some of them may appear in different groups, further suggesting the fluidity of dramatic character as conceived by Chekhov.

The sense of disorientation caused by the lack of knowledge about the meaning of life affects most characters in Chekhov's plays. Minor characters—Sorin in *The Seagull*, Chebutykin in *The Three Sisters*, and Charlotta in *The Cherry Orchard*—become emblematic of this sense of epistemological anxiety and uncertainty about the meaning of life. As discussed in chapters 4 and 6, Chebutykin's existential and epistemological anxiety ("I don't know," "I know absolutely nothing") is linked to his misplaced temporality and ignorance, which culminates in doubt about his own existence. Similarly, the governess Charlotta's angst takes on a broader symbolic dimension when she confesses her ignorance of her origins and her real age. This ignorance results in an almost complete lack of identity or awareness of who she really is. Alienated from her life and from the people around her, Charlotta emerges as a complete stranger: "I don't have a real passport, I don't know how old I am, and I keep thinking I'm young. . . . I don't know where I'm from or who I am . . . Who my parents are, maybe they never got married . . . I don't know. (*Takes a cucumber out of her pocket and eats it.*) I don't know anything" (13:215). The stage directions reinforce the sense of absurdity this scene creates and point to the comic incongruity between her existential anxiety and the fact that she carries a cucumber in her pocket—not the most appropriate or typical place to keep it. Her very existence seems as out of place as the cucumber that she takes out of her pocket. It is literally outside of place and time. Charlotta's loneliness symbolizes the human predicament in general, as Chekhov sees it: "All alone, alone, I have no one and . . . And who I am, why I am, I don't know" (13:216). At the end of the play, Charlotta leaves the estate, as do the other characters in the play, but she has nowhere to go: "So you please find me a place. . . . I have nowhere to live in the city. I have to leave" (13:248). She goes, literally, nowhere.

What kind of dramatic composition results from Chekhov's ironic view of truth and skepticism about the possibility of any ultimate knowledge? How does this skepticism affect the structure and plot of his plays? The characters' epistemological and existential anxiety is never limited to their debates and musings about the meaning of life—it leads to a peculiar notion of theatrical plot and movement. The lack of knowledge, which is a common theme of Chekhov's plays, creates a distinctive plot structure characterized by open-ended denouements and character de-heroization—that is, the refusal to endow any one character or even a small group of characters with exceptional validity. Furthermore, Chekhov's plays raise the question of the relationship between knowledge, plot, and genre. Although his characters seem preoccupied with a lack of knowledge and struggle to find meaning in their existence, the plots and structures of the plays do not depend on withholding knowledge from either the characters or the audience. Traditional plays rely on some form of knowledge manipulation, but Chekhov does not seem to conceal any information from either the characters or the audience. By the end of *The Seagull*, we learn nothing substantially new about Arkadina, Trigorin, Masha, or Treplev. Perhaps only Nina undergoes some changes, but these changes are not based on any particular event or factual information revealed to her or to the viewer but on her inner growth. In *Uncle Vania*, Voinitsky becomes disillusioned with his life in act 1 and remains so in act 4. The three sisters' dreams of going to Moscow are ironically questioned from the very beginning of the play. While Olga and Irina fantasize about Moscow ("Yes! As soon as possible, off to Moscow. . . . Masha will come to Moscow every year for the whole summer" [13:120]), their hopes are undermined by carefully planted stage directions: "Chebutykin and Tuzenbach laugh," "Masha quietly whistles a tune" (12:120). Although at the end of the play the sisters are stripped of their previous illusions, they gain no substantial new insight about their situation other than the dim realization that most of their hopes will never come true. They resolve to live without knowing why they are living and suffering. The impending sale of Ranevskaia's estate is no secret and is announced in the first act of *The Cherry Orchard*. From a purely factual point of view, nothing particularly new happens in the course of the play. But ironically, whenever Chekhov's characters proclaim they know something, this "knowledge" is presented as a delusion and causes the audience to smile ironically at its inadequacy or even absurdity. Such is our reaction to Irina's naïve claim that all is clear to her, that she knows "how one ought to live" and that she knows "everything" (13:123). Claims of knowledge are always presented in Chekhov's works as either naïve or absurd and turn out to be extreme ignorance. (Compare Solyonyi as discussed in chapter 6.) Most of the characters in Chekhov's plays become victims of their false knowledge, and "knowing" always emerges as a deception (e.g., Vania's belief that he is serving a higher purpose or the three sisters' conviction that life in Moscow would be better than in the town where they live). The pursuit of knowledge, not knowledge itself, is the driving force of meaningful existence and the organizing principle of Chekhov's plays.

In classical comedies and tragedies, the audience knows or discovers things that the main characters initially do not know or learn about only belatedly. Both tragedies and comedies are based on some form of final revelation, leading to the realization of characters' errors or hubris, or the removal of misunderstandings and obstacles on the way to a happy reconciliation (comic revelation, movement from illusion to reality). But Chekhov's plays are structured differently. The later plays contain no unexpected developments and almost no element of surprise. Chekhov reduces the discontinuity between anticipated and actual outcome and consistently eliminates the elements of reversal and surprise that he used extensively in his early one-act plays, and even in *Ivanov*. The spectator possesses no superior knowledge as compared to the plays' characters, and the characters never achieve significant insights, tragic or comic. Whereas Aristotelian *anagnorisis* presupposes a transition from ignorance to knowledge, or the critical discovery of a certain truth about oneself and the world, with few exceptions, Chekhov's characters move from ignorance to ignorance. In *The Seagull*, Treplev suffers from not knowing why he lives or for whom he writes: "I still keep on drifting in a maelstrom of dreams and images, not knowing what it's for or who needs it. I don't have faith and I don't know what my calling is" (13:59). By the end of the play he has not gained a new understanding of life and only succeeds in what he has already tried before—suicide. Arkadina, Trigorin, and Masha all fail to acquire any new insight about life and about themselves.

A good example of how differently Chekhov treats the device of withholding of information from either characters or the audience (dramatic irony) is his reworking of Molière's *Tartuffe* in *Uncle Vania*. In Molière's comedy, the audience knows that Tartuffe is a crook, and the characters discover this truth by the end of the play. In Chekhov's play the audience has no superior knowledge of what kind of person Professor Serebriakov (the Tartuffe of the play) is. Nor do the characters derive a better understanding of whether or not he is a fraud. Moreover, Voinitsky does not, strictly speaking, go from illusion to reality. Because he has already been stripped of his previous illusions when we first meet him, what we witness at the end of the play is a time when he is forced to come to terms with and live with that reality. Whereas in the comedy the illusion is created and dispelled, in *Uncle Vania* the illusion is problematized as a human predicament. What matters is not the discovery of illusion as such but the question of how to live with this discovery. There is no *cognitio*, only *re-cognitio*.

Traditionally, lack of knowledge, in whatever form it manifests itself, drives the plots of tragedies and comedies and creates what is known as dramatic irony. In Chekhov's plays, by contrast, the understanding of events or individuals on the part of the audience or readers does not surpass that of the play's characters. Do we know a solution to Vania and Sonia's predicament? Do we have better ideas than the Prozorov sisters about how to live life within the constraints imposed on us by death and circumstance? While there may be a slight asymmetry of knowledge here and there (Lopakhin knows that the estate will be sold if nothing is done, while Ranevskaia and Gaev refuse to acknowledge this reality), factual information as such is not what drives the plot. Ultimately, Lopakhin does not have a better understanding of life and the fundamental questions of human existence than the other characters in the play, and the audience's awareness of the situation in which the plays' characters exist does not differ substantially from that of the characters. There is not a single character who is endowed with a deeper knowledge and understanding. Perhaps the sole exception to this pattern is Nina, who seems to develop a new understanding of her role in life as an actress: "I now know and understand, Kostya, that in our craft—it is all the same whether we play onstage or write—the main thing is not fame, not glitter, not what I dreamed of, but the ability to endure. Be able to bear your cross and have faith" (13:58). The irony of this truth, however, is that it does not point to the gaining of ultimate knowledge or truth but to a particular attitude toward this truth. In other words, the desire or thirst for knowledge—

with full awareness of the impossibility of ever decisively achieving it—is the only form of truth available to humanity.

Chekhov's plays are peculiarly lacking in dramatic irony (i.e., irony based on the withholding and disclosure of information). Harai Golomb suggests that dramatic irony functions in a special way in Chekhov's plays because "the knowledge granted to the perceivers and withheld from the personages is psychological rather than factual, it is withheld from the latter not because it is inaccessible to them, but because of basic flaws in their ability for self-awareness."[4] However, even if the audience can better understand the specific circumstances in which the characters find themselves, such as the futility of the three sisters' dream of going to Moscow, they do not possess the comprehensive, fuller knowledge that the sisters crave. For Olga's last words, "If only we could know" (*esli by znat'*), do not refer to specific information or knowledge about specific events or even choices but instead reflect her epistemological anxiety, her longing to understand the meaning of life and being in this world and her awareness that we are inherently limited in our ability to know. It is true that Chekhov is far more interested in psychological knowledge than in factual knowledge, but even in regard to psychological knowledge the public is hardly in a privileged position, and the reader has no special access to such knowledge. Thus, instead of dramatic irony, the plays produce an irony of a different kind, one that stems from the discrepancy between the pursuit of truth and knowledge and the impossibility of achieving them. Chekhov's plays operate not on specific factual information but on knowledge of being as a whole, of the very realm of existence (see chapter 6). Without the driving force of factual knowledge, Chekhov's plays grow into existential dramas.

Northrop Frye's taxonomy of plot structures is a useful vantage point for considering the ironic mode and its divergences from satire, and how its modal properties are present in Chekhov's plays. Viewing satire as "militant irony," Frye insists that irony, by contrast, conceals the author's attitude and "is consistent both with complete realism of content and with the suppression of attitude on the part of the author."[5] Although he does not delve deeply into Chekhov's plays, Frye aptly calls his particular kind of theatrical form an ironic play, inferring that its irony stems from the depiction of the stifling of human activity by outside pressure, and a "disorganized soul" within. Thus he maintains that in the last act of *The Three Sisters*, "we are coming about as close to pure irony as the stage can get."[6] Indeed, this drama creates a powerful ironic effect by juxtaposing Olga's assertion that the military band "plays so joyfully, so happily" and her hope to understand "why we live, why we suffer" with the play's stage directions—gestures and sounds that undermine any possibility of straightforward optimism: "The music sounds more and more softly; Kulygin, happy, smiling, brings the hat and cape [of Masha], Andrei wheels the baby carriage in which Bobik is sitting" (13:188). The "joyful and happy" music fades. Kulygin's "happiness" hardly convinces—he knows about Masha's affair with Vershinin, though he may be relieved that her lover is leaving. Finally, Andrei's marital happiness, as he pushes a stroller with Bobik and his wife's lover takes care of their daughter, deceives no one, including himself. The curtain falls on Olga repeating "if only we could know, if only we could know!" and the audience inevitably partakes in this lack of knowledge.

Although Chekhov repeatedly stated that his intention was to show how badly people live (a form of satirical intent), his plays are largely governed by an ironic mode that never actually evolves into satire. In his discussion of different modes of emplotment in historical narratives, Hayden White, elaborating on Frye's ideas, sees satire as a mode of emplotment that thrives on subversion: "Satire represents a different kind of qualification of the hopes, possibilities, and truths of human existence revealed in Romance, Comedy, and Tragedy respectively. It views these hopes, possibilities, and truths Ironically, in the atmosphere generated by the apprehension of the ultimate inadequacy of consciousness to live in the world happily or to comprehend it fully."[7] Chekhov's plays tend to resist and subvert traditional tragic, comic, or melodramatic structures, and indeed view those "truths" ironically. Yet they do not develop into satire, for the author always conceals his attitude toward the characters and events.

Not with a Bang but a Whimper

Scholars, stage directors, general audiences, and readers have observed and widely discussed the fact that Chekhov's plays do not fit neatly into genres such as comedy, tragedy, melodrama, and farce. Their generic ambiguity is particularly evident in Chekhov's first major play, *The Seagull*, and his last, *The Cherry Orchard*. While designated as comedies, both plays defy traditional comedic denouements. *The Seagull* ends with Treplev's suicide and *The Cherry Orchard* with the loss of the family nest—a far cry from the traditional comic closures that involve some form of final reconciliation. In fact, a peculiar aspect of a Chekhov play is that it creates a series of illusory conflicts and reconciliations. Vania can quarrel and make peace with Serebriakov, but his conflict is not with Serebriakov—it is an inner conflict with himself. Any conflict and "reconciliation" between the two are therefore inconsequential. After the passionate outburst against Arkadina and her thespian practices, Treplev reconciles with her, but this reconciliation is transient and does not alleviate his psychologically torturous relationship with his mother. Nor does it resolve his own conflict, which is ultimately not with his mother but with himself as an artist. Similarly, Ranevskaia and Petia Trofimov have short outbursts and moments of tension, even amounting to what we might call scandal scenes (see chapter 4 on the role of scandals in Chekhov's plays), but the ensuing reconciliations function only as a diffusion of conflict—Petia and Ranevskaia are not antagonists, and their brief clashes never develop into real conflicts. The real conflicts in Chekhov's plays are not external, not between characters, but internal, within them. That is why reconciliations in Chekhov's plays are never complete, even when the characters are forced to resign themselves to their conditions, like Vania, Sonia, and the three sisters at the endings of their respective plays. Their conditions are not situational but essentially eternal. Refusing to end his comedies with the reconciliations and sense of unity and integration that the comedic mode normally generates, Chekhov consistently opts for a peculiar denouement (regardless of the plays' generic designation)—departure. Professor Serebriakov, Yelena, and Astrov go away, leaving Vania and Sonia to their daily routine of drudgery. The Prozorov sisters leave their family home. With the exception of old Firs, who is forgotten and locked up in the house, all the characters in *The Cherry Orchard* disperse and leave their beloved estate. Chekhov's obsession with the trope of departure—which also figures prominently in his later short stories—emphasizes his search for an open ending and his rejection of conventional denouements. An arrival-departure motif, on the one hand, offers a conventional framework but, on the other hand, creates a sense that the beginning and the end are essentially superfluous, as the action is centered in the middle. This is not to say that Chekhov did not carefully think about how to end his plays. He did. Every word, every gesture and sound is carefully chosen. But Chekhov sought to eliminate the sense of finality that the curtain traditionally imposes on the audience. Upon completing *The Seagull*, he wrote to his friend Suvorin: "Well, I've finished the play. I started it forte and finished it pianissimo—contrary to all the rules of dramatic art." Does his play really end, then?

Closure in theater is always more pronounced than in prose, if only because the curtain rises and falls. The audience must leave as the curtain falls.

Chekhov, however, tried to synchronize the departure of the audience with the departure of the characters. Rather than creating a sense of finality, this synchronization generates a sense of continuity as both the characters and the spectators return to their lives. Closure normally implies that something is not just over—like an audience's visit to the theater or the characters' presence onstage—but has been resolved and is now complete. Chekhov's plays, however, do not allow for this kind of closure and completeness. That the infinite complexities of real life do not lend themselves to simple closures was a problem that Russian novelists, especially Tolstoy and Dostoevsky, were fully aware of, and they tried to find innovative ways to end their narratives.[8] Chekhov's approach to dramaturgy was as radical as Tolstoy's iconoclastic interpretation of historiography and its flaws. Much like Tolstoy, who dismissed hero-centric narratives and believed that history is made by ordinary individuals and minute, imperceptible changes, Chekhov rejected the idea of "main" protagonists in a play and sought to endow many of his characters with equal validity. Like Tolstoy, who believed that history is made not on the battlefield but in the day-to-day existences of unremarkable people, Chekhov chose to disrupt the hierarchy of what is traditionally considered important or unimportant. What happens during such mundane activities as drinking tea or playing cards is no less important than what we consider "dramatic" or important events—getting married or shooting oneself or each other. Therefore, in Chekhov's plays, these traditionally dramatic events frequently take place offstage. Like Tolstoy, he was skeptical of the ability of particular genres to reflect life truthfully. Specific genres always lie, Tolstoy believed (see his attack on so-called war stories).[9] Chekhov's generic anxiety is undoubtedly deeply rooted in the Russian tradition. Chekhov felt that life is as limitless and amorphous as the Russian steppe, and therefore cannot easily fit into any fixed genre. That is why his first venture into the longer form, "The Steppe," was a watershed in his evolving ideas about fictional narrative structures, as manifest in theater and prose fiction. Calling Chekhov a "man of the field" (*chelovek polia*), Alexander Chudakov argued that this positioning of himself between opposing poles implied absolute freedom with respect to final destinations and boundaries. Chekhov was intent upon showing us the never-ending movement within the field. Chudakov explains that "the position of the man of the field—not only not reaching, but in principle not approaching the poles (this also applies to more specific philosophical and ideological concepts such as radicalism-conservatism, idealism-materialism)—the position of being in an unfixed

and ideologically not sharply demarcated point of the field had a significant influence on the structure of Chekhov's artistic world at all its levels."[10]
Chudakov does not explore in detail how this position affects Chekhov's
structure and plot, but we may say that it undoubtedly leads Chekhov to a
rejection of firm closures, and to his frequent use of the departure paradigm.

Chekhov was deeply concerned with the illusion of an ending that was
inherent in fictional narratives. As he complained in a letter to Suvorin
(July 4, 1892), "I have an interesting plot for a comedy, but I have not yet
invented an ending. Whoever invents new endings for plays will usher in
a new era" (P 5:72). Rejecting traditional comedic and tragic endings—
"The hero either gets married or shoots himself, there is no other choice"—
Chekhov tried to focus on life as a process, as a flux, and so chose the departure of the characters as an emblem of transience. Frank Kermode suggests
that in order to make sense of our lives, we need to find some kind of "con-
sonance" between the beginning, the middle, and the end. Endings function
to create a sense of meaning and purpose. Yet while real endings are impossible in life, novels provide a sense of ending that is missing in life.[11] Chekhov questioned the notion of the ending as a generator of meaning, or as
a final moment that retroactively endows human life with the illusion of a
pattern. Rather, he repeatedly depicted life not as a story with a beginning
and an end, nor as a classical journey involving departure, initiation, and
return, but as an open, inconclusive journey through life (the most typical
examples of this vision in his prose are "The Steppe," "The Beauties," "The
Lady with the Lapdog," "The Student," "The Bishop," and "The Bride"; in
theater we observe this paradigm in all his major plays). Chekhov's intention to experiment with open endings goes as far back as his writing of "The
Steppe," about which he wrote to D. V. Grigorovich: "I deliberately wrote it
so that it gave the impression of an incomplete work. It is, as you will see,
similar to the first part of a longer novella" (P 2:190). Not only was Chekhov not satisfied with the artificiality of endings, but he even attempted to
destroy what Kermode called "the sense of an ending." Instead, he created a
sense of non-ending and mercilessly mocked any attempt to impose an artificial ending or beginning on the story of human life. When, at the end of
The Cherry Orchard, Ania cheerfully exclaims "Farewell, old life," and Petia
echoes her enthusiasm with "Hello, new life," the audience is acutely aware
of the irony inherent in their naïve optimism—the transition from "old life"
to "new life" is a long, painful, and continuous process and does not occur
simply by turning a switch from "farewell" to "hello."

Chekhov questions the neat narrative closures and opts for ambiguity and uncertainty. In real life, Chekhov argued, people do not shoot themselves every day, or say clever things. But in real life it is also impossible to determine where and at which point things begin and end, unless one chooses conventional disruptors such as birth and death, or a variation on the birth and death theme—arrival and departure. Arrivals and departures in Chekhov's plays serve to make a point that life is a process, for the action of leaving suggests only the start of a new journey. For much of his life Chekhov tried to reconcile the totalitarian impulse of story to impose a pattern and paradigm on human life with the non-narrative aspect of life as he saw it. This tension resulted in the continuous subversion of available narrative structures, including plot, conflict, and endings. Harai Golomb proposes an ingenious way of interpreting the inherent ambiguity of Chekhovian closures, suggesting that Chekhov essentially creates a series of potential endings rather than a conclusive denouement. Golomb thus offers a compelling discussion of the multiplicity of various potential endings in *The Cherry Orchard* (he distinguishes at least eleven) and identifies "alternative skeleton-plot endings" in the main body of the play.[12] While I agree with Golomb's interpretation of how each potential ending retroactively offers the possibility of looking at the entire play differently, I believe that Chekhov's main goal was to create a sense of non-ending, which is consistent with his skeptical attitude toward any final knowledge or discovery.

Indeed, all of Chekhov's major plays convey a sense of non-ending, of disruption, disunity, and dispersal. Even the finality of Treplev's suicide in *The Seagull* is presented not as an ultimate act—the "bang"—that concludes the play (as in *Ivanov*) but as a transient moment in the lives of the characters. We do not know how Treplev's suicide will affect their lives, but we can assume that they will live, for the most part, as before: Nina will continue to be an aspiring actress, Trigorin will continue to write his novels, and Arkadina will continue to boast of her theatrical success. This strategy of undermining the sense of finality that is usually conveyed by the end of an individual life (a death, a murder, a suicide) in narrative closures is further developed in *The Three Sisters* and *The Cherry Orchard*. Tuzenbach's death in the duel is relatively inconsequential for the lives of the sisters, and Firs's impending death at the abandoned estate is unlikely to affect the characters of *The Cherry Orchard*. In fact, the deaths that occur in Chekhov's plays lack a tragic core: they are presented either as part of the natural and therefore inevitable cycle of life (consistent with his medical training) or as inconsequential, having no significant impact on the action of the play.[13] The death and suffering that the characters experience are merely part of the immutable cycle of nature—Firs will die, but he is very old and will have to die, as will Sorin. The suffering of the characters is part of the general conditions of life that apply to all people, and therefore it does not make any character's fate uniquely tragic. The unfortunate events dissolve into the sustained irony of the plays.

What prevents us from perceiving the potential tragic events of the plays as tragic is the absence of the classical element of tragedy—fear, for the misfortunes and even the deaths of the characters seem either natural or preventable to us. It is worth noting that modern tragicomedies, such as those by Samuel Beckett, evoke feelings of fear and sometimes even horror. In Chekhov's plays, however, there is no sense of fear, only uncertainty. Chekhov replaces the fear and pity of classical tragedy with the laughter and pity of his peculiar comedy, which evokes a deep but ironic compassion for the human predicament in general. The comic in Chekhov does not make the tragic seem even more devastating than, for example, the comic in Ibsen's plays. Nor does the Chekhovian play become an absurdist tragicomedy, in which laughter is the only response left when the individual is faced with the tragic emptiness and meaninglessness of existence (as in Beckett). Chekhov never wallows in scenes of grim despair but instead simply portrays the human condition as he sees it—with humor, mild sadness, compassion, and a glimmer of hope. His seemingly nonchalant attitude toward the deaths of his characters is not accidental; it is deeply rooted in Chekhov's general philosophy of life, which refuses to consider death as a tragic event—and, therefore, to depict it in forte. Instead, he views it as a cyclical process, merely a transient moment in the never-ending stream of life. What Dr. Dorn expresses somewhat cynically and bluntly—"According to the laws of nature, all life must have an end"—and what in Vershinin's formulation sounds like a platitude—"Everything has an end"—also resonates in Chekhov's own humorous reflections in his letter to his sister Masha (November 13, 1898): "All the same, summer is followed by winter, youth is followed by old age, happiness is followed by misfortune and vice versa; a man cannot be healthy and cheerful all his life, losses are always awaiting him, he cannot avoid death, even if he was Alexander the Great—and one should be ready for everything and treat everything as inevitably necessary, sad as it is. One must only do one's duty to the best of one's ability, and nothing else" (P 7:327). The contradiction between the inevitability of death and suffering, human folly and delusion, on the one hand, and the realization that through effort and perseverance, perhaps a slightly better future is possible, though not guaranteed, on the other, is profoundly ironic. This philosophical stance does not allow for a sense of end and emphasizes cyclicality, which in narrative form is better conveyed through the paradigm of recurrent arrivals and departures—Chekhov's favorite trope for denoting continuity.

Despite the uncertainty and ambiguity that these non-endings generate, Chekhov's plays, regardless of their generic designations, are decidedly not tragic or sad. The question of genre becomes almost as unimportant to Chekhov as the question of what life is that, as we recall, he compares to the question of what is a carrot (P 12:93). Chekhov was interested in exploring human existence in his theatrical productions, but how that existence might be embedded within a plot—in comedy, tragedy, farce, melodrama, or tragicomedy—was not as essential to him as his desire to break down generic constraints for the sake of a truthful representation of life. All conventional genres, including tragedy, melodrama, comedy, and romance, represented for him an inadequate vision of the world because they imposed artificial plot structures (beginnings, conflicts, culmination points, and denouements) on human life, which did not lend itself to demarcation by these traditional fictional means. Instead, he sought to convey the irony of a life that defied generic taxonomy, and so he cast his plays in the ironic mode. Rejecting romantic, comic, and tragic denouements, Chekhov opted for an overarching irony that exposed the fatuity of these "generic" conceptions of the world. The audience is left with a peculiar mixture of laughter and pity (or at least compassion), defying both tragic and comic ethos. Nothing is resolved in Chekhov's plays. They do not settle the dramatic potentials inherent in their narrative arcs and, in fact, pose more questions than they answer. The audience simply walks away with new questions, mirroring the characters' comings and goings and returning to their daily routines. The theatrical experience becomes like a train ride: the audience meets the characters as passengers, but both the audience and the characters eventually leave for their own destinations. The repeated phrase "They've gone" at the end of *Uncle Vania* is paradigmatic of the transient state of human life, in which both characters and viewers are merely passengers. In *The Three Sisters*, Olga and Masha repeat a similar phrase when Vershinin and the other officers leave town: "They are going away." We also know that the sisters will leave the family home. At the end of *The Cherry Orchard*, all the characters except the old and abandoned Firs go out to board the train that will take them to their various destinations, while Firs repeats the paradigmatic phrase: "They've gone." Even in *The Seagull*, which ends with Treplev's offstage suicide, the departure of the heroine, Nina, evokes the paradigm of life's journey as a train ride. As she embarks on her journey as an actress, Nina leaves Treplev, the lake, and the place of her childhood and youth, and takes a third-class train to the provincial town of Elets.

Non-firing Guns and the Thespian Relay: Chekhov's Contextualism

Chekhov's profound suspicion of endings—his persistent attempt to "devise new endings for plays"—and his awareness "that it all has to come to an end someday" ("Lady with the Lapdog") lead him to a peculiar strategy as a playwright: he constantly returns to the same key concerns and issues that he addresses in his major plays, creating variations on a theme. Emphasizing the cyclicality of his artistic vision, Chekhov also frequently frames his stories and plays with references to cyclical processes in nature (morning—day—evening—night; spring—summer—fall—winter). The same theme is refracted in his major plays in different tonalities and different contexts, a strategy that emphasizes Chekhov's epistemic modesty. Chekhov's plays flow one into the other, creating complex patterns with varying degrees of self-similarity. Scholars have commented extensively on the connections between the plays and the recurrent motifs, and even the phrases that reverberate in them. This chapter does not purport to describe and summarize them all but gives only a few examples. As in much of his work, the themes of the plays overlap in relation to what Chekhov considers universal human predicaments—the quest for knowledge, frustrated expectations, unrequited love, feelings of abandonment and alienation, the need to work, and anxiety about the meaning of life in the face of existential uncertainty.

Certain characters, situations, motifs, and collisions "migrate" from one play to another, creating complex contextual variations. For example, the figure of the doctor migrates from *Ivanov* to *The Seagull*, *Uncle Vania*, and *The Three Sisters*, with Dr. Astrov and Dr. Chebutykin amplifying or developing some of the latent potentialities of Dr. Lvov and Dr. Dorn. The variation in the theatrical parts of these doctors points to the multiplicity of potentialities that Chekhov presents contextually, emphasizing the perspectival nature of all perception and understanding.

Chekhov's profound contextualism leads him to reject definitive conclusions and a strategy of considering problems and issues from different angles, in cycles (cf. Bakhtin's concept of "incompleteness" in regard to Dostoevsky). Perhaps what Dostoevsky achieves within his novels, Chekhov achieves within his cycles. Truth can be glimpsed at not in its unity and completeness but in its rawness and multiplicity. Most of his plays depict highly dysfunctional families, with selfish, narcissistic mothers (Arkadina, Maria Vasilievna Voinitskaia, Ranevskaia) or mothers absent from their children's lives (in the case of Sonia, the Prozorov sisters, and Charlotta), or families with egotistical or absent fathers (Professor Serebriakov; Nina's neglectful father; and the absent fathers of Treplev, the Prozorov sisters, and Ania). The fatherlessness motif (cf. his earliest unfinished play, *Bezottsovshchina*, also known as *Platonov*) culminates in the figure of Charlotta, whose parents died when she was a child and who does not even know how old she is or whether her parents were married.[14] The theme of "fatherlessness" develops into existential anxiety and a sense of uprootedness or groundlessness in his later plays. There are no happy or even stable families in Chekhov's theater: death, infidelity, unrequited love, celibacy, failed proposals, bachelorhood, broken marriages, and out-of-wedlock births mark the characters' family relationships. With the dissolution of families and fulfilling relationships also comes a sense of greater disconnection and alienation in society, along with a sense of completely breaking with the past and traditions, which Chekhov believes was characteristic of his era. While Lev Shestov extolled such "groundlessness" as an "apotheosis" leading to "adogmatic thinking" and the possibility of "creation from the void," Chekhov was more cautious in his assessments of these trends.

Many of his characters separate from their environment—hence the frequent theme of departure—but this detachment is always ambiguous: it can be a promise for renewal, as in Nina's case, or a less likely path to fulfillment, as in Irina Prozorova's; or it can lead literally "nowhere," as in the case of Charlotta, who has no sense of identity, nationality, place, time, or attachments. Complaining that she has "nobody to talk to" and does not know who she is, she appears as a universal trickster, a mysterious Harlequin-like figure performing acrobatic and magical tricks. Her physicality and her outfits indicate her distant heritage and origin from commedia dell'arte (note that she was born into the family of traveling circus performers): she wears a rifle attached to a leather strap and a man's old cap (cf. Harlequin's wooden sword hanging from a leather belt), or a gray top hat and checkered pantaloons. But this modernist jester ultimately becomes not only a comic character but also a tragic one and grows into an emblem of estrangement, signifying the existential loneliness and anxiety of the modern age. It is no coincidence that Chekhov originally planned that the part of Charlotta—this strange character, an outsider without a nationality or even a passport—would be played by his wife, Olga Knipper (P 11:258). As Chekhov wrote to her, "Ah, if only you played the governess in my play. That's the best part. I don't like the others" (P 11:258).[15] The character of Charlotta undoubtedly endows the play both with a universal quality, a comedic nature reminiscent of the timeless comedy played out in public squares, and an ironic and even tragic undertone. It is this character, as well as other less prominent ones (cf. the *zanni* of commedia dell'arte), that reflects Chekhov's unique thespian handwriting: an amalgamation of psychological realism, harlequinade, and slapstick. It is significant that Chekhov was upset when Stanislavsky asked him to cut several of Charlotta's original lines from act 2: "The act seemed to us drawn-out, and we, when Chekhov arrived in Moscow, asked him for permission to cut it down. Apparently this request hurt him, his face saddened" (P 11:338). Perhaps Stanislavsky, with his emphasis on psychological realism and naturalism, could not fully appreciate those elements of Chekhov's dramaturgy that emphasized pantomime, buffoonery, modernist grotesque, and a type of character and acting not based on verisimilitude. Charlotta seemed alien, a generic other in his interpretation of the Chekhovian mood as based on truthfulness of psychology. As the only character who goes off in an unknown direction (the audience never learns where she is going), Charlotta creates a sense of non-ending and ambiguity that is central to Chekhov's theatrical experiments.

The sense of uncertainty associated with the societal breakup and the awareness of the need for transition permeate all of Chekhov's plays and are presented differently in each of them, but Chekhov's plays are not structured in terms of the progression and cumulative development of a particular motif or type. All his plays are variations on the theme of the human condition as a whole, but none of them pretends to present an exhaustive picture of it. Chekhov approaches the human condition contextually and with epistemic humility, as a series of case studies that never add up to a definitive conclusive vision and do not lend themselves to the determinism of expectations. The world and all aspects of human life are infinitely malleable to different interpretations. Thus, Chekhov, for example, experiments with the dramatic staple of tragedy—death, murder, or suicide—as represented symbolically in the sound of a gunshot. Scholars have noted a progression of diminishing tragic elements, such as death onstage, in Chekhov's plays from *Ivanov* to *The Cherry Orchard*. However, it would be more appropriate to speak not of a progression, but of his "case study" approach to writing. Gunfire is present in almost all of his major plays, but it functions differently in each of them. Ivanov shoots himself onstage. Treplev first shoots the seagull, then slightly wounds himself, and finally kills himself backstage. But the sound of the shot in *The Seagull* is conveyed in a distinctly understated way. Arkadina refers to the sound of the shot as "click-click" in the bandage scene ("And when I'm gone you are not going to do click-click, are you?"), and Dr. Dorn explains Treplev's final suicide shot as "a bursting bottle of ether." In *Uncle Vania*, the gunshot is presented in a similarly parodic and slightly mocking way: it is first mentioned as the sound of a shot offstage in the farcical scene when Vania is chasing Professor Serebriakov, and is then mimicked by Vania, who shouts "Bang!" as he shoots the professor. In *The Three Sisters*, Tuzenbach's death in a duel is conveyed through curt stage directions: "There is heard a faint shot, far off." Only *The Cherry Orchard* seems to avoid the ubiquitous gunshot, but firearms are still present in the background of the play, as Charlotta carries a rifle and Epikhodov a revolver. Although Chekhov is known for his frequently quoted words that a gun must fire if it is mentioned in the text, these words obviously cannot be taken literally: "You can't put a loaded rifle on the stage if no one means to fire it. One can't promise" (letter to Aleksandr Lazarev [Gruzinsky], November 1, 1889; P 2:273). While guns are fired in other plays, in *The Cherry Orchard* Chekhov seems to do just the opposite of what he professes: neither Charlotta's rifle nor Epikhodov's revolver is ever fired. Why, then, does Charlotta carry her rifle? Or Epikhodov his revolver? Isn't this simply a violation of the stage rule of not promising something that won't be performed? Does Chekhov include unnecessary extraneous details? While traditional expectations are clearly subverted here, these silent guns also serve an important function by questioning the audience's dramatic assumptions and their tendency to view life in terms of well-defined plots and conventional genre designations. Chekhov's non-firing guns are no less significant and no less "dramatic" than those that do fire. By subverting expectations of tragedy, they elucidate the open potentiality inherent in life and question the predictability of traditional endings. Actions, conflicts, and images have no fixed meaning but are presented contextually.

Chekhov's programmatic contextualism leads him to another artistic strategy: his plays can be seen as a cycle in which he creates chains of interlinked potentialities, engaging in a playful relay race of certain motifs. Thus, for example, what Chekhov merely mentions as a potential topic for a play in *The Seagull*—the plot Sorin offers Treplev about "L'homme qui a voulu"—is realized in his own later plays. Treplev does not write this novella, but Sorin, so to speak, "passes the baton," which Chekhov picks up in his later plays. The story of "l'homme qui a voulu" is further developed in the character of Voinitsky from *Uncle Vania* as well as the characters of the three Prozorov sisters. They all "want" something in their lives but have to live with frustrated hopes and expectations and unrealized potential. Each case is slightly different from the others, as are the circumstances. Sorin, who aspires to marry and become a writer but fails to realize any of his desires, remains a marginal character on the periphery of *The Seagull* and is even forced to live on the periphery geographically—in the country, not in the city, where he wishes to live. Voinitsky, on the other hand, who complains that he could have been a Dostoevsky or Schopenhauer, takes center stage in *Uncle Vania*. But instead of living his own life, he lives vicariously, serving his idol, Professor Serebriakov, and is now forced to face the meaninglessness of his wasted years. The three sisters also follow the theme of "l'homme qui a voulu": they hope to go to Moscow, fall in love, get married, and work, but these hopes remain unrealized and their expectations are thwarted. Sorin may be an extreme case of an unfulfilled life and of marginalization, but this relatively minor character anticipates themes and motifs developed in later plays. One of these is the theme of death, which is presented "not with a bang but a whimper." In the fourth act of *The Seagull*, we learn that all the characters have gathered at Sorin's estate because he is apparently dying. His condition must be critical, as Arkadina has been summoned by telegram. However, not only does Treplev's death overshadow the significance of Sorin's pending death, but the characters are as oblivious to his condition as the audience. They forget about Sorin, just as the characters of *The Cherry Orchard* forget about Firs. Sorin exemplifies the human predicament that is rooted in desire and volition but inevitably faces the limits of possibility and, ultimately, mortality.

Nevertheless, Chekhov's plays are not hopeless in the sense that all desires are inevitably obstructed and thwarted. Wishes, not as misguided and grandiose as Vania's but aimed at improving life around them, bring the characters a degree of fulfillment, if not necessarily happiness. Astrov, who is planting trees to preserve the environment, Marina and Sonia, who find meaning in their simple daily activities, and Nina, who is willing "to carry her cross," succeed in a limited way.

Treplev's futuristic interest in life in two hundred thousand years is picked up and elaborated upon by Chekhov in *The Three Sisters* in the discussion of Vershinin and Tuzenbach about life in two or three hundred years. The metaphysics of Treplev's play within the play—the struggle between the devil and the world's soul, or between inertia (matter) and spirit—are replayed on the larger stage of Chekhov's plays in a realistic key as the human need to resist the forces of inertia and inaction. While Sonia and Vania resolve to work and the three sisters resolve to live, the refusal by the characters of *The Cherry Orchard* to cultivate their garden leads to destruction—not as complete as envisioned by Treplev but destruction nevertheless, for any renewal is only possible through cultivation. Although Treplev's play has been criticized for its lack of dramatic action, the struggle with inertia becomes the focus of Chekhov's dramatic attention. Chebutykin's inaction, reflected in his refrains "it's all the same" and "it does not matter," is refracted in the passivity of the owners of the cherry orchard and the pathological idleness of many characters in Chekhov's plays.

One more "relay plot" that is worth mentioning is the theme about a schoolteacher suggested to Trigorin by Medvedenko: "But, you know, it would be good to describe in a play and then perform it onstage, how our brother, the teacher, lives. It's a hard, hard life!" (act 1, 13:15). Again, although Trigorin remains apparently uninterested in this theme, it is further developed by Chekhov in the characters of Kulygin and Olga, and to some extent Irina (who also plans to become a teacher) in *The Three Sisters*. On the other hand, the plot proposed by Trigorin—Trigorin's famous "subject for a short story" about a man ruining an innocent girl's life—is not actually developed in Chekhov's plays because of its melodramatic basis, which contradicts Chekhov's artistic vision. Chekhov consistently tried to purge his plays of simple dichotomies of villains and angels, adversaries and victims, suggesting instead that each person is responsible for his or her own life.

By treating themes, characters, and situations cyclically, Chekhov suggests an approach deeply embedded within the context that is constituted by the acts of seeing and understanding. Rejecting the accessibility of absolute essential truth and being deeply skeptical of all accepted "worldviews," he suggests that knowledge of something is always partial and bound to the interpretive perspective of the observer, and that the methods of science are not the only legitimate ways of gaining knowledge. Chekhov had great respect for the scientific method, but the idea that scientific knowledge is also perspectival and dependent on the scientist's experiences was deeply ingrained in his philosophical outlook.[16] Having been trained as a physician, Chekhov was fully aware that scientific knowledge was also necessarily partial and incomplete. He had even less patience for loudly proclaimed philosophical truths. By the mid-1800s, he began to lose faith in those political, social, economic, and religious institutions that claimed to represent "truth." Chekhov's epistemic pluralism was at variance with some of his Russian contemporaries who sought to be moral teachers and strove to convey essential, universal truths. He referred to them as despotic "generals." "All the great sages are as despotic as generals, and as ignorant and as indelicate as generals," Chekhov wrote, in reference to Tolstoy, but, as we have discussed in previous chapters, he also objected to the philosophical "immodesty" of Dostoevsky. To the epistemic arrogance of Tolstoy and Dostoevsky, as he understood them (or misunderstood them), he contrasted his perspectival humility, which implied that there was no privileged position that reigned supreme above all others. A true intellectual precursor of modernism, he questioned the certainties that sustained traditional modes of social organization and morality as well as traditional ways of conceiving of the human self. Deeply sensitive to the pervasive sense of loss, disillusionment, and even despair of modern man, he sought to break out of tradition and convention through experimentation with new literary forms and a new kind of theater focused on the everyday experience that constitutes the world of the individual. Recall again his ideas about what a theater event should represent (chapter 6). The absence of any definite knowledge appears to Chekhov to be the very essence of human existence. The only "knowledge" available to his characters and the audience is life as we see it and as we experience it. His characters are desperate to find the meaning of life, but the irony of their situation is that the only meaning of life is life itself. As Masha Prozorova muses at the end of *The Three Sisters*, "we are left alone, to begin our life over again. We must live . . . We must live." Nina and Olga echo her: "We must live . . . We shall live, we shall!" The end is a new beginning—not in the comic sense that implies reconciliation or relief, but only as a sense of continuity. It is this life, this existence that Chekhov wanted to bring to the stage.

In explaining his new approach and its difference from the earlier literary tradition, Chekhov assumed a position of humble resignation to the need to write and create differently because of a different perception of reality by modern man—with no clear sense of direction and no teleology (letter to Suvorin, November 25, 1892; P 5:133–34; quoted in chapter 1). Out of modesty, Chekhov simply said that one cannot be an artist without a well-defined worldview rather than suggesting that this new position should generate a new type of art. Perhaps Chekhov fits more with "adogmatic" existentialist thinkers such as Shestov and with the modernist sensibility in general, of which Nietzsche's perspectivism and his call for "*more* eyes, different eyes ... to view this same matter" is a vivid example. Chekhov's own artistic perspectivism allowed him to respond with "more eyes"—not with a monistic vision of the world but with a plurality of his theatrical variations—to what he considered the dominant state of mind of modern man: a state of alienation, separation from society or even from one's own self, detachment from the meaning of his work, and lack of a sense of satisfaction from that work. Chekhov's theater reflects his core philosophical (or, perhaps, anti-philosophical) approach put into practice. His plays are an attempt to stage existence as he sees it—in its fragmentariness, variability, and plurality; without linear sequential development, but in its discontinuity, with gaps and fractures; without "heroes," only with actors who have their individual points of view; without closures, only with departures; without endings—only with final curtains.

NOTES

INTRODUCTION

1. Kataev, "Istinnyi mudrets," 69–70. Many scholars have noted the metaphysical and philosophical aspects of Chekhov's fiction and his interest in the problem of human existence. See, in particular, Dolzhenkov, "Chekhov i pozitivizm"; Bocharov, "Chekhov i filosofiia"; Tabachnikova, *Anton Chekhov through the Eyes of Russian Thinkers*; and Kibalnik, "Khudozhestvennaia fenomenologiia Chekhova." About the existential themes in Chekhov and his interest in the problems of being, see also Sobennikov, "*Mezhdu 'est' Bog' i 'net Boga.'*"

2. Gertsen, *Polnoe sobranie sochinenii v 30 tomakh*, 7:300.

3. Scholars have described this aspect of Chekhov's artistic sensibility using such terms as "a man of the field" (Chudakov, "Chelovek polia"), "the poetics of middle ground" (de Sherbinin, "The Poetics of Middle Ground"), and "the poetics of inbetween-ness" (Lapushin, *"Dew on the Grass"*). See also Evdokimova, "Russian Binaries and the Question of Culture."

4. Sergei Kibalnik links Chekhov's artistic perception of the world to the phenom-enological tradition in Western and Russian thought but limits his discussion to a few examples from Chekhov's prose (Kibal'nik, "Khudozhestvennaia fenomenologiia Chekhova").

5. Berkovskii, "Chekhov, povestvovatel' i dramaturg," 965.

6. Sartre, "On *The Sound and the Fury*," 79.

CHAPTER 1. CHEKHOV'S (ANTI-)PHILOSOPHY

1. Merezhkovskii, *Vechnye sputniki*, 300.

2. All references to Chekhov's writings are to the complete academic edition, A. P. Chekhov, *Polnoe sobranie sochinenii i pisem*. References to this edition are indicated in the text by volume number followed by page number. References to the twelve volumes of letters are preceded by *P*. Unless otherwise noted, all translations are mine. This passage from Chekhov's notebooks attracted considerable attention among scholars. It made Alexander Chudakov conclude that Chekhov is a "man of the field" (*chelovek*

polia) in reference to his rejection of simple dichotomies in questions of faith (Chudakov, "Chelovek polia"). Chudakov's article, in turn, generated a series of studies dedicated to Chekhov's rejection of extreme positions. See, in particular, Julie W. de Sherbinin, "The Poetics of Middle Ground." See also a very fine study by Radislav Lapushin, *Dew on the Grass.* Lapushin aptly sums up Chudakov's application of the expression "man of the field" to Chekhov: "At no point in life, according to Chudakov, was Chekhov able to identify with any one of these extremes ('God exists' or 'there is no God'). He is always 'in-between,' inside of this 'immense field'; so too are Chekhov's 'favorite' protagonists" (28).

3. To be sure, one could easily explain Chekhov's remark about the body as a tribute to his medical profession, with its approach to the human body as an object of biological study and his respect for positivist science. The dualistic division of body and soul was alien to Chekhov, who seemed to endorse the classical tradition of *mens sana in corpore sano*, a tradition that to some extent was restored only by Edmund Husserl and especially Merleau-Ponty, who insisted on the corporeity of perception, in opposition to the predominant dualistic ontology of body and reason of Descartes. Human body and corporeity, the meaning of subjectivity as an existential basis of reality, are at the very center of Chekhov's attention—similar to the overall modernist tendency in literature and visual arts to present the subject through its corporeity. For a more detailed discussion of Chekhov's use of the phrase *mens sana in corpore sano*, see Evdokimova, "Fenomenologiia 'chelovecheskogo tela' v poetike Chekhova." See also Evdokimova, "Chekhov's 'Holy of Holies.'"

4. On the question of Chekhov's concern for aesthetics, see Evdokimova, "An *Intelligent* in Everyday Life."

5. For a detailed discussion of Chekhov's "A Daughter of Albion," which juxtaposes two types of behavior, Russian and British, and other examples, see Evdokimova, "Russian Binaries and the Question of Culture."

6. This section of chapter 1 is based on my previously published essay "Philosophy's Enemies: Chekhov and Shestov."

7. See Berdiaev, "Lev Shestov i Kirkegaard," 376. See also Berdiaev, "Osnovnaia ideia filosofii Shestova," 8.

8. Shestov, "Tvorchestvo iz nichego," 3.

9. See Bunin, *About Chekhov*, 65.

10. Shestov, "Tvorchestvo iz nichego," 29.

11. Ibid., 5.

12. For comparison, see Kataev, *Proza Chekhova*, 217.

13. Shestov, "Tvorchestvo iz nichego," 50.

14. Ibid., 30–31.

15. Ibid., 31.

16. Ibid., 39.

17. Camus, *The Myth of Sisyphus and Other Essays*, 28.

18. Ibid., 19.

19. Ibid., 23.

20. In his article on Chekhov and Rozanov, Kataev points out the centrality of the theme of the lack of understanding and comprehension of the world among Chekhov's

characters. He concludes that the "lack of understanding (inability or unwillingness to understand the other) and false understanding are the main causes of human unhappiness in Chekhov's universe." See Kataev, *Chekhov plius*, 283. On the role of epistemological questions in Chekhov, see also Popkin, "*Historia Morbi* and 'the Holy of Holies.'"

21. For comparison, see Popkin, "*Historia Morbi* and 'the Holy of Holies.'"

22. See Chekhov's autobiography sent in his letter to G. I. Rossalimo (October 11, 1899): "My experience with natural sciences and the scientific method has always kept me on my guard; I have tried wherever possible to take scientific data into account, and where it has not been possible I have preferred not to write at all. Let me note in this connection that the principles of creative art do not always allow full accord with scientific data. . . . I do not belong to those writers who negate the value of science and would not wish to be one of those who try to figure out everything on their own" (16:271).

23. Shestov, *Afiny i Ierusalim*, 570.

24. "I think, Chekhov created for the whole world new, entirely new forms of creative writing, unlike anything I have ever encountered. . . . One can no longer compare Chekhov as artist to previous Russian writers—to Turgenev, Dostoevsky or myself. Chekhov has his own unique form of writing, similar to that of the impressionists" (Sergeenko, *Tolstoi i ego sovremenniki*, 226, 228).

Chapter 2. Life without a Plot

1. Eikhenbaum, *O proze*, 365.

2. Goldenveizer, *Vblizi Tolstogo*, 68–69.

3. In *The Seagull*, one of Chekhov's minor characters, Medvedenko, humorously suggests a similar idea, that the theater should be more down-to-earth and feature less "heroic" themes and characters: "You know, it would be great to describe and then stage a play about our fellow the schoolteacher" (13:15).

4. Feider, Chekhov, *Literaturnyi byt i tvorchestvo po memuarnym materialam*, 160.

5. For the term "prosaics" and its application to Tolstoy, see Morson, *Hidden in Plain View*.

6. Serebrov, *Vremia i liudi*, 219.

7. The following section of this chapter is based on my series of articles on Chekhov and the conventions of melodrama, including "Unmelodramatizing Drama: Čechov's Experiment" and "Chekhov's Anti-Melodramatic Imagination: Inoculation against the Diseases of the Contemporary Theater."

8. For a classical discussion of melodrama's generic characteristics, see Balukhatyi, "K poetike melodramy."

9. Brooks, *The Melodramatic Imagination*, 36.

10. Mann, "The Stature of Anton Chekhov."

11. On "communication failure" in Chekhov's prose and drama and "dialogues of the deaf," see Stepanov, *Problemy kommunikatsii u Chekhova*.

12. See also Chekhov's sketch "Fashionable Effects" ("Modnyi effekt").

13. See Chudakov, "Chelovek polia." Referring to Chekhov as a "chelovek polia" ("man of the field") who is "infinitely free" because he does not place himself at any of the two poles, Chudakov hinted at the importance of the middle ground vision for

Chekhov's poetics: "In its significance this phenomenon is comparable to the dialogic worldview of Dostoevsky; in its influence on art it may be even more important, as it marks the beginning of the twentieth century's literature and theater" (308).

14. Quoted in McGuinness, *Maurice Maeterlinck and the Making of the Modern Theater*, 217.

15. Boris Eikhenbaum writes extensively about the importance of Chekhov's training in natural sciences for his literary method, in both his 1914 and 1944 essays. I am grateful to Alexandar Mihailovic for drawing my attention to the fact that Eikhenbaum was also in a sense referring to Chekhov's method of "inoculation" when he argued that Chekhov often sought to examine the lowly and repulsive in real life for its ability to trigger resistance to it: "and in this contact with the low, the vulgar, the terrible, so that the reaction impulse into the dream realm would be stronger, is the main alcohol of Chekhov's art." In this "process of repulsion" he sees the basis of Chekhovian naturalism (Eikhenbaum, "O Chekhove," 965). Scholarly work addressing Chekhov's background as a scientist and doctor is substantial. Among many studies, one could mention Evgenii Meve, *Meditsina v tvorchestve i zhizni A. P. Chekhova*. An important work on epistemological implications of Chekhov's training as doctor has been done by Cathy Popkin, including her excellent essay "*Historia Morbi* and the 'Holy of Holies'" and an essay coauthored with Louise McReynolds, "The Objective Eye and the Common Good." See also Finke, *Seeing Chekhov*, 51–138.

16. In his essay "Melodramaticheskie klishe v dramaturgii Chekhova i Zudermana," Ivan Kuznetsov lists some of the melodramatic clichés that Chekhov uses in his plays, such as the topos of the family nest, characters' analysis and self-analysis of their emotions, the principle of contrast, among other characteristics of melodrama as outlined in S. D. Balukhatyi's "Poetika melodramy," included in *Voprosy poetiki*. Although Kuznetsov does not analyze in detail the function of specific melodramatic devices in Chekhov, he correctly observes that the melodramatic clichés are used in Chekhov's plays as a distancing device, as a way to dissociate the author's point of view from the plays' characters ("Melodramaticheskie klishe," 70). About the remnants of melodrama in Chekhov's plays, see also Odesskaya, "Chekhov's *Tatiana Repina*." Odesskaya notes that "Chekhov exploited several clichés of melodrama, but … having placed them in a different semiotic context or system, he fractured the stereotypes. As is well known, Chekhov actively engaged his literary predecessors in dialogue, employing their popular subjects, heroes, and devices as material for parody" (479).

17. Compare with Boris Zingerman's observation: "They push Ivanov into an old worn-out net of human relations—into the parameters of an old theatrical system" (*Teatr Chekhova i ego mirovoe znachenie*, 227).

18. Melodrama may be at the same time interpreted as democratic in its attempt to make its representation clear and accessible to everyone. See Brooks, *The Melodramatic Imagination*, 15.

19. Serebrov, *Vremia i liudi*, 225.

20. Brooks, *The Melodramatic Imagination*, 5.

21. For comparison, see the excellent essay by Carol Strongin "Irony and Theatricality in Chekhov's 'The Seagull.'"

22. Turgenev, *Sobranie sochinenii v desiati tomakh*, 5:331.

23. Ibid., 332.

24. Ibid., 333.

25. Ibid., 335–36.

26. Ibid., 341.

27. Ibid., 346.

28. Ibid., 333.

29. Ibid., 346.

Chapter 3. A Seagull Is a Seagull Is a Seagull

1. Of the many studies dedicated to Treplev's suicide as nontragic, see, in particular, Gilman, *Chekhov's Plays*, 99. In his seminal article on *The Seagull*, Robert Louis Jackson concludes, "Like so many Chekhovian heroes, his [Treplev's] tragedy consists in his inability to rise to the level of tragedy" ("Chekhov's Seagull," 3).

2. Jackson, "Chekhov's Seagull," 3.

3. Among the host of studies dedicated to literary allusions in *The Seagull*, see, in particular, Rayfield, *Chekhov: The Evolution of his Art*, 204–5, and the fundamental study of Sergei D. Balukhatyi, *Problemy dramaturgicheskogo analiza*, 103–5.

4. Zinovy Paperny calls *The Seagull* "a tragedy of heart mismatches" and a "labyrinth of infatuations" having no exit (Papernyi, *"Chaika" Chekhova*, 12).

5. Scholars have extensively analyzed the discussion of art in the play as represented by Treplev and Trigorin. Among many others, see Richard Peace, who argues that both writers, Treplev and Trigorin, show affinities with Chekhov's own creative method (*Chekhov*, 33).

6. Flath, "The Seagull," 502.

7. Chekhov wrote an unpreserved parody of this play and overtly mocked it: "We've seen and inhaled *Fumes of Life*, a drama by a well-known Moscow fop" (2:535).

8. Gorodetskii, "Mezhdu 'Medvedem' i 'Leshim,'" cited in *Letopis' zhizni i tvorchestva Chekhova*.

9. Memoirs of Ilia Gurliand, in *Teatr i iskusstvo* (1904, no. 28), quoted in Chekhov's *Polnoe sobranie sochinenii i pisem* (12:316). See chapter 2 for a full quotation.

10. Chekhov frequently mocks the grandiose theatrical effects of contemporary melodrama. See his 1884 parody "Nechistye tragiki i prokazhennye dramaturgi" and his review "Modnyi effekt" (1886), among many others (2:319–22; 16:230–32).

11. Meierkhol'd, *O teatre*, 24.

12. Eikhenbaum, "O Chekhove," 962.

13. Zola, *Le Roman Expérimental*, 95.

14. Ibid., 103–5.

15. On the most recent scholarship on Chekhov and Zola, see the informative article by Melissa Miller "Chekhov and Zola's Naturalism." Scholars have noted that Chekhov's "medical" approach to fiction writing might have some affinity with Zola's approach to literature. See, for example, Chekhov's frequently quoted letter to Kiseleva, in which he proclaims that writers should be as objective as chemists and not be afraid of the "dung heaps" of life (January 14, 1887; P 2:10–14). On Chekhov and naturalism, see Grossman, "Naturalizm Chekhova," 294. Grossman asserts, perhaps too categorically, that Chekhov was a positivist and a materialist, believing that "humans are animals."

See also Kuleshov, "Realizm Chekhova," 21–37. Dolzhenkov disagrees with Grossman's assessment of Chekhov's unconditional adherence to Zola's concept of the "human beast" and offers instead a much more nuanced discussion of Chekhov's relation to positivism (Dolzhenkov, *Chekhov i pozitivizm*).

16. Jackson, "Chekhov's Seagull," 4.

17. Tolstaia, *Poetika razdrazheniia*, 312.

18. Alla Golovacheva, "'Dekadent' Treplev i blednaia luna," 189.

19. Ibid., 194.

20. Bocharov, "Chekhov i filosofiia," 146–59.

21. Solov'ev, "Obshchii smysl iskusstva," 399.

22. Flath, "The Seagull," 495.

23. Allusions to *Hamlet* figure prominently in Chekhov's theater and prose and have been discussed extensively in Chekhov's criticism. See, in particular, Winner, "Chekhov's *Seagull* and Shakespeare's *Hamlet*." See also Rayfield, *Chekhov*; Peace, *Chekhov*. Most of Chekhov's plays, from *Platonov* and *Ivanov* to *The Cherry Orchard*, contain allusions to *Hamlet*. Scholarship dedicated to the subject of Chekhov and Shakespeare is substantial. A recent volume, Gulchenko et al., *Chekhov i Shekspir* (*Chekhov and Shakespeare*), includes a wide range of useful essays on the subject.

24. As Jackson observed, Treplev "finds himself trapped in the 'oedipal situation.'" Yet, as opposed to Oedipus and Hamlet, his entrapment does not lead him to "self-discovery in art or action" (Jackson, "Chekhov's Seagull," 13). Apollonio shows how "the plot takes much of its power from hints at the timeless Oedipal paradigm" (Flath, "The Seagull," 492).

25. In her excellent article on the play, Carol Apollonio shows how those Oedipal tensions and "deeper personal conflicts" "erupt in what is ostensibly an argument over aesthetic views" (Flath, "The Seagull," 493).

26. For comparison, see Chekhov's letter to Suvorin of April 1, 1890: "Of course, it would be nice to combine art with preaching, but for me personally it is extremely difficult and almost impossible due to the conditions of literary technique" (P 4:54).

27. Here Chekhov quotes himself from his story "The Wolf." He clearly valued this narrative strategy as follows from the advice he gave to his brother Alexander: "In my opinion, the descriptions of nature should be very brief and have a character à propos. . . . For example, you'll get a moonlit night if you write that a glass from a broken bottle flashed brightly on the mill dam and a black shadow of a dog or wolf rolled in a ball, etc." (P 1:242). The fact that he generously makes Trigorin a master of this literary device indicates that he wanted him to share some of the artistic principles he valued himself.

28. Chekhov's memoirists and scholars pay considerable attention to this quote. For a more detailed discussion of Nina's medallion and its reference to Dostoevsky, see chapter 4 of this book. See also Harai Golomb's nuanced and comprehensive discussion of the medallion scene in Golomb, *A New Poetics of Chekhov's Plays*, 322–50.

29. This phrase is used mockingly in Chekhov's story "The Neighbors." For more on the sources of this quote and its connection to the flirting literary game between Chekhov and Lidia Avilova, see chapter 4 of this book.

30. In his *Sakhalin Island*, Chekhov referred to this phenomenon: "The most common name among vagrants is Ivan, and the surname Nepomniashchii [literally, one without memory]" (14:69).

31. Ginzburg, *Clues, Myths, and the Historical Method*, 101.

32. "The Swedish Match" is a story not so much about discovery of the crime but about the investigative methods. The young detective Diukovsky bases his investigation on marginal and seemingly insignificant details, a Swedish match. I have written on the importance of the "evidential paradigm" for Chekhov's poetics and on this story in "Chekhov: Poetika ulik," 177–87.

33. Vatsuro, *A. P. Chekhov v vospominaniiakh sovremennikov*, 226.

34. Vainshtein, *Dendi*, 325–26.

35. Gorodetskii, "Mezhdu 'Medvedem' i 'Leshim,'" cited in *Letopis' zhizni i tvorchestva Chekhova*.

36. This section of chapter 3 is based in part on my previously published essay "'Chaika': 'Chto eto znachit?'"

37. See his letter to M. O. Menshikov of October 12, 1892, in which he censures his correspondent for not paying attention to "the nature of language" and shares his ideas about the ways language enriches itself (P 5:114–15). Sergei Komarov suggests that Chekhov may have been familiar with Alexander Potebnja's study *Thought and Language* (1862) (Komarov, "O 'slozhnosti prostoty' A. P. Chekhova-dramaturga," 24).

38. Potebnia, *Estetika i poetika*, 147. As observed by Komarov, in one of his letters Chekhov seems to rely on Potebnja's ideas about the "inner form" (Komarov, "O 'slozhnosti prostoty' A. P. Chekhova-dramaturga," 24).

39. Potebnia, *Estetika i poetika*, 114.

40. Carol Apollonio argues that there is a metonymical connection between life and art in *The Seagull*. She concludes that this explains why the play's major symbols—the dead seagull and the lake—are not easily interpretable, for they are metaphorically related to reality (Flath, "The Seagull," 507).

41. Jakobson, "On Realism in Art," 25.

42. Jakobson, "Two Aspects of Language," 111.

43. Bunin, *Sobranie sochinenii v shesti tomakh*, 6:156. Compare with Chekhov's criticism of those who, like Gorky, lacked restraint in their descriptions of nature and indulged in anthropomorphism. See his letter to Gorky: "The sea breathes, the sky looks, the steppe lazes, nature whispers, speaks, grieves, etc. Such likenesses make descriptions somewhat monotonous, sometimes saccharine, sometimes obscure; colorfulness and expressiveness in nature descriptions are achieved only by simplicity, by such simple phrases as 'the sun went down,' 'it got dark,' 'it rained,' etc." (P 8:11–12). Likewise, Serebrov recalls Chekhov's words: "The sea doesn't laugh, it doesn't cry, it murmurs, it splashes, it sparkles. . . . Look at Tolstoy's works: the sun rises, the sun sets, the birds sing. . . . No one weeps or laughs. And that's the most important thing, simplicity" (Serebrov, *Vremia i liudi*, 219).

44. Stein, "Poetry and Grammar," 316. Stein was fascinated with nouns as proper names:

When I said.

A rose is a rose is a rose is a rose.

And then later made that into a ring I made poetry and what did I do I caressed completely caressed and addressed a noun. (327)

45. The introduction to *Four in America* by Thornton Wilder (Stein, *Four in America*, v).

46. Mandel'shtam, *Sobranie sochinenii v chetyrekh tomakh*, 2:254–55.

47. Stein writes: "'now listen! Can't you see that when the language was new—as it was with Chaucer and Homer—the poet could use the name of a thing and the thing was really there? He could say 'O moon,' 'O sea,' 'O love' and the moon and the sea and love were really there" (*Four in America*, v). Mandelshtam, for his part, praises Walt Whitman, who resembled a new Adam and "Homer himself" in that he "[gave] names to things" (Mandel'shtam, *Sobranie sochinenii v chetyrekh tomakh*, 251).

Chapter 4. Dostoevsky's Graft

1. See Stepanov, *Problemy kommunikatsii u Chekhova*, 63–64.

2. Numerous studies have analyzed the "intertextual" dimensions of Chekhov's oeuvre. See, in particular, Kataev, *Literaturnye sviazi Chekhova*. See also Sukhikh, *Problemy poetiki Chehova*.

3. See an important book chapter discussing allusions to Dostoevsky in Chekhov's works (Gromov, "Chekhov i Dostoevskii," 246–88). A recent collection of essays, *Chekhov i Dostoevskii*, offers a wide array of different approaches to the problem of Dostoevsky and Chekhov. A significant part of this chapter is based on my article "Simpaticheskie chernila Chekhova (Dostoevsky?)," included in that collection; the chapter also uses material from "Ne sotvori sebe Tartiuffa (Mol'er, Dostoevsky, Chekhov)."

4. Eikhenbaum, "O Chekhove," 963.

5. Nazirov, "Dotoevskii i Chekhov," 164-67.

6. Kibal'nik, "Chekhov 'chitaet' Dostoevskogo," 114–30.

7. See Nabokov's letter to Edmund Wilson of 1956 (Nabokov and Wilson, *The Nabokov-Wilson Letters*, 297). On Nabokov's attitude to Chekhov, see Karlinsky, "Nabokov and Chekhov."

8. See Nabokov, "Sartre's First Try": "Somewhere behind looms Dostoevsky at his worst, and still farther back there is old Eugene Sue, to whom the melodramatic Russian owed so much" (Nabokov, *Strong Opinions*, 229).

9. Nivat, "Nabokov and Dostoevsky," 400.

10. The refraction of this irritation with Dostoevsky in Nabokov's texts is beyond the scope of this book, whose focus is primarily Chekhov.

11. Gromov, "Chekhov i Dostoevskii," 259.

12. Dostoevskii, *Polnoe sobranie sochinenii v tridtsati tomakh*, 6:326–27.

13. In her memoirs, "A. P. Chekhov in My Life" ("A. P. Chekhov v moei zhizni"), Lidia Avilova recalls how Chekhov promised to respond to her sending him her medallion with reference to his story from the stage during the production of his play *The Seagull* (184).

14. See, for example, Stepanov, *Problemy kommunikatsii u Chekhova*, 167–74.

15. Quoted in full in chapter 2 of this book.

16. See chapter 1 of this book for a full quotation and interpretation of this letter.

17. See Shestov, "Umozrenie i Apokalipsis (Religioznaia filosofiia V. Solov'eva)." Andrea Oppo discusses Shestov's polemic with Solovyov and critique of Solovyov's peculiar dismissal of the Russian literary tradition (including Chekhov) in his article "Shestov i Solov'ev."

18. Shestov, "Tvorchestvo iz nichego," 24.

19. Shestov, *Afiny i Ierusalim*, 656.

20. Robin Feuer Miller offers a detailed overview of the story's interpretations and literary subtexts and an excellent analysis of the story's close ties with Dickens's *Christmas Carol* and "The Dream" as a meta-Christmas story (Miller, "Dostoevsky's 'The Dream of a Ridiculous Man,'" 95).

21. Dostoevskii, *Polnoe sobranie sochinenii v tridtsati tomakh*, 25:105.

22. Indeed, the phrase "all the same" (*vsio ravno*) is inseparably connected with Kirillov's worldview and his concept of suicide and freedom from fear and pain, which he believed would make him God himself (Dostoevskii, *Polnoe sobranie sochinenii v tridtsati tomakh*, 10:93–94). Trying to persuade Kirillov to write a suicidal note in which he would take upon himself all the blame for Shatov's death, Pyotr Verkhovensky refers to his concept of "all the same": "After all, it's all the same to you; and this is my special request. . . . Well, if it does not matter to you; and you keep saying that it's all the same to you" (ibid., 292). Throughout the novel and before his suicide Kirillov frequently uses this phrase (ibid., 466). Moreover, the phrase *vse ravno* often is used in quotation marks, referring specifically to a particular worldview. For example, Verkhovensky thinks the following thoughts about Kirillov: "and Kirillov, therefore, would 'no longer care' [*budet uzhe vse ravo*]; at least, that is how Pyotr Stepanovich reasoned" (ibid., 444–45).

23. In Dostoevsky's last novel, *The Brothers Karamazov*, the concept "nothing matters" evolves into the concept "everything is permitted." The meaninglessness of the world emerging from the rejection of God leads Ivan Karamazov to the consideration that "everything is permitted." According to him, the loss of higher metaphysical values gives rise to the conclusion that all human ideas are valueless and therefore all actions become "allowable." Similarly, Nietzsche anticipated that philosophical nihilism would become widespread and was already "at our door." Indeed, it figured prominently in twentieth-century thought, from Sartre, Camus, and Heidegger to Cioran and Derrida (cf. Cioran's nonfictional work *On the Heights of Despair*, which includes chapters titled "Nothing Is Important" and "Nothing Matters").

24. See Durkin, "Chekhov's Response to Dostoevskii."

25. Critics have analyzed Dr. Ragin's worldview in the context of the philosophy of Marcus Aurelius and the ideas of Schopenhauer and Tolstoy. On Marcus Aurelius and the philosophy of the Stoics in Chekhov's works, see Skaftymov, "O povestiakh Chekhova 'Palata No 6' i 'Moia zhizn'"; Kapustin, *"Chuzhoe slovo" v proze A. P. Chekhova*, 223; Sobennikov, "'Palata No 6' Chekhova"; Sobennikov, "Chekhov i stoiki"; Golovacheva, "'Razmyshleniia Marka Avreliia' v filosofskikh sporakh geroev A. P. Chekhova"; Kashcheev, "'Razmyshleniia imperatora Marka Avreliia Antoniia'"; and others.

26. For an excellent discussion of the Aristotelian concepts of fear and pity in "Ward Six" and the characters' failure to accept similarities among themselves, which prevents them from experiencing fear and pity in a healthy way, see Knapp, "Fear and Pity in 'Ward Six.'"

27. According to Marcus Aurelius, while we cannot control external circumstances, we can control the way we respond to them: "If you are grieved about anything external, 'tis not the thing itself that afflicts you, but your judgment about it; and it is in your

power to correct this judgment and get quit of it" (Aurelius, *Meditations*, 103). See also other sections of his *Meditations* (bk. 8, 40; bk. 7, 4; bk. 4, 49).

28. Dostoevskii, *Polnoe obranie sochinenii v tridtsati tomakh*, 25:107.

29. Ibid., 25:117

30. Ibid., 10:92–93.

31. Ibid., 25:107.

32. Ibid., 25:110.

33. Referring to Marcus Aurelius, Dr. Ragin proclaims: "Marcus Aurelius said: 'Pain is the vivid representation of pain; if you make an effort of will, in order to change this representation, if you reject it and stop complaining, the pain will disappear'" (8:100). "If you reflect on this more often, you will realize how insignificant all the external things which agitate us really are. One must strive for comprehension of life—therein lies the true good" (8:101).

34. Compare with Chekhov's comments about how "practice" may refute "theory" and his emphasis on the centrality of physical perceptions. In his letter to Suvorin of March 24, 1894, he writes: "Tolstoy's moral philosophy has ceased to move me. . . . Since childhood I acquired my belief in progress and couldn't help believing in it, because the difference between the time when they flogged me and the time when they stopped flogging me was enormous" (P 5:283). In "Ward Six" Dr. Ragin's opponent, Gromov, appeals to the same argument of physical pain and the "difference" between being flogged or not being flogged (8:102).

35. Dostoevskii, *Polnoe sobranie sochinenii v tridtsati tomakh*, 25:119.

36. The Ridiculous Man anticipates here the ideas expressed by Ivan and Alyosha Karamazov in *The Brothers Karamazov*: "—To love life more than its meaning?—Certainly so, to love before logic, as you say" (ibid., 14:210).

37. As opposed to Descartes's lasting legacy of viewing mind and body as completely distinct ("mind-body dualism"), as a doctor and artist Chekhov was skeptical of this dualism and had a more phenomenological *avant la lettre* perspective focusing on the idea of what later was identified as "lived experience" (see the later work of Merleau-Ponty and his notion of the "lived-body"). Since phenomenology has been practiced in various guises for centuries, there is no need to present Chekhov as a thinker in the tradition of the early twentieth-century philosophers, such as Husserl, Heidegger, Sartre, Merleau-Ponty, and others, although he might have shared intuitively some of the ideas that were part of the "air" he was breathing at the time.

38. See Morson's excellent essay on second-person narration in Tolstoy's "Sebastopol in December," "The Reader as Voyeur."

39. Shestov, "Tvorchestvo iz nichego," 46.

40. Ibid., 47.

41. Note, however, that "nothing matters" (*vse ravno*) is used only once in *The Seagull* and in *Uncle Vania*, and twice in *The Cherry Orchard*. The frequency of the phrase in *The Three Sisters* clearly points to the particular importance and semantic significance of this concept for the play. In his book on Chekhov's plays and vaudevilles, Zinovy Paperny catalogs most of the uses of *vse ravno* in *The Three Sisters* and notes that the phrase expresses a variety of meanings and nuances, depending on the character and context (Papernyi, "*Vopreki vsem pravilam*," 180–83).

42. Dostoevskii, *Polnoe sobranie sochinenii v tridtsati tomakh*, 25:108.

43. Ibid., 104.

44. Chekhov uses the incomprehensible refrain of this popular music hall tune in his 1893 story "The Two Volodyas" ("Volodia bol'shoi i Volodia malen'kii"), which was published two years after the show appeared in Paris. *Tararabumbiia* in this story also stands for abracadabra and conveys a sense of the absurd: "'You, Volodya, are a clever man,' . . . Tell me something convincing. Say one word.'—'One word? Here you are: *tararabumbiia*'" (8:223). The "little" Volodya's *tararabumbiia* in response to Sofia Lvovna's melodramatic rhetoric and request of advice implies that he has dismissed her histrionics as ludicrous blabber. *Tararabumbiia* is his way to say "nonsense." He sings the tune as Sofia continues her insincere and pretentious rambling on the big questions of life and death. The song was widely popular, and Chekhov may even have heard it when he traveled to Paris in 1891, sampling the city's nightlife and visiting its *cafés-chantants*.

45. The idea of the Golden Age figures prominently in Dostoevsky's fiction ("The Dream of the Ridiculous Man," *Demons*, *The Adolescent*, and other texts) and is always presented in a complex and ambiguous light. Consider also Dostoevsky's critique of the utopian dream of the Crystal Palace in *Notes from the Underground* and his polemic with Chernyshevsky's socialist utopian vision. Chekhov does not engage in a philosophical discussion of the idyll—past, present, or future—but presents his characters' dreams of an ideal future life as naïve, idle, and facile philosophizing that turns people away from the practical work of self-improvement and amelioration of living conditions.

46. Golovacheva commented on Uncle Vania's allusions to *The Village of Stepanchikovo* in her book *Pushkin, Chekhov i drugie*, 134–40.

47. See Mochul'skii, *Dostoevskii*, 143. For a detailed comparison of Opiskin with Tartuffe, see Danowski, "Opiskin and Tartuffe."

48. For various Russian and European sources of parody in Dostoevsky's novella, see Kibal'nik, *Problemy intertekstual'noi poetiki Dostoevskogo*, 89–159. Many scholars, including M. Bakhtin, interpreted Dostoevsky's portrayal of Foma Fomich Opiskin as a parody of Gogol's *Selected Passages from a Correspondence with Friends* (Bakhtin, *Problems of Dostoevsky's Poetics*, 163). See Tynianov, *Dostoevskii i Gogol'*, 27–47. On Opiskin as a parody of Belinsky, see Mackiewicz, *Dostoevsky*, 5. On the connection with Molière's Tartuffe, see Chulkov, *Kak rabotal Dostoevskii*, 47.

49. See, by comparison, Golovacheva's observations about the semantics of the word "uncle" in Chekhov's play and in Dostoevsky's novella (Golovacheva, *Pushkin, Chekhov i drugie*, 134, 137).

50. Dostoevskii, *Polnoe sobranie sochinenii v tridtsati tomakh*, 3:6–7.

51. Ibid., 3:6.

52. Ibid., 3:14.

53. Ivanov, *Freedom and the Tragic Life*, 11–12.

54. Dostoevskii, *Polnoe sobranie sochinenii v tridtsati tomakh*, 15:491.

55. Bakhtin, *Problems of Dostoevsky's Poetics*, 17.

56. Among the many studies addressing Dostoevsky's indebtedness to Greek tragic drama, see George Steiner's classic essay *Tolstoy or Dostoevsky*. Steiner emphasizes the dramatic energy and compression of Dostoevsky's art.

57. Bakhtin, *Problems of Dostoevsky's Poetics*, 17.

58. As Igor Sukhikh observes, Chekhov was not at the center of Bakhtin's interests and, apart from some inconsequential asides, he makes only one major reference to Chekhov (Sukhikh, *Problemy poetiki Chekhova*, 285–86).

59. Bakhtin, *Problems of Dostoevsky's Poetics*, 18.

60. Ibid., 163.

61. On Dostoevsky's interest in theater, see Alekseev, "O dramaticheskikh opytakh Dostoevskogo," 54–60. K. V. Mochulsky, among many others, observed the dramatic element of Dostoevsky's art (Mochul'skii, *Gogol', Solov'ev, Dostoevskii*, 436–47). Dostoevsky's theatricality has been frequently discussed by other scholars as well. See, for example, analysis of the theatricality of Dostoevsky's "Uncle's Dream" in Chulkov, *Kak rabotal Dostoevskii*, 67. See also Tunimanov, *Tvorchestvo Dostoevskogo*, 17–25; Berzaite, "K voprosu o teatral'nosti." Dostoevsky's early theatricalized texts foreshadow the scenic dialogical structures of Dostoevsky's major novels.

62. Bakhtin, *Problems of Dostoevsky's Poetics*, 146.

63. In his brief essay "Dva skandala: Dostoevskii i Chekhov," Igor Sukhikh notes the prominence of scandals in Chekhov's prose and drama. He suggests that although Chekhov's scandals follow a similar pattern to Dostoevsky's scandalous scenes, ultimately they lead to an almost "opposite interpretation." He further points out that Chekhov's scandals, in opposition to Bakhtin's interpretation of them in Dostoevsky's novels as moments that "free human behavior from its predetermining norms and motivations," function in a different way: they "confirm the inviolability of both the picture of the world and established relationships" (Sukhikh, *Ot . . . i do*, 491).

64. For a detailed discussion of this one-act play and its connection to Gogol's play *Marriage* (*Zhenit'ba*, 1832), see my article "Metafizicheskii vodevil."

65. Remizov, "Potainaia mysl'," 189.

66. Gottlieb, *Chekhov and the Vaudeville*, 150–51.

67. Simonov, *S Vakhtangovym*, 56.

68. Bakhtin, *Problems of Dostoevsky's Poetics*, 155.

69. Remizov, "Potainaia mysl'," 201.

Chapter 5. Homo Laborans

1. Gor'kii, *Sobranie sochinenii v vosemnadtsati tomakh*, 15:281.

2. Dostoevskii, *Polnoe sobranie sochinenii v tridtsati tomakh*, 4:20.

3. Ibid., 4:20.

4. Ibid., 4:20.

5. Ibid., 4:20.

6. Ibid., 4:80.

7. Ibid., 4:173.

8. Camus, *The Myth of Sisyphus and Other Essays*, v.

9. Scholars have discussed Chekhov's "existentialism" mostly only in terms of common themes and motifs. Thus, for example, Pyotr Dolzhenkov in his book *Chekhov and Positivism* (*Chekhov i pozitivizm*) dedicates to this question a brief sub-chapter titled "Chekhov and Existentialism" and mentions several "existentialist themes" in Chekhov's works, such as alienation, angst, the problem of the meaning of life in the face of human

suffering, a sense of abandonment, and so forth. Dolzhenkov limits his discussion to those "themes" in Chekhov's prose and his drama *The Three Sisters*. See Dolzhenkov, *Chekhov and Positivism*, 161–73. See also Spivak, "Chekhov i ekzistentsializm."

10. A small part of this section of chapter 5 draws on my previously published essay "Work and Words in 'Uncle Vanja.'"

11. Marx, *Economic and Philosophical Manuscripts of 1844*, 110–11.

12. Walzer, *The Revolution of the Saints*, 210.

13. Jones, "British Protestantism," 138.

14. Gertsen, *Sobranie sochinenii v deviati tomakh*, 5:458.

15. Tolstoi, *Polnoe sobranie sochinenii v devianosta tomakh*, 29:186.

16. Ibid., 29:186.

17. Ibid., 25:375.

18. Ibid., 64:84. The letter is tentatively dated October 3, 1887.

19. In *The Seagull*, for example, Arkadina calls her son a "sponger" in a fit of anger. In *Uncle Vania*, Telegin, who lives on Sonia's estate, announces to Elena, "If you may have noticed, I dine with you every day." Telegin (nicknamed Waffles) complains that he has been called a "sponger" by a shopkeeper (13:106). But the nurse Marina consoles him, saying that "we are all spongers on God" (*vse u Boga prizhivaly*). Marina's comment points to Russia's almost religious perception of dependency as something not necessarily inherently negative but more like a universal human condition. In *The Three Sisters*, Chebutykin is a semi-sponger, for he lives in the Prozorovs' house but "forgets" to pay the rent and intends to settle near them for life upon his retirement. In *The Cherry Orchard*, the impoverished landowner Simeonov-Pishchik owes money to everyone around ("vsem dolzhen") and is also a "freeloader" of sorts (13:249).

20. Goncharov, *Sobranie sochinenii v shesti tomakh*, 4:189.

21. Flath, "Art and Idleness," 456.

22. Annenskii, *Knigi otrazhenii*, 137.

23. Camus, *The Myth of Sisyphus and Other Essays*, v.

24. Ibid., 3, 27.

25. Ibid., 31.

26. Kluge, "O smysle ozhidaniia," 144.

27. Ibid., 145.

28. Dolzhenkov, *Chekhov i pozitivizm*, 171–72.

29. Ibid., 173.

30. Camus, *The Myth of Sisyphus and Other Essays*, 21.

31. Ibid., 31.

32. On the relation of Chekhov's ideas to Shestov and other philosophers of a phenomenological-existential orientation, see Stepanov, "Lev Shestov on Chekhov," 169–74. See also Kibal'nik, "Khudozhestvennaia fenomenologiia Chekhova," 18–28. In his recent comprehensive study of Lev Shestov, Andrea Oppo makes a series of insightful remarks on Shestov's interpretation of Chekhov and Chekhov's influence on his own aesthetics (Oppo, *Lev Shestov*, 85–90).

33. Shestov, "Tvorchestvo iz nichego," 67–68.

34. Camus, *The Myth of Sisyphus and Other Essays*, 120–21.

35. Ibid., 121.

36. Ibid., 121–22.

37. Ibid., 122

38. Ibid., 123.

39. Ibid., 27.

40. Gary Saul Morson, for example, in his article "Sonia's Wisdom," views Sonia as "the most admirable and wisest character" and suggests that "what is heroic about Sonia, is what she is doing in the present" (70–71).

41. Dostoevskii, *Polnoe sobranie sochinenii v tridtsati tomakh*, 10:272–76. It is not clear who authored the poem "Svetlaia lichnost'" in *The Devils*, but, as Vladislav Khodasevich correctly observes, it is likely Pyotr Verkhovensky's own creation, even though he attributes it first to Shatov and later to Alexander Herzen (Khodasevich, "Poeziia Ignata Lebiadkina," 200). Scholars suggest this is a parody of Nikolai Ogarev's poem "Student" (Dostoevskii, *Polnoe sobranie sochinenii v tridtsati tomakh*, 12:303). The extent to which this expression was marked as reflecting a particular ideology and had become a trite epithet could be seen in Vladimir Korolenko's *History of My Contemporary* (*Istoriia moego sovremennika*, 1921). Commenting on the progressivist writers of the younger generation, Korolenko criticizes them for their lack of literary skills and their artificial, strained characters: "In general, these were not individuals as in Turgenev's, Pisemsky's and Goncharov's works, but personalities [lichnosti] with an addition of a widely spread epithet: 'enlightened personalities'" (Korolenko, *Sobranie sochinenii v desiati tomakh*, 316). In 1909 E. P. Karpov, who was closely associated with populist movements, published his comedy titled *Svetlaia lichnost'*.

42. Tolstoi, *Polnoe sobranie sochinenii v devianosta tomakh*, 29:179.

43. Even the successful writer Trigorin (*The Seagull*) despondently laments his essentially Sisyphean plight (13:29). More cogently, this idea of perseverance, of living and creating "in the midst of the desert," is expressed by Nina Zarechnaia at the end of *The Seagull*: "The main thing isn't fame, glamour, the things I dreamed about, but knowing how to endure. Know how to shoulder one's cross and have faith. I have faith and it's not so painful for me, and when I think about my calling, I'm not afraid of life" (13:58). Nina's cross and Sisyphus's boulder help them to follow their calling and not to be afraid of life.

44. We may recall this well-known passage from Marx's *Capital*: "A spider conducts operations that resemble those of a weaver, and a bee puts to shame many an architect in the construction of her cells. But what distinguishes the worst architect from the best of bees is this, that the architect raises his structure in imagination before he erects it in reality. At the end of every labour process, we get a result that already existed in the imagination of the labourer at its commencement" (178).

45. Annenskii, *Knigi otrazhenii*, 84–85.

46. In his book *Russia's Capitalist Realism*, Vadim Shneyder discusses some of Chekhov's works showing the effects of the rising industrialization and capitalism in Russia during the late nineteenth century but does not mention *The Three Sisters* and many other important texts. See his analyses of several Chekhov stories, including "The Peasants," "A Woman's Kingdom," "Three Years," "In the Ravine," and "A Case History" (Shneyder, *Russia's Capitalist Realism*, 154–72).

47. Dostoevskii, *Polnoe sobranie sochinenii v tridtsati tomakh*, 4:177.

48. Annenskii, *Knigi otrazhenii*, 88.

49. Ibid.

50. Zaitsev, *Chekhov: Literaturnaia biografiia*, 219–20.

51. Compare with Tolstoy's interest in Laozi and the concept of "non-activity."

CHAPTER 6. *THE THREE SISTERS*

This chapter is based on my essay "Being as Event, or the Drama of *Dasein*: Chekhov's *The Three Sisters*."

1. There have been several studies, including my own, that treat Chekhov in the context of phenomenological or existential thought, but most of them are limited in scope. See Evdokimova, "Philosophy's Enemies." See also Kibal'nik's "Khudozhestvennaia fenomenologiia Chekhova," which draws parallels between Chekhov's philosophical outlook and Russian and Western "phenomenologists." See also Kataev, *Proza Chekhova*, 26–30; Spivak, "Chekhov i ekzistentsializm." Igor Sukhikh dedicates a chapter of his 2007 book to "Khudozhestvennaia filosofiia Chekhova" (Sukhikh, *Problemy poetiki Chekhova*, 302–37).

2. *The Three Sisters* has been interpreted as a philosophical play more often than any of Chekhov's theatrical works. For a particularly insightful interpretation of the metaphysical aspect of the sisters' search for knowledge, see Radislav Lapushin's excellent article "'. . . Chtoby nachat' nashu zhizn' snova.'"

3. That *The Three Sisters* deals with questions of human existence and the meaning of life has not gone unnoticed among Chekhov scholars. However, the concept of being as it relates to the play has not been addressed in explicitly philosophical terms.

4. Boris Zingerman correctly observes that "each of Chekhov's plays has its own 'plot structure' [*siuzhetnyi riad*]; in reality, his plays are full of events" (*Teatr Chekhova i ego mirovoe znachenie*, 17).

5. For a discussion of Chekhov's treatment of events, see Chudakov, *Poetika Chekhova*, 217–24. For the narratological aspect of the concept of event, see Volf Shmid [Wolf Schmidt], *Narratologiia*, 16–20. Nina Ishchuk-Fadeeva also makes a good point about Chekhov's approach to plot structure in her discussion of *The Three Sisters*, insisting that "the 'plot-hero' system undergoes fundamental changes as compared to the Aristotelean drama: an event serving as a basis of a traditional dramatic plot leading to a denouement stops being a generic goal of the play" ("Tri sestry," 53).

6. Zingerman, *Teatr Chekhova i ego mirovoe znachenie*, 16–17.

7. Ibid.,19.

8. Margarita Odesskaia has observed that *The Three Sisters* has two planes, which she identifies as "the plane of objects and events and the symbolic plane, which is connected with the world of metaphysical ideas" ("'Tri sestry,'" 150).

9. See Wiles, *The Theater Event*, 37–65.

10. Brustein, *The Theater of Revolt*, 152.

11. In his discussion of the concept of eventfulness in narratology, Konstantin Barsht mentions Chekhov, whose allegedly "weakened eventfulness" concerns only the eventfulness of fabula and plot. Barsht suggests, however, that in Chekhov's texts it is precisely the intense "meta-eventfulness" that seems to be predominant ("O trekh urovniakh sobytiinosti," 77–80).

12. For the theme of knowledge, see Golomb, "'Esli by znat'.'" As Golomb points out, Chekhov "shows that man's unquenchable thirst for knowledge and understanding of the world and the human condition is an existential driving force in the endless human journey to infinity" (128). Kataev also points out the centrality of the theme of the lack of understanding and comprehension among Chekhov's characters, including their inability to comprehend the world. He concludes that the "lack of understanding (inability or unwillingness to understand the other) and false understanding are the main cause of human unhappiness in Chekhov's universe" (Kataev, *Chekhov plius*, 283).

13. Lapushin, "'. . . Chtoby nachat' nashu zhizn' snova,'" 28.

14. In one of his notes for *The Three Sisters*, Chekhov writes: "Until he finds his own God, man will be disoriented, will search for an aim, and will remain dissatisfied. One cannot live for the sake of children or mankind. And if there is no God, there is nothing to live for, one must die. Man must either have faith or search for faith, otherwise he is a shallow person" (17:215–16). Chekhov dismisses all human goals, higher aims, philosophies, and even the sense of duty as not fully inadequate for the task of life. They are merely substitutes for the Truth.

15. Heidegger, *Being and Time*, 11.

16. Alla G. Golovacheva discusses some of the possible literary sources of *The Three Sisters*, including Zhukovsky's essay "The Three Sisters," which presents the three sisters as Past, Present, and Future. She also mentions the connection with Shakespeare's three witches (sisters) in *Macbeth*. See Golovacheva, "'Proshedshei noch'iu vo sne ia videl trekh sester.'"

17. Chekhov's treatment of time in his plays and in *The Three Sisters* in particular has attracted scholarly attention. Commentators have pointed out the importance of the stage setting and stage directions in heightening the audience's awareness of the passage of time. See Turner, "Time in Chekhov's *Tri sestry*." Turner makes a useful distinction between "real" time and the inner, psychological time. See also Zingerman, *Teatr Chekhova i ego mirovoe znachenie*, 5–62. For an interesting discussion of the interplay between fictional time and theatrical time in Chekhov, see Marsh, "Two-Timing Time in *Three Sisters*."

18. Heidegger, *Being and Time*, 311.

19. Heidegger, *On Time and Being*, 11.

20. Ibid., 11–15.

21. Odesskaia writes about the alienation felt by almost all the characters of *The Three Sisters*, including Chebutykin, who is alienated from himself, or "from his own life," and loses all sense of self-identity (Odesskaia, "'Tri sestry,'" 152).

22. At the end of Chekhov's last play, *The Cherry Orchard*, Charlotta echoes Chebutykin's "it doesn't matter" by exposing the landowners' lack of responsibility. She is neglected and left alone: "I have nowhere to live in town . . . I must leave. . . . (*Hums*) It doesn't matter" (13:248).

23. Heidegger, *On Time and Being*, 19.

24. Ibid., 21.

25. I find Timothy Wiles's observation that Stanislavsky derived his method of acting from Chekhov's plays to be consistent with my discussion of Chekhov's ontological

concept of event. According to Wiles, Stanislavsky found "in the process by which Chekhov's characters discover themselves an analogue for his technique by which the actor discovers his characterization. For Chekhov's characters, life is a process of self-realization" (*The Theater Event*, 39).

26. Stanislavski, "The Art of the Actor and the Art of the Director," 81.

Chapter 7. The Temptations of the Nursery

An earlier version of this chapter was previously published as "What's So Funny about Losing One's Estate, or Infantilism in *The Cherry Orchard*."

1. Senelick, *Anton Chekhov*, 124–25.

2. Stanislavskii, *Sobranie sochinenii*, 7:265–66.

3. In her article "Chekhov vs. Gor'kii and the Moscow Arts Theater," Anna Linden argues that the directors of the Moscow Art Theater revised *The Cherry Orchard* to accord with "public preference for contemporary melodrama" (504).

4. See Senelick, "Chekhov on Stage." See also Carnicke, "Stanislavsky's Production of *The Cherry Orchard* in the U.S."

5. "Many modern directors have tried to bring out the comedy; Brook was one of the few to do so without descending to farce, and one of the few to create a true ensemble" (Senelick, "Chekhov on Stage," 225). This is how Brook himself defined this task: "It must be approached as a theatrical movement purely played. A false Chekhovian manner that is not in the text, and sentimentality, must be avoided. *The Cherry Orchard* is not gloomy, romantic, long and slow but a comic play about real life" (Hunt and Reeves, *Peter Brook*, 234). See also Borden, "Chekhov on the Contemporary Stage of Moscow and St. Petersburg"; LeBlanc, "Liberating Chekhov or Destroying Him?"

6. Valency, *The Breaking String*, 271.

7. Ibid., 179–80.

8. Styan, *Chekhov in Performance*, 315.

9. Senelick, *The Chekhov Theater*, 333–34.

10. LeBlanc, "Liberating Chekhov or Destroying Him?," 60.

11. In discussing Chekhov's fiction, Harvey Pitcher distinguishes four main types of the comic in Chekhov: comedy of situation, comedy of subversion, comedy of surprise, and comedy of the absurd. It is the comedy of the absurd that surfaces, according to Pitcher, most often in Chekhov's four major plays. Pitcher convincingly demonstrates the affinity of the comic-absurd in Chekhov's plays with the earlier Chekhonte type of humor ("Chekhov's Humour," 100–102). Karl Kramer offers an interesting insight on the source of the comic in *The Cherry Orchard*. He places it in the "discord itself, in the moment of total incomprehension between an order receding and an order still uncertain of its ascendancy" ("Love and Comic Instability," 306). LeBlanc provides an excellent analysis of the farcical characters in the play and suggests that these are used by Chekhov "to defuse the earnestness and seriousness that we might otherwise feel inclined to attach to the characters or their situations in Visnevyj sad" ("Two-and-Twenty Misfortunes," 150). However, it is clear the source of the comic in Chekhov's plays and in *The Cherry Orchard* specifically resists classification. Thus, Richard Gilman feels compelled to use such hardly helpful qualifications as "a comedy in Chekhov's meaning" (*Chekhov's Plays*, 237).

12. Igor Sukhikh aptly observes that beneath the surface of comedy, these words recall Hamlet's famous "To be or not to be" (Sukhikh, *Problemy Poetiki,* 211). I would add that Epikhodov also emerges as an absurdist, modernist version of the lovesick Pierrot—a sad clown, pining for love of his "Columbine," Duniasha, but also characterized by existential anguish. Tongue-tied (cf. Pierrot's poignant lapses into mutism), he presents himself as a perpetual loser and fellow sufferer and is a far more ambiguous and complex figure than a merely cardboard stock type. Note also that in act 2, Epikhodov pretends to be playing a mandolin (compare Léon Comerre's painting of Pierrot playing the mandolin, 1884; see also Aubrey Beardsley's *Pierrot with Mandolin,* 1894, among others).

13. Gor'kii, *Sobranie sochinenii v vosemnadtsati tomakh,* 18:14.

14. Styan, *Chekhov in Performance,* 336.

15. Williams, *Peter Brook,* 325.

16. While pursuing a set of somewhat different issues in his very stimulating article "The Machine in Chekhov's Garden," Stephen L. Baehr has also posited a similar connection between the characters' immaturity and the demise of the pastoral in *The Cherry Orchard.* Baehr views the cherry orchard as a "shattered Oblomovka that tries to freeze time but fails" (102).

17. Alpers, *What Is Pastoral,* 28–37.

18. Kermode, *English Pastoral Poetry,* 13.

19. Durkin, "Pastoral and Anti-Pastoral in Chekhov," 676.

20. See, for example, Boas, *The Cult of Childhood,* 11.

21. See Senelick's discussion of Strehler's approach to the nursery question (*The Chekhov Theater,* 270–72). In literary criticism, one should mention an analysis by John Tulloch, who acknowledges the significance of the image of the nursery and notes that the shepherd's pipe at the end of act 1 "is a sound which evokes the enclosed nostalgia of the nursery" (*Chekhov: A Structuralist Study,* 189). See also Peace, *Chekhov,* 123; Baehr, "The Machine in Chekhov's Garden," 102.

22. Tolstoi, *Sobranie sochinenii v dvadtsati dvukh tomakh,* 1:52–54.

23. As opposed to other major characters in the play, Gaev's childishness has received much attention in Chekhov criticism (see, for example, Pitcher, "Chekhov's Humour," 174–75; Peace, *Chekhov,* 123–24, 131; LeBlanc, "Two-and-Twenty Misfortunes," 147–48).

24. It is surprising that some critics assume that Lopakhin is able to quote from *Hamlet* in English and do not consult the original of Chekhov's play. Gilman writes: "Lopakhin quotes *Hamlet*—'get thee to a nunnery'—saying 'Amelia' for Ophelia. . . . Lopakhin again quotes *Hamlet*—'nymph in thy orisons,' saying 'horizons' instead" (*Chekhov's Plays,* 230). The pun "orisons/horizons," which Gilman is so eager to discover, is present only in the English translation of Chekhov's play, for Lopakhin never uses the word "horizons." Lopakhin, to be sure, quotes *Hamlet* in Russian and slightly changes not only Ophelia's name but also Hamlet's request of Ophelia to remember his "sins" in her "orisons": "Okhmeliia, idi v monastyr'"; "Okhmeliia, o nimfa, pomiani menia v tvoikh molitvakh!" (as compared to Shakespeare's "The fair Ophelia! Nymph, in thy orisons / Be all my sins remember'd"). The latter change, however, is consistent with some of the Russian translations of Shakespeare's text. See, for example, a translation

by N. Kh. Ketcher (1873): "O nimfa, pomiani menia v svoikh molitvakh" (Shekspir, *Gamlet*, 568). For comparison, see also a translation by A. Sokolovskii (1883): "O nimfa, pomiani menia, proshu, v sviatykh svoikh molitvakh" (Shekspir, *Gamlet*, 570). In Russian theater, however (up to the beginning of the twentieth century), the most widely used translation was that of N. Polevoi (1837), who preserves the reference to "sins": "Milaia Ophelia! o nimfa! / Pomiani grekhi moi v molitvakh!" (Shekspir, *Gamlet*, 166). The most popular literary translation was that of A. Kroneberg (1844): "Ophelia! o nimfa! pomiani / Moi grekhi v tvoei sviatoi molitve" (Shekspir, *Gamlet*, 267).

25. In his famous speech "Hamlet and Don Quixote" (1860), Ivan Turgenev sums up and solidifies the Russian tendency to view Hamlet as a type of a skeptic gnawed by reflection. See chapter 2 in this book. Gradually, a type of Russian Hamlet emerges who is closely associated with the so-called superfluous man (Turgenev coins the term in his "Diary of the Superfluous Man," 1850). In the last decades of the nineteenth century, Shakespeare's *Hamlet* and Russian Hamletism became so popular that the critic Nikolai Mikhailovsky insisted on the need to separate Shakespeare's Hamlet from "little Hamlets" (*gamletiki*) and "Hamletizing piglets" (*gamletiziruiushchie porosiata*). Russian Hamletism is an important topic in Chekhov's prose and drama. For a detailed discussion of Russian Hamletism and especially its reflection in *The Seagull*, see essays by Thomas Winner, Harai Golomb, and Hanna Scolnicov (Winner, "Chekhov's *Seagull* and Shakespeare's *Hamlet*"; Golomb, "Hamlet in Chekhov's Major Plays"; Scolnicov, "Chekhov's Reading of *Hamlet*"). Chekhov mocks Russian Hamletism most explicitly in his 1891 feuilleton "In Moscow" ("V Moskve"). The narrator, who identifies himself as the Moscow Hamlet, complains: "I am a rotten rag, a good for nothing, a whiner; I am the Moscow Hamlet. Drag me to the Vagankovo cemetery!" (7:507). As early as 1882 Chekhov, however, protested against interpreting Shakespeare's Hamlet as a weak and whining character. In his review "*Hamlet* on the Pushkin Theater Stage" ("'Gamlet' na Pushkinskoi stsene"), he criticizes the actor Ivanov-Kozelsky for "whining" too much: "Hamlet was incapable of whining. A man's tears are valuable, and especially those of Hamlet; and one must not waste them onstage" (16:20).

26. Without developing the analogy between Lopakhin and Podkolesin, Richard Peace correctly identifies the Gogolian subtext in the scene of Lopakhin's failed proposal (*Chekhov*, 120).

27. In her dissertation, "The Endless Passage: The Making of a Plot in the Russian Novel," which offers a stimulating discussion of the unfulfilled quest for adulthood, Ksana Blank observes that "the Russian hero's lack of maturity is manifested most clearly in his indecisive behavior with women" (2).

28. Chernyshevsky, "The Russian at the *Rendez-vous*," 123.

29. For comparison, see Valency: "She is the secret love of his life, his ideal of womanhood, and perhaps the true reason why he will not compromise by marrying Varya" (Valency, *The Breaking String*, 273). See also Styan: "Chekhov's character is not the one to say defiantly, 'I'm master now!' when it comes to forcing Varya to sell herself to the only bidder" (Styan, *Chekhov in Performance*, 129–30). In addition, see Pitcher, "Chekhov's Humour," 203. Kramer suggests that "this potential marriage exists only in Liubov' Andreevna's terms" ("Love and Comic Instability," 297).

30. Kramer, "Love and Comic Instability," 299.

31. Bergson uses the term "mechanical inelasticity" to describe what triggers laughter (*Laughter*, 10).

32. Senelick, *Anton Chekhov*, 121.

33. As Schopenhauer insists, "laughter itself is just the expression of this incongruity" (*The World as Will and Idea*, 76). To be sure, there exists an extensive literature on the psychology and philosophy of laughter and humor, which is beyond the scope of this book. Although there are many cases of incongruity, which are not humorous, infantile behavior for the most part does constitue a sort of incongruity that causes laughter. Among numerous studies that may support my interpretation of childishness as an embodiment of incongruity that may potentially arouse laughter, see, for example, Martin, "Humor and Aesthetic Enjoyment of Incongruities"; Clark, "Humor and Incongruity" and Morreall, "The New Theory of Laughter." Paul Lewis makes an important point that "because it contributes to both maturity and maturation, humor frequently arises in convincing literary treatments of growth or enlightenment" (*Comic Effects*, 75).

34. Ronald LeBlanc has provided a very interesting psychoanalytic reading of several Russian texts that use gastronomic images to portray Russia's tendency "to retreat from 'growing up'" ("Food, Orality, and Nostalgia for Childhood," 246). He shows how food imagery is used by Gogol, Goncharov, and Kvitka-Osnovianenko to convey the sense of nostalgia for childhood, both personal and national (the childhood of Russia as a country).

Chapter 8. Back to the Cherry Orchard Itself

1. Timiriazev, *Istoriko-statisticheskii obzor promyshlennosti Rossii*. Useful information about the extent of cherry cultivation could also be found in P. F. Kalaidovich's article "About the City of Vladimir's Orchards" ("O sadakh Vladimirskikh"), in which the author reports the striking number of cherry orchards in and around this city (56–61).

2. Stanislavskii, *Sobranie sochinenii*, 1:269.

3. For comparison, see Styan, *Chekhov in Performance*, 241; for the cherry orchard as a symbol of nineteenth-century society, see Peace, *Chekhov*, 136–37.

4. Rayfield, *Understanding Chekhov*, 248.

5. For a dichotomy of pastoral and industrialization, see Baehr, "The Machine in Chekhov's Garden."

6. Balabanov, "Razvedenie dokhodnykh vishnevykh sadov," 140–41.

7. On Chekhov's passion for gardening, see Bartlett, "Seeds of the Real Cherry Orchard." In her biography of Chekhov, Rosamund Bartlett also observed Chekhov's particular love of cherry trees. On Chekhov's gardens in Melikhovo, see Bartlett, *Chekhov*, 191–211.

8. Chekhov's memoirists note his love of gardening. Among other authors, see, in particular, Chlenov, "Chekhov i kul'tura." See also Chekhov's letter to Nemirovich-Danchenko: "My Yalta dacha came out very comfortable. It's cozy, warm and the view is good. The garden will be extraordinary. I plant it myself, with my own hands. I planted a hundred roses, all of the noblest, most cultivated varieties. 50 pyramidal acacias, lots of camellias, lilies, tuberoses, etc., etc." (P 8:309).

9. Chekhov's attitude to Trofimov is clearly ironical and detached. Recalling Chekhov's comments about revolutionary students, A. N. Tikhonov (Serebrov) quotes his words, which perfectly apply to Trofimov as well: "'Students rebel in order to be seen as heroes and make it easier to have success with the ladies.'... 'Nowadays students, instead of studying, either write novels or engage in revolution'" (Serebrov, *Vremia i liudi*, 221).

10. For more on the concept of culture in Chekhov, see Evdokimova, "Chekhov i problema kul'tury." See also Evdokimova, "Russian Binaries and the Question of Culture."

11. Robert L. Jackson, "'What Time Is It?,'" 136–49. The motif of the garden and its symbolic function in Chekhov have been frequently addressed by scholars. See Jackson, "Chekhov's Garden of Eden.'" See also Rayfield, "Orchards and Gardens in Chekhov." On the religious symbolism of the Garden of Eden in "The Black Monk," see Pavlov, "Paradise Lost."

12. Voltaire, *Candide and Other Stories*, 88.

13. In his memoirs about Chekhov, Serebrov (Tikhonov) recalls Chekhov's irony about revolutionary rhetoric of the Russian intelligentsia and its calls for marching forward. In his biting criticism of Gorky's "Song of the Stormy Petrel" and "Song About the Falcon," he writes: "I know you're going to tell me—this is politics! But what kind of politics is that? 'Going forward without fear or doubt'—that's not yet politics. ... And which way forward is unknown ... If you call for movement forward, you must specify the goal, the path, the means. Nothing has ever been done in politics by 'the madness of the brave' alone. It is not only frivolous, it is harmful" (Serebrov, *Vremia i liudi*, 218–19).

Conclusion

1. Mann, "The Stature of Anton Chekhov." Mann's original essay, "Versuch Über Tschechow" (1954), was written for the fiftieth anniversary of the death of Chekhov.

2. Mann, *Essays*, 269.

3. This reference is discussed in chapter 1 of this book.

4. Golomb, *A New Poetics of Chekhov*, 100.

5. Frye, *The Anatomy of Criticism*, 224.

6. Ibid., 285. Bert States echoes Frye and sees him as "the drama's first master of the ironic play" (*Irony and Drama*, 102).

7. White, *Metahistory*, 10. See also Frye, *The Anatomy of Criticism*, 158–238.

8. See, for example, Morson on *War and Peace*'s "absent ending" (*Hidden in Plain View*, 62–65).

9. For comparison, see Tolstoy's words about the generic peculiarity of *War and Peace*, which he insisted did not fit the system of European fictional genres: "There is not a single work of prose fiction in the new period of Russian literature that rises at least a little above mediocrity that fits perfectly into the form of a novel, poem, or novella" (Tolstoi, *Sobranie sochinenii v dvadtsati dvukh tomakh*, 7:356–57).

10. Chudakov, "Chekhov i vera," 192.

11. Kermode, *The Sense of an Ending*.

12. Golomb, *A New Poetics of Chekhov's Plays*, 240.

13. Kataev notes that "vaudeville with suicide, comedy with suicide—the original genre oxymoron in Chekhov's oeuvre" (*Literaturnye sviazi Chekhova*, 115).

14. The fact that most of the families in Chekhov's plays are dysfunctional is further confirmed by the relatively large number of illegitimate children: Natasha and Protopopov's daughter in *Three Sisters*; most likely Masha Shamraeva, whose mother is in an ongoing relationship with Dr. Dorn; perhaps Irina Prozorova (we know that Chebutykin passionately loved the sisters' mother and that this love may have been mutual; he was also obviously very attached to Irina, and this explains his extravagant gift to her: "My dearest child, I have known you since the very day you were born . . . I carried you in my arms . . . I loved your dead mother"); and finally, Charlotta, who says she is not sure her parents were wedded.

15. A. P. Skaftymov, among many others, paid particular attention to the figure of Charlotta. See Skaftymov, "O edinstve formy i soderzhaniia v 'Vishnevom sade' A. P. Chekhova," 351.

16. See Chekhov's "Autobiography": "Familiarity with natural sciences, with the scientific method always kept me on my guard. . . . I should note, by the way, that the conditions of artistic creativity do not always allow complete agreement with scientific data" (16:271–72). About the role of science for Chekhov the artist, see Romanenko, *Chekhov i nauka*.

BIBLIOGRAPHY

Alekseev, A. P. "O dramaticheskikh opytakh Dostoevskogo." In *Tvorchestvo Dostoevskogo*, edited by L. P. Grossman, 54–60. Odessa: Vseukrainskoe gosudarstvennoe izdatel'stvo, 1921.

Alpers, Paul. *What Is Pastoral?* Chicago: University of Chicago Press, 1996.

Annenskii, Innokentii. *Knigi otrazhenii*. Seriia "Literaturnye pamiatniki." Moscow: Nauka, 1979.

Aurelius, Marcus. *The Meditations of the Emperor Marcus Aurelius Antoninus*. Translated by Francis Hutcheson and James Moore. Indianapolis: Liberty Fund, 2008.

Avilova, Lidiia. "A. P. Chekhov v moei zhizni." In *Chekhov v vospominaniiakh sovremennikov*, edited by N. L. Brodsky, 148–216. Moscow: Gosudarstvennoe izdatel'stvo khudozhestvennoi literatury, 1952.

Baehr, Stephen L. "The Machine in Chekhov's Garden: Progress and Pastoral in *The Cherry Orchard*." *Slavic and East European Journal* 43, no. 1 (1999): 99–121.

Bakhtin, Mikhail. *Problems of Dostoevsky's Poetics*. Edited and translated by Caryl Emerson. Minneapolis: University of Minnesota Press, 1984.

Balabanov, M. S. "Razvedenie dokhodnykh vishnevykh sadov." *Progressivnoe sadovodstvo i ogorodnichestvo* 10 (1908): 140–41.

Balukhatyi, S. D. "Poetika melodramy." In *Voprosy poetiki*, 30–79. Leningrad: Izdatel'stvo Leningradskogo universiteta, 1990.

Balukhatyi, Sergei. "K poetike melodramy." In *Poetika: Sbornik statei*, 63–86. Leningrad: Academia, 1927.

Balukhatyi, Sergei. *Problemy dramaturgicheskogo analiza: Chekhov*. Leningrad: Academia, 1927.

Barsht, Konstantin. "O trekh urovniakh sobytiinosti." In *Sobytie i sobytiinost': Peterburgskii sbornik*, edited by Vladimir Markovich and Wolf Schmid, 77–80. Moscow: Intrada, 2010.

Bartlett, Rosamund. *Chekhov: Scenes from a Life*. London: Free Press, 2004.

Bartlett, Rosamund. "Seeds of the Real Cherry Orchard." *The Daily Telegraph*, June 30, 2018.

Berdiaev, Nikolai. "Lev Shestov i Kirkegaard." *Sovremennye zapiski* 62 (1936): 376.

Berdiaev, Nikolai. "Osnovnaia ideia filosofii L'va Shestova." Introduction to *Umozrenie i Otkrovenie*, by Lev Shestov, 5–9. Paris: YMCA-Press, 1964.

Bergson, Henri. *Laughter: An Essay on the Meaning of the Comic.* Translated by Cloudesley Brereton and Fred Rothwell. New York: MacMillan, 1911.

Berkovskii, Naum Ia. "Chekhov, povestvovatel' i dramaturg." In *A. P. Chekhov: Pro et Contra. Lichnost' i tvorchestvo A. P. Chekhova v russkoi mysli XX veka (1914–1960),* 2:930–73. St. Petersburg: Izdatel'stvo Russkoi khristianskoi gumanitarnoi akademii, 2010.

Berzaite, Dagne. "K voprosu o teatral'nosti, ili chto nachinaetsia v povesti F. M. Dostoevskogo 'Diadiushkin son'?" *Literatūra* 61, no. 2 (2019): 36–48.

Blank, Ksana. "The Endless Passage: The Making of a Plot in the Russian Novel." PhD diss., Columbia University, 1997.

Boas, George. *The Cult of Childhood.* London: University of London Press, 1966.

Bocharov, Sergei. "Chekhov i filosofiia." In *Vestnik istorii, literatury, iskusstva: Otdelenie istoricheskikh-filologicheskikh nauk Rossiiskoi Akademii nauk,* 146–59. Moscow: Sobranie, Nauka, 2005.

Borden, Richard. "Chekhov on the Contemporary Stage of Moscow and St. Petersburg." In *Chekhov Then and Now: The Reception of Chekhov in World Culture,* edited by J. Douglas Clayton, 93–101. New York: Peter Lang, 1997.

Brooks, Peter. *The Melodramatic Imagination: Balzac, Henry James, Melodrama, and the Mode of Excess.* New Haven, CT: Yale University Press, 1976.

Brustein, Robert. *The Theater of Revolt: An Approach to Modern Drama.* Boston: Little, Brown, 1962.

Bunin, Ivan. *About Chekhov: The Unfinished Symphony.* Edited and translated by Thomas Gaiton Marullo. Evanston: Northwestern University Press, 2007.

Bunin, Ivan. *Sobranie sochinenii v shesti tomakh.* Vol. 6. Moscow: Khudozhestvennaia literatura, 1988.

Camus, Albert. *The Myth of Sisyphus and Other Essays.* Translated by Justin O'Brien. New York: Vintage, 1991.

Carnicke, Sharon Marie. "Stanislavsky's Production of *The Cherry Orchard* in the U.S." In *Chekhov Then and Now: The Reception of Chekhov in World Culture,* edited by J. Douglas Clayton, 19–30. New York: Peter Lang Publishing, 1997.

Chekhov, Anton P. *Polnoe sobranie sochinenii i pisem. Sochineniia,* 18 vols. *Pis'ma,* 12 vols. Moscow: Nauka, 1974–83.

Chekhov i Gogol': K 200-letiiu so dnia rozhdeniia N. V. Gogolia. Chekhovskie chteniia v Ialte, no. 14. Simferopol: "Dolia," 2009.

Chernyshevsky, Nikolai. "The Russian at the *Rendez-vous.*" In *Belinsky, Chernyshevsky, and Dobrolyubov: Selected Criticism,* edited by Ralph E. Matlaw, 108–29. New York: E. P. Dutton, 1962.

Chlenov, Mikhail. "Chekhov i kul'tura." In *Chekhov v vospominaniiakh sovremennikov,* edited by N. L. Brodsky, 465–67. Moscow: Gosudarstvennoe izdatel'stvo khudozhestvennoi literatury, 1952.

Chudakov, A. P. "Chekhov i vera." *Novyi mir* 9 (1998): 186–92.

Chudakov, Aleksandr. "Chelovek polia." In *Anton P. Čechov—Philosophie und Religion in Leben und Werk*, edited by Vladimir Kataev, Rolf-Dieter Kluge, and Regine Nohejl, 301–8. Munich: Otto Sagner, 1997.

Chudakov, Aleksandr. *Poetika Chekhova*. Moscow: Nauka, 1971.

Chulkov, Georgii. *Kak rabotal Dostoevskii*. Moscow: Iurait, 2018.

Clark, Michael. "Humor and Incongruity." In *The Philosophy of Laughter and Humor*, edited by John Morreall, 139–55. Albany: State University of New York Press, 1987.

Clyman, Toby W., ed. *A Chekhov Companion*. Westport, CT: Greenwood Press, 1985.

Danowski, Grzegorz. "Opiskin and Tartuffe: Tyranny and Freedom in Dostoevsky's *The Village of Stepanchikovo*." *Toronto Slavic Quarterly*. http://sites.utoronto.ca/tsq/14/danowski14.shtml.

de Sherbinin, Julie. "The Poetics of Middle Ground: Revisiting 'The Lady with the Little Dog.'" In *Chekhov: Poetics—Hermeneutics—Thematics*, edited by J. Douglas Clayton, 179–91. Ottawa: Slavic Research Group, 2006.

Dolzhenkov, Petr. *Chekhov i pozitivizm*. Moscow: Izdatel'stvo "Skorpion," 2003.

Durkin, Andrew. "Chekhov's Response to Dostoevskii: The Case of 'Ward Six.'" *Slavic Review* 40, no. 1 (1981): 49–59.

Durkin, Andrew. "Pastoral and Anti-Pastoral in Chekhov." In *Anton P. Čechov: Werk und Wirkung*, edited by Rolf-Dieter Kluge, 675–87. Wiesbaden: Otto Harrasswitz, 1990.

Dostoevskii, F. M. *Polnoe sobranie sochinenii v tridtsati tomakh*. Edited by V. G. Bazanov et al. Leningrad: Nauka, 1972–90.

Eikhenbaum, Boris M. "O Chekhove." In *A. P. Chekhov: Pro et Contra. Tvorchestvo A. P. Chekhova v russkoi mysli kontsa XIX–nachala XX veka (1887–1914)*, 961–68. St. Petersburg, 2002.

Eikhenbaum, Boris M. *O proze*. Leningrad: Khudozhestvennaia literatura, 1969.

Evdokimova, Svetlana. "Being as Event, or the Drama of *Dasein*: Chekhov's *The Three Sisters*." In *Chekhov for the 21st Century*, edited by Carol Apollonio and Angela Brintlinger, 57–78. Bloomington, IN: Slavica, 2012.

Evdokimova, Svetlana. "'Chaika': 'Chto eto znachit?'" In *Chekhovskaia karta mira: Materialy mezhdunarodnoi konferentsii, Melikhovo, 3–7 iiulia 2014*, edited by A. A. Zhuravleva and V. B. Kataev, 332–43. Moscow: Melikhovo, 2015.

Evdokimova, Svetlana. "Chekhov i problema kul'tury." In *Izuchenie chekhovskogo naslediia na rubezhe vekov: Vzgliad iz XXI stoletiia*, 13–31. Simferopol: Arial, 2019.

Evdokimova, Svetlana. "Chekhov: Poetika ulik." In *Obraz Chekhova i chekhovskoi Rossii v sovremennom mire*, 177–87. St. Petersburg: "Petropolis," 2010.

Evdokimova, Svetlana. "Chekhov's Anti-Melodramatic Imagination: Inoculation against the Diseases of the Contemporary Theater." In *Chekhov the Immigrant: Translating a Cultural Icon*, edited by Michael Finke and Julie de Sherbinin, 207–17. Bloomington, IN: Slavica, 2007.

Evdokimova, Svetlana. "Chekhov's 'Holy of Holies': The Poetics of Corporeity." In *Chekhov's Letters: Biography, Context, Poetics*, edited by Carol Apollonio and Radislav Lapushin, 263–67. Lanham, MD: Lexington Books, 2018.

Evdokimova, Svetlana. "Fenomenologiia 'chelovecheskogo tela' v poetike Chekhova." In *Filosofiia Chekhova*, 77–90. Irkutsk: Irkutsk University Press, 2016.

Evdokimova, Svetlana. "An Intelligent in Everyday Life: Chekhov on the Ethics and Aesthetics of Behavior." In *Sankirtos: Studies in Russian and East European Literature, Society and Culture (In Honor of Tomas Venclova)*, edited by Lazar Fleishman. Frankfurt am Main: Peter Lang, 2007.

Evdokimova, Svetlana. "Metafizicheskii vodevil': 'Zhenit'ba' Gogolia i 'Svad'ba' Chekhova." In *Chekhov i Gogol': K 200-letiiu so dnia rozhdeniia N. V. Gogolia. Chekhovskie chteniia v Ialte*, vyp. 14, 48–61. Simferopol: "Dolia," 2009.

Evdokimova, Svetlana. "Ne sotvori sebe Tartiuffa (Mol'er, Dostoevsky, Chekhov)." In *Chekhov na mirovoi stsene i v mirovom kinematografe. XXXVII mezhdunarodnaia konferentsiia "Chekhovskie chteniia v Ialte,"* 40–48. Simferopol: Arial, 2017.

Evdokimova, Svetlana. "Philosophy's Enemies: Chekhov and Shestov." In *Anton Chekhov through the Eyes of Russian Thinkers*, edited by Olga Tabachnikova, 219–46. London: Anthem Press, 2010.

Evdokimova, Svetlana. "Russian Binaries and the Question of Culture: Chekhov's True Intelligent." In *Chekhov's Letters: Biography, Context, Poetics*, edited by Carol Apollonio and Radislav Lapushin, 173–92. Lanham, MD: Lexington Books, 2018.

Evdokimova, Svetlana. "Simpaticheskie chernila Chekhova (Dostoevsky?)" In *Chekhov i Dostoevskii*, 322–38. Moscow: GTsTM im. A. A. Bakhrushina, 2017.

Evdokimova, Svetlana. "Unmelodramatizing Drama: Čechov's Experiment." In *Anton P. Čechov—der Dramatiker: Drittes internationales Čechov-Symposium Badenweiler im Oktober 2004*, edited by Regine Nohejl and Heinz Setzer, 404–12. Munich: Otto Sagner, 2012.

Evdokimova, Svetlana. "What's So Funny about Losing One's Estate, or Infantilism in *The Cherry Orchard*." *Slavic and East European Journal* 44, no. 4 (Winter 2000): 623–48.

Evdokimova, Svetlana. "Work and Words in 'Uncle Vanja.'" In *Anton P. Čechov—Philosophische und Religiöse Dimensionen im Leben und im Werk: Vorträge des Zweiten Internationalen Čechov-Symposiums, Badenweiler, 20–24 Oktober 1994*, edited by Vladimir B. Kataev, Rolf-Dieter Kluge, and V. Regine Nohejl, 119–27. Munich: Verlag Otto Sagner, 1997.

Feider, Valeriia. *Chekhov, Literaturnyi byt i tvorchestvo po memuarnym materialam*. Leningrad: Academia, 1928.

Finke, Michael C. *Seeing Chekhov: Life and Art*. Ithaca, NY: Cornell University Press, 2005.

Flath, Carol A. [Apollonio]. "Art and Idleness: Chekhov's 'The House with a Mezzanine.'" *Russian Review* 58, no. 3 (July 1999): 456–66.

Flath, Carol A. [Apollonio]. "The Seagull: The Stage Mother, the Missing Father, and the Origins of Art." *Modern Drama* 42, no. 4 (1999): 491–510.

Frye, Northrop. *The Anatomy of Criticism: Four Essays*. Princeton, NJ: Princeton University Press, 1957.

Gertsen, Aleksandr I. [Alexander Herzen]. *Polnoe sobranie sochinenii v tridtsati tomakh*. Vol. 7. *O razvitii revoliutsionnykh idei v Rossii. Proizvedeniia 1851–1852 godov*. Moscow: Izdatel'stvo Akademii Nauk SSSR, 1956.

Gertsen, Aleksandr [Alexander Herzen]. *Sobranie sochinenii v deviati tomakh*. Vol. 5. Moscow: Khudozhestvennaia literatura, 1956.

Gilman, Richard. *Chekhov's Plays: An Opening into Eternity.* New Haven, CT: Yale University Press, 1995.

Ginzburg, Carlo. *Clues, Myths, and the Historical Method.* Translated by John and Anne C. Tedeschi. Baltimore: Johns Hopkins University Press, 1989.

Goldenveizer, Aleksandr. *Vblizi Tolstogo.* Moscow: Khudozhestvennaia literatura, 1959.

Golomb, Harai. "'Esli by znat'—Knowledge, Art and 'Philosophizing' in Čechov's Later Plays [An Abstract]." In *Anton P. Čechov—Philosophie und Religion in Leben und Werk,* 127–28. Munich: Verlag Otto Sagner, 1997.

Golomb, Harai. "Hamlet in Chekhov's Major Plays: Some Perspectives of Literary Allusion and Literary Tradition." *New Comparison* 2 (1986): 69–88.

Golomb, Harai. *A New Poetics of Chekhov's Plays: Presence through Absence.* Brighton: Sussex Academic Press, 2014.

Golovacheva, Alla, ed. *Chekhov i Dostoevskii: Po materialam Chetvertykh mezhdunarodnykh Skaftymovskikh chtenii (Saratov, 3–5 2016).* Moscow: GTsTM im. A. A. Bakhrushina, 2017.

Golovacheva, Alla. "'Dekadent' Treplev i blednaia luna." In *Chekhoviana: Chekhov i "serebrianyi vek,"* edited by M. O. Goriacheva and A. P. Chudakoov, 186–94. Moscow: Nauka, 1996.

Golovacheva, Alla. "'Proshedshei noch'iu vo sne ia videl trekh sester.'" In *Chekhoviana: "Tri sestry"—100 let,* edited by M. O. Goriacheva, 69–82. Moscow: Nauka, 2002.

Golovacheva, Alla. *Pushkin, Chekhov i drugie: Poetika literaturnogo dialoga.* Simferopol: Dolia, 2005.

Golovacheva, Alla. "'Razmyshleniia Marka Avreliia' v filosofskikh sporakh geroev A. P. Chekhova." In *Lichnaia biblioteka Chekhova: Literaturnoe okruzhenie i epokha. Materialy mezhdunarodnoi nauchnoi konferentsii, Taganrog 2015,* 17–29. Rostov: Foundation, 2016.

Goncharov, Ivan. *Sobranie sochinenii v shesti tomakh.* Vol. 4. Moscow: Pravda, 1972.

Gor'kii, Maksim. *Sobranie sochinenii v vosemnadtsati tomakh.* Vol. 18. Moscow: Khudozhestvennaia literatura, 1963.

Gorodetskii, D. "Mezhdu 'Medvedem' i 'Leshim.' Iz vospominanii o Chekhove." *Birzhevye vedomosti,* no. 364 (July 18, 1904).

Gottlieb, Vera. *Chekhov and the Vaudeville.* Cambridge: Cambridge University Press, 1982.

Gromov, Mikhail. "Chekhov i Dostoevskii: Velikoe protivostoianie." In *Kniga o Chekhove,* 246–88. Moscow: Sovremennik, 1989.

Grossman, Leonid P. "Naturalizm Chekhova." In *Ot Pushkina do Bloka: Etiudy i portrety.* Moscow: Sovremennye problemy, 1926.

Gulchenko, V. V., et al., eds. *Chekhov i Shekspir* [Chekhov and Shakespeare]. Moscow: GTsTM, 2016.

Heidegger, Martin. *Being and Time.* Translated by Joan Stambaugh. Revised by Dennis J. Schmidt. Albany: State University of New York Press, 2010.

Heidegger, Martin. *On Time and Being.* Translated by Joan Stambaugh. Chicago: University of Chicago Press, 1972.

Hunt, Albert, and Geoffrey Reeves. *Peter Brook.* Cambridge: Cambridge University Press, 1995.

Ishchuk-Fadeeva, Nina. "Tri sestry"—roman ili drama?" In *Chekhoviana: "Tri sestry"— 100 let*, edited by M. O. Goriacheva, 44–53. Moscow: Nauka, 2002.

Ivanov, Viacheslav. *Freedom and the Tragic Life: A Study in Dostoevsky.* Wolfeboro, NH: Longwood Academic, 1989.

Jackson, Robert Louis. "Chekhov's Garden of Eden, Or, The Fall of the Russian Adam and Eve: 'Because of Little Apples.'" *Slavica Hierosolymitana* 4 (1979): 70–78.

Jackson, Robert Louis. "Chekhov's Seagull: The Empty Well, the Dry Lake, and the Cold Cave." In *Chekhov's Great Plays: A Critical Anthology*, edited by Jean-Pierre Barricelli, 3–17. New York: New York University Press, 1981.

Jackson, Robert Louis. "'What Time Is It? Where Are We Going?' Chekhov's *The Cherry Orchard*: The Story of a Verb." In *Close Encounters: Essays on Russian Literature*, 130–52. Boston: Academic Studies Press, 2013.

Jakobson, Roman. "On Realism in Art." In *Language in Literature*, edited by Krystyna Pomorska and Stephen Rudy, 19–27. Cambridge, MA: Belknap Press of Harvard University Press, 1987.

Jakobson, Roman. "Two Aspects of Language and Two Types of Aphasic Disturbances." In *Language in Literature*, edited by Krystyna Pomorska and Stephen Rudy, 94–114. Cambridge, MA: Belknap Press of Harvard University Press, 1987.

Jones, Malcolm. "British Protestantism as a Factor in the Development of Nineteenth-Century Russian Literature: A Preliminary Sketch." In *Russian Thought and Society, 1800–1917: Essays in Honour of Eugene Lampert*, edited by Roger Bartlett. Staffordshire: University of Keele, 1984.

Kalaidovich, Petr. "O sadakh Vladimirskikh" [About the City of Vladimir's Orchards]. *Vestnik Evropy* 17, no. 59 (1811): 56–61.

Kapustin, N. V. *"Chuzhoe slovo" v proze A. P. Chekhova: Zhanrovye transformatsii.* Ivanovo: Izdatel'stvo Ivanovskogo gosudarstvennogo universiteta, 2003.

Karlinsky, Simon. "Nabokov and Chekhov." In *The Garland Companion to Vladimir Nabokov*, edited by Vladimir E. Alexandrov, 389–97. New York: Garland, 1995.

Kashcheev, V. I. "'Razmyshleniia imperatora Marka Avreliia Antoniia o tom, chto vazhno dlia samogo sebia': Chekhovskii ekzempliar knigi." In *Lichnaia biblioteka Chekhova: Literaturnoe okruzhenie i epokha* , 30–40. Rostov: Foundation, 2016.

Kataev, Vladimir. *Chekhov Plius . . . Predshestvenniki, sovremenniki, preemniki.* Moscow: Iazyki slavianskoi kul'tury, 2004.

Kataev, Vladimir. "Istinnyi mudrets." In *Filosofiia A.P. Chekhova*, 68–75. Irkutsk: Izdatel'stvo Irkutskogo gosudarstvennogo universiteta, 2008.

Kataev, Vladimir. *Literaturnye sviazi Chekhova.* Moscow: Izdatel'stvo Moskovskogo universiteta, 1989.

Kataev, Vladimir. *Proza Chekhova: Problemy interpretatsii.* Moscow: Izdatel'stvo Moskovskogo universiteta, 1979.

Kermode, Frank, ed. *English Pastoral Poetry: From Beginnings to Marvell.* New York: W. W. Norton, 1972.

Kermode, Frank. *The Sense of an Ending: Studies in the Theory of Fiction.* Oxford University Press, 1967.

Khodasevich, Vladislav. *Sobranie sochinenii v chetyrekh tomakh.* Vol. 2, *Poeziia Ignata Lebiadkina.* Moscow: Soglasie, 1996.

Kibal'nik, Sergei "Chekhov 'chitaet' Dostoevskogo (ot kruga chteniia k strategiiam pis'ma)." In *Filosofiia Chekhova: Materialy tret'ei mezhdunarodnoi konferentsii, Irkutsk, 28 iiunia–2 iiulia 2015*, 114–30. Irkutsk: Izdatel'stvo Irkutskogo universiteta, 2016.

Kibal'nik, Sergei. "Chekhov protiv Dostoevskogo." In *Chekhovskaia karta mira: Materialy mezhdunarodnoi konferentsii, Melikhovo, 3–7 iiulia 2014*, edited by A. A. Zhuravleva and V. B. Kataev, 221–36. Moscow: Melikhovo, 2015.

Kibal'nik, Sergei. "Khudozhestvennaia fenomenologiia Chekhova." In *Obraz Chekhova i chekhovskoi Rossii v sovremennom mire*, edited by V. B. Kataev and S. A. Kibal'nik, 18–28. St. Petersburg: Petropolis, 2010.

Kibal'nik, Sergei. *Problemy intertekstual'noi poetiki Dostoevskogo*. St. Petersburg: Petropolis, 2013.

Kluge, Rolf-Dieter. "O smysle ozhidaniia (Dramaturgiia Chekhova i 'V ozhidanii Godo' Bekketa)." In *Chekhoviana: Chekhov i Frantsiia*, 140–45. Moscow: Nauka, 1992.

Knapp, Liza. "Fear and Pity in 'Ward Six': Chekhovian Catharsis." In *Anton Chekhov*, edited by Harold Bloom, 209–18. Philadelphia: Chelsea House, 1999.

Komarov, Sergei. "O 'slozhnosti prostoty' A. P. Chekhova-dramaturga." *Filologicheskii klass* 24 (2010): 25–29.

Korolenko, Vladimir. *Sobranie sochinenii v desiati tomakh*. Vol. 5. Moscow: Khudozhestvennaia literatura, 1954.

Kramer, Karl D. "Love and Comic Instability in *The Cherry Orchard*." In *Russian Literature and American Critics*, edited by Kenneth Brostrom, 295–307. Papers in Slavic Philology 4. Ann Arbor: University of Michigan, 1984.

Kuleshov, Vasilii. "Realizm Chekhova v sootnoshenii s naturalizmom i simvolizmom v russkoi literature kontsa XIX–nachala XX vekov." In *Chekhovskie chteniia v Ialte*, 21–37. Moscow, 1973.

Kuznetsov, Ivan. "Melodramaticheskie klishe v dramaturgii Chekhova i Zudermana." In *Chekhov i Germaniia*, edited by V. B. Kataev and R.-D. Kluge, 61–70. Moscow: Moscow State University, 1996.

Lapushin, Radislav. "'. . . Chtoby nachat' nashu zhizn' snova' (Ekzistentsial'naia i poeticheskaia perspektivy v 'Trekh sestrakh')." In *Chekhoviana: "Tri sestry"—100 let*, edited by M. O. Goriacheva, 19–33. Moscow: Nauka, 2002.

Lapushin, Radislav. *"Dew on the Grass": The Poetics of Inbetweenness in Chekhov*. New York: Peter Lang, 2010.

LeBlanc, Ronald D. "Food, Orality, and Nostalgia for Childhood: Gastronomic Slavophilism in Mid Nineteenth-Century Russian Fiction." *Russian Review* 58 (1999): 244–67.

LeBlanc, Ronald. "Liberating Chekhov or Destroying Him? Joel Gersmann's Farcical Production of *The Cherry Orchard*." In *Chekhov Then and Now: The Reception of Chekhov in World Culture*, edited by J. Douglas Clayton, 53–61. New York: Peter Lang, 1997.

LeBlanc, Ronald. "Two-and-Twenty Misfortunes: Epixodov, Farce, and the Subversive Nature of Laughter in *Vishnevyj sad*." *Russian Language Journal* 49, no. 162–64 (1995): 141–60.

Letopis' zhizni i tvorchestva Chekhova. http://chehov-lit.ru/chehov/bio/letopis/letopis-1889-7.htm.

Lewis, Paul. *Comic Effects: Interdisciplinary Approaches to Humor in Literature*. Albany: State University of New York Press, 1989.

Linden, Anna L. "Chekhov vs. Gor'kii and the Moscow Arts Theater." *Russian History/ Histoire Russe* 18, no. 4 (1991): 501–28.

Mackiewicz, Stanisław. *Dostoevsky*. London: Orbis, 1947.

Mandel'shtam, Osip E. *Sobranie sochinenii v chetyrekh tomakh*. Vol. 2. Moscow: Terra, 1991.

Mann, Thomas. *Essays*. Vol. 6, *Meine Zeit 1945–1955*. Frankfurt: S. Fischer, 1997.

Mann, Thomas. "The Stature of Anton Chekhov." *New Republic*, May 16, 1955. https:// newrepublic.com/article/78215/the-stature-anton-chekhov.

Marsh, Cynthia. "Two-Timing Time in *Three Sisters*." In *Anton Chekhov—New Edition*, edited by Harold Bloom, 99–108. New York: Infobase Publishing, 2009.

Martin, Mike W. "Humor and Aesthetic Enjoyment of Incongruities." In *The Philosophy of Laughter and Humor*, edited by John Morreall, 172–86. Albany: State University of New York Press, 1987.

Marx, Karl. *Capital*. Vol. 1. Translated by S. Moore and E. Aveling. London: Lawrence and Wishart, 1970.

Marx, Karl. *Economic and Philosophic Manuscripts of 1844*. Edited by Dirk J. Struik. Translated by Martin Milligan. New York: International Publishers, 1964.

McGuinness, Patrick. *Maurice Maeterlinck and the Making of Modern Theater*. Oxford: Oxford University Press, 2000.

McReynolds, Louise, and Cathy Popkin. "The Objective Eye and the Common Good." In *Constructing Russian Culture in the Age of Revolution: 1881–1940*, edited by Catriona Kelly and David Shepherd, 57–105. Oxford: Oxford University Press, 1988.

Meierkhol'd, Vsevolod [Vsevolod Meyerhold]. *O teatre*. St. Petersburg: Prosveshchenie, 1913.

Merezhkovskii, D. S. *Vechnye sputniki: Portrety iz vsemirnoi literatury*. St. Petersburg: "Nauka," 2007.

Meve, Evgenii. *Meditsina v tvorchestve i zhizni A. P. Chekhova*. Kiev: Gosudarstvennoe meditsinskoe izdatel'stvo SSSR, 1961.

Miller, Melissa. "Chekhov and Zola's Naturalism." *Russian Review* 79, no. 2 (2020): 179–83.

Miller, Robin Feuer. "Dostoevsky's 'The Dream of a Ridiculous Man': Unsealing the Generic Envelope." In *Freedom and Responsibility in Russian Literature: Essays in Honor of Robert Louis Jackson*, edited by Elizabeth Cheresh Allen and Gary Saul Morson, 86–104. Evanston, IL: Northwestern University Press, 1995.

Mochul'skii, K. V. *Dostoevskii: Zhizn' i tvorchestvo*. Paris: YMCA-Press, 1980.

Mochul'skii, K. V. *Gogol', Solov'ev, Dostoevskii*. Moscow: Respublika, 1995.

Morreall, John. "The New Theory of Laughter." In *The Philosophy of Laughter and Humor*, edited by John Morreall, 128–38. Albany: State University of New York Press, 1987.

Morson, Gary Saul. *Hidden in Plain View: Narrative and. Creative Potentials in "War and Peace."* Stanford, CA: Stanford University Press, 1987.

Morson, Gary Saul. "The Reader as Voyeur: Tolstoi and the Poetics of Didactic Fiction." *Canadian-American Slavic Studies* 12, no. 4 (1978): 465–80.

Morson, Gary Saul. "Sonia's Wisdom." *A Plot of Her Own: The Female Protagonist in Russian Literature*, edited by Sona Stephan Hoisington, 70–71. Evanston, IL: Northwestern University Press, 1995.

Nabokov, Vladimir, and Edmund Wilson. *The Nabokov-Wilson Letters: Correspondence between Vladimir Nabokov and Edmund Wilson 1940–1971*. Edited by Simon Karlinsky. Hagerstown, NY: Harper and Row, 1979.

Nabokov, Vladimir. "Sartre's First Try." *New York Times*, April 24, 1949.

Nabokov, Vladimir. *Strong Opinions*. New York: Vintage International, 1973.

Nazirov, Roman. "Dostoevskii i Chekhov: Preemstvennost' i parodiia." In *Russkaia klassicheskaia literatura: Sravnitel'no–istoricheskii podkhod issledovaniia raznykh let*, 159–68. Ufa: RIO BashGU, 2005.

Nietzsche, Friedrich. *On the Genealogy of Morals*. Oxford: Oxford University Press, 1996.

Nivat, Georges. "Nabokov and Dostoevsky." In *The Garland Companion to Vladimir Nabokov*, edited by Vladimir E. Alexandrov, 398–402. New York: Garland, 1995.

Odesskaya, Margarita [Odesskaia]. "Chekhov's *Tatiana Repina*: From Melodrama to Mystery Play." *Modern Drama* 42 (1999): 475–90.

Odesskaia, Margarita. "'Tri sestry': Simvoliko-mifologicheskii podtekst." In *Chekhoviana: "Tri sestry"—100 let*, edited by M. O. Goriacheva. Moscow: Nauka, 2002.

Oppo, Andrea. *Lev Shestov: The Philosophy and Works of a Tragic Thinker*. Boston: Academic Studies Press, 2020.

Oppo, Andrea. "Shestov i Solov'ev: Antipody russkoi religioznoi filosofii." *Solov'evskie issledovaniia* [Solovyov Studies] 1, no. 65 (2020): 79–90.

Papernyi, Zinovii. *"Chaika" Chekhova*. Moscow: Khudozhestvennaia literatura, 1980.

Papernyi, Zinovii. *"Vopreki vsem pravilam . . ." P'esy i vodevili Chekhova*. Moscow: Iskusstvo, 1982.

Pavlov, Svetoslav. "Paradise Lost: Biblical Parallels and Autobiographical Allusions in Chekhov's Story 'The Black Monk.'" *Toronto Slavic Quarterly* 43 (Winter 2013): 102–14.

Peace, Richard. *Chekhov: A Study of the Four Major Plays*. New Haven, CT: Yale University Press, 1983.

Pitcher, Harvey. "Chekhov's Humour." In *A Chekhov Companion*, edited by Toby W. Clyman, 87–103. Westport, CT: Greenwood Press, 1985.

Popkin, Cathy. "*Historia Morbi* and the 'Holy of Holies'—Scientific and Religious Discourse and Čechov's Epistemology." In *Anton P. Čechov—Philosophische und religiöse Dimensionen im Leben und im Werk*, edited by Vladimir B. Kataev, Rolf-Dieter Kluge, and Regine Nohejl, 365–73. Munich: Verlag Otto Sagner, 1997.

Potebnia, Aleksandr A. [Alexander Potebnja]. *Estetika i poetika*. Moscow: "Iskusstvo," 1976.

Rayfield, Donald. *Chekhov: The Evolution of His Art*. London: Paul Elek, 1975.

Rayfield, Donald. "Orchards and Gardens in Chekhov." *Slavonic and East European Review* 67, no. 4 (1989): 530–45.

Rayfield, Donald. *Understanding Chekhov: A Critical Study of Chekhov's Prose and Drama*. Madison: University of Wisconsin Press, 1999.

Remizov, Aleksei. "Potainaia mysl'." *Ogon' veshchei: Sny i predson'e. Gogol', Pushkin, Lermontov, Turgenev, Dostoevskii*. Paris: Opleshnik, 1954.

Romanenko, V. T. *Chekhov i nauka*. Kharkov: Kharkovskoe knizhnoe izdatel'stvo, 1962.

Sartre, Jean-Paul. "On *The Sound and the Fury*: Time in the Work of Faulkner." In *Literary and Philosophical Essays*, 79–87. Translated by Annette Michelson. London: Ride and Company, 1955.

Schopenhauer, Arthur. *The World as Will and Idea*. Vol. 1. Translated by R. B. Haldane and J. Kemp. London: Tribner & Co., Ludgate Hill, 1883.

Scolnicov, Hanna. "Chekhov's Reading of *Hamlet*." In *Reading Plays*, edited by Hanna Scolnicov and Peter Holland, 192–205. Cambridge: Cambridge University Press, 1991.

Senelick, Laurence. *Anton Chekhov*. Houndmills, England: Macmillan, 1985.

Senelick, Laurence. "Chekhov on Stage." In *A Chekhov* Companion, edited by Toby W. Clyman, 209–32. Westport, CT: Greenwood Press, 1985.

Senelick, Laurence. *The Chekhov Theater: A Century of the Plays in Performance*. Cambridge: Cambridge University Press, 1997.

Serebrov, Aleksandr [A. N. Tikhonov]. *Vremia i liudi: Vospominaniia, 1898–1905*. Moscow: Khudozhestvennaia literatura, 1955.

Sergeenko, Petr Alekseevich. *Tolstoi i ego sovremenniki*. Moscow: Izdanie V. M. Sablina, 1911.

Shekspir, Uil'iam [William Shakespeare]. *Gamlet (Hamlet, Prince of Denmark)*. Izbrannye perevody. Moscow: Raduga Publishers, 1985.

Shestov, Lev. *Afiny i Ierusalim*. Vol. 1 of *Sochineniia v dvukh tomakh*. Moscow: Nauka, 1993.

Shestov, Lev. "Tvorchestvo iz nichego." *Nachala i kontsy: Sbornik statei*. St. Petersburg, 1908.

Shestov, Lev. "Umozrenie i Apokalipsis (Religioznaia filosofiia V. Solov'eva)." In *Umozrenie i otkrovenie*, 23–91. Paris: YMCA Press, 1964.

Shmid, Vol'f [Wolf Schmidt]. *Narratologiia*. Moscow: Iazyki slavianskoi kul'tury, 2003.

Shneyder, Vadim. *Russia's Capitalist Realism. Tolstoy, Dostoevsky, and Chekhov*. Evanston, IL: Northwestern University Press, 2021.

Simonov, Ruben. *S Vakhtangovym*. Moscow: Iskusstvo, 1956.

Skaftymov, A. P. "O edinstve formy i soderzhaniia v 'Vishnevom sade' A. P. Chekhova." In *Nravstvennye iskaniia russkikh pisatelei*, 339–80. Moscow: Khudozhestvennaia literatura, 1972.

Skaftymov, A. P. "O povestiakh Chekhova 'Palata No 6' i 'Moia zhizn.'" In *Nravstvennye iskaniia russkikh klassikov: Stat'i i issledovaniia o russkikh klassikakh*, 381–403. Moscow: Khudozhestvennaia literatura, 1972.

Sobennikov, Anatolii. "Chekhov i stoiki." In *Filosofiia Chekhova: Materialy Mezhdunarodnoi nauchnoi konferentsii, 27 iiunia–2 iiulia 2006*, 168–80. Irkutsk: Izdatel'stvo Irkutskogo universiteta, 2008.

Sobennikov, A. S. *"Mezhdu 'est' Bog' i 'net Boga'": O religiozno-filosofskikh traditsiiakh v tvorchestve A. P. Chekhov)*. Irkutsk: Izdatel'stvo Irkutskogo universiteta, 1997.

Sobennikov, Anatolii. "'Palata No 6' Chekhova: Geroi i ego ideia." In *Chekhovskie chteniia v Ottave*, 86–95. Tver'-Ottawa: Liliia Print, 2006.

Solov'ev, Vladimir. "Obshchii smysl iskusstva." In *Sochineniia v dvukh tomakh*, vol. 2. Moscow: Mysl, 1988.

Spivak, R. S. "Chekhov i ekzistentsializm." In *Filosofiia A. P. Chekhova*, 193–208. Irkutsk: Irkutskii gosudarstvennyi universitet, 2008.

Stanislavski, Constantin [Konstantin Stanislavskii]. "The Art of the Actor and the Art of the Director." In *Stanislavski's Legacy*, edited and translated by Elizabeth Reynolds Hapgood, 182–94. New York: Theater Arts Books, 1958.

Stanislavskii, Konstantin. *Sobranie sochinenii.* 8 vols. Moscow: Iskusstvo, 1954.

States, Bert O. *Irony and Drama. A Poetics.* Ithaca, NY: Cornell University Press, 1971.

Stein, Gertrude. *Four in America.* Introduction by Thornton Wilder. New Haven, CT: Yale University Press, 1947.

Stein, Gertrude. "Poetry and Grammar." In *Writings 1932–1946*, edited by Catharine R. Stimpson and Harriet Chessman, 313–36. New York: Library of America, 1998.

Steiner, George. *Tolstoy or Dostoevsky: An Essay in the Old Criticism.* New Haven, CT: Yale University Press, 1996.

Stepanov, Andrei. "Lev Shestov on Chekhov." In *Anton Chekhov through the Eyes of Russian Thinkers*, edited by Olga Tabachnikova, 219–45. London: Anthem Press, 2010.

Stepanov, Andrei. *Problemy kommunikatsii u Chekhova.* Moscow: Iazyki slavianskoi kul'tury, 2005.

Strongin, Carol. "Irony and Theatricality in Chekhov's 'The Seagull.'" *Comparative Drama* 15, no. 4 (1981–82): 366–80.

Styan, J. L. *Chekhov in Performance: A Commentary on the Major Plays.* Cambridge: Cambridge University Press, 1971.

Sukhikh, Igor'. *Ot . . . i do . . . Etiudy o russkoi slovesnosti.* St. Petersburg: Rodnik, 2015.

Sukhikh, Igor'. *Problemy poetiki Chekhova.* St. Petersburg: St. Petersburg University Press, 2007.

Tabachnikova, Olga, ed. *Anton Chekhov through the Eyes of Russian Thinkers.* London: Anthem Press, 2010.

Timiriazev, Dmitrii. *Istoriko-statisticheskii obzor promyshlennosti Rossii.* Vol. 1, *Sel'sko-khoziaistvennye proizvedeniia, ogorodnichestvo, sadovodstvo i domashnie zhivotnye.* St. Petersburg: Tipografiia A. S. Suvorina, 1883.

Tolstaia, Elena. *Poetika razdrazheniia: Chekhov v kontse 1880-kh—nachale 1890-kh godov.* Moscow: Radiks, 1994.

Tolstoi, Lev. *Polnoe sobranie sochinenii v devianosta tomakh.* Vol. 29, *Proizvedenia 1891–1894.* Moscow: Khudozhestvennaia literatura, 1954.

Tolstoi, Lev. *Sobranie sochinenii.* 22 vols. Moscow: Khudozhestvennaia literatura, 1978–85.

Tulloch, John. *Chekhov: A Structuralist Study.* New York: Barnes & Noble Books, 1980.

Tunimanov, Vladimir. *Tvorchestvo Dostoevskogo, 1854–1862.* Leningrad: Nauka, 1980.

Turgenev, Ivan. *Sobranie sochinenii v desiati tomakh.* Vol. 10. Moscow: Khudozhestvennaia literatura, 1962.

Turner, C. J. G. "Time in Chekhov's *Tri sestry.*" *Canadian Slavonic Papers* 28 (1986): 64–79.

Tynianov, Iurii. *Dostoevskii i Gogol' (K teorii parodii).* Petrograd: Izdatel'stvo "Opoiaz," 1921.

Vainshtein, Ol'ga. *Dendi: Moda, literatura, stil' zhizni.* Moscow: NLO, 2006.

Valency, Maurice. *The Breaking String: The Plays of Anton Chekhov.* New York: Schocken Books, 1983.

Vatsuro, Vadim, et al., eds. *A.P. Chekhov v vospominaniiakh sovremennikov.* Moscow: Khudozhestvennaia literatura, 1986.

Voltaire. *Candide and Other Stories.* Oxford: Oxford University Press, 2006.

Walzer, Michael. *The Revolution of the Saints: A Study of the Origins of Radical Politics.* New York: Atheneum, 1974.

White, Hayden. *Metahistory: The Historical Imagination in Nineteenth-Century Europe.* Baltimore: Johns Hopkins University Press, 1973.

Wiles, Timothy J. *The Theater Event: Modern Theories of Performance.* Chicago: University of Chicago Press, 1980.

Williams, David, ed. *Peter Brook: A Theatrical Casebook.* London: Methuen, 1988.

Winner, Thomas, G. "Chekhov's *Seagull* and Shakespeare's *Hamlet*: A Study of a Dramatic Device." *American Slavic and East European Review* 15 (February 1956): 103–11.

Zaitsev, Boris. *Chekhov: Literaturnaia biografiia.* New York: Izdatel'stvo imeni Chekhova, 1954.

Zingerman, Boris. *Teatr Chekhova i ego mirovoe znachenie.* Moscow: RIK Rusanova, 2001.

Zola, Émile. *Le Roman Expérimental: Notes et Commentaires de Maurice Le Blond.* Paris: François Bernouard, 1928.